About the Author

Mark Conway Munro is an entrepreneur who turned a software-writing hobby into Mark was born in Indiana and raised in Ohio. In 1986, Mark moved to New York City. As the manager of Louis Tannen's Magic Store in New York City, he taught himself the Macintosh Computer and FileMaker Pro while building a database of inventory, which eventually led to the development of a networked order processing solution. From there he went on to work for the Jack Morton Company, where he was the Network and Telecommunications Manager. He began developing custom solutions with HyperCard and FileMaker Pro in his spare time. After the release of AppleScript in 1992, he refocused his experience with computer networking, training, technical support, database development, and custom application development. He quickly transitioned from HyperTalk to AppleScript and began building custom workflow automation solutions.

Mark founded Write Track Media in 1994, where he continues to develop innovative solutions that eliminate repetition and optimize computerized workflows. Write Track Media has since become known for its reputation for excellence, and has developed complex automated solutions for companies in a variety of industries all across the country including Adobe Systems, The Associated Press, BMG, Dreyfus, Entertainment Weekly, Epson, KraftMaid, McCann-Erickson, The Miami Herald, MYOB, Nabisco, NASA, Nikon, Random House, Reader's Digest, Sony Music Entertainment, and many other companies.

Currently Mark resides in Pennsylvania, where Write Track Media is located. In his spare time, he enjoys hiking and nature photography.

Contents at a Glance

Contents

Part IV: Using Subroutines and Open-Ended Programming 409

Foreword

Twelve years ago Mark Munro asked me to write something for the Web site he was building for his company, Write Track Media. I had already been working with him for about three years: me as an editor and in-house FileMaker developer at the country's second-largest record company, and Mark as outside FileMaker and AppleScript developer. He had helped build the departmental Mac-based database of discs, tapes, and videos with up-to-date listings of all their artists, prices, genres, formats, and so on. But the major part of the project, and where Mark was proving so invaluable, was in the system's output.

We needed to produce a monthly pocket-sized catalog of the active product — about 13,000 data records. Mark automated production so that I could generate a 180-page complexly styled catalog — using FileMaker Pro, AppleScript, and Quark — at the push of a button. We needed to constantly produce multipage order forms with elaborate line listings and scannable barcodes. Mark automated these so that one button would trigger the form to build from scratch: Quark firing up, new blank documents opening, text boxes being created and placed, text flying into the boxes, picture boxes being created, AppleScript running off and building barcode images for each product, bringing them back, dropping them into the picture boxes, sizing them to fit…. All this looked like magic to the IT guys that would drop by occasionally, none of them Mac users, with no idea that an application like AppleScript existed that could make the programs all "talk" to each other. It was magic to us, too: the documents were data driven, accuracy was better than it ever had been, and the automation was saving countless hours of typing, page layout, and proofreading every week.

New record formats were coming into being; sales needs and the documents supporting them were changing often. I was pressed for time and got to work with Mark a lot. The thrill was that I could call him and tell him what I needed and he'd never get nervous or show hesitation, and he'd never say it couldn't be done. There was always a way, and for him, always a good way. He worked fast and methodically, kept me briefed, and generally delivered ahead of his target date. I would send lists of fields, find and sort rules, and layout requirements. He would send code. I wrote for his Web site, "There seems to be no limit to the complexity of the scripting and automation jobs they are able to take on, and they do it with an energy, focus, speed, and level-headed aplomb that are to be admired." "They," of course was all Mark himself, and I feel the same twelve years later.

It's not surprising to me that Mark, early in his career, was a performing magician who got his start with databases when he decided to computerize the inventory at Tannen's, the New York City magic supply mecca where he was working. I don't mean this in the hokey, "Oh, this guy works magic" sense; I mean that like a skilled performer he has brought to his work in these intervening years a rigorous, practiced, polished, and intensely methodical approach. He has developed a remarkable overview of the effects he wants to achieve. He has codified a highly refined aesthetic and has devoted himself to the rigorous practice that it takes to express it.

I went to the Apple Store last night and happened to mention to a young clerk that my friend was writing a developer guide to AppleScript. I was floored when he said, "Oh AppleScript — nobody talks about that around here — I think there's one guy that knows something about it and was thinking of using it to automatically update his phone, but he only knew how to get it to turn on and off." Luckily, that's just ignorance, even if it's coming from an Apple employee: AppleScript remains an unparalleled development tool for desktop automation. It's not easy, and that's why there are specialists like Mark Munro. Sometimes it's hard to envision what it's capable of because it takes effort to zoom out, like a movie camera craning overhead, to get a real sense of what's possible to automate. Then building the solution can be daunting and time-consuming. It takes an effort to stop what you're doing by rote, and to devote time to changing direction. The resulting time savings and ease of operation can be thrilling.

I've heard a professional developer say, "What is good code? Good code is code that works." I don't think Mark would say that. There's code that works and there's good code that works. It's not a fussy, perfectionist approach, either, just a sense of the intrinsic RIGHTness of an approach. He abhors wasted time and repetition of effort and spends remarkable effort in streamlining his FileMaker development practices and templates. This is to save time and money for his clients and, I think, to keep himself moving forward. It's obvious to me why his company's motto is: "Write Track Media creates solutions that eliminate repetition and allow our clients to focus on their highest potential."

As a fledgling FileMaker developer, I have to admit that working with Mark over the years has been an occasional wellspring of inferiority feelings: "Is this the standard? Can I ever be a developer who's worth his salt if I'm not as good as Mark?" Maybe I can relax a little. I've come to believe that in all likelihood Mark's unique: perhaps there's no one as methodical and philosophically rigorous at what he does. But now that he's taking the time to codify his theories and his method, maybe we can get a little closer.

Walker Stevenson
FileMaker Developer

Acknowledgments

Writing this book was a tremendous effort and would not have been possible without the support, contributions, and encouragement of many people.

First, I want to thank John Thorsen, Jr., for the development opportunities he provided me many years ago. He is a constant source of advice, knowledge, and humor that would be difficult to find anywhere within a single human being. Also, thanks goes to Rob Vanderwerf for reviewing the manuscript with a keen eye for technical consistency and accuracy. His feedback led to many key improvements that greatly enhanced the quality of the material. To my friend, Walker Stevenson, for his meticulous nature, a willingness to discuss technical details, and for writing a foreword that makes it sound like I know what I'm doing. And to Aaron Black, Katharine Dvorak, and everyone at Wiley for providing me with this opportunity and for all their hard work.

Finally, a special thanks to all of my wonderful clients, especially those who have worked with me as an extension of their staff for many years. They have presented me with one challenge after another, constantly forcing me to push beyond my comfort zone. Many of the advanced concepts in this book would not exist without them.

Introduction

In the early 1990s, I was working as a Computer Network and Telecommunications Manager at the New York City headquarters of a company now known as Jack Morton Worldwide. In addition to my other responsibilities, I was tasked with creating FileMaker Pro databases to help manage the office's information. At that time, FileMaker was still somewhat crude, and had been since I began using it in the late 1980s.

During this time, I learned how to program HyperCard and was having a lot of fun building custom applications. Then I received a copy of the AppleScript Developer's Toolkit and Scripting Kit, an add-on piece of software for the Macintosh Operating System. I began converting the HyperTalk scripts in my applications to AppleScript. Almost immediately HyperCard was relegated to my archives in favor of AppleScript.

This was still a year or two before the Internet exploded in popularity. Finding documentation and sample scripts was difficult, and very few applications supported scripting. These difficulties led to many frustrating and yet ultimately rewarding, struggles to figure out how to successfully automate one task after another. However, as support for scripting spread out into the Mac OS and in third-party software, it became clear that workflow automation on a Mac was going to be a huge phenomenon.

This was a driving factor for founding Write Track Media in 1994 to specialize in the development of workflow automation solutions. Since that time, I have worked with many wonderful clients in a variety of different industries. Many times since then, I have entertained the notion of writing a book on AppleScript. Some of the techniques and ideas that I used daily, many created out of the necessity of the moment, seemed good enough to share. Believing that good ideas only become great when they are shared with others was a driving factor that led me to avail myself of the opportunity to write this book.

I tried to structure this book to appeal to programmers of any skill level, including those who have never programmed before. I start with the basics and gradually work toward more advanced material to make this book beneficial to all. It is laced with advice, ideas, and techniques gleaned from years of trial and error. Hopefully, you will find these useful and encouraging in your future automation endeavors.

AppleScript is a wonderful language to know and is powerful enough to automate virtually any task. It was a rewarding experience to focus on the language in a systematic fashion while writing this book. I hope you enjoy reading it as much as I have writing it.

Please let me know about issues you find in the book or offer suggestions for subjects you'd like to see covered in a future edition. Visit `www.writetrackmedia.com/contact/` to send me an e-mail.

Getting the Most Out of This Book

The chapters in this book are organized into five parts. They are organized with the assumption that a reader will read the book from cover to cover. The material starts with the basics and gradually moves to more advanced material.

Part I, "AppleScript: The Power of Automation" includes an introduction and history of AppleScript as well as discussions of workflow automation with AppleScript and script deployment options. It also includes a presentation of a comprehensive set of naming and usage standards.

Part II, "Learning the AppleScript Language" begins with a chapter on AppleScript basics followed by chapters detailing each class of data that can be manipulated with scripts. From there, chapters discuss logical branching with if-then statements, repeat loops, error containment and management, and an in-depth look at how the standard scripting addition extends AppleScript's functionality.

Part III, "Using Scripts to Control Applications" reveals AppleScript's capability to tap into the functionality of standard, off-the-shelf software to create powerful multi-application workflows. Also, the three "faceless" applications — Image Events, Database Events, and System Events — included with the Macintosh operating system that provide additional functionality for AppleScript are covered in detail.

Part IV, "Using Subroutines and Open-Ended Programming" contains chapters that discuss the creation of subroutines, writing open-ended code, and an advanced discussion of using a hierarchical method for dividing code into subroutines.

Part V, "Organizing Code into Modules and Libraries for Multi-Module Solutions" continues to push into more advanced topics, discussing the development of complex AppleScript solutions that are spread across more than one script file.

Parts III–V contain several versions of an Image Batch Processing script that evolves over five chapters. Each successive version of the script is improved with concepts that are introduced in that chapter.

All of the code in this book was created and tested in Mac OS X 10.6.

Using the Book's Icons

There are four margin icons that are used throughout the book to provide additional information, tips, warnings, or indications of where to find additional information.

NOTE

Notes highlight useful information that you should take into consideration.

TIP

Tips provide additional bits of advice that make particular features quicker or easier to use.

CAUTION

Cautions warn you of potential problems before you make a mistake.

CROSS-REF

Watch for the Cross-Ref icon to learn where in another chapter you can go to find more information on a particular topic.

Accessing the Book's Web Site

Several of the longer scripts presented in this book are available for download on Wiley's companion Web site. Visit `www.wileydevreference.com` for more information and to download the script files.

AppleScript: The Power of Automation

Introduction to AppleScript Programming

AppleScript is an Open Scripting Architecture (OSA)–compliant command language that can communicate with and control scriptable applications and scriptable features of Macintosh Operating System (Mac OS) X.

The OSA is a mechanism within the Mac OS that provides a library of functions and allows inter-application communication and control by sending and receiving messages called Apple Events.

An *Apple Event* is a basic message exchange system of the OSA that is used to send instructions to an application and optionally, send back a result. Apple Events can be used to control inter-process communication within an application, between applications on a single computer, and between applications on a remote computer. Figure 1.1 illustrates the path of an Apple Event message.

Since 1994, when System 7.5 was released, most Mac users have been unaware that they send Apple Events every day. For example, each time they double-click a document to open it, an Apple Event is responsible for instructing the appropriate application to launch and to open the file, as shown in Figure 1.2.

AppleScript provides an easy to learn, English-like language that enables users to write scripts that send and receive Apple Events. Each script acts like a new feature of the OS or an application. Scripts can integrate third-party applications, creating custom solutions that perform very specific tasks.

Because of its English-like syntax, even novice programmers can build scripts to perform virtually any function. With pervasive support of AppleScript throughout the Mac OS and many third-party applications, it is the ideal platform to create efficiency-rich, workflow automation solutions.

This amazing and award-winning technology provides a simple and affordable way to automate repetitive computing tasks and leave users free to focus their attention on more creative tasks.

In This Chapter

An introduction to AppleScript

Locating AppleScript applications and other resources

Looking at AppleScript's resources and unique characteristics

Who uses AppleScript and what they automate

Looking at AppleScript's influence

Figure 1.1

The path of an Apple Event message sending a command to an application

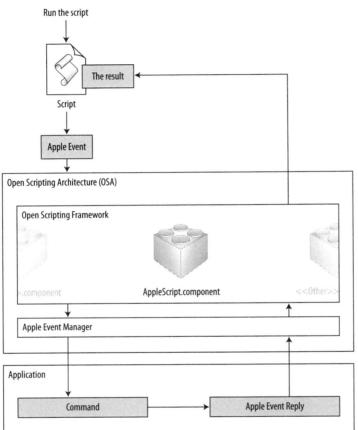

Figure 1.2

The underpinnings of an Apple Event opening a document

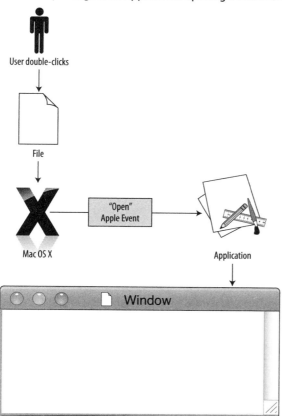

A Brief History of AppleScript

AppleScript and its associated tools were conceived, designed, and implemented between 1989 and 1993. It was a long-term investment in fundamental infrastructure that matured over a span of several years (see Figure 1.3).

Figure 1.3

A timeline of the history of AppleScript

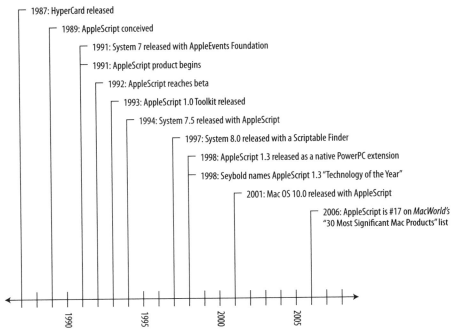

Often considered a precursor to and inspiration for AppleScript, HyperCard was released in 1987. This software enabled novice programmers to rapidly create custom tools that would carry out a set of specific processes. Featuring an easy-to-learn, English-like scripting language called HyperTalk, it was easier to learn and use than other programming languages available at that time.

AppleScript was officially conceived in 1989 as a research project by the Advanced Technology Group (ATG) at Apple Computer and was code-named "Family Farm." The research team was led by Larry Tesler and included Mike Farr, Mitchell Gass, Mike Gough, Jed Harris, Al Hoffman, Ruben Kleiman, Edmund Lai, and Frank Ludolph. Their goal was to create a new system-level development environment for the Mac OS that would allow for inter-application communication and control and provide a user-level language. The original group was disbanded in mid-1990 and new teams were assembled to design and implement the ideas first conceived.

The first step was the development of Apple Events, which is the inter-application communication foundation of AppleScript in the OS. Written in Pascal, like much of the Mac OS at the time, this foundation needed to be in place before the development of AppleScript could begin. The AppleScript project officially began in April 1991, just months before Mac OS 7, when the new Apple Events foundation was released.

NOTE
The AppleScript project was code named "Gustav" after a team member's dog.

In September 1992, AppleScript reached beta. However, in January 1993, the original team was disbanded when several leaders left the project. It wasn't until April of that year that the AppleScript 1.0 Developer's Toolkit shipped as a stand-alone product that could be installed on any Mac running System 7. In September, AppleScript version 1.1 was included as part of System 7.1.1 (System 7 Pro). In December, the first "end user" release — AppleScript 1.1 Developer's Toolkit and Scripting Kit — was released. Finally, in 1994, AppleScript was ready to revolutionize how people use computers when it took its place as an official part of Macintosh System 7.5.

Since that time, AppleScript has slowly evolved into the invaluable tool that we know today. In 1997, the Macintosh Finder finally became scriptable, eliminating the need to use the Finder scripting extension. When Macintosh OS 8.0 was released in July 1997, it included AppleScript version 1.1.2 with many minor improvements.

NOTE
In 1997, Apple had plans to eliminate AppleScript in order to cut expenses but, thankfully, this plan was thwarted by a campaign by loyal users of the technology.

In October 1998, AppleScript 1.3 was released, recompiled as a native PowerPC extension and included Unicode support. In that year, Steve Jobs demonstrated AppleScript at Seybold, and *Macworld* magazine named AppleScript 1.3 the "Technology of the Year." In 2006, AppleScript held position #17 on *Macworld*'s list of the 30 most significant Mac products ever.

NOTE
Read the entire history of AppleScript at `www.cs.utexas.edu/~wcook/Drafts/2006/ashopl.pdf`.

A 1999 technology study by research firm GISTICS estimated that AppleScript produced more than $100 million in annual savings for North American media firms. Today, Google returns more than two million results when searching for the word "AppleScript."

In Mac OS 10.6, released in 2009, AppleScript, Standard Additions, and all AppleScript-related system applications, such as System Events, are now 64-bit capable.

The technology has flourished and now boasts a thriving and happily efficient user base.

Finding AppleScript Resources

AppleScript is made up of various elements located on each Mac computer. These elements include applications, scripting additions, and components.

Applications

AppleScript developers use two applications: the AppleScript Editor and the Folder Actions Setup application.

NOTE
Mac OS 10.5 included a folder called "AppleScript" inside the `/Applications/` folder that contained three applications: Script Editor, AppleScript Utility, and Folder Action Setup. Mac OS 10.6 doesn't include this folder. The Script Editor is now the "AppleScript Editor" and is in the `/Utilities/` folder; the options accessible from the AppleScript Utility are now in the Editor's preference panel; and Folder Action Setup is now in the `/System/Library/CoreServices` folder.

AppleScript Editor

Probably the most important application in the AppleScript toolbox is the AppleScript Editor, which is located in the `/Applications/Utilities/` folder. This application is used to create, write, edit, compile, run, and save scripts. It contains many features that assist a developer in learning the language, writing scripts, and exploring the command library of scriptable third-party applications.

CROSS-REF
See Chapter 6 for more information about using the AppleScript Editor.

Folder Actions Setup

The Folder Actions Setup application, located in `/System/Library/CoreServices/`, is used to assign script actions to folders. This enables a script to respond to various folder actions, such as the arrival or removal of a file or folder, and perform a sequence of automated tasks on it.

NOTE
You can access the Folder Actions Setup application by clicking a folder while pressing the Ctrl key or by clicking the right button on your mouse and selecting the Folder Actions Setup option from the contextual menu.

The Folder Actions Setup window, shown in Figure 1.4, lets you enable and disable folder actions globally as well as add, show, and remove folders on a computer. Once you have added a folder, you can attach one or more scripts to it.

CROSS-REF
See Chapter 16 for more information about using Folder Actions.

Figure 1.4

The Folder Actions Setup window

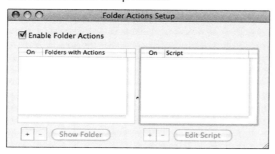

Scripting additions

A *scripting addition* is used to extend the AppleScript language by providing a set of additional commands. Scripting additions can be stored in several locations on a computer. Apple includes several scripting additions in the OS and you can find additional third-party scripting additions on the Internet.

CROSS-REF

See Chapter 16 for more information about installing and using scripting additions.

TIP

A set of sample scripts provided by Apple and installed as part of the Mac OS 10.6 installation is located at `/System/Library/Scripts/`.

Components

Components are files that provide basic functionality for AppleScript, Apple Events, and other OSA–related languages. While the process of using or developing scripts does not require you to be concerned with these components, they are provided in this book for informational purposes only. Except when adding or removing additional language components, such as JavaScript, you should never attempt to remove, modify, or be concerned with the whereabouts of any of these components.

The Apple Event Manager provides an application programming interface (API) for sending and receiving Apple Events, thereby providing support for the creation of scriptable applications.

It exists as part of the `CoreSErvices.framework` and is called the `AE.framework`. This is important for those creating scriptable applications but not important for those writing scripts with AppleScript.

Likewise, the `OpenScripting.framework` is a part of the `Carbon.framework` and is not something AppleScript users and developers need to worry about. It defines data structures, routines, and resources that support scripting components regardless of the language. It also compiles, executes, loads, and stores scripts.

The `AppleScript.component` file, the default OSA scripting language component provided by Apple, enables a computer to use the AppleScript language. It is located at `/System/Library/Components`.

Other OSA component files, such as the `JavaScript.component`, can be installed in `~/Library/Components` for each user account that will use it. If your computer is connected to an office network, you may need to contact your network administrator before installing additional OSA components.

Understanding the Unique Characteristics of AppleScript

While old-fashioned macro recording utilities were quite useful in their time — they could simulate a series of literal keystrokes and mouse clicks, respectively — it was difficult to use them in a dynamic and practical manner. With AppleScript you can not only automate a sequence of literal actions, but also you can create a dynamic script that includes logical branches, variable content, and options for different behavior depending on specific conditions. This gives AppleScript the power of a real programming language.

AppleScript possesses more unique characteristics that add to its appeal, such as its English-like syntax, the fact that it is universally open-ended, its deep level of access into the Mac OS framework and the frameworks of third-party applications, and its consistency between OS updates.

English-like syntax

One of the most unique characteristics of AppleScript is its English-like syntax. While some detractors might say it is not even close to "natural spoken English," most would agree that it is certainly more like a spoken language than most other scripting and programming languages. The difference in syntax can be illustrated with a few simple examples.

The following examples present a sort of Rosetta Stone of programming languages. The code in each example performs exactly the same function: It builds a text-based list of numbers within a range specified by two variables. At the end of each script, the resulting value will be a sequence of numbers from 25 to 30 with a carriage return after each number.

Listing 1.1 illustrates the English-like language used in AppleScript. Notice how setting the content of a variable doesn't require any code-like declarations or explicit identification of the initial value's data class. Also, there is no need to worry about line endings; just type a return and keep on typing.

Listing 1.1

AppleScript

```
set numLength to 5
set numStart to 25
set textResults to numStart as string
if numLength > 1 then
    repeat with a from 1 to numLength
        set numStart to numStart + 1
        set textResults to textResults & return & numStart
    end repeat
end if
```

The code script shown in Listing 1.2 performs the same functions with JavaScript. Putting a value into a variable is a little less English-like. Like many other languages, JavaScript requires a special line ending, which in this case is a semi-colon. Also, the repeat loop is more cryptically phrased and, therefore, less clear than the AppleScript example.

Listing 1.2

JavaScript

```
var numLength = 5;
var numStart = 25;
var textResults = numStart;
for (var a=numStart+1; a<=(numStart+numLength); a++) {
    textResults=textResults + '<br>' + a;
}
```

The code in Listing 1.3 performs the same functions using the REALBasic language. Notice that the variable declarations are more complicated and require the data class of each must be specifically stated prior to placing a value within them.

Listing 1.3

REALBasic

```
Dim numLength as Integer
Dim numStart as Integer
Dim textResults as String
Dim a as Integer
numLength = 5
numStart = 25
textResults= str(numStart)
if numLength > 1 then
  For a=1 to numLength
    numStart=numStart+1
    textResults = textResults + Chr(13) + str(numStart)
  Next
end if
```

Finally, the code shown in Listing 1.4 performs the same functions with PHP (Hypertext Preprocessor). Like JavaScript, it requires line endings and brackets enclosing a more cryptic combination if-then and repeat function.

Listing 1.4

PHP

```
$numLength = 5;
$numStart = 25;
$textResults = $numStart;   //no coercion is necessary
if ($numLength > 1) {
for ($a = $numStart+1; $a <= ($numStart + $numLength); $a++) {
    $textResults = $textResults . "<br>\n". $a;

}
}
```

Certainly, the development time required to build a script always depends on the complexity of the tasks to be automated. However, AppleScript's English-like language and automatic handling of many fundamental programming chores significantly reduce the time required to develop a solution.

NOTE

The code in Listings 1.1, 1.2, 1.3, and 1.4 are available for download from the book's Web site at `www.wiley`
`devreference.com`.

Universally open-ended

Another important characteristic of AppleScript is its success as an open-ended, universal
scripting language. Before AppleScript, the few applications that enabled users to automate
tasks each had their own way of doing things. In today's modern Internet-driven world full of
standard languages, it is hard to imagine a time when each application had its own set of rules.
Imagine a nightmarish world in which every Web site had its own language and, therefore, its
own browser. Perhaps that is a bit dramatic, but that is not totally unlike the way things were
with automation.

In a world without AppleScript, each application would need its own macro language and features. To use them, you would have to learn and remember each of them from any number of
applications. Creating a macro that works across multiple applications would be difficult to virtually impossible. Some software might try to bridge this gap, but it could break with each OS
upgrade and generally would be more trouble than it's worth.

AppleScript addresses such nightmares by implementing a universal language with which any
and all applications could communicate. An application possesses its own object model that
can be automated by AppleScript, specifying the objects, properties, and commands that it can
work with. In a way, each application's script dictionary becomes an extension of the
AppleScript language, offering its unique services to a script in a familiar way.

Today, virtually every application developed for the Mac has some scriptable features. Widely
used applications like Adobe's Creative Suite have extensive support for automating almost
every conceivable feature. For those applications that don't support scripting, or to access a
command not made accessible to AppleScript, Apple developed *System Events*. This amazing
scripting addition enables AppleScript to simulate mouse clicks, keystrokes, and menu selections in many un-scriptable applications, thereby allowing you to script the un-scriptable.

CROSS-REF

See Chapter 20 for more information about System Events.

Deep level of access

AppleScript enables scripts to tap into many of the technologies of Mac OS X with its unique
ease of use. For example, the `do shell script` command in the Standard Scripting Additions
enables a script to run any shell script.

CROSS-REF
See Chapter 16 for more information about using AppleScript to perform shell scripts.

AppleScript also has access to many of the frameworks created by Apple for their applications and for third-party developers. These are made available to scripts with Scripting Additions. The Image Events scripting addition enables scripts to access the Core Image framework of the OS. Also, soon after the Core Data framework was developed, the Database Events scripting addition became available.

Consistency maintained between updates

Because AppleScript is built as a clean and easy-to-use layer on top of the OS that obscures the complex connection to the lower-level architecture, scripts typically continue to work from one OS update to the next. While major OS changes typically require bug fixes or complete overhauls of third-party applications, scripts are usually immune to such things. Even the transition from the "Classic" OS (System 9) to Mac OS X didn't require much more than a recompiling and resaving of older scripts.

When third-party applications require major rewrites or make changes to their object model and command libraries, it can break scripts. However, most applications eventually maintain a relatively consistent language for objects, their properties, and the commands they support.

CROSS-REF
See Chapter 17 to learn about the object model of third-party applications.

Exploring the Uses and Users of AppleScript

As a flexible, inter-application scripting language, AppleScript has a virtually unlimited number of uses and can be used by every user of a Mac computer. Even though many users will not take the time to learn the language and write their own scripts, they can still use the scripts written by others.

TIP
Always use caution when using scripts written by someone else. Be sure they are reputable or have a personal connection to you. A script could potentially perform malicious or virus-like behavior.

Scripts can react to various stimuli. Double-clicking a script application can begin an automated process while another application begins processing files a user drops on it. Scripts can be attached to the script menu, embedded into application menus and palettes, and on a Finder window toolbar. They can be launched by an iCal alarm or whenever files or folders appear in a watched folder. Scripts can talk to other scripts on a user's computer or other computers across the office or the Internet. Scripts can run day and night, constantly watching, checking, processing, and reporting on anything that anyone takes the time to develop.

CROSS-REF

See Chapter 3 to learn more about AppleScript deployment options.

Uses for AppleScript

While some scripts may possess wider appeal and mass-market usefulness, typically most focus on a specific company's unique workflow. They can integrate third-party applications in ways that would not be practical or economical for mass production. Every manual task performed on a Mac computer can be automated with AppleScript, leaving its limitations to that of your imagination.

The following examples provide a glimpse of the limitless activities that can be automated with AppleScript.

File processing

There are numerous ways to streamline user interaction with files:

- **Image files can be opened, resized, flattened, modified with filters, and saved into one or more new files.** A script can automatically create preview images for the Web and high-resolution files for print. It can make "decisions" and vary the processing tasks based on a characteristic of the file, such as the file name, layer names, size, or page orientation. Individual files can be merged into a preview sheet or split into separate files. Any of these tasks can be automatically performed on a folder of 10 images or 10,000.

- **PDF files can be manipulated with AppleScript to suit the needs of even the most complex workflow.** Scripts can add or remove pages, stamps, comments, and more. Separate files can be merged into a single file while multiple page files can be split into individual files. A script can generate PDFs, print them, and place them in a folder for human review. The content of the files can be resumes, books, instruction manuals, fact sheets, and countless others. A script can detect and process each with a separate set of business logic.

- **Scripts can manipulate text-based data files of any type.** They can change delimiters to comma, tab, or fixed width text. They can extract specific rows or columns based on date ranges, product numbers, or customer name and then generate a new file with only the desired information. The files can be resorted, have data added or removed, and can be checked for common errors. Characters can be replaced with other characters to conform to importing regulations of databases, hypertext markup language (HTML) language rules or your company business rules.

E-mail processing

On an automated e-mail account or a user's computer, AppleScript can help manage a crowded inbox and assist in sending bulk e-mail:

- **Scripts can scan, read, and take predetermined actions on incoming messages in many popular e-mail applications.** They can also help you prepare, create, and customize messages to a batch of contacts.

- **Scripts can detect, read, parse, and route data from a Web form to a database.** On a user's computer, this can be done with a mail rule that runs an AppleScript when Mail detects a web form email. A server with a fully autonomous script and dedicated e-mail account can constantly monitor the inbox for various messages from different Web forms. Once an incoming message has been processed, an alert can be sent to key personnel notifying them of the new information.

- **Scripts can help send e-mail, especially in batches.** Sending a single e-mail message to a huge list can be less impersonal by a script that sends a separate e-mail to each person on a list with a personalized greeting. Scripts can even build a unique e-mail based on customer ordering patterns, available material, and encoded business rules that describe how the recipient and the personal message should be matched up.

Desktop publishing automation

Using scripts to automate laborious desktop publishing tasks could fill endless volumes. Scripts can build simple pages with a variety of styles or build complex pages with hundreds or thousands of specific business rules encoded. They can build catalogs, complex tables, and charts, and automatically import text and images from various sources. They do all of this while reducing errors, improving consistency, and flawlessly enforcing style guidelines. In addition:

- **Scripts can build catalog files of any type.** Even a catalog with uniform styling and formatting can be a burdensome task to build by hand. A user must copy, paste, position, and style text, then search for and import the appropriate artwork or images. When catalog pages vary by category or product data, scripts eliminate the need to remember numerous layout design rules. They can quickly and accurately locate the text and images necessary to build richly styled and dynamically spaced product information into a copy of the appropriate template. Watching for changes in category or other group fields, a script can diverge the styles and structure based on the appropriate rules. For example, each product category could require the insertion of a title page with a leading blank page or it might prompt the creation of an entire new document for each section.

- **Scripts can scan documents and build indexes or tables of contents.** They can cross-reference products across corresponding documents, such as a catalog that has a separate price book.

Some processes are too daunting to contemplate without scripts, such as modifying hundreds of price changes or adding or removing products. Instead of manually updating pricing and squeezing new products into spaces left by old ones, a script enables you to simply build an entirely new catalog.

Monitoring sales performance of a catalog or other advertisement can be difficult when simply looking at the numbers. The context of the sale — such as the page the customer was reading when ordering — can be just as important to determine which strategies are working and which are not. A script can open documents, color-code product information based on actual sales, expand the page size, and integrate key sales data right on the page. Imagine the advantage of not just knowing how well a product did but also why it did so well when placed in a certain location on a page.

Central processing and resource monitoring

Even as a script saves you time, it might be wasting it. Rather than sitting idle, mesmerized as you watch a script take control of the applications on your computer, you might consider setting up an automation server. Just as a file server, mail server, or Web server centrally processes information for its respective services, an *automation server* is a shared computer on a network that centrally processes all of your automated activity.

TIP

A Windows-based company can still benefit from AppleScript automation with a single Mac acting as an automation server. All of the scripts process incoming files and then push them back out to the users. This can even be a great way to help convince management to consider a full switch to Mac OS X.

Instructions can be sent to an automation server is many different ways. The most common is to simply move files for processing into folders that are being watched by a script. When a new file appears, the script "wakes up" and begins processing them. Likewise, users might indicate through a database or a small custom script which catalog they want to build. The script would receive these instructions and begin the process. With an automation server watching folders, multiple users can send files dozens or hundreds of files at the same time. They are queued up in the watched folder and are processed while users work on other tasks, go to lunch, or leave for the day. The scripts keep on working.

Scripts that monitor valuable resources and ensure that key systems are up and running are best suited when they are running on an automation server. For example:

- **Scripts can search, sort, and extract data from databases and then create and send periodic e-mail reports to key personnel.** A script can send a daily sales report, tabulated survey data, a summary of sales leads, and any other kind of report you can generate manually. This saves users the time it takes to locate, open, and create a report query, and a report can even be generated early in the morning before the staff arrives.

- **A script can scan a file server to ensure that folder structure rules are being followed.** If misfiled items are detected, it might send an e-mail alert listing the offending items and can even include a URL link so the reader can quickly navigate to the item to remedy the situation. It might send one e-mail to graphic artists informing them that images are supposed to be in a subfolder called Product Images and another to the sales team indicating that spreadsheets need to be in the Reports folder. Managers can be CC'd on these, notifying them of issues and empowering them when they need to enforce compliance.

Users of AppleScript

While the AppleScript language is designed to be accessible for casual programmers of varying skill level to write scripts, it can be used by anyone. Scripts built with AppleScript can dramatically increase a user's productivity while simultaneously reducing stress and errors and increasing adherence to business rules Scripts free up users to focus on details that cannot be automated and require human attention.

Individuals

Whether an employee works for a small, family-owned business or a Fortune 500 corporation, he can use AppleScript solutions to streamline any repetitive task. Any task, large or small, involving at least some repetition can typically benefit from automation. These custom tools can be built to help remind, assist, and notify this employee with his daily work.

Teams

As part of a team, individuals need to focus not only on their work but also keep in mind how their work integrates with their co-workers and the goals of the team. When each member of the group has access to a well-designed set of tools that helps her get her work done quickly while adhering to company policy, the team will benefit enormously. Scripts can help team members navigate project folders; store files in the correct location, with approved naming conventions; and notify others about their status. Scripts can remove much of the stressful and redundant tasks that can sap the creative effort a team needs to thrive. An overworked team might rejoice over more work as long as they have the tools necessary to get it done.

Companies

The breadth of a scripted solution has no limitations. As long as it is worth the development effort required, automation can provide solutions to individuals, teams, divisions, and more. Any and every department within a company can benefit by automation. Whether it is sales, marketing, design, inventory, shipping, or any other department, AppleScript provides a powerfully scalable technology that can be a solution to almost every repetitive problem you can imagine, regardless of the industry. Scripts enable companies to improve the quality and quantity of work while reducing costs, errors, and stress, leaving in their wake an environment conducive to creative thought.

Respecting the Power of AppleScript

In the past, especially the early years of its genesis, AppleScript was often given a bad rap. Some would say it was only a script language, not a programming language. Others referred to it as buggy, slow, or weak. Some even predicted its obsolescence once Apple's OpenDoc technology emerged. Ironically, it was OpenDoc that was scraped in 1997.

Sometimes the criticism would come from programmers who promoted costly development in other languages, while other times, it came from developers or users who were "Windows centric" and looked down on the Mac and Apple. In this age of iPods, iPhones, and the witty "Mac versus PC" commercials, it may be difficult to believe this, but at the time, it was quite fashionable to predict doom and gloom for Apple and all of her wares, both hard and soft.

Admittedly, at least some of the criticism may have been earned, at least at first. There were bugs and speed issues in the early years, but the same was true of the Mac OS. It relied a lot on third-party scriptable applications, which were slow to embrace it. But slowly, over time, the bugs were fixed, the computers became faster, and the scriptable applications began appearing everywhere. The language made the transition to the new and modern OS X and continued to evolve and to embrace new technologies.

AppleScript survived and, more importantly, it flourished. It won awards, was the focus of "return on investment" studies, and finally silenced the critics. Today a skillful developer can automate a large portion of a workflow, creating an unprecedented boom in efficiency.

It is finally time that AppleScript gets the respect it is due as a truly unique, powerful, and revolutionary technology that remains hard pressed to find an adequate rival on any platform. It is easy to learn, easy to use, and can do almost anything. It has been used to build countless catalogs, brochures, and factsheets. It has processed images, text, numbers, and more. It has been the workhorse of the computer age, doing the heavy lifting between applications, processes, and users. All indications show it will continue doing so for the foreseeable future.

Summary

In this chapter, you were introduced to AppleScript. I discussed its historic design and gradual percolation into many corners of the Mac OS. You became acquainted with the location of key resources, including applications and scripting additions. I also discussed the unique characteristics of AppleScript and explored the uses for, and users of, this amazing technology.

Workflow Automation with AppleScript

Before delving into the intricate details of designing, developing, and deploying AppleScript workflow solutions, take a step back and consider the various ways the solution might be used in the future. Such reflection will give you a much richer grasp of the benefits of AppleScript and what it can help you achieve.

A *workflow* is an ordered sequence of individual steps that are performed together to achieve an overall task. Although the term can refer to any task, in this chapter, only tasks performed on a computer are relevant.

Before you can automate a workflow, you need to abstract the workflow steps from the other unrelated tasks with which they intersect. You must also delimit your focus to avoid being caught up in the folly of automating everything.

For example, suppose you were presented with the challenge of automating a catalog production workflow. At first it might sound easy. After all, there are only three or four steps. Material is created, placed into a page layout document, proofed, and then converted into a portable document format (PDF) file for print. However, each of these steps can be considered an entire workflow on its own. The text and images that eventually find their way into a page layout program might go through dozens of steps, from concept to completion, before getting to the page layout step. Further, some of the steps that occur during concept and completion might be defined as separate, smaller workflows. If you reduced the entire process down into the smallest individual steps, there might be thousands or millions of them.

2 ▸ **In This Chapter**

Defining workflow automation

Exploring reasons to automate a workflow

Understanding why AppleScript is the best language for workflow automation

When defining a workflow for eventual automation, it is important to focus on a reasonable portion of the "big picture" process. But you also need to choose processes that lend themselves to automation. Appropriate processes must have a lot of repetitive activity and not a great amount of creativity. Writing a script that places and styles text according to static business rules is a much more sensible choice for automation than trying to make a script perform the creative writing process necessary to generate the text in the first place.

Another factor to consider when searching for a workflow to automate is who performs the work manually. If your script will perform a handful of functions that you or your co-workers currently do manually, there isn't much to consider. However, some workflows might involve tasks performed by dozens of people. Those people might work for the same company or be diverse members of different companies, offices, departments, or disciplines. In such a case, you must consider the human factor as part of your definition of the workflow to ensure that you don't try to automate a workflow with a single script that must somehow pause and wait for people to perform a few steps. Instead, there should be multiple scripts, one for each discrete portion of the work. In essence, you want to automate tasks "between" people and not "through" them.

It can be a challenge to untangle a process from all the other processes and the people involved while simultaneously considering all the variables. Successful developers need to be able to alternate their focus from the isolated details of a process and the full context in which it exists. This skill is crucial for developers defining a workflow for automation.

Defining Workflow Automation

Workflow automation is the creation of a technological solution to automatically perform some or all of the tasks within a given workflow. Although the focus here is on automating manual activity performed with software on a computer, the term applies to anything that increases the efficiency of the user. This includes everything from an electric pencil sharpener to programmable welding robots building car frames, or even to the computers used to control the International Space Station.

The personal computer itself is an example of workflow automation. Expanding on past tools such as calculators and slide rules, computers eliminate enormous amounts of manual work and save time. With spreadsheets, we no longer needed to punch numbers into a calculator and write them on paper. With word processors, we can make edits in a single document rather than having to type up an entirely new version to reflect changes. Countless other examples of automated workflows, such as steps in image processing and desktop publishing software, have lifted enormous burdens from our hands and have freed us to do more creative work. However, it doesn't just end there. The time you save today is invested in making possible the more advanced tools of tomorrow. Workflow automation is a continuing step in the process.

Busting some myths about automation

Many of the myths about automation might seem a little dated today, but that alone won't quell them.

Automation will take my job

In today's world of gadget-crazed consumers, it's hard to imagine that only a few decades ago there was a lot of computer phobia, especially when it came to discussing automation. Many people feared that computers would end up replacing humans while they watched Captain Kirk repeatedly make computers spontaneously self-destruct by presenting them with a logical paradox.

While any technological advance can displace and even eliminate certain jobs, in the long run, it often creates far more jobs than it replaces. For example, someone has to design, build, market, sell, program, and maintain the robots that autonomously weld car frames.

If you are asked to automate a task currently performed by people, being sensitive to how the change will be viewed is certainly a good idea. Sometimes a complex solution might displace a few jobs. However, the majority of the time automated solutions are just another tool that people will use to reduce the burden of mundane and repetitive work. Artists can spend more time on the creative aspects of their jobs when they are relived from saving hundreds of images in three different sizes and formats for a Web site. Page layout experts can focus on the unique aspects of a catalog rather than tediously copying and pasting thousand of product descriptions onto catalog pages.

NOTE

It is important to remember that workflow automation with AppleScript is another way of making better tools and does not automatically mean that people will lose their jobs.

Automation will fix our problems

Perhaps the worst myth of all is that automation will fix problems. We should look to automation to amplify our strengths rather than to disguise our faults.

By itself, the act of automating a process does not guarantee an improvement to the process. While automation can magnify the efficiency of a process, it can also magnify any inefficiency that may exist. If business rules are not explicitly understood, documented, and communicated for a manual workflow, a workflow automation solution can inherit those flaws. If some of the steps required to carry out a certain task are forgotten or improperly embedded into scripts, the solution will not spontaneously correct those problems. This is one of the reasons why it is advisable to begin with smaller scripts and focus on familiar tasks, and then gradually take steps to advance to more complex situations.

The more removed you are from the end user, the more danger there is of someone assuming scripts can "just do things" without explicitly stating what those things are and the rules that guide them. If the end user has never performed the tasks manually, the danger of this myth increases exponentially. Be sure that everyone understands that while your scripts might seem magical, they aren't, and that you need clear details for even the smallest step in the process you are automating.

In the decades since the invention of the personal computer, we have witnessed amazing technological solutions to many problems that brought about many great benefits. But our relatively new "age of technology" is riddled with the corpses of horribly designed solutions. The majority of the time the fault lies in the belief that if we build it, it will "just work."

I can automate it and forget it

The notion that you can build a complex piece of software that endures throughout time is another dangerous myth. Custom solutions must interact with various pieces of hardware, software, and business rules that inevitably change and, therefore, require monitoring, maintenance, upgrades, and enhancements over time. With every operating system or third-party application upgrade, a scripted solution needs to be retested and tweaked to ensure that it will continue performing as designed.

Certainly, a script can be left to run autonomously and will not require as much attention as a fully manual workflow. However, creating a script that creates a catalog file does not mean the catalog will be "perfect" and not require proofing. It uses data written by people and images processed, cropped, resized, and named by people. In some cases, the result of an automated task requires more proofing to ensure that the scripts are working correctly. However, that additional proofing time may be offset many times over by the enormous time saved during assembly.

Automation is easy

Computers are so easy to use that they sometimes spoil us a little too much. Hidden from sight in the millions of lines of code is all of the effort needed to make them work well and keep our lives so carefree. The same is true of automation, which leads us to false conclusions that automated processes are easy to build.

Another culprit for the notion that writing scripts should be easy is our own brain. People are often amazed at the time involved to build a script that will automatically do things that they take for granted. Many of the mental tasks we perform so easily are very difficult to "teach" a computer. Deciding if a photo needs to be rotated or not is an instantaneous decision we make subconsciously. Picking a color to match a color scheme in a room is, at least for some, a simple task. However, these kinds of things are nearly impossible to program into a script.

N O T E
To write a script, you need to know every detailed step in the process, including all the decision-making logic that users might take for granted.

Automation will make us appear less personal with clients

The idea that automation shows or requires a lack of concern for personal interaction with clients or vendors is another common myth. Those who believe this fallacy have had too much exposure to poorly developed solutions. Everything from voice-mail systems that seem to be designed to keep us from every reaching a human being to cryptically formatted e-mails with "Do not reply" stamped in them makes some people leery of automating their interactions with their clients. However, these failures should be used as an inspirational call to arms.

T I P
Any poorly implemented solution can certainly appear cold and impersonal. However, if done well, automated solutions can present you and your company as a technologically proficient and efficient vendor, which is always a plus. Most of the time, automated solutions can be completely concealed from view.

A piece of technology, by itself, isn't impersonal. It all depends on how you use it. When the telephone was first introduced, there were probably some who complained that it reduced face-to-face meetings. However, it also enabled people to "meet" more often. E-mail likely raised the same fears initially, but now it's clear how it has dramatically increased the amount of information we can quickly communicate.

Databases need to operate with a serial number assigned to each client. However, that doesn't mean you should forget your client's name and refer to the client only by the number.

Automation doesn't automatically turn a company into a cold, uncaring box. Instead, it makes possible a new level of personalized client communication. Product announcements can be created based on a client's individual profile, giving them a brochure specifically designed for them. Customized project status reports can be created to keep the client up to date and well informed about their project. Using a person's name in the Reply To address and taking care to format the data in a friendly, easy-to-read manner should just be common sense.

Exploring reasons to automate a workflow

Automated solutions are, in a lot of ways, just like any other cost-saving policy a company might adopt. They can save time and reduce costs while increasing quality and capacity. However, unlike some new and oppressive rules and regulations dreamed up by "efficiency consultants," automation can achieve these goals while simultaneously reducing stress, improving morale, and allowing staff members to focus on more rewarding creative work rather than mundane, repetitive chores. In this way, well-designed workflow automation solutions can be mutually beneficial for both a company and its employees. Rather than viewing cost saving directives as punitive, employees and their company can use automation to obtain the same goals in a more rewarding way.

Improve consistency

One of the first things to be affected when people are overworked is consistency. It is hard to step back and look at the big picture when you are crunching out a batch of files as quickly as possible. The thought of stopping just to remind yourself of a naming convention for Web site files or the correct column order for a sales report can be grueling when the clock winds down and you still have dozens of items on an urgent to do list.

An automated solution with all the company business logic correctly encoded within it applies those conventions every single time it executes, and does so dispassionately. Many human errors caused by fatigue, stress, or carelessness magically disappear.

Improve quality

Automation can have a huge effect on quality. When a script frees employees from frantically working through lists of manual chores to meet a deadline, they can spend more of their time thinking about how they work and discovering new areas where automation might help improve their jobs. In short, they can focus on quality.

For example, if a script automatically assembles desktop publishing files, the layout designer can focus more attention on fine-tuning the master pages, style sheets, and artwork of the template. If a photographer doesn't have to manually save each photo in ten different sizes, each in a different file format and with a different naming convention, she is free to spend more time tweaking her photographs before sending them on to the next department.

Increase project size and capacity

Automation also can make it possible to increase the size and capacity of projects. New services that are prohibitively labor intensive suddenly become a possibility. Because a computer can run constantly day and night, and on weekdays, weekends, and holidays, it can be continually building, processing, informing, and managing a variety of automated tasks from a massive queue in a folder. Massive tasks can be assigned to a fleet of automated servers, each responsible for one or more of a group of automated tasks.

NOTE
When a script cuts the effort required for a particular project by some significant percentage, additional projects loaded onto the same staff are not as oppressive as they would be without automation.

Reduce stress

Stress is a human response to adverse conditions. In business, people can experience elevated levels of stress when they have too much pending work, are too close to a deadline, or do not have the proper tools to complete the work. Under stress, people often begin to rush, cut corners, forget procedures, make typos, and worse.

The most common "solution" to such a situation is to reduce an employee's workload. Automation makes it possible to shift the focus to tools that allow the work to be completed more easily, creating less of a burden on an employee.

Scripts can help remind, encourage, and even autonomously enforce naming and other business conventions. They work tirelessly to perform routine tasks while the user is out to lunch, in a meeting, or at home for the evening. An inbox full of messages informing you that your documents have been successfully processed and are now waiting for your review is far more welcoming than strict and ominous reminders that you have work due.

Well-designed automated solutions can be a huge stress relief to every user involved in a given workflow.

Encourage employee innovation

Sometimes people hide in their cubicles, never making any suggestions for improvements because they don't want to create more work for themselves or others. Any suggestion for improvement to a company's products, services, or some part of their workflow often results in more work for someone, usually the one with the idea.

Workflow automation can have an opposite effect, making employees fountains of innovative ideas. Once users realize that automation creates tools that help them be more valuable employees while doing less manual work, their enthusiasm for innovation may be difficult to contain.

Using AppleScript for Workflow Automation

There are many reasons to choose AppleScript as the programming platform for automating a workflow. After all, the language was specifically designed to allow users to create custom solutions to automate workflows of any size, shape, and form. Other technology is hard pressed to boast the return on investment (ROI) and quality improvements that are proven with AppleScript every day.

Understanding the scalability of AppleScript

AppleScript is highly scalable in size and scope. Scripts can start out small, automating a single task with a few lines of code. Over time, they can grow into multifunctional tools and awesomely complex applications. They can also be designed to adapt as business rules and requirements change. Understanding some of the different form factors a script can take is beneficial knowledge to have.

Transition scripts

A *transition script* is a small script that provides a simple way to transition from one context to another. These scripts might only save a few seconds each time they are used, but over time those seconds add up.

An example of a transition script is a small script that enables users to quickly open a server folder of their choice. A button on a contact record in FileMaker Pro that uses a small script to locate and open a related folder is another. A text "cleaning" script might manipulate text in the clipboard in a variety of different ways, such as removing or adding hard returns, sorting the paragraphs, adding or removing prefixes or suffixes, or quickly saving the data into a text file in a folder the user chooses.

If a user forwards or replies to e-mail with standard responses or instructions, a simple script can automatically prepare the e-mail for review. Or if a selected file needs to be sent to a group of people, it can be dropped on a script that gives the user a choice of e-mail, FTP (File Transfer Protocol), or some other method of delivery and of a list of recipients.

TIP

People often underestimate how much time is lost navigating around a server or typing out commonly used instructions into e-mail messages again and again. Small transition scripts can make a huge impact on a workflow, especially when they are used by a large number of people.

Script tools

A *script tool* is a script that performs some specific function or set of functions. While the size and scope of the automated task can vary dramatically and can evolve over time, a script tool is narrowly focused, much like the tools you use in your everyday life in the garage or kitchen. They are meant to be executed on users' machines while they wait, setting them apart from fully autonomous solutions intended to run on a servers or dedicated computers.

NOTE

Script tools are probably the most popular type of scripts built with AppleScript. They are relatively easy to design and develop and they have an immediate positive effect on the user's work. Simple tools can cross the line into transition scripts while more complex ones might blur the distinction between tools and full-blown solutions.

One of the best examples of a script tool is a batch processor script. Batch processor scripts perform a limited set of functions on any number of files. They might add layers, flatten or resize images, modify file names, generate reports, look for errors, convert file types, merge or parse PDF pages, and many more similar functions.

CROSS-REF

Chapter 18 and Chapters 22–25 contain a detailed example of an image batch processing script evolving from a simple tool to a robust solution as new concepts are applied to the script in each successive chapter.

Script tools can do just about anything. Some might create a complex folder structure for a new project or help copy standard files into a new user directory. Others may help a user create a new product sheet from one of a group of available templates. Script tools can help search documents for text overflow errors or help users connect to servers in the morning. There really is no limit to the kinds of tools a thoughtful developer can dream up.

Script solutions

A *script solution* is made up of one or more scripts that automate highly complex and often lengthy processes. While the size and scope of solutions can vary like script tools, a script solution is more broadly focused on a larger sequence or quantity of tasks. While a script tool might help a user create a paragraph for a catalog page, or tabulate some data, a script solution can assemble an entire catalog file from start to finish. Besides the size of the scripts, the major distinction between a tool and a solution is that the latter is intended to run with minimal to no human intervention.

A script solution might start out small and gradually expand. In fact, many times a group of script tools can merge and evolve into a solution. As they become more complex and begin to control more steps of a workflow, script solutions can expand into a multi-module solution made up of dozens or hundreds of individual script files that are managed by a primary module that orchestrates a complex workflow.

CROSS-REF

Chapters 24 and 25 discuss techniques for creating multi-module, open-ended solutions.

The most common type of script solution is desktop publishing automation. For example, a script can perform multiple find, sort, and export routines to gather product information from a database that will be placed and styled in a page layout document. Next, the script can find image files on a server and import, size, and position them. Throughout this process, countless business and style rules are consistently applied. Product subcategories are automatically started on a new page or in a new document. Spacing is dynamically adjusted based on the amount of content for each product. Once the file has finished building, the script can save it for review or print it to a PDF file. It might also cross-reference products and price lists, and scan the document for text overflows or other issues and report them in a dialog box, text log, e-mail, or any other communication software. The same process can apply to any type of file, including brochures, flyers, reference guides, catalogs, and more.

Script solutions can take many other forms. Some might watch folders for files to process or instructions to carry out. Others might monitor file servers and report misplaced files to administrative personnel and performance issues to technical personnel. Others may merge photos into a time-lapse movie or contact sheet. Solutions can alert, analyze, build, create, compile, convert, delete, export, import, modify, or report just about anything.

Quantifying the return on investment potential of AppleScript

Many of the arguments for the adoption of workflow automation in general and AppleScript automation in particular might seem obvious. However, it is always nice to be objective and simply present established facts to support such claims, especially when you are attempting to convince those who control a budget that it is worth the investment.

As fortune would have it, in 1999 GISTICS, a research firm that investigates new technology adoption and the strategic role that third-party developers play in maximizing the payback of new technologies, created seven informative publications analyzing Apple's technology. One of them was titled "AppleScript Payback Assessment — Return-on-investment Calculations for the Deployment of AppleScript by Smart Media Producers". Although it is now more than ten years old, this 54-page document highlights some very impressive results from using AppleScript to automate a workflow. I have derived most of the factual data I present here from that report.

CROSS-REF

You can view the entire GISTICS AppleScript Payback Assessment at `www.wtmedia.com/services/applescript/AppleScript-ROI.pdf`.

An Automation Case Study

At my company, Write Track Media (`www.wtmedia.com`), we spend each day creating solutions that make our clients more efficient. In this particular case, the results the client reported were truly astonishing.

Before this particular client's collaboration with Write Track Media, they were developing QuarkXPress files manually. In 2002, two full-time employees and one part-time employee manually generated 15 catalogs with an average of 94 pages and a total of 3,700 products. They had a total of 62 human errors. They had to place text and images by hand and cross-reference data between a specification book and a price book.

In 2006, using a Write Track Media workflow automation solution, two full-time employees generated 26 catalogs with an average of 180 pages and more than 15,000 products. They had a total of eight human errors.

Managing four times as many products in almost twice as many catalogs, fewer employees were able to perform the work much faster and more accurately using our custom optimized workflow solution.

Assembling a single catalog manually used to take multiple people weeks and months. Now, an automated solution can automatically build and cross-reference the two book sets in less than four hours! The staff now focuses its time on proofing and managing data rather then the tedious, time-consuming tasks of building a catalog by hand.

This is another example of the power potential of a database-driven, desktop publishing solution automated with AppleScript.

Monetary savings

Deploying AppleScript solutions can yield return on investment (ROI) figures anywhere from a typical five-fold annual ROI to an astonishing 24 times ROI realized in the first year of AppleScript deployment. In 1998, AppleScript produced an estimated $100,630,500 in total savings for North American media producer firms. One firm, after an investment of 500 hours developing a suite of scripts, derived $500,000 to $1.2 million in annual savings.

Improved quality

When deploying AppleScript as a strategic platform by which to reengineer and systematize business processes for profit, executives and owners derive higher quality production at significantly lower costs and shorter production cycles. Scripts don't forget even the smallest rules they are "taught" and the attention to detail never fluctuates, no matter how tedious the task.

Increased productivity

Simple tasks can be performed three to ten times faster by using AppleScript. For example, AppleScript can reduce complex tasks such as the composition of a catalog from a nine-person workweek to less than one hour.

Increased workload and profit

AppleScript creates more predictable workflows, enabling firms to accept larger jobs and faster cycle times.

Rapid implementation

Compared to the time required to plan and develop solutions built with programming languages such as C++ or Visual Basic, AppleScript solutions can be built very quickly. Time-saving ideas can become part of your daily production process in a much shorter time frame and require less development and troubleshooting than other languages can offer.

Summary

In this chapter, you learned about the benefits of automating a workflow. Reasons for using AppleScript were discussed, including its amazing return on investment (ROI) potential.

AppleScript Deployment Options

A script is considered *deployed* when it is distributed to users to utilize in their daily workflows. Scripts can be deployed in a variety of file formats and locations on a user's computer or networked file server.

A script's deployment options should be considered during both the design and development phases of a script. Some file formats are best suited for small script tools while other formats are more appropriate for larger solutions that may be made up of multiple script files. Likewise, certain installation or usage locations for scripts vary their compatibility with certain file types. All of these issues affect how a user interacts with a script and should be taken into consideration as early in the development phase as possible.

CROSS-REF
This chapter focuses only on the formats available when saving scripts and locations into which to deploy scripts. For more information about the AppleScript Editor application and working with scripts, see Chapter 6.

Exploring AppleScript Formats

The AppleScript Editor's Save As dialog box, shown in Figure 3.1, provides formats and options when saving a script.

Figure 3.1

The AppleScript Editor's Save As dialog box

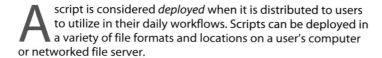

In This Chapter

Looking at the formats and options available when saving scripts

Looking at script deployment locations

Charting user interaction options in each deployment location

Four formats are available: Script, Script bundle, Application, and Text (see Figure 3.2). Each of these choices creates a file with a corresponding extension and icon, as shown in Figure 3.3.

Figure 3.2

Four file formats are available in the File Format pop-up window.

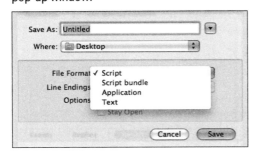

Figure 3.3

Script output formats

Saving scripts as files

A *script file* is a file that contains a single script. AppleScript documents can be saved and deployed as one of three types of files: text, compiled script, and compiled script bundle. Each of these formats has different properties that you should consider when deciding how to deploy a script.

NOTE

In most circumstances, you would not want to deploy a script as any script document unless it will be attached to a menu or palette of another application where it can be run without the need to open it in the AppleScript Editor. Instead, saving a script as an application enables any user, especially non-programmers, to interact with the script just as he would with any other application on his computer.

Saving a script as plain text

Saving a script as a text file enables you to open and edit the script with any application that can read text files. Because the script has an extension of `.applescript`, it will open in the AppleScript Editor when double-clicked; however, it will also open in any text-based application, such as TextEdit, if you drop it on the application icon or choose it through application's File ⇨ Open menu. Figure 3.4 shows a text-based script open in TextEdit. Because it is a text file, you can edit the script and save it regardless of the application you use to open it.

Figure 3.4

An example of a script text file opened in TextEdit

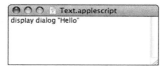

If you open the file with the AppleScript Editor, you can compile and run a script like you would any other script file although the file will continue to be saved as plain text. Due to this condition, it is not practical to deploy a script as a text file. Instead, use a text file to save a script that is under development and can't yet be compiled.

When saving a script as a plain text file, you can specify the line endings by selecting the desired option from the corresponding popup window in the Save As dialog box (see Figure 3.5). The choices include Unix (LF), Mac (CR), Windows (CRLF), and Preserve Line Endings, each of which is described here:

- **Unix (LF).** Choosing this option inserts a line feed character (Unicode ID 10) to mark line endings.
- **Mac (CR).** Choosing this option inserts a carriage return character (Unicode ID 13) to mark line endings.
- **Windows (CRLF).** Choosing this option inserts a combination of a line feed and carriage return character (Unicode ID {10,13}) to mark line endings.
- **Preserve Line Endings.** Choosing this option retains the existing line endings.

Figure 3.5

You can choose the type of line endings you want to use in the Line Endings popup window.

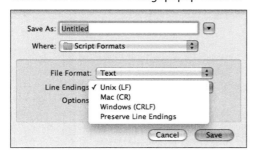

Saving a script as a compiled script file

 A *compiled script file* is a file that contains both a single editable, text-based version of a script and a compiled, machine-code version within the same physical file. The file has an extension of `.scpt` and opens directly into the AppleScript Editor application when double-clicked. This format is the most commonly used of the three types of script files. In fact, it is the default option the AppleScript Editor presents when saving a new script document.

When opened with the AppleScript Editor, a script saved as a compiled script file is already compiled and ready to run. It does not have to be recompiled unless changes are made.

Unlike a script saved as a text file, a compiled script file will not be readable or editable when opened in another text editor. It will be a jumble of code, as shown in Figure 3.6.

Figure 3.6

An example of a compiled script file opened in TextEdit

You can save the compiled script as run only by selecting the corresponding option in the Save As dialog box. When choosing this option, the resulting script file will no longer be editable with the AppleScript Editor or any other program and will display the error message shown in Figure 3.7.

TIP

Be sure to save a separate, editable copy of the script for future development.

Figure 3.7

An error message indicating that a script file was saved as run only

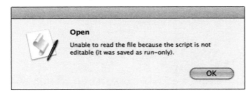

Saving a script as a compiled script bundle

A *compiled script bundle* is a script file similar to a compiled script, but with an embedded folder structure called a "package". The file has an extension of `.scptd` and opens directly into the AppleScript Editor application when double-clicked. Like a compiled script, a script bundle is already compiled when opened, so there is no need to recompile it unless changes are made.

The embedded folder of a script bundle can contain any material required by the script to perform its function, such as graphics, templates, and text-based data. This enables a script to appear to a user like a "regular" file, while keeping all of the resources tucked safely within it. This provides a great method to ensure essential resources will always be available when running the script. However, when scripts are distributed to many users, it is not practical to store data requiring frequent changes within a bundle.

CROSS-REF

Accessing items contained within the embedded folder structure of a script bundle is discussed in Chapter 16.

Once saved, the embedded folder structure is accessible through the AppleScript Editor's document window or directly through the Finder.

To open the folder structure from the script document window, click the Bundle Contents button in the toolbar to open a "drawer" on the side of the document window that displays the internal Resources folder (see Figure 3.8). The Action button at the top of the drawer provides a menu of actions that enable you to create new folders and open, reveal, duplicate, delete, and rename items within the contents folder.

To open the folder structure in the Finder, click the script bundle while holding down the Control key or click the right mouse button. Select Show Package Contents from the contextual menu to open the bundle as a folder and add folders or files. Unlike the toolbar button access in a script document, opening the folder structure directly requires you to navigate down to the Resources folder.

Figure 3.8

A compiled script bundle's embedded folder structure

As with a compiled script, you can choose to save a compiled script bundle as run only by selecting the corresponding option in the Save As dialog box. If you choose this option, the resulting script file will no longer be editable with the AppleScript Editor. Be sure to save a separate copy of the script for future development. Other files, including scripts that are added to the bundle package, will still be editable. Scripts can be individually saved as run only before being added to the package.

Saving scripts as applications

A *script application* is a script that is saved as an application. Users can interact with it like they would any other application they encounter in Mac OS X. They can double-click it to launch it, or once it is enabled, they can drop files or folders onto it for processing.

N O T E

Prior to Mac OS X 10.6, a script application could be saved as a "plain" application or an application bundle, which includes a folder structure within the application file. As of version 10.6, all script applications are bundles.

Although there is only a single choice for application in the Save As dialog box, there are two types of applications into which a script can be saved: as a run application or as a drop application (which is sometimes called a *drop*let). The two options are shown in Figure 3.9.

Figure 3.9

Scripts can be saved as one of two types of applications.

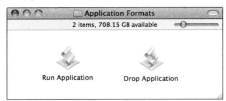

To edit a script application, simply drag and drop it onto the AppleScript Editor. Like a script bundle, applications contain a hidden internal folder structure, which can be opened in the Editor by clicking the Bundle Contents button in the toolbar and in the Finder by Control+clicking the file and choosing Show Package Contents.

Saving a script as a run application

A *run application* is any script that is saved as an application. When a user double-clicks the script application file, the file launches and executes the script's code. This enables a user to interact with the script as an application rather than as a bunch of code in a document.

Saving a script as a drop application

A *drop application* is any script that is saved as an application with an on open command handler subroutine. When a user drops files or folders onto a drop application, the script application file launches and processes each dropped item with the script's code. This enables a user to specify what material should be processed without having to select it through dialog boxes as they would with a run application.

Drop applications have an arrow superimposed on their icon, which helps signify to users that files or folders can be dropped on the script. You can do this by placing the following on open subroutine into the script and resaving it as an application:

```
on open listItems
     -- Add code to process the dropped items here
end open
```

The listItems parameter will automatically contain any files or folders that the user dropped onto the script application.

NOTE

While the application icon will now allow you to drop items onto it, no processing will take place because no specific processing code is included in this example.

CROSS-REF

Subroutines, including on open, are discussed in Chapter 21.

Saving a script with additional options

Three additional options are available when saving a script as an application: Save the script as run only, include a start-up screen when the application is launched, and keep a script application open after it has been executed.

Run Only

Like a compiled script, you can choose to save a script application as run only by selecting the Run Only check box in the Save As dialog box. If you choose this option, the resulting script application will no longer be editable with the AppleScript Editor. Be sure to save a separate copy of the script for future development. Other files, including scripts that are added to the application bundle, will still be editable unless they are saved as run only before being added to the package.

Start-up screen

You can choose to include a start-up screen when the application is launched. The start-up dialog box enables a user to run or quit the script. If you did not enter a description before saving the script, a default start-up screen, shown in Figure 3.10, will automatically be displayed. It will use the name of the script application for the title of the dialog box.

Figure 3.10

The default script application start-up screen

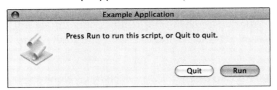

If the script has a description, the description will be displayed in a modified start-up screen, as shown in Figure 3.11. This is an ideal method of communicating information about the script to the user. You might include a description of what tasks the script will perform, what software is required, and any other short instructions a user might need to know when running the script.

Figure 3.11

A custom script application start-up screen based on the script description

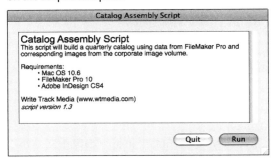

Stay Open

Selecting the Stay Open check box enables a script application to remain open even after it has been executed. This enables you to use the script again without having to re-launch it. It also enables a script to continuously "wake up" and execute at predetermined intervals when using the `idle` command.

CROSS-REF

The `idle` command is discussed in Chapter 21.

Exploring Script Deployment Locations

As Mac OS X has evolved over the last ten years, the number of places to store or attach scripts has gradually increased. Today, there are many places to store or attach scripts tucked away within the folder structures and user interface. There are two groups of deployment locations: those that provide an installation location and those that provide user access to scripts that are installed elsewhere.

While some locations are more practical than others, there is no "right" or "wrong" place to put a script. However, the deployment location you choose determines how a user finds and interacts with the script and, in some cases, can render certain features inoperable. Thus, it is important to explore and understand the available locations for script deployment.

Mac OS X installation locations

An *installation location* is a place on a computer where a script can be physically copied and then accessed in some way by a user. Some locations provide practical access directly from their location while others will be less accessible in a folder structure and you will need to use an alias or other interface element to navigate to them.

Applications folder

The most suitable location for most scripts saved as applications is in the Applications folder, where they will be grouped with other applications and be available to all user accounts. Figure 3.12 shows a script application named Catalog Assembly Script that is installed in the Applications folder.

Figure 3.12

A script application in the
Applications folder

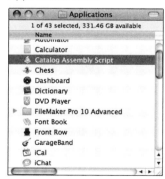

A user can access the script as he would any other application. For example, this script can be kept in the dock by manually placing it there or by choosing Options ⇨ Keep in Dock when clicking on it in the dock while it is running (see Figure 3.13). Also, an alias to the script can be placed on the desktop to aid in dragging and dropping items onto a script.

Figure 3.13

A script application Keep in Dock menu option

User Applications folder

Script applications used only by specific user accounts can be saved into an Applications folder inside the user's Home folder. While this folder is not automatically created with a new user account, it can be manually created and used for scripts or other applications specific to a user account.

Once installed, the user can launch the script through her home folder in the dock, as shown in Figure 3.14.

Figure 3.14

Opening an application through the user's Home folder in the dock

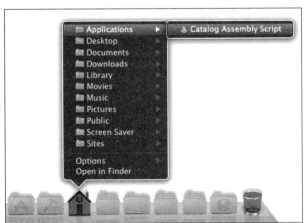

Desktop

From an organizational point of view, the desktop is not the best place to install scripts. However, it eliminates the need to remember where the script is stored and helps keep the dock free from clutter while still providing a quick and easy way to run or drop items onto a script application.

When more than a few scripts are used, it is best to install them elsewhere or merge them into a multi-module solution represented by a single script on the desktop.

CROSS-REF
Learn more about multi-module solutions in Chapter 24.

Script menu

The Script menu, shown in Figure 3.15, is an optional Mac OS X menu icon that provides users with a quick way to choose from a list of scripts. By default the Script menu is disabled and must be enabled in the AppleScript Editor's General preferences tab. This tab also enables the option to show the "Computer scripts," which are script examples provided by Apple.

TIP
The example scripts provided by Apple can be hidden with a setting located in the General preferences tab, reducing clutter in the menu without deleting the examples.

Figure 3.15

The default Script menu

CROSS-REF
The AppleScript Editor preferences are discussed in Chapter 6.

While the Script menu is a great place to deploy scripts of any size, it is well suited for large numbers of small scripts. They can be organized into a nested folder structure making them easy to locate and access. The Script menu is visible no matter which application a user has in front, so they are only a click away. The scripts can be visible in every application or can be configured to only appear when a specific application is in the front, which is discussed later in this chapter.

A downside to using the Script menu is that a user cannot drop files or folders onto a script for processing. However, a script that processes files or folders can automatically use the items currently selected in the Finder or can ask the user to make a selection using the `choose folder` or `choose file` commands.

CROSS-REF
The Choose a Folder and Choose a File dialog boxes are discussed in Chapter 16.

If a Script menu item is a compiled script document, when selected, it will run without opening the AppleScript Editor. However, if a script is saved as an application, it will launch when selected. This allows a startup screen to be displayed and the script application to stay open after it has finished processing the immediate task, making subsequent executions faster because it doesn't have to be launched each time it is used.

Script menu folder structure

The entire content of the Script menu is dynamically populated based on several folders that exist on the computer. This can be referred to as *using the Finder as a database*. Adding or removing files from the Script menu is as easy as adding or removing them from the corresponding folder. Any changes to the folder structure are instantly applied to the Script menu.

Two primary folders, shown in Figure 3.16, are used to populate the Script menu. These folders are referred to as:

- **Computer scripts.** These scripts are located in /Library/Scripts/ and are provided by Apple as part of the Mac OS X installation.
- **User scripts.** These scripts are located in: ~/Library/Scripts/. This folder is empty by default and ready for your custom scripts.

The User scripts folder can be configured to only show scripts that pertain to a single application when that application is in the front. This is accomplished by creating an Applications folder inside the user scripts folder. Within this folder, all scripts for the Finder will go into a subfolder named Finder. All scripts for FileMaker Pro will go into a folder named FileMaker Pro. The scripts in these folders will only appear in the scripts menu when their corresponding application is in the front.

The Script menu will even create these folders for you. The first menu item, Open Scripts Folder, is a submenu that contains three items. The first one will always dynamically open the current application's scripts folder, creating it if one does not yet exist. With the Finder in the foreground, this menu item will be named Open Finder Scripts Folder. If the AppleScript Editor is in front, it will be named Open AppleScript Editor Scripts Folder. When you select this item, it will open a folder for the front application in `~/Library/Scripts/Applications/`, automatically creating the folder if needed. This relationship between the front application and its corresponding folder inside the Applications folder in the user scripts folder is shown in Figure 3.17.

Script menu naming techniques

Once a group of scripts in the menu includes more than a handful of items, you run the risk of having a visually cluttered and counterproductive menu, like the one shown in Figure 3.18. With each script you add, the situation becomes more intolerable.

Splitting scripts into subfolders is a good first step to address the issue. In doing so, you can name folders so they contain part of the description of what actions the enclosed scripts will perform. Because the folders the user navigates to include much of this information, the script names can be shortened.

Figure 3.16

These folders provide content for the Script menu.

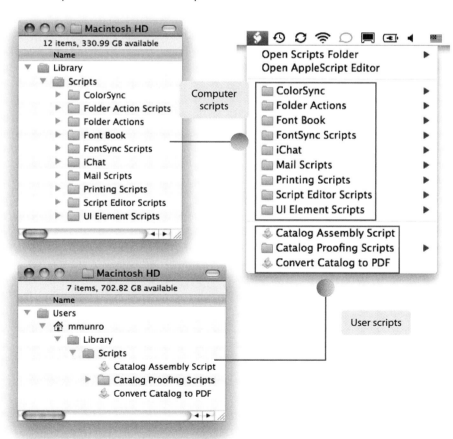

Figure 3.17

The Finder subfolder items are visible in the Script menu when the Finder is in front while other application scripts are not shown. The computer scripts are hidden for clarity.

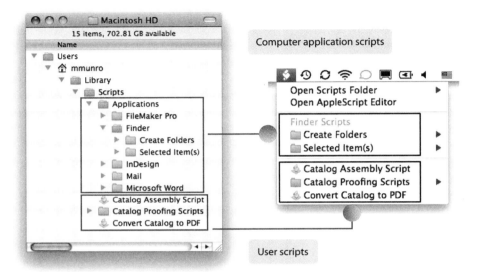

Figure 3.18

A list of Finder scripts in the Script menu

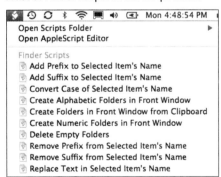

Consider a hypothetical instance where a script will rename the selected items in the finder by adding a prefix to each. In this scenario, the script might be named Add Prefix to Selected Finder Items. Another script that removes a prefix from the selected items might be named Remove Prefix from

Selected Finder Items. Once you begin adding other scripts that add or remove suffixes, change case, and replace characters, you may begin naming them in a way to group them together. For example, you might rename them Finder Selection – Prefix Add, Finder Selection – Prefix Remove, Finder Selection – Suffix Add, and Finder Selection – Suffix Remove. This makes them "sort friendly" because they will sort so all prefix and suffix modifying scripts appear together.

CROSS-REF
Naming subroutines to make them "sort friendly" is explained in Chapter 4.

The ability to organize these scripts inside of a hierarchical folder structure enables you to extend the "sort friendly" naming by splitting the names into parts with the "grouping" portions of the name as a folder. For example, within the Application folder, Finder, which contains scripts that will only show up when the Finder is in front, you can add a folder called Selected Item(s). Inside of this will be a folder called Rename, inside of which will be the script files with shortened names like Prefix Add, Prefix Remove, Suffix Add, and Suffix Remove, as shown in Figure 3.19.

This method uses the subsequent folders not only for organizational purposes but also to keep the list of available scripts in any one group to a minimum and increase ease of use.

Figure 3.19

A set of Finder scripts shown in hierarchical folders

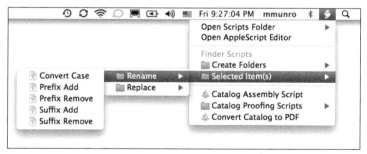

Attached to folders

A *Folder Action script* is a script that has been attached to a folder and will execute in response to a variety of activities, including adding or removing files or folders.

CROSS-REF
Creating and attaching folder actions to folders is discussed in Chapter 16.

Library folders

Both the computer and the user have a Library folder that can be a great place to store scripts, especially libraries of subroutines or generic modules that will be shared among multiple scripts installed elsewhere. The Library folders are also an ideal place to store scripts that will be made available through a user interface usage location such as the Finder toolbar, iCal, and other locations discussed later in this chapter.

In both cases, the Library folder is located immediately inside the corresponding folder. A hypothetical folder structure is shown in Figure 3.20. In this folder structure, logs, script applications, shared libraries, and shared modules can be conveniently stored in either Library folder. You may also add folders for templates and other resources that are locally stored.

CROSS-REF
Creating subroutine libraries and designing multi-module solutions is discussed in Chapters 24 and 25.

Figure 3.20

A hypothetical folder structure for centralized storing of script libraries, modules, and shared resources

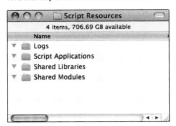

Where you decide to put the folder in either of the two Library folders is completely up to you. However, creating your own folder will help to insure that there is no conflict with other resources in other default OS X folders. For example, you don't want to put them into the Scripts folder unless you want them to be available from the Scripts menu mentioned earlier.

When naming the main folder that will contain your script resources, be sure to plan ahead for the inclusion of resources for many different scripts. Naming it something generic like Script Solution Resources is better than Image Processing Resources or Catalog Builder Scripts, which are too specific. Creating an open-ended subfolder structure that allows for expansion over time will save you from future headaches.

CROSS-REF
Learn more about designing open-ended solutions in Chapter 22.

File server

Similar to Library folders, storing scripts and script resources on a central file server is a great way to make them available to any number of users on a network. This enables users to instantly receive updated resources when they are updated on the server.

NOTE

Server-based material should be limited to scripts and resources that a script on a user's computer might load or copy. It should not include script applications that more than one user might launch at the same time.

Mac OS X usage locations

A *usage location* is a location within the user interface where a user can access a script that resides elsewhere, kind of like an alias.

Finder window toolbar

The Finder window toolbar can be customized to contain scripts. The toolbar, shown in Figure 3.21, offers a simple way to make a script universally available to a user no matter what window a user is browsing. In addition to launching the script with a click, if the script is deployed as a drop application, users can drop files or folders onto it for processing.

While convenient, using the Finder window toolbar as an access point for scripts can quickly become impractical. First, the toolbar does not typically offer much horizontal real estate and it can become cluttered with just a couple of scripts. In an attempt to solve the clutter, selecting to show icons only in the toolbar leaves you with icons that all look the same. Also, if a user chooses to hide the toolbar, the scripts become hidden as well and difficult to access.

Figure 3.21

The Catalog Assembly Script application in the Finder window toolbar

Finder window sidebar

Depending on a user's preference, the Finder window sidebar can contain Devices, Shared Servers, Places, and Smart Searches. Like the Finder toolbar, the Places section of the sidebar can include scripts.

Mail rule

Apple's Mail application enables users to create rules for handling e-mail based on numerous criteria. One of the actions that can be performed when a message adheres to a given criteria is to run an AppleScript, as shown in Figure 3.22.

Figure 3.22

The available actions to perform on a Mail message, including Run AppleScript

Once you select Run AppleScript, click the Choose button, shown in Figure 3.23, and select the script that should be executed as the action portion of the Mail rule.

Figure 3.23

The Choose AppleScript Mail rule controls

As a Mail rule, a script can perform any number of tasks. It can move content of a message into an e-mail archive database, link it to a contact record, file the message into a folder, and automatically create a reply to confirm receipt of the message. Another script rule might detect e-mail messages that contain Web form data or some other structured data and parse it for other uses such as a database or spreadsheet. It could also send alerts out to coworkers via e-mail, chat, or other scriptable communication mechanisms.

Print Dialog PDF menu

The Print Dialog PDF menu, shown in Figure 3.24, is a menu of functions that appear when you click the PDF button at the lower-left corner of the Print dialog box.

Figure 3.24

The Print Dialog PDF menu

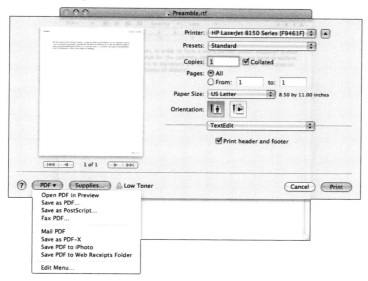

The Print Dialog PDF menu is a great example of an open-ended feature or a feature with built-in functionality that can be infinitely customized. Rather than adding a few predetermined menu items, Apple created an expandable menu to which you can attach scripts. You can add scripts that open, rename, and modify PDF files; merge PDF files together; parse PDF pages apart; copy to an archive; and any number of other tasks you might desire.

By default, the menu contains four permanent options and four optional ones. Selecting Edit Menu at the bottom opens a dialog box that enables you to add or remove items from the optional items listed at the bottom (see Figure 3.25).

To create a script that can be used with the PDF menu, it must include an `on open` command handler, or subroutine. This is required because the Print process of the operating system will generate the PDF in a temporary folder and then "drop" it onto the selected script. From then on, it is up to the script to perform whatever tasks are required.

Figure 3.25

You can add or delete AppleScripts
in the Edit PDF Menu dialog box.

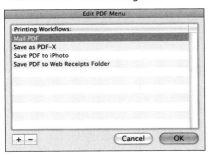

The following example accepts the dropped item, displays a dialog of its location, and then tells
the Preview application to open the file. While this example doesn't have much practical value,
it demonstrates the basic process involved.

```
on open pathToPDF
      activate
      display dialog pathToPDF
      tell application "Preview"
            open pathToPDF
      end tell
end open
```

CROSS-REF

The previous example is provided as a basic example of scripts used in the PDF menu but uses programming topics that
will be explained in later chapters. Learn more about the `display dialog` command in Chapters 6 and 16, and
the `on open` and other command hander subroutines in Chapter 21.

Once an appropriate script is saved as an application, it needs to be added to the PDF menu. To
do this, follow these steps:

1. **Open any document.**

2. **Choose Edit Menu from the PDF menu.**

3. **Click the plus (+) symbol in the dialog box.**

4. **Choose the script and then click OK to close the dialog box.** You should see the
   script in the menu, as shown in Figure 3.26.

Figure 3.26

The custom PDF Sample Script after
being added to the PDF menu

If you choose the new script from the menu, the dialog box shown in Figure 3.27 appears, displaying the path to the temporarily generated PDF file. The PDF will then open in the Preview application, shown in Figure 3.28.

Figure 3.27

A dialog box showing the newly generated
PDF file's location in a temporary folder structure

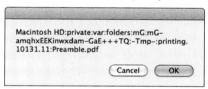

Figure 3.28

The newly generated PDF file open in the Preview application

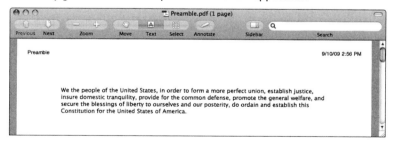

Like the Finder toolbar and Mail rule actions, a PDF script is a usage location only and the actual script file must be saved elsewhere. If you attach the script to the menu and then delete the script file, it will still be listed in the menu and will result in an error if selected.

CDs & DVDs preferences

The CDs & DVDs preferences panel enables a user to specify how his computer will react when disks are inserted. Typically, the preferences panel is used to select the preferred application to launch for playing the disk. However, one option for each of the five disk situations is to Run script, shown in Figure 3.29, which enables a script to be attached to a disk insertion event. This location for script usage has a fairly narrow focus and may only be practical from an automation point of view for those that might automate multiple disk duplications.

Figure 3.29

The options available in the CDs & DVDs preferences panel

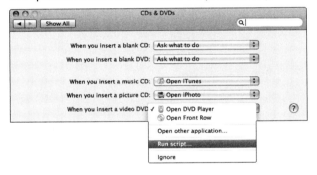

Mouse button preferences

The Mouse preferences panel enables a user to configure each of the four buttons on Apple's mouse to perform mouse or other functions. The Other option for each of the four button configuration popup menus, shown in Figure 3.30, enables an AppleScript application to be linked to a button. While it is not advisable to replace the left or right clicks with a script, the center button is a prime candidate for launching a commonly used script.

iCAL alarms

Apple's calendar program, iCal, enables a user to add an alarm to an event. The popup menu of alarm options, shown in Figure 3.31, includes Run Script. This can be used to automatically open documents and applications related to the scheduled event or to create an automation server that executes scripts repeatedly using iCal as the scheduling interface.

Figure 3.30

The button options available in the Mouse preferences panel

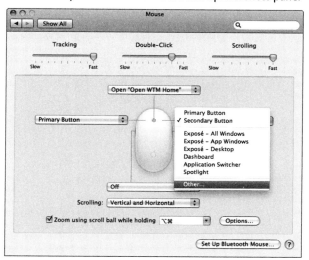

Figure 3.31

iCal's alarm options popup menu

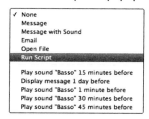

Third-party application locations

In addition to enabling scripts to access data and control actions, many applications developed for the Mac OS by third parties enable scripts to be embedded or attached. While it would be impossible to list them all, here are a few worth mentioning.

CROSS-REF

Using scripts to control applications is discussed in Chapter 21.

Adobe InDesign

Adobe InDesign CS4 has a script palette accessible by choosing Windows ➪ Automation ➪ Scripts. The palette, shown in Figure 3.32, has two categories: Application and User. The application scripts are samples in both AppleScript and JavaScript. The user category displays any scripts that are installed in the InDesign user preferences folder: `~/Library/Preferences/Adobe InDesign/Version 6.0/en_US/Script/`. To open this folder, click the User Scripts folder in the palette while holding down the Control key. In the contextual menu that appears, choose Reveal in Finder.

Figure 3.32

The default Adobe InDesign CS4 Scripts palette

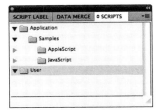

This is a great way to provide convenient access to scripts that perform activities primarily within InDesign documents. They can be organized into nested folder structures to help users quickly locate the script they need.

FileMaker Pro

AppleScripts embedded in databases can be executed with the Perform AppleScript option in FileMaker Pro scripts. This enables a database to reach out to the file structure of disks or any other application and access information from, and perform activity in, other applications. For example, with a click of a button, a user can instantly navigate to a project folder for the current customer record. Click in another button might open a proposal document for the current project record.

The FileMaker script step can perform a native AppleScript, or code that is typed directly into the Perform AppleScript step, as shown in Figure 3.33. When the script shown runs, AppleScript will perform the script, creating a dialog box with the text, "Hello World."

CROSS-REF

Learn how to create a "Hello World" dialog in Chapter 6.

More impressive is the Perform AppleScript step's capability to run a script that is the result of a calculation. The calculation can simply refer to a field that contains some static code or dynamically construct the contents of the script by incorporating information from fields from local or related tables and from variables. Figure 3.34 shows a simple example of displaying a dialog box that contains text from a FileMaker Pro field.

Figure 3.33

The FileMaker Pro Perform AppleScript script step with static "native" code

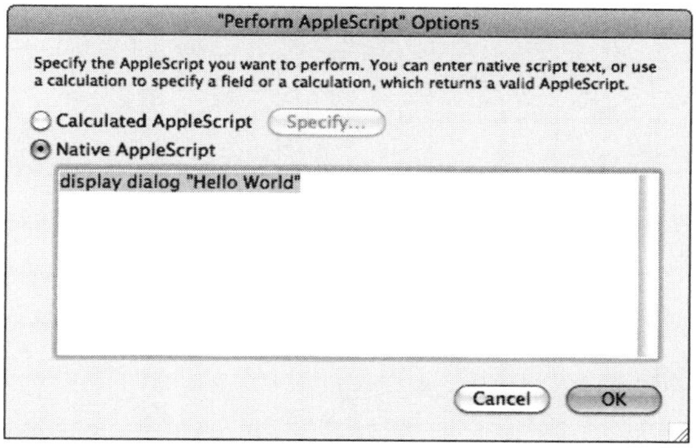

A skilled AppleScript developer can write an embedded script to save and load data to and from fields in the database, creating a seamless integration of scripts into a database.

Microsoft Word

Some applications, like Microsoft Word, include an integrated Script menu. The menu, shown in Figure 3.35, has only one item by default: About This Menu. When selected, it displays a dialog box that provides a button to open the scripts folder from which the menu is populated. This folder exists in the user documents folder at `~/Documents/Microsoft User Data/Word Script Menu Items/`. The choice of folder is somewhat unfortunate and really shows a lack of understanding of the Mac OS X folder structures. Applications really shouldn't store information in the documents folder, even when the user provides it. Such data should really be located in a subfolder of `~/Library/Application Support/`.

Any compiled script document or application placed into the folder will appear in the menu. Script applications in this menu will not launch as applications; they will be run like scripts within Word. The scripts in the folder can be organized into nested folders, which will appear as submenus in the scripts menu.

Figure 3.34

The FileMaker Pro Perform AppleScript script step forming dynamic code that incorporates a database field

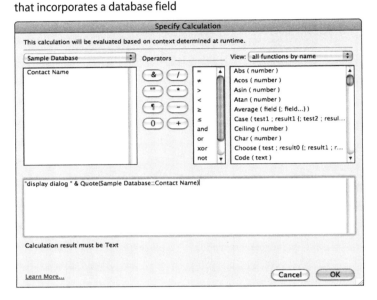

Figure 3.35

The Microsoft Word script menu

Choosing a Format and Location

Understanding the types of script formats available, the various locations into which they can be installed, and how a user interacts with them is only the first step. Assimilating all of these choices can be rather daunting, especially to a newcomer. Table 3.1 integrates the user action (run or drop) and, in some cases, script action (load or folder action) with script formats and deployment locations to provide an overview of the options available.

Table 3.1 Deployment Options by Script Type

Deployment Location	Text	Script	Script Bundle	Run App	Drop App	User Action
AppleScript Editor	√	√	√	√	√	Run
	–	–	–	–	–	Drop
Application Folder and Dock	–	–	–	√	√	Run
	–	–	–	–	√	Drop
Desktop	–	–	–	√	√	Run
	–	–	–	–	√	Drop
Script Menu	–	√	√	√	√	Run
	–	–	–	–	–	Drop
Finder Folder Actions	–	√	√	√	–	Actions
Library Folders	–	–	–	√	√	Run
	–	–	–	–	√	Drop
	–	√	√	√	√	Load
File Servers	–	–	–	√	√	Run
	–	–	–	–	√	Drop
	–	√	√	√	√	Load
Finder Window Toolbar	–	–	–	√	√	Run
	–	–	–	–	√	Drop
Finder Window Sidebar	–	–	–	√	√	Run
	–	–	–	–	√	Drop
Mail Rule	√	√	√	√	√	Run
	–	–	–	–	–	Drop
Print Dialog PDF Menu	–	–	–	–	–	Run
	–	–	–	–	√	Drop
CD/DVD Preference Actions	–	√	√	–	–	Run
	–	–	–	–	–	Drop
Mouse Button Preferences	–	–	–	√	–	Run
	–	–	–	–	–	Drop
iCal Alarm	–	√	√	–	–	Run
	–	–	–	–	–	Drop
InDesign CS4 Script Palette	√	√	√	√	–	Run
	–	–	–	–	–	Drop

continued

Table 3.1 Continued

Deployment Location	Script File Format					User Action
	Text	Script	Script Bundle	Run App	Drop App	
FileMaker Pro Field	√	–	–	–	–	Run
	–	–	–	–	–	Drop
Microsoft Word Script Menu	–	√	√	√	√	Run
	–	–	–	–	–	Drop

Summary

In this chapter, I discussed the various file formats and options available when saving a script. Many deployment locations were explored, including installation, usage, and third-party locations.

Making the Case for Standardization

T his chapter defines and discusses the need for AppleScript naming and usage standards and proposes a set of standards to follow. It contains a discussion about the benefits and the flexibility of standards, including the option of defining your own. In addition, special attention is given to the presentation of a specific set of naming standards for variables and subroutines.

Understanding the Benefits of Standards

The need for AppleScript programming standards may not be immediately clear, especially to those new to software development. To most developers, writing "good code" is a description of how well that code carries out the tasks assigned to it rather than how the code is formatted and what naming conventions are used for its various components.

Anyone who has sifted through a folder full of hundreds of poorly named files, or tried to remember which of dozens of Adobe Photoshop layers is which, should understand the need for clearly naming things and organizing them from the start. What seems like a laborious waste of time at first pays dividends later when you need to quickly locate and reuse some old work. In the end, it is a habit well worth that initial investment.

Standards for writing scripts are more important than file or layer organization. The need to open an old Photoshop file and find a specific layer may never arise, but at some point an old script will need to be upgraded, expanded, tested, or reused in a new script.

Because AppleScript uses an English-like syntax that is intended for use by any Mac user, it lends itself to somewhat sloppy results. Even experienced programmers might carry forward some lingering habits of the "old days" when memory was limited and abbreviated and cryptic naming was required. Also, many programmers passively absorb the naming and usage standards, or lack thereof, that they see in books and sample code written by others. It is important to realize that many books, including this one, often use shorter naming conventions in order to keep code readable on the dimensions of a printed page. In the "real world" scripts are not small, neatly packaged, examples of one or two basic concepts.

In This Chapter

Looking at the benefits of AppleScript naming and usage standards

Looking at the flexibility of standards

Identifying AppleScript naming standards

Identifying AppleScript usage standards

A developer struggling to learn the AppleScript language or trying to create a proof of concept for some new automated task may rightly not focus on a set of standards. However, as an AppleScript solution begins to grow, needs upgrading, or becomes a resource when collaborating with other developers, the need for and benefits of standardization becomes more pronounced.

Whether you write small scripts or complex multi-script solutions, understanding some of the benefits of standardization will help illustrate their vital importance.

Consistency

Perhaps the most important benefit of naming and usage standards is the way they encourage consistency from one piece of code to the next. In fact, the very act of standardization could be said to be nothing more than simply being consistent. It makes possible all the other benefits: efficiency, collaboration, and repurposing code for new scripts; and it enables you to see relationships between code that would otherwise be obscured. When you write code in a consistent manner, you need to rely less on your memory to keep track of which variable contains what value, thus enabling your focus to shift to quality, new features, enhanced performance, and more.

Repurposing

Eventually, every good developer will reuse old code for new scripts. If that code is months or years old, you may need to reverse engineer it just to recall how it worked and what values the poorly named variables contain.

By creating consistently well-commented and clearly named code from the start, you will be able to harvest generic code, merge it into libraries, and reuse it countless times with little or no additional effort.

Enhanced efficiency

The time you save by reusing well-designed code can be enormous. You can build new solutions that use previously written code in much less time and without the need to recall the specialized naming fads of the moment. You can use the time you save to improve the quality and feature set of the new code. You can also improve your efficiency, even when a script requires all new code. Navigating through a script, tracing a variable, and troubleshooting is much easier when you are working with well-designed code.

Improved quality

Standards help to promote good programming practices at the most basic level. If code can be reused without retesting, you will have `more` time to work on the new portions of a script, which results in a higher quality, full-featured solution.

Collaboration

Naming and usage standards enable multiple developers to collaborate on projects in a way that would otherwise be inefficient and in some cases not possible. If everyone agrees on naming and usage standards, a team can create solutions much faster and more efficiently.

Automation

Standards make it possible to develop automated systems that harvest and store subroutines in a database for future reuse. Without standards, it would be a grueling manual task to identify valuable subroutines, assemble them into libraries, and use them again in the future.

Professionalism

The final and all encompassing benefit of naming and usage standards is a more professional solution made up of high quality, consistent, and reusable code that requires less troubleshooting and is easier to expand and reuse.

Exploring the Flexibility of Standards

A code of standards should be viewed as a set of principles that can be applied to situations as they arise rather than a strict set of rules that must be obeyed. If it is a good set of standards, it will have a clear solution for each set of circumstances that may arise. However, even then, you may find situations that are exceptions or decide to modify the standards to meet your own individual needs.

Applying standards within a context

One example of when you might loosen the standards is with naming variables. If your script's only function is to build a very specific report, a generic variable name will be fine. When your script grows in size and includes several report-related variables, you will need to begin naming them with longer and more distinctive names. The overall context of the script and the types of activity it automates must be taken into consideration.

When a script contains only a few lines of code, there is no reason to group code into subroutines or include script comments describing what functions it performs. In fact, it would be a waste of time to do so. When a script approaches a dozen lines or more, you should begin to include comments. Consider using subroutines if a script grows beyond that.

CROSS-REF

Subroutines are groups of code segregated from other code. See Chapter 21 for more information.

NOTE

There is not necessarily an "exception to every rule" as some are fond of saying. However, you should apply principles with conscious thought and a keen understanding of the goals they are trying to achieve.

Setting your own standards

The standards presented in this chapter are those designed for and used by developers at my company, Write Track Media. They were developed in opposition to the default "standards" adopted, and promulgated, by almost every AppleScript developer, often without their conscious knowledge. In a perfect world, every developer of AppleScript would agree on a single set of universal standards, such as these; however, you should feel free to use, modify, or ignore them depending on your individual needs.

Defining AppleScript Naming Standards

Several script components can benefit from comprehensive naming conventions, including variables, subroutines, subroutine parameters, and properties. Each shares a set of goals that guides how they are named.

CROSS-REF

I discuss these topics in more detail throughout this book, so you may find it useful to reread this chapter when you are finished with the book. Variables are discussed in Chapter 5, properties are discussed in Chapters 5 and 22–24, and subroutines and subroutine parameters are discussed in Chapter 21.

The goals of naming standards

You should consider several primary goals when defining a set of naming conventions. These goals will guide you through the development of specific naming rules.

A Note About Case

Both the naming standards and all of the examples in this book use the style known as *camel case*, which is the practice of writing compound words with no spaces and with the first letter of each word capitalized except for the first. This is the prevailing method for writing names for AppleScript variables and subroutines. Examples include:

```
textReportData
dateOfExpiration
```

Using all upper- or lowercase is not common because it is difficult to read. Another method that is somewhat difficult to read is to use a delimiter (such as an underscore) between each word. For example:

```
text_Report_Data
date_Of_Expiration
```

Clarity

The primary goal of naming objects is to make sure that each name describes the object in a clear and consistent manner. Variable names should explain what kind of data they contain, what that data relates to, and how it might be used. Subroutine names should help group them with other similar subroutines, describe what material they process, and what kinds of actions they can perform.

If you have a variable that contains invoice data, you might name it `theData`. If there is only one piece of data for the entire script, this might seem like an acceptable name. However, if your script grows in size to handle multiple data objects or you return to the script after months of focusing on other projects, `theData` is too generic. While you know the variable contains data, the name doesn't tell you what kind of data. It might contain text, numbers, lists, records, and more. It also doesn't tell you what the data relates to. It could be data for invoices, scheduling, resumes, balance sheets, and more. Changing the name to `textInvoiceData` or `textInvoicePastDue` makes it quite clear what kind of data the variable contains.

Likewise, a subroutine named `makeText()` doesn't say enough about what kind of text will be created. Renaming it something like `makeInvoiceReport()` provides more information about what the subroutine is doing.

Non-cryptic

Abbreviating too much may be a remnant from the days when computer memory was limited or is a misguided attempt at brevity. Regardless of why people do it, shortening names into super-compact abbreviations is not only unnecessary but also unwise. The more often you make up cryptic abbreviations, the more of a drag it will be to your productivity as you gradually forget what they stood for.

Except for some rare cases when an abbreviation is universally known or established as a standard for all naming, it is best to avoid abbreviations altogether. When confronted with a name made up of too many long words, try rephrasing rather than using an acronym or abbreviation.

A variable that contains the number of people attending a meeting might be named cryptically `peepsAtMeet`; however, `meetingAttendees` is a better name. The amount of annual revenue might be called `dollsAnnRev`, which later might sound like a toy doll named "Ann"; something like `annualRevenue` is better.

A subroutine that counts the number of text boxes on a page would be too cryptic if it was called `pgTBxCnt()`. There is no reason not to expand the name to `pageTextboxCount()`.

Concise

The opposite of unclear and non-cryptic naming is not long and super-detailed names. Both are equally counterproductive. While longer names seem to be "clear," they visually clutter a page of code and overload the conscious mind, making them a bad idea. Names should be limited to three to six words and contain no more than 25 characters.

If a variable will contain the names of all the people who attend a meeting and `numPeeps` seems too cryptic and `listNames` too unclear, you might be tempted to use something like `listOfPeopleWhoAttendedTheMeeting`. However, this is much too long to be an effective name. Instead, you could name it either `listAttendees` or `listMeetingAttendees`.

A subroutine that puts styled text into a text box on a specific page in a desktop publishing document might be named `addTextToTextBoxInPageOnQuarkDocument()`. In this case, including the entire hierarchy of objects is unnecessary. Because a text box must be on a page in a document and you would be putting text into it, it must be a text box. So, it would be better to use something like `textAddWithStyle()`.

Professional

Keep names serious and professional by avoiding the use of acronyms and "cute" expressions based on slang, pop culture, or your own personal interests. These add to the length of names without adding any descriptive value or are unclear, distractive, and unprofessional. Slang and fads change over time and might even be offensive.

TIP

It may be tempting to display your personality in your scripts or to show off how cleverly you can obfuscate your meaning. However, if you want your clients and co-workers to take you seriously, keep your script names professional.

A variable that contains a list of late items should be called `listLateItems` rather than `yoStuffIsLateDog`. A subroutine that plays a selection of music in iTunes should be called `itunesSelectionPlay()` rather than `playFunkyMusicDude()`.

Consistent

A little naming consistency can make a huge impact on the quality of your scripts. When referring to objects, content, or activity of the same type, try to use the same terms universally. When you start mixing terms that refer to the same kind of thing, it can become a little confusing.

If you're describing the act of creating a new object, whether it is a folder in the Finder, a record in a database, or some text in a document, choose a term and stick with it. For example, use "create," "make," or "new," but not a combination of these. It often doesn't matter which term you choose just as long as you remain consistent. So, rather than using `finderFolderCreate()` and `quarkBoxMake()`, make the terms consistent by changing the latter to `quarkBoxCreate()`.

Also, try to keep the order of things consistent. For example, if you have one variable that contains overdue items and another than contains items that are on time, name them in a similar manner. So, instead of naming them `listLateItems` and `listItemsOnTime`, name them `listItemsLate` and `listItemsOnTime`. The consistent prefix `listItems` unifies them.

Case-sensitive

Keeping the case of names consistent adds to the professionalism and visual appeal of your code. You would not want to name variables `TEXTreport`, `DataREPORT`, and `listitemslate`, each of which uses a different case style. Instead, keep the case style consistent by naming them `textReport`, `dataReport`, and `listItemsLate`.

Naming variables

The general formula for naming variables is:

«Prefix»«Type»«Description»«…»

Both the prefix and type portion of the naming standards include abbreviations that are considered acceptable as universal standards. They add additional information about the type of variable and the content it contains without impinging too greatly on the rest of the name.

N O T E

All of the naming examples used thus far do not adhere to the naming formula described in this section in order to focus on specific issues. All names from this point on will adhere to the naming formula as long as space allows them to fit on a page.

Prefix

The «Prefix» is optionally used to differentiate certain types of variables. Table 4.1 lists the prefix naming variables. These are intentionally short and cryptic so they do not use up space for the more descriptive parts of the names.

Table 4.1 Prefix Naming Variables

Prefix	Description
c	Used to identify a temporary variable that contains some current data that will change on the next loop or its next instance. For example, in a repeat loop, if a variable contains the current item extracted from a list it might be named cNameFile, cNumToProcess, or cPathToStatusFile.
g	Used to identify a global variable. For example, a library global might be named gLibFinder while the root path to a solution folder might be named gPathToRoot.
p	Used to identify a property. For example, a property might be named pPathToOutput or pTextTemplate.
dev	Used to identify a variable that is used only when in development mode and should not be accessed or used in any way for the final release of a solution. Typically, these will be removed before the release or they will be contained within code that only executes when a developer allows it to.

Type

The «Type» portion of the variable name indicates the kind of data that is contained within the variable. Table 4.2 lists the type naming variables.

C R O S S - R E F

Learn more about the different data classes in Chapters 7–12.

Table 4.2 Naming Variables

Type	Description
alias	Used for variables that contain an alias to a file. Examples include `aliasToProjectFolder` and `aliasLogFile`.
bln	Used for variables that contain a boolean true or false value. Examples include `blnImageFileFound` and `blnMountServer`.
data	Used for variables that might contain more than one type of data. This is useful when receiving a value from a subroutine that could be a string, list, or number depending on the success or failure of the subroutine's code. Examples include `dataResults` and `dataToProcess`.
int	Used to denote an integer from a real number. However, if your scripts don't need the distinction, you can use `num` for all number-related variables.
lib	Used for variables that contain an entire subroutine library script. Typically, this is always used in global variables that make the library universally accessible within one or more script files. Examples include `gLibFinder`, `glibChartBuilder`, and `glibClientStyleRules`.
list	Used for variables that contain a list of data. A list of file paths might be called `listFilesToProcess` or `listPathsToProcess`, while a list of user names might be called `listUserNames`.
name	Can be used in place of `text` when a variable contains an actual name. Examples include `nameUser`, `nameFolder`, and `nameFile`.
num	Used for variables that contain numeric values. Examples include `numFilesToProcess`, `numRecordCount`, and `numPage`.
path	Used for variables that contain a text-based path and should typically include a second word such as "To" or "Of". Examples include `pathToHomeFolder` and `pathOfSourceFile`.
real	Used to denote a real number (a number that can include a fractional value) from an integer (a whole number). However, if your scripts don't need the distinction, you can use `num` for all number-related variables.
rec	Used for variables that contain records of information, such as `recDataToProcess` or `recServerLogonInfo`.
ref	Used for variables that contain a reference to an application object, such as `refWindow` or `refPage`.
rgb	Used for variables that contain an RGB (red, green, blue) value, such as `rgbBlack` or `rgbWhite`
script	Used in place of `lib` when a script module is contained within a variable, such as `scriptTemplate`, `scriptPageBuilder`, or `scriptModule`. For an explanation of the difference between a library and module, see Chapter 24.
text	Used for variables that contain a text value, such as `textToProcess`, `textInstructions`, `textMessage`, or `textReport`.

Description

The «Description» portion of the variable name should be a clear and concise description of what is contained within the variable. There are no specific rules for the description except for the general naming rules (short, clear, no abbreviations, consistent, and so on). The description can be one or more words as needed to adequately describe the data. For example, `pathToProject-Folder` contains a two-word description while `pathToServer` contains only one. Other examples include `recInvoiceData`, `refPage`, and `numPlanetsToVisit`.

As a script evolves, you might find your descriptions being expanded, contracted, or reordered, depending on the growing context of other variables. So, a variable might start out as `recInvoiceData` and then, when another variable is required and named `recScheduleData`, you might decide to move the data shared part of the description in front of unique part making `recDataSchedule` and `recDataInvoice` or, perhaps, `recDataForSchedule` and `recDataForInvoice`.

Naming subroutines

The formula for naming subroutines is:

```
«Group»«Object»«...»«Property»«...»«Action»()
```

The extra parameters «...» indicate that more than one word can be included for the object and property portions of the name of a complex subroutine.

One aspect of these naming standards most likely to be misunderstood and perhaps even maligned is the arrangement of parts in the subroutine naming formula. Ignoring the «Group» for now, the rest of the formula translates to noun-verb rather than verb-noun, which is the first instinct of AppleScript programmers. So, it might make sense to name a subroutine `create-Folder()` because it sounds like a sentence. However, the previous naming formula requires that you name the subroutine `folderCreate()`.

As your scripts grow in size and you begin separating code into subroutines the reason for this becomes more apparent. When looking at a list of subroutines in the AppleScript Editor, this naming formula organizes subroutines by object rather than by action. This also applies to lists of subroutines you may view in a database. So, all subroutines that perform actions to a folder would be sorted together as `folderCreate()`, `folderDelete()`, `folderRename()`, `folderNameGet()`, and `folderNameSet()`.

Figure 4.1 shows both naming philosophies side by side. The left is the verb-noun, or "sentence," form while the right column shows the noun-verb. While the proposed approach may not suit everyone, when your scripts begin to grow in size and you gather subroutines into libraries, you might find that its benefits justify acceptance.

Group prefix

The first part of the naming formula is the «Group» prefix. This can be the name of a functional group or subroutine library to which the subroutine is a member. Primarily its purpose it to do what it says — to group similar subroutines together. This is especially useful when viewing them in a list in the AppleScript Editor's navigation bar.

There are three recommended grouping methodologies you can use as needed: group by application name; function; and project or client.

Figure 4.1

Examples of naming subroutines. On the left is the verb-noun "sentence"; on the right is the noun-verb format.

```
on DeleteFinderItem                on finderItemDelete
on DoesFinderItemExist             on finderItemExists
on CreateFinderItem                on finderItemCreate
on GetFinderItemName               on finderItemNameGet
on SetFinderItemName               on finderItemNameSet
on OpenFinderItem                  on finderItemOpen
on CopyFinderItem                  on finderItemCopy
on MoveFinderItem                  on finderItemMove
on DeleteFolder                    on finderFolderDelete
on DoesFolderExist                 on finderFolderExists
on CreateFolder                    on finderFolderCreate
on GetFolderName                   on finderFolderNameGet
on SetFolderName                   on finderFolderNameSet
on OpenFolder                      on finderFolderOpen
on GetFolderContents               on finderFolderContentsGet
on GetTextContents                 on finderFolderContentsDelete
on SetTextContents                 on textContentsGet
on DeleteTextContents              on textContentsSet
on SettextStyle                    on textContentsDelete
on GetTextStyle                    on textContentsStyleSet
on CountTextCharacters             on textContentsStyleGet
on CountTextParagraphs             on textContentsCharactersCount
```

Group by application name

When naming low-level subroutines that perform a single function or a relatively small group of functions in a single application, the group should be either the application name or type.

Subroutines that perform functions with an application that has no alternative, like the Finder, should start with the shortest possible name for the application. For example, Finder subroutines should start with the group prefix of "finder."

Subroutines that perform functions with an application that has an alternative should start with the shortest possible unique name for the type of application. For example, subroutines that perform basic desktop publishing functions should start with "dp" rather than "quark" or "indesign." This is important for interchangeable subroutines, enabling the same name to be used for subroutines that perform the identical functions in another application of the same type.

CROSS-REF

For more information about naming interchangeable subroutines, see Chapter 25.

For example:

- db is used for database applications such as FileMaker Pro.
- dp is used for desktop publishing functions for applications such as Adobe InDesign and QuarkXPress.
- finder is used to group all subroutines that perform functions within the finder.
- ftp is used to group subroutines that perform functions with any file transfer software.

- `image` is used for photograph or image software such as Photoshop.
- `mail` is used for e-mail applications such as Apple's Mail and Microsoft Entourage.
- `word` is used for word processing applications such as Apple's Pages and Microsoft Word.

Group by function

When naming subroutines that perform non-application specific functions, the group should be the shortest possible name for the type of function that it performs. These may include all kinds of text, date, time, number, and other functions, all of which do not interact with any application.

For example:

- `date` is used to group all subroutines that perform date related functions.
- `number` is used to group all subroutines that perform math and numeric related functions.
- `text` is used to group all subroutines that perform text manipulations.
- `time` is used to group all subroutines that perform calculations of time.

TIP

For a subroutine that calls a variety of low-level application-specific subroutines for different applications, the group should be named by the type of function rather than the type of data. For example, if you have a subroutine that interacts with some FileMaker Pro and Adobe InDesign subroutines, you may want to name it based on the function it performs, such as `catalog` or `brochure`.

Group by project or client

Subroutines that perform functions specific to a particular client solution can be grouped together with a prefix of the client or project name. These can include simple or complex subroutines that work with a variety of applications, call a variety of other subroutines, or perform a variety of different functions. Typically, this type of grouping should only be used for new subroutines that are not open-ended enough for eventual inclusion in another generic and non-project specific library; that is, they will not be harvested for reuse.

Object

The second part of the subroutine naming formula is the «`object`». This should be the name or type of the primary object that will be manipulated or investigated by the subroutine. For example, a subroutine that manipulates a folder in the finder would start with `finderFolder`, with `finder` as the group and `Folder` as the object. A subroutine that manipulates a record in a database would start with `dbRecord`, with `db` as the group and `Record` as the object.

Some Finder object examples include `File`, `Folder`, `Item,` and `Window`. Database object examples include `Database`, `Field`, `Record`, and `Script`.

Whenever the object being manipulated is part of a hierarchy of objects, it is permissible to list some or all of that hierarchy. This kind of situation may occur in complex applications, such as desktop publishing where some text is in a sentence of a paragraph in a text box, on a page, on a spread, in a document.

An example of this is a subroutine that manipulates text in a desktop publishing application. You may want to differentiate subroutines that manipulate a paragraph of text from a character of text yet still want to group the two under the text object. You might name the subroutine:

```
dpTextParagraph«action»()
dpTextCharacter«action»()
```

In the previous example, `dp` is the group and `TextParagraph` is the object — a paragraph of text.

To avoid extremely long subroutine names, the object portion of the name should not contain more than one to three words. Unlike the examples shown earlier, you would not want to try to include every step of the hierarchy like this:

```
dpDocumentPageFrameTextFlowParagraphSentanceWord«action»()
```

Remember, most of the hierarchy can simply be implied. After all, if you are manipulating text in InDesign, it should be clear that the text must be in a box on a page and in a document. Any implied level of the object hierarchy can be excluded from the name. You should include only enough information as needed to clearly communicate the type of object to which the subroutine refers. In fact, the only reason to include `text` in the example `dpTextParagraph` is for sorting purposes, to keep it grouped with the character, word, sentence, line and text flow related subroutines.

Property

The third part of the subroutine naming formula is the optional «property». If needed, it should specify the property or properties of the object being manipulated or accessed. If a subroutine were going to manipulate or access the text format style of a word in a desktop publishing application, you might name it:

```
dpTextWordStyle«Action»()
```

In this example, `dp` is the group, `TextWord` is the object, and `Style` is the property or attribute of the object that will be manipulated or accessed.

If a subroutine were going to access the modification date of a file in the finder, you might name it:

```
finderFileDate«Action»()
```

In this example, `finder` is the group, `File` is the object, and `Date` is the property or attribute of the file that will be accessed.

Whenever the property of an object being manipulated is part of a hierarchy of properties, it is permissible to list some or all of that hierarchy as shown with the «Object» portion of the name. For example, if the previous subroutine were going to get the date format, you would want to list both properties for clarity naming it:

```
finderFileDateFormatGet()
```

Action

The fourth part of the subroutine naming formula is the «Action». As it sounds, it should specify the action being performed to the object. The most common actions for low-level, single function subroutines are Get, Set, Create, Delete, List, and Run. In addition to these, a complex subroutine might also have actions like Build, Calculate, Collect, and Process.

For example, getting or setting the style of a word of text in a desktop publishing application would be performed by subroutines that might be named:

```
dpTextWordStyleGet()
dpTextWordStyleSet()
```

Or, running a script in a FileMaker Pro database would be performed by a subroutine that might be named:

```
dbScriptRun()
```

Defining AppleScript Usage Standards

The AppleScript language enables you to write code to perform actions in a variety of different ways. While it typically doesn't matter which method you use, you need to consider several things when establishing a set of standards.

The goals of usage standards

Many of the goals of usage standards are similar to those for naming. They include functionality, consistency, and clarity.

Functionality

Obviously all code should be written so that it functions correctly and is not overly slow or buggy. Some of the usage standards presented in the next section help ensure that a script runs smoothly and is easy to read.

Consistency

Once again, whichever standards a developer uses, it is important he use it consistently. The same goal applies to code usage. If code is in a familiar format (structured the same as other similar code), browsing, reading, testing, and searching code will be less strenuous and, therefore, more efficient.

Clarity

It is important to avoid usage that makes code more difficult to read and understand. When presented with a choice between two formatting options, choose the one that is easier and faster to visually comprehend. There are reasons that books break text into paragraphs, sections, and chapters. The same reasons apply to writing code. You want your code to be laid out neatly and be easy to read.

AppleScript usage standards

First and foremost, code must carry out the functions it is intended to perform. Beyond that, these usage standards will help improve the consistency and clarity of your code, making it less visually cluttered and, therefore, easier to navigate, edit, share, and review.

Avoid line wraps

If a line of code is too long to fit the AppleScript Editor window that is set to your preferred width, try shortening or splitting the code into more than one line. AppleScript provides a method for making a line wrap regardless of the window width; however, short lines of code can be perused much faster than long wrapping ones.

In this example, a variable `listOfValues` is being set to contain the list of three text values.

```
set listOfValues to {"This is some sample text", "More text for
    wrapping", "Hopefully this will explain the issue"}
```

By contrast, this example achieves the same end without wrapping:

```
set text1 to "This is some sample text"
set text2 to "More examples of text for multi-line code wrapping"
set text3 to "Hopefully this will help explain the problem"
set listOfValues to {text1, text2, text3}
```

Removing the wrap makes the code easier to read. However, it also takes up more vertical space. Developers must find their own preference for avoiding or tolerating line wraps.

Compress vertical space

Sometimes a line of code can be compressed from a multi-line structure to a single line. For example, an `if-then` statement of five lines can be downsized to two lines, making it much more readable. Of course, if this should never be done if it makes the compressed lines wrap.

This example shows a simple `if-then` statement setting a single variable to one of two style sheet names:

```
if nameReport = "Sales" then
  set nameStyleSheet to "Sales Style"
else
  set nameStyleSheet to "Inventory"
end if
```

Because there are only two options available and the variable must be set to one of those, the code can be flattened from five lines to two. This example shows setting the variable to one of the two values and then adding a single line `if-then` command to change it to the opposite value if needed.

```
set nameStyleSheet to "Inventory"
if nameReport = "Sales" then set nameStyleSheet to "Sales Style"
```

As long as it doesn't cause line wrapping, less vertical space helps keep a script more compact and visually accessible.

CROSS-REF
For more information about `if-then` commands, see Chapter 13.

Avoid nested tells to multiple applications

A *nested tell* is the use of multiple `tell application` commands to several different applications, one after the other without an `end tell` before starting the next `tell`. This creates a situation where one application is talking to another application, which is talking to a third application, and so on.

CROSS-REF
For more information about `tell application` statements, see Chapter 17.

When using the `tell application` command to instruct more than one application to perform a sequence of tasks, avoid having one application talk directly to another application, as shown in Figure 4.2. Even though the code might function correctly, nesting `tell application` commands to multiple applications can have some drawbacks. It can make your code visually confusing, difficult to follow, and, if the script is complex enough, it could slow down the script and it might even fail.

Figure 4.2

The script is talking to the second application through the first one.

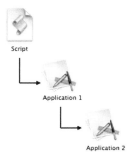

Instead of nested tells, you should treat the script like the manager of the process, as shown in Figure 4.3. The script talks to one application, and gets information or performs actions and then `end tell`. Then the script talks to a second application, performing actions and then stopping.

Figure 4.3

A script talking directly to applications instead of talking to the second one through the first one

Listing 4.1 shows a series of nested `tell application` commands. First, the Finder is getting the user selection. Then, the Finder is telling Pages to open the selected file. Then, the Finder is telling Pages to tell the Finder to get the name of the file, and so on. While the code will function, as it should, this type of nesting should always be avoided. With longer scripts carrying out more complicated commands, over-nesting can become visually confusing and could slow down a script and cause failures.

Listing 4.1

A script with multiple nested tell application commands

```
tell application "Finder"
  set pathToFile to the selection as string
  tell application "Pages"
    open file pathToFile
    tell application "Finder"
      set nameFile to the name of file pathToFile
      tell application "Pages"
        tell document 1
          set numPages to count of pages
          close
        end tell
        tell application "Finder"
```

```
            set nameFileNew to numPages & nameFile
            set the name of file pathToFile to nameFileNew
        end tell
      end tell
    end tell
  end tell
end tell
```

The code in Listing 4.2 shows the same commands performing the same tasks without the unnecessary nesting.

Listing 4.2

A script with un-nested tell application commands

```
tell application "Finder"
  set pathToFile to the selection as string
  set nameFile to the name of file pathToFile
end tell
tell application "Pages"
  open file pathToFile
  tell document 1
    set numPages to count of pages
    close
  end tell
end tell
tell application "Finder"
  set nameFileNew to numPages & nameFile
  set the name of file pathToFile to nameFileNew
end tell
```

Once a variable has been set, it continues to contain that value even if you manipulate it outside of the `tell application` command as long as the contents is not an object that is unique to the application. Because the `pathToFile` variable contains a file path in the form of a text string, the script and other applications are able to manipulate or use that value as needed. It does not have to remain inside of the `tell application` command.

Also, notice that the set `nameFile` command is in a different location. By moving it up into the first `tell application "Finder"` command, it removes the need for a second `tell` command.

When a script contains a `tell application` command woven with an `if-then` command and/or a `repeat` command, there is a natural temptation toward nesting.

The code in Listing 4.3 shows the same activity as the last two examples with the addition of a `repeat` loop. The Finder gets a list of files in a folder, has Pages open the file to count the number of pages, and then has Pages close the file. Finally, the Finder renames the file with the number of pages before moving on to the next one.

Listing 4.3

A script with multiple nested tell application commands

```
tell application "Finder"
  set pathToFolder to the selection as string
  set listItemPaths to every file of folder pathToFolder
  repeat with a from 1 to count items of listItemPaths
    set pathToFile to item a of listItemPaths as string
    set nameFile to the name of file pathToFile as string
    tell application "Pages"
      open file pathToFile
      tell document 1
        set numPages to count of pages
        close
      end tell
    end tell
    set nameFileNew to numPages & nameFile as string
    set the name of file pathToFile to nameFileNew
  end repeat
end tell
```

Because the `tell application "Finder"` command has a `repeat` loop within it, you can't put an `end tell` before the Pages commands, which forces you into a nest. Once again, the code works but would become much more visually confusing and potentially buggy as it grows.

Listing 4.4 shows the same commands without the nest.

Listing 4.4

A script with un-nested tell application and repeat commands

```
tell application "Finder"
  set pathToFolder to the selection as string
  set listItemPaths to every file of folder pathToFolder
end tell
repeat with a from 1 to count items of listItemPaths
  set pathToFile to item a of listItemPaths as string

  tell application "Finder"
    set nameFile to the name of file pathToFile
  end tell
```

```
    tell application "Pages"
      open file pathToFile
      tell document 1
        set numPages to count of pages
        close
      end tell
    end tell

    tell application "Finder"
      set nameFileNew to numPages & nameFile as string
      set the name of file pathToFile to nameFileNew
    end tell
  end repeat
```

By adding an `end tell` before the `repeat` and adding a `tell application "Finder"` and `end tell` just inside the `repeat` to get the name of the file, the nested issue is gone.

Avoid nested indentation overload

Indentation overload is a situation in which there is a large amount of commands standing between each instance of a nested `if-then` or `repeat` command. This obscures the beginning and end of each step in the overall command, making it difficult to know to which condition a particular line belongs.

The code in Listing 4.5 demonstrates four `repeat` commands nested one inside another. It has one «Code 1» comment placeholder between each `repeat` level, representing an area that one or more lines of actual code might be placed. This example assumes that each `listOf` variable has already been given a value, which is not shown.

Listing 4.5

Nested repeat statements

```
repeat with a from 1 to count items of listOfSections
  --   «Code 1»
  repeat with b from 1 to count items of listOfChapters
    --   «Code 2»
    repeat with c from 1 to count items of listOfParagraphs
      --   «Code 3»
      repeat with d from 1 to count items of listOfSentances
        --   «Code 4»
      end repeat
    end repeat
  end repeat
end repeat
```

As it stands, this example is a justified nested `repeat`. Nothing is wrapping, and it is a short, concise expression. Each `repeat` command is indented automatically by AppleScript, clearly showing each level.

However, imagine the same code with dozens or hundreds of command lines at each `repeat` step in place of the «Code» comments. In such a case, each level of the `repeat` command would span several pages and make it very difficult to know which level you are editing.

Like other usages standards, the code will perform its task as intended but it is obscured over several pages. A good rule is to limit this distance by what is viewable on a single page, or around a dozen lines at each `repeat` level.

The same applies to the nested `if-then` commands in this example. Listing 4.6 assumes that each `blnProcess` variable has already been given a value, which is not shown.

Listing 4.6

A script with nested if-then statements

```
if blnProcessSections = true then
   --   «Code 1»
   if blnProcessChapters = true then
      --   «Code 2»
      if blnProcessParagraphs = true then
         --   «Code 3»
         if blnProcessSentances = true then
            --   «Code 4»
         end if
      end if
   end if
end if
```

Rarely, you can avoid these nests by rearranging your code. Typically, the only solution available is to compress an overloaded nested `if-then` and `repeat` command by using subroutines to compress the space between each level down to a few lines.

 CROSS-REF

For more information, see Chapter 14 for **repeat** commands, Chapter 13 for **if-then** commands, and Chapters 21–23 for using subroutines.

Use subroutines as often as possible

When a script begins to exceed several dozen lines, it is time to consider subroutines. A *subroutine* is a grouping of code that can be run by calling it from other groups of code. A script with three-dozen lines of code might be broken into three subroutines with a dozen lines each. The primary part of the script then becomes three lines that each call one of the three subroutines. This enables you to break large, visually cluttered blocks of code into small portable chunks. As shown in Listing 4.7, the top level of the script can call these subroutines with a single command keeping the height of the overall statement to a minimum.

Listing 4.7

A script with nested if-then statements calling subroutines

```
if blnProcessSections = true then
  performSubroutine1()
  if blnProcessChapters = true then
   performSubroutine2()
    if blnProcessParagraphs = true then
     performSubroutine3()
      if blnProcessSentances = true then
        performSubroutine4()
      end if
    end if
  end if
            end if
```

CROSS-REF

For more information about using subroutines and how and where to divide code into subroutines, see the detailed discussions in Chapters 21–23.

Choose parameter passing over global variables

A *global variable* is a variable that is globally available to all code regardless of the subroutine or file that contains them. In order to write reusable subroutines, it is best to use subroutine parameters and limit the use of global variables.

CROSS-REF

For more information about global variables, see Chapter 5. For more information about using parameters instead of global variables, see Chapter 23.

Use script comments

A *comment* is one or more lines of text placed inline with code that does not execute. Comments are a great way to improve your script and make it easier to write, test, troubleshoot, and more.

CROSS-REF
Comments are covered in more detail in Chapter 5.

Summary

In this chapter you learned about the benefits of good code writing practices, were given a comprehensive naming convention guide, and were shown numerous examples of usage standards. While you are free to adopt all, part, or none of the concepts provided, these standards are used in all of the examples throughout the rest of this book.

Learning the AppleScript Language

Exploring AppleScript Basics

B efore you begin to write code in AppleScript, it is important to become familiar with related terminology and concepts. In this chapter, I cover common terms in the AppleScript language. I also provide an overview of the topics that will be explored in more detail throughout the remaining chapters of this book.

Understanding AppleScript Terminology

Like any programming language, AppleScript has a language syntax that establishes rules for the terms used to write code. Understanding commonly used terms is a vital first step in learning the language.

The AppleScript language consists of commands, literals, keywords, operators, object classes, variables, statements, subroutines, and scripts. An AppleScript developer can declare custom variables, which can contain any object class. Data can be converted into other classes in a process often called *coercion*.

All of these language elements are grouped to form expressions and statements, both of which can be evaluated to produce a result. Statements can be grouped together to form *compound statements*. Statements can also be controlled by other statements, which are called *control statements*.

Statements can manipulate data in variables, the functions of scriptable applications, and the objects they contain. They can be grouped together into subroutines and scripts.

Objects have properties that help define their characteristics and specifiers or references that point to them, defining their location. Objects can be contained within other objects and be containers themselves.

Scripting additions extend the language by adding new objects and commands that are not part of the core language. Both application and scripting additions contain dictionaries, which document their automation capabilities.

In This Chapter

Learning the rules of AppleScript terminology

Looking at the uses and benefits of script commenting methods

Planning an AppleScript project

Finally, scripts can be saved as files or applications, which can be distributed to users who will use them to increase the efficiency of their tasks. Scripts can also be placed on an automation server where they will autonomously perform tasks embedded in their code. Scripts can also be joined together to form complex multi-module solutions.

Commands

A *command* is a word or sequence of words that requests the execution of a predefined action. Commands are always directed at a target, which can be an application object, including those in Mac OS X, or a script object.

There are four types of commands:

- **AppleScript command.** Five AppleScript commands are built into the language: `get`, `set`, `count`, `copy`, and `run`. All the commands except `copy` are typically included in most scriptable applications. These are discussed later in this chapter and throughout Part II.
- **Scripting addition command.** A scripting addition command is a command provided by a scripting addition. This includes the default Mac OS X Standard Additions and any third-party scripting additions that are installed on the computer running the script. Scripting additions are discussed in Chapter 16.
- **User-defined command.** A user-defined command is a developer-defined group of code statements packaged into a subroutine. Subroutines are discussed in Chapter 21.
- **Application command.** An application command is an application-defined command within an application that provides access to a scriptable feature of the application. The application can be part of Mac OS X, an Apple-branded application, or any third-party application. Using scripts to control applications is discussed in Chapter 17.

A *command parameter* is an additional keyword that can be included with a command to identify the object being manipulated, the property being manipulated, or the type of action to be taken. A parameter that specifies an object is called an *object specifier*.

Literals

A *literal* is a value that is interpreted as it is written and, therefore, always evaluates to itself. For example, a piece of text like `"Hello World"` is a text literal. A number such as `2010` is a number literal. Any value that is literally typed into code and is not a placeholder for another value is a literal. AppleScript provides two literals shown in Table 5.1. Developers can hardcode literal values into their scripts as needed.

Table 5.1 AppleScript Literals

Keyword	Description
true	A boolean literal
false	A boolean literal

Keywords

A *keyword* is a word or a two-word phrase that is reserved by the AppleScript language. Keywords are always made up of lowercase letters from a–z. These words, along with commands, constants, and operators, all shown in separate tables in this chapter, make up the AppleScript language and your code should not attempt to redefine them by treating them like a variable.

The keywords listed in Table 5.2 are control statement keywords.

Table 5.2 Control Statement Keywords	
Keyword	*Description*
`considering, ignoring, with, without, but`	Used when comparing text values (Chapter 7).
`if, then, else`	Used to create logical branching statements (Chapter 13).
`repeat, times, until, while, exit`	Used to create repeat loops that process code more than once (Chapter 14).
`tell`	Used to route commands to scripts, applications, and application objects (Chapter 17).
`try, error`	Used to protect code and capture errors programmatically (Chapter 15). The `error` keyword can also be used to generate an error.
`timeout`	Used to protect code by extending the amount of time AppleScript waits before issuing a timeout error (Chapter 17).
`transaction`	The transaction statement sends all commands within it as a single unit to an application that supports it. This is used to ensure that the object being modified doesn't become "busy" with another user's task in the middle of an automated processes.
`end`	Used to terminate any control statement and subroutines.
`on`	Used to initiate several control statements and subroutines.

The keywords in Table 5.3 are subroutine parameter labels, which are discussed in Chapter 21.

Table 5.3 Subroutine Parameter Label Keywords	
Keyword	*Notes*
`about`	
`above`	
`against`	
`apart`	
`around`	
`aside`	

continued

Table 5.3 Continued

Keyword	Notes
at	
below	
beneath	
beside	
between	
by	Also used as an operator
for	
from	Also used to specify a range (For example, from 1 to 10)
given	
instead of	
onto	
out of	
over	
since	

The keywords in Table 5.4 are positional indication keywords, which enable AppleScript to refer to a specific position within an object like text, lists, or other application objects.

Table 5.4 Postional Indication Keywords

Keyword	Description
first	Identifies the first position
second	Identifies the second position
third	Identifies the third position
fourth	Identifies the fourth position
fifth	Identifies the fifth position
sixth	Identifies the sixth position
seventh	Identifies the seventh position
eighth	Identifies the eighth position
ninth	Identifies the ninth position
tenth	Identifies the tenth position
middle	Identifies the middle position
last	Identifies the last position
some	Identifies a random position

The keywords in Table 5.5 are a miscellaneous group of keywords that do not belong to another logical group.

Table 5.5 Miscellaneous Keywords

Operator	Description
as	Used to convert a value from one class to another
back, in back, behind	Used to describe a position
beginning, front, in front	Used to specify a point at the beginning of a container
continue	Resumes a command that has been interrupted by a command subroutine
every	Used to specify every object in a container
it, its	Refers to the current target
me, my	Refers to the current script
of	Used to build object specifiers (object «name» of location «name»)
return	Used to exit a subroutine
the	Used to make statements appear more English-like
through, thru	Used to specify a range of values
to	Widely used in many types of statements
where, whose, that	Used to filter values

Operators

An *operator* is a symbol, word, or phrase that is used to generate a value from another value or a pair of values. An *operation* is an evaluation of an expression that contains one or more operators.

An example of an operator-laden expression is any mathematical equation like this:

```
15 + 15
```

When this expression is evaluated, the operator instructs AppleScript to create a new value that is the sum of the two numbers. The operator — the plus symbol (+) — indicates that the new value should be the sum of the two numbers if added together. Therefore, the result of the expression is 30.

Operators are not limited to numeric equations. They can be used to compare any two objects, as demonstrated by this expression, which will return a false value, indicating that the comparison of the two text strings do not equal one another:

```
"Hello" equals "World"
```

In addition to math and comparison, operators can also be used to join values, convert values, and generate a reference to an object. Table 5.6 contains a list of AppleScript operators.

Table 5.6 AppleScript Operators

Operator	Description
and	Used to combine two boolean equations. The result of the entire equation is true only if the results of both equations are true.
or	Used to combine two boolean equations. The result of the entire equation is true if the result of either equation is true.
&	Used to join two values. For example, two pieces of text can be merged into one using this operator. It can also merge two lists or records. If the operator is used to merge numbers, the result will be a list containing the two numbers.
= is equal equals is equal to	Used to compare two values for similarity. The equation will be true if the two values are equal.
≠ is not isn't isn't equal to is not equal to doesn't equal does not equal	Used to compare two values for dissimilarity. The equation will be true if the two values are not equal.
> is greater than comes after is not less than or equal to isn't less than or equal to	Used to compare two value's relative alphabetical or numerical positions. The equations will be true if the value on the left is greater than the value on the right.
< [is] less than comes before is not greater than or equal [to] isn't greater than or equal [to]	Used to compare two value's relative alphabetical or numerical positions. The equations will be true if the value on the left is less than the value on the right.
≥ >= [is] greater than or equal [to] is not less than isn't less than does not come before doesn't come before	Used to compare two value's relative alphabetical or numerical positions. The equations will be true if the value on the left is greater than or equal to the value on the right.

Operator	Description

≤
`<=`
`is less than or`
`  equal to`
`is not greater than`
`isn't greater than`
`does not come after`
`doesn't come after`
	Used to compare two value's relative alphabetical or numerical positions. The equations will be `true` if the value on the left is less than or equal to the value on the right.

`start[s] with` `begin[s] with`	Used to compare a value to a portion of another value. The equation will be `true` if the value on the left starts with the value on the right.
`end[s] with`	Used to compare a value to a portion of another value. The equation will be `true` if the value on the left ends with the value on the right.
`contains`	Used to compare a value to a portion of another value. The equation will be `true` if the value on the left contains the value on the right.
`does not contain` `doesn't contain`	Used to compare a value to a portion of another value. The equation will be `true` if the value on the left does not contain the value on the right.
`is in` `is contained by`	Used to compare a value to a portion of another value. The equation will be `true` if the value on the left is found within the value on the right.

`is not in`
`is not contained by`
`isn't contained by`
	Used to compare a value to a portion of another value. The equation will be `true` if the value on the left is not found within the value on the right.

`+`	The number or date on the left will be added to the number or date on the right.
`-`	The number on the right will be subtracted from the number or date on the left.
`*`	The number on the right will multiply the number to the left.
`/`	The number on the right will divide the number to the left.
`div`	The integral part of the result of the number on the left divided the number to the right.
`mod`	The remainder of the result of the number on the left divided the number to the right.
`^`	Raises the number on the left by the power of the number on the right.
`as`	Used to convert an object to another class.
`not`	Used to negate a result of the equation to its left. The result will be false if the equation is true and vice versa.
`reference to`	During runtime, returns a reference object that specifies the location of object on its right.

Object classes

As an object-oriented language, everything a script works with is an instance of an object, and every object is a member of a *class*. The AppleScript language defines many object classes, including the `script` object and all the AppleScript data classes.

AppleScript includes three types of objects:

- **AppleScript objects.** There are seventeen AppleScript objects, which include the following object classes: `alias`, `application`, `boolean`, `class`, `constant`, `date`, `file`, `integer`, `list`, `number`, `real`, `record`, `reference`, `RGB color`, `script objects`, `text`, and `unit types`.
- **Mac OS X objects.** A Mac OS X object is an object defined by any application of the Macintosh operating system, including the Finder, Database Events, Image Events, System Events, and more.
- **Third-party application objects.** A third-party application object is an object defined by an application created by anyone other than Apple.

Object properties

An *object property* is a characteristic of the object that is represented by a name. For example, an object might have a name or a location.

CROSS-REF
Object properties are discussed throughout Part II.

AppleScript-defined object classes

The AppleScript language defines fifteen object classes: `class`, `constant`, `alias`, `file`, `RGB color`, `text`, `number`, `unit types`, `dates`, `boolean`, `list`, `record`, `reference`, `application`, and `script`.

Class

A *class* is a read-only property of an object class, which is always `class`. In other words, the class of each object class is `class`. In addition to being somewhat confusing, it has limited usage. It can be used to convert data from one class to another and to get the class of an object.

These examples show that the class of an object class is `class`:

```
class of text -- result = class
class of date -- result = class
```

The class of a value will be its object class:

```
class of "Hello World" -- result = text
```

CROSS-REF
Converting data from one class to another is discussed later in this chapter and throughout Part II.

Constant

A *constant* is a predefined value that is globally available to any script. A constant's value is fixed and constant, hence the name. Although AppleScript constants are read-only, a script can temporarily overwrite them for the duration of an executing script. Each constant is represented by a reserved keyword, which represents it within a script's code. Table 5.7 lists the AppleScript constants.

Table 5.7 AppleScript Constants	
Keyword	*Description*
current application	The name of the application executing the script
false	A boolean constant of false
hyphens	Used when considering or ignoring properties during text comparisons
linefeed	A line feed character, which is Unicode ID 10
missing value	A placeholder for a missing or uninitialized value
pi	The ratio of a circle's circumference to its diameter: 3.14159265359
quote	A quote character, which is Unicode ID 34
return	A paragraph return character, which is Unicode ID 13
space	A space character, which is Unicode ID 32
tab	A tab character, which is Unicode ID 9
text item delimiters	A list containing an empty string, which is used to parse and merge text
true	A boolean constant of true
result	Automatically contains the result of the last code statement to be executed
version	The version of AppleScript or of a scriptable application
white space	Used when considering or ignoring properties during text comparisons

Alias

An *alias* has dynamic reference to an existing disk, file, or folder accessible to or located anywhere on a computer.

CROSS-REF
Aliases are discussed in Chapter 11.

File

A *file* is a reference to a file on a computer.

CROSS-REF

Files are discussed in Chapter 11.

RGB color

A *RGB color object* is a three-item list of integers that specify a color object by its red, green, and blue portions.

CROSS-REF

RGB Color is discussed in Chapter 11.

Text

A *text object* is an ordered series of Unicode values. Text can be made up of a single character, word, sentence, paragraph, or more. It can contain names, products, descriptions, warnings, messages, shopping lists, and more.

With AppleScript, you can manipulate text in various ways. Two or more pieces of text can be merged into a new combined text value. You can parse text out into separate values or search for a value within the text. You can count characters, words, sentences, and paragraphs.

CROSS-REF

For more information on working with text objects, see Chapter 7.

Number (integer and real)

A *number object* is a numeric value, which is either an integer or real number. A number object can contain prices, quantities, and measurement values such as length, area, volume, weight, and temperature.

With AppleScript you can manipulate numbers in various ways. Numbers can be added, subtracted, multiplied, divided, and more. You can compare, convert, and manipulate them in all kinds of ways.

CROSS-REF

For more information on working with numbers, see Chapter 8.

Unit types

Unit types are measurement groups that enable numeric values to be converted from one type to another. Unit types include length, area, cubic volume, liquid volume, weight, and temperature.

CROSS-REF
For more information about working with unit types, see Chapter 8.

Dates

A *date object* contains a date and time value. Date objects can represent events, deadlines, schedules, due dates, or any other information.

With AppleScript you can manipulate dates in various ways. Specific data about a date can be extracted such as the month, month name, day, day name, year, hour, minute, and seconds. You can compare dates and calculate the span of time between them. Dates can also be converted into text.

CROSS-REF
For more information about working with dates and times, see Chapter 9.

Boolean

A *boolean* is a true or false value. Booleans are the result of object comparisons and can be used in a variety of different ways.

CROSS-REF
For more information about working with booleans, see Chapter 10.

List

A *list object* is any variable that contains a sequence of one or more values grouped together. A list might contain a list of text objects, numbers, or dates, or a mix of any class of variable. A list can even contain a list of lists.

With AppleScript you can manipulate lists in various ways. A list can be parsed into separate smaller lists or merged with other lists. Items can be added to or removed from a list. You can search within a list for one ore more values or modify a specific value within a list.

CROSS-REF
For more information about working with lists, see Chapter 11.

Record

A *record object* is any variable that contains one or more unordered collections of labeled properties. Like a database record, an AppleScript record variable can be made up of one ore more records, each with data stored within multiple user defined "fields." Each field can contain text objects, numbers, dates, lists, or a mix of any class of variable. A field in a record can even contain another record.

With AppleScript you can manipulate records in various ways. You can compare records and search within them for specific values. You can add, modify, replace, and remove data from a record. The fields contained within a record are completely user definable. In fact, a record is the only variable class that allows user-definable properties.

CROSS-REF
For more information about working with records, see Chapter 12.

Reference

A *reference* is any variable that contains a "pointer" to an application object. A reference might specify the location to a folder of file in the Finder, a record in a database, or a text box on a page of a desktop publishing application.

CROSS-REF
For more information on working with references, see Chapter 10.

Application

An *application* is a file that contains executable code. AppleScript can send commands to, manipulated objects in, and get information from a scriptable application or an application that is designed to communicate with AppleScript.

CROSS-REF
For more information about controlling applications with scripts, see Chapter 17.

Script

A *script* is a collection of AppleScript statements joined together to perform a function.

CROSS-REF
Learn about scripts later in this chapter and in Chapter 24.

Class conversion

Object classes can be converted to another class in a process called *coercion*. Table 5.8 shows the classes each class can be converted into.

CROSS-REF
Converting classes is discussed throughout Part II.

Table 5.8 AppleScript Class Conversion

Class	Conversion Details
`alias`	`Single item list` and `text` class
`application`	`Single item list` class
`boolean`	`integer`, `single item list`, and `text` class
`class`	`Single item list` and `text` class
`constant`	`Single item list` and `text` class
`date`	`Single item list` and `text` class
`file`	`Single item list` and `text` class
`integer`	`Single item list`, `real`, and `text` class
`list (single item)`	Can convert to any class that the value within the list can be converted to
`list (multi-item)`	`text` class, but only if each item in the list can be converted to text
`POSIX file`	`Single item list` and `text` class
`real`	`integer` (dropping any fraction portion) and `single item list` class
`record`	`list` class (without its labels)
`reference`	Any class that the referenced object can be converted to
`script`	`Single item list` class
`text`	`Single item list` class and, if the text represents a number, `real` or `integer` class
`unit types`	`integer` class, `single item list`, `real`, and `text` class, and between unit types (for example, feet to meters)

Variables

A *variable* is a letter, word, or phrase that represents a value it contains. As the name implies, the data placed in a variable can vary and can be any value you choose. Every script you write will use variables to store data, compare data, get or set data, manipulate data, and more. They are the lifeblood of any script.

Naming variables

Variable names must start with an upper- or lowercase letter and can contain any of these characters:

```
ABCDEFGHIJKLMNOPQRSTUVWXYZabcdefghijklmnopqrstuvwxyz0123456789_
```

After the first letter, a variable can be any combination of these characters, forming any word grouping you desire as long as it isn't a command, constant, or value reserved by the AppleScript language. For example, a variable can be named x, aNumberToUse, someLogicalPhrase, sevenOf9, or ship1701D. Of course, these are illustrations of the fact that a variable name can be any character or phrase and are not necessarily appropriate for use in a real script.

CROSS-REF
Professional variable naming standards are discussed in Chapter 4.

Declaring variables

AppleScript has two types of variables: local and global. As its names suggest, local variables are only available locally to the piece of code in which they were declared. Global variables are available to any code within a script file and to any other script that is loaded into a variable within a script file, as long as both scripts contain an identical declaration.

To declare a global variable, use the keyword local or global followed by the name of the variable, like this:

```
local «variable name»
global «variable name»
```

CROSS-REF
Properties, which are very similar to variables, are discussed later in this chapter.

A global variable that contains a path to the root level of a script folder is declared like this:

```
global gPathToRoot
```

A local variable that contains a date is declared like this:

```
local dateToStart
```

To declare additional variables, follow the same pattern on a new line or add additional variables to the same line with a comma between each. This example demonstrates a combination of these:

```
global gPathToRoot
local dateToStart, dateToStop
global gLibFinder, glibLog, gPathToResources
```

A declared variable is undefined until a code places a value within it. This is accomplished with the `copy` or `set` command, as shown here:

```
global gPathToRoot
copy "Maintosh HD:Applications:myApplication.app" to gPathToRoot
set gPathToRoot to "Maintosh HD:Applications:myApplication.app"
```

Although local variables can be declared, it is not required. Instead, the `copy` or `set` command can declare them and initialize them all in one step:

```
set nameCompany to "Write Track Media"
```

NOTE
If the `set` command is used again to place a value into the same variable, the previous value will be overwritten.

CROSS-REF
Variables are used throughout Part II and the rest of this book. Learn how to load a script file and place it into a variable in Chapter 16. Learn more about global variables in Chapters 21–23.

Statements

A *statement* is a sequence of commands, constants, expressions, keywords, variables, operators, and any other AppleScript language element. When a statement is executed, AppleScript reads the statements and carries out the instructions they contain. Following are five sample statements, which are explained in more detail in forthcoming chapters:

```
"Some Text"
10 + 100
beep
display dialog "Hello World"
set nameCompany to "Write Track Media"
```

Generating a result

When executed, some statements generate a result. When this happens, the resulting value is placed into an AppleScript constant called the `result`. A statement can include instructions about what to do with the result. For example, the result can be placed into a variable in a statement immediately following the statement that produced it, as shown here:

```
10 + 100
set numTotal to the result
```

As soon as the next statement that produces a result is executed, a new result will replace the previous one. In this example the `numTotal` variable will contain the result, "Write Track Media":

```
10 + 100
set nameCompany to "Write Track Media"
set numTotal to the result
```

The result can also be placed into a variable on the same line as the statement. For example, here the resulting number from the mathematical equation is immediately placed into a variable:

```
set numTotal to 10 + 100
```

In this case, even after other statements execute, the result of the equation is preserved in the variable.

NOTE
The result of one statement, if placed into a variable, can be used or manipulated by a future statement, creating a script flow.

Using control statements

A *control statement* is a statement that wraps around one or more other statements and exerts some control over how these statements perform. AppleScript control statements include:

- **considering/ignoring.** A `considering` or `ignoring` statement is used to determine if specific characteristics are considered or ignored when making comparisons of two text values. (See Chapter 7.)

- **if-then.** An `if-then` statement controls which of one or more statements will be executed based on an equation's result. `if-then` statements allow logical branches. (See Chapter 13.)

- **repeat.** A `repeat` statement enables one or more statements to be executed more than once. (See Chapter 14.)

- **try.** A `try` statement enables a script to run one or more statements in a protected environment that captures any errors that might occur. This enables a script to perform special code in the event of an error. (See Chapter 15.)

- **tell application.** A `tell application` statement enables a script to route commands to a scriptable application. (See Chapter 17.)

Nesting control statements

Control statements can be nested within other statements. For example, a `repeat` statement can be nested within another `repeat` statement, which can be nested inside of a `tell application` statement.

A script can have any number and combination of nested commands, although it is good practice to avoid nesting `tell application` commands for reasons discussed in Chapter 4.

CROSS-REF

Nesting `if-then` and `repeat` commands are discussed in Chapters 14 and 15.

Subroutines

A *subroutine* is a collection of AppleScript statements that are grouped together and can be executed from one or more locations within a script.

CROSS-REF

Subroutines are discussed in Chapter 21.

Scripts

A *script* is a collection of properties, variables, statements, and subroutines. A *script file* is a collection of these elements that are stored in a file as one of the available AppleScript file types.

CROSS-REF

AppleScript file types are discussed in Chapter 3.

Script properties

A *script property* is a characteristic of a script that has a single value and is represented by a name. Properties are declared at the beginning of a script with the keyword `property` followed by the name of the property, a colon, and the value of the property, as shown here:

```
property nameCompany : "Write Track Media"
```

Property names must follow the same rules as variables. The value can be a literal value, like the one shown previously, or a variable that contains a value. The value of a property can be any object class and it can be modified using the `set` or `copy` command.

Script objects

A *script object* is an instance of a script. It may be a multi-line statement beginning with the word `script` and ending with `end script`, or an entire script file, which has an implied start and end. It can also be a script that is loaded into a variable.

CROSS-REF
Scripts, loading a script into a variable, and embedded script objects are discussed in Chapter 24.

Looking at AppleScript Comments

A *comment* is one or more lines of text that appears with your code but is ignored by AppleScript and, therefore, does not execute. Comments provide instructional details for the lines of code that they precede. They may also be used to temporarily disable one or more lines of code during a troubleshooting or testing process.

Good code commenting is one of the easiest ways to improve the quality of your scripts. Comments can help you troubleshoot problems, restructure your code design, and navigate to specific areas within your code; and they encourage good code organization. They are great reminders of what tasks each block of code performs and are crucial when a script begins to grow longer and more complex. When you collaborate with other developers, good comments become a much greater necessity.

Considering the small investment of time required to write clear, concise, and informative comments, the return can be staggering. Understanding the goals and benefits of good comments can make a huge difference in the viability of your AppleScript solutions.

Commenting methods

There are two types of comments in AppleScript: single line comments and multi-line comments.

Commenting on a single line

To create a single line comment, type two dashes (--) in front of the text of the comment. When you compile the script, the dashes and the code on the same line will become gray, indicating a comment.

Here is an example of a single line script comment:

```
-- This is a comment
```

A single line comment doesn't have to be on a line by itself; it can also be used at the end of a line of code. While you shouldn't do this if it causes a line to wrap and make a script look cluttered, it is a good way to add a short note about a single line of code. For example:

```
set nameCompany to "Write Track Media" -- This is a comment
```

When using the single line commenting method, any comments that require two lines must have dashes in front of them like this:

```
-- This is the first line of a comment
-- This is the second line of a comment
```

Commenting multiple lines

To create a multi-line comment, type a left parenthesis (( ) and an asterisk (*) to start the commented area and an asterisk followed by a right parenthesis ( )) to terminate the area. Any text that falls between these two will become a comment.

Here is an example of a multi-line script comment:

```
(*
 This is a comment first line
 This is a comment second line
*)
```

Multi-line comments are particularly useful for "commenting out" a block of code while troubleshooting another part of a script. In that case, the commented section is not meant to be a documented developer note or reminder but code that is temporarily not used.

Uses for comments

Comments can be used as a form of documentation and for many other purposes. You can use them to do the following:

- Provide script information
- Separate sections of code
- Describe functions of a group of code

- Define a complex record variable
- Outline a script in development
- Comment to-do items

Providing script information

Comments are great for providing information about a script. This information might include the name of the script, a description of the material it processes, and/or the actions the script performs. Developer information can be included as well. For example:

```
-- Script Name: Create Project Folder Structure
-- This script will build a folder structure in
--    Server:Projects:«Client Name»:«Project»
-- Subfolders:
--    Proposal, Specification, Development
-- Last update: August 1, 2009
-- Write Track Media, Inc (www.wtmedia.com)
```

While your client or end user may never see these comments, having them embedded in your scripts can be useful. They can remind you of certain details or provide information should another developer eventually inherit your script.

Separating sections of code

Comments are also good for segregating sections of a script. One comment might highlight the start of the script properties and global variables while another might highlight the primary script functions. A third might separate an area for subroutines. Here is an example of a script with section comments, not including any of the code that would be placed under each one:

```
-- Script Information
-----------------------------

-- Main Subroutine
-----------------------------

-- Subroutine Library
-----------------------------
```

Describing functions of a group of code

The most common use for comments is to describe the functions performed by several lines of code. In this case, a comment should be fairly brief, preferably a single line. It should describe the functions of the code without simply reiterating each step of the code.

The following example shows five lines of code with two comments. Each comment provides a short description of what the code it precedes will perform:

```
-- Gather company data
set nameCompany to "Write Track Media"
set textIndustry to "Computer Programming"
set textURL to "www.wtmedia.com"
-- Create marketing report
set nameReport to "WTM Marketing Report"
set textData to nameCompany & return & textURL
```

Defining a complex record variable

A complex record variable containing multiple values should always be defined with a script comment. This is especially important when the code that will manipulate the record is located in a different subroutine or script file from were it is originally defined. A comment can eliminate the need to jump between two points in a script or two script files. In this case, the comment should list each field and a description of what kind of data it contains and how that data is formatted.

This example defines the format of `recData` that gets a record of information from a fictitious subroutine:

```
set recData to wtmDataUploadGet()
-- recData =
--    {
--    nameCompany : ""
--    textIndustry : ""
--    textURL : ""
--    }
```

Outlining a script in development

Comments can be a great way to create a quick outline for the script you are planning to write. They can remain in place as you build out actual code and test each part of your script. You can delete them when you're finished or use them to create permanent comments that will remain in your code.

TIP

When using this method, it is a good idea to format your outline comments from comments meant to provide documentation. The easiest way to do this is to remove any spaces between the dashes and the comment so that they will stand out when compared to comments that will remain in the script after the outline is gone.

Obviously, any outline comments you use can be vague and roughly phrased because they are not meant to be permanent. Here is an example of how you might use comments as an outline:

```
--get data from databases
--open the marketing template
--build the brochure
--save it to the desktop
```

Commenting to-do items

Similar to outlining, comments can be a great tool for a developer to leave instructional notes about tasks that remain unfinished for a portion of script. Sometimes, when writing a script, you don't have all the information you need right in front of you. Rather than stopping the development process until you have the information, you can just leave a note about what remains unfinished and then move on to developing other parts of the code. Here is a somewhat exaggerated example that shows three developer to-do comments:

```
-- Open the marketing database
set nameDatabase to "Marketing Materials"
set textPassword to "" -- PENDING: get the password
set listFields to {} -- PENDING: get the field list
-- Open the template
--PENDING: get a sample of the template
```

A consistent prefix indicating to-do–style comments is easy to find and ensures that you don't overlook any unfinished work. In a collaborative development environment, you can leave instructional to-do requests for other developers.

Frequency of comments

Deciding how frequently to use comments requires a keen understanding of the use of comments. Comments should help clarify what code will do. Also, they should help break up a long script into smaller chunks, making the script more visually organized and accessible.

Adding a comment for every line of code would unnecessarily lengthen the overall size of a script and make a visual mess. A good rule of thumb is to have one comment for every seven lines of code on average.

NOTE

The actual location of the division between groups of code needs to be decided based on the code in question. Sometimes it will make sense to comment four lines and other times it will make sense to comment nine lines.

Sample Script Result Comments

Throughout this book, examples often show a comment like the one that follows. These examples are used to show the resulting value of the code statement directly above it.

```
-- result = «value»
```

In this example, the result of the mathematical equation is displayed in the result comment:

```
Set numResult to 10 * 15
-- result = 150
```

Try to divide your code along functional lines. If you have three lines pulling data from one location and five lines manipulating that data, you could divide the lines by function. Or, if you have a few lines that get and manipulate data from a contacts database and then a few lines that do the same for a projects database, you might separate them by database.

One way to gauge how well you are doing is by the length of a comment. If your comment is very short, you might be using it in front of too few lines of code and the opposite might be true if your comment is quite long. Judging the length of a comment isn't a guaranteed way of splitting code into sections because some comments might simply be poorly phrased, though it can often provide you with some guidance.

Commenting usage conventions

As a developer you must adopt your own approach to commenting. However, to be clear, concise, and fully effective, you should consider several usage conventions and avoid some common mistakes. As with all of the usage conventions outlined in Chapter 4, feel free to use or ignore them as you see fit.

T I P

Even if you are the only developer who will see your code, write comments clearly as if someone else will rely on them for guidance or will edit them for you.

Add visual breaks to single line comments

When creating a single line comment to describe several lines of code, always put an empty line above the comment. This will create a pleasing visual break between each block of code and make your code much easier to read and navigate.

Limit comments to about six to eight words and always use sentence case for your comments, unless you are mentioning a named object or application. If they need to be longer, be sure that they do not wrap. Instead, create a second single line comment directly below the first and continue the thought.

Also, put a tab between the dashes and the comment text. This makes it more readable and ensures that the text is not mistaken for an outline comment or a developer to-do comment.

Use inline comments when possible

When a comment only refers to a single line of code and is very short, it can be placed at the end of the line. It should be no longer than a few words.

Instead of a tab, place a single space between the dashes and the comment text. This helps keep the overall line short and avoids wrapping.

Remove comments used as an outline

If you are using comments to form an outline of a script you are planning to write, you can use any form you like as long as you reformat them so they're more formal before finalizing your script or remove them when permanent comments are added.

NOTE

Any comment that is part of your outline should only have a single space between the dashes and the text to help distinguish it from permanent documentation-style comments.

Determine a reminder keyword

When using comments to place reminders, decide on a single word that indicates the comment is a reminder. Always make this first word all capitals so that it stands out from the rest of the script. Something like PENDING or FINISH does the job nicely. Reminders should have a single space between the dashes to further differentiate them from permanent documentation comments.

Avoid literal comments

Comments should describe what tasks a group of code is performing and not rephrase the actual script steps being performed. This common commenting mistake is shown here, with a comment is explaining every step of the script exactly how you might read the script lines themselves:

```
-- Put company name, industry and url into variables
set nameCompany to "Write Track Media"
set textIndustry to "Computer Programming"
set textURL to "www.wtmedia.com"
```

It is obvious that the three lines are putting data into variables. Rather than describe the technical steps, try explaining what the data is for, where it comes from, or what it will be used for.

Avoid cryptic comments

Comments should be informative and clear. If they are too vague, they are just taking up space without offering much in return. In this example, the comment is too short and obscure. It says nothing about which data is being set up and what it is being set up for:

```
-- Setup info
set nameCompany to "Write Track Media"
set textIndustry to "Computer Programming"
set textURL to "www.wtmedia.com"
```

TIP

Avoid abbreviations, acronyms, and slang to keep your comments clear, informative, and professional.

Avoid verbose comments

When comments become too verbose, they can be counterproductive. They may appear to be thorough and informative; however, they often take up too much space, add visual clutter, and may not focus on only the group of code they describe. When you find your comments wrapping or more than six to eight words, like in the following example, you may need to be more concise:

```
-- Set up the company information for the marketing report on
   Tuesday, which we will send around the world and beyond.
set nameCompany to "Write Track Media"
set textIndustry to "Computer Programming"
set textURL to "www.wtmedia.com"
```

Maintain consistency

Being consistent in naming and commenting can go a long way to help your efficiency and make collaborative projects friendlier. It is not as important which words you use to describe a certain action, but once you pick one style, try to stick with it. As in the inconsistently commented example that follows, if you are commenting three parts of a script that will gather data from various sources, you could describe that as "getting data," "accessing data," and "finding data." Any one of those is fine. All three in a script creates inconsistent commenting and can be confusing.

```
-- Get company data
set nameCompany to "Write Track Media"
set textIndustry to "Computer Programming"
set textURL to "www.wtmedia.com"
-- Access product information
set textLanguage to "AppleScript"
set textDatabase to "FileMaker Pro"
-- Go find other stuff
```

Planning Scripts

When it comes to starting a script, having a plan is always better than not having a plan. While each developer must find his or her own method of planning a script, several techniques may be beneficial.

Pre-coding steps

Before opening the AppleScript Editor, you should take several steps gather details about what you will automate. These can help you focus your energy on a specific set of tasks.

Choosing a workflow

Before you can automate a workflow, you must decide which aspects of a workflow you want to automate. In some cases, you may not have a choice because the decision will come from a supervisor or a client. However, when it is up to you, there are a few techniques to consider.

It is always best to choose something that is familiar to you, especially for your first project. The more you know about the process, the more clarity you will have up front. This can be a critical factor in the success or failure of your coding. It is difficult to outline a well-designed script when you know little about the tasks it will automate. If you are working for a client, be sure you have contact with people who can answer important questions about the workflow and the related business rules.

Another important factor in your decision should be to choose something that involves a lot of repetition. There will be less variation for uniformly repetitive processes and a higher return on investment potential for the resulting script.

It is a good idea to limit the scope of a script. Nothing is more difficult than starting out trying to automate "everything." Instead of trying to automate an entire catalog production workflow, try focusing on one phase. For example, automate the assembly of page layout documents, data preparation, or image processing, but not all of them at once. If you must work on a large workflow, break it into pieces and start form the one with the most repetition, or the one that you are most familiar with.

Finally, whichever workflow you select, be sure the applications involved are scriptable.

Gathering notes

Once you have chosen a workflow for your automation project, the next step is to gather notes and goals for the project. In some cases, you may be able to immediately begin writing code; however, it is typically a good idea to write out the basic steps involved in the workflow. A good design can save you a lot of time once you start coding.

Start with the big picture. Write out each major task the script must perform. Then gradually work your way down to more detailed information, describing each step. During this process, many pieces of information will arise for which you will need to find answers. These include the names and locations of resources, find and sort criteria, business rules, style sheets, and more, depending on the type of task you are automating. Having as much of this detailed information readily available when you start increases your efficiency when your write the code.

Diagramming the workflow

One secret to a well-designed AppleScript solution is having a good grasp of the big picture. It is important to be able to visualize the entire process in as much detail as possible before typing your first command. Having some form of a workflow diagram is an important step in the planning process.

Workflow diagrams vary from one developer to the next. Some developers may doodle some rough boxes with arrows on paper or a white board while others will create a neatly detailed flowchart. Whatever method you choose, be sure that it helps you to understand the logical processes you are panning to automate.

Coding steps

Once you have gathered as many details about the process you will be automating as you can and have a good sense of what the process involves, it is time to open the AppleScript Editor and get started.

Outlining the script

Before you write any actual code, you can create a script outline that translates your notes into the framework of a script. Using comments, you can plot out the major sections and put in loads of detail about the commands the script will perform and the objects it will manipulate. The outline provides the same kind of overview for coding that a diagram and notes provide during planning.

As you enter comments, you might find some portions are just easier to write in code. These might be the start and end of a `repeat`, `if-then`, or `tell application` statement. Also, you can often type subroutines and calls to them at this stage. It is perfectly fine to enter them as code, as well. You can enter a hybrid of outline comments, pseudo code, and actual code quickly and it can help you visualize the flow of the script, like the one in Listing 5.1. You might enter some comments out of order; for example, a note "here" might indicate something that needs to be "there."

Listing 5.1

A sample of a script outline with some actual code structure in place

```
-- open the product database
-- find every record for the current catalog
-- sort records by category, group, name
-- count the records
-- set up variables for tracking category changes and available page
   space
set numProducts to "PENDING"
-- process each record
repeat with a from 1 to numProducts
    -- start a new page, if needed
    -- get data for the current product
    -- start a new page if the category changes
    -- enter the product data
    -- place the images (if there are any)
end repeat
```

Outline comments don't need to be well written or concise. They are not intended to be permanent comments that help organize and explain your code. Instead they are inline notes that help form a framework to aid you in writing code more effectively. As such, try to format them differently than you do your actual comments. Use all lowercase and make them as verbose as needed so they remind you of any pertinent details when you start writing actual code.

Writing the code

Once you have a code outline that includes of the majority of your notes, you are ready to write the script. You can start from the top and work your way down, or start with the easy portions and work your way out to more complex areas. Whatever method you choose, a good planning and design process can be a valuable asset.

Summary

This chapter covered many of the fundamentals of working with AppleScript. It provided a broad overview of AppleScript terminology, explored adding comments to code, and presented an introduction to planning a script project.

Getting Started with the AppleScript Editor

 he *AppleScript Editor* is an application used to create, edit, test, and run AppleScripts. It exists on every Mac running System 7.5 through every version of Mac OS X.

You will find the AppleScript Editor in the AppleScript folder in the Applications folder located in the root level of your hard drive: `/Applications/Utilities/Script Editor.app`. The AppleScript Editor application icon is shown in Figure 6.1. Launch the application to start learning the AppleScript Editor user interface.

> **NOTE**
> The AppleScript Editor was renamed in Mac OS 10.6. Previously, it was named Script Editor.

Figure 6.1

The AppleScript Editor application icon

Exploring the AppleScript Editor User Interface

The AppleScript Editor user interface is very similar to any document-based application you have used in Mac OS X. It enables you to create, open, open recent, close, edit, save, save as, and print documents. In addition to these basic functions, the AppleScript Editor interface also has many unique features that enable a developer to write, compile, run, and troubleshoot AppleScripts.

Becoming familiar with the user interface of the AppleScript Editor is the first step to writing scripts.

The script document window

When you launch the AppleScript Editor, you will see a new untitled script document, as shown in Figure 6.2. Each AppleScript Editor document contains one script. A script can be a few lines or thousands of lines depending on the functions it must perform.

Figure 6.2

The AppleScript Editor's document window

Take a look at the elements of the document window starting from the top and working your way down.

Toolbar

The script document window features a standard Mac OS X toolbar. You can hide and show the toolbar by clicking the button in the top-right corner of the window. The default toolbar is configured with five buttons, from left to right:

- **Record.** This button makes a script begin monitoring and recording any manual activity you perform and attempt to write a script based on that activity. While the results of recording a script can vary, it can sometimes be useful when learning how to automate a feature for the first time.

- **Stop.** This button makes the script stop running or recording.

- **Run.** This button attempts to compile and run the script contained within the script document. If the script doesn't compile, it alerts you with an error and stops.

- **Compile.** This button compiles the code contained within the script document.

- **Bundle Contents.** This button opens a "drawer" on the side of the script window showing the contents embedded within the script bundle. This button is only enabled when the script you are editing has been saved as a script bundle.

C R O S S - R E F

See Chapter 3 and Chapter 24 for more information about script bundles.

Like most toolbars found in Mac OS X applications, the AppleScript Editor's toolbar is customizable. To do so, click on the View menu and choose Customize Toolbar. The customize toolbar dialog box window opens, as shown in Figure 6.3.

Figure 6.3

The AppleScript Editor's customize toolbar dialog box

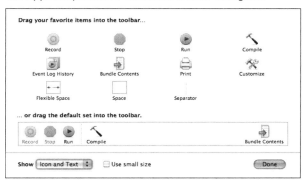

In the customize toolbar dialog box, you can add, remove, or reorder any individual item by dragging and dropping. You can also drag the default toolbar group to reset the toolbar in a single motion.

To control the appearance of the toolbar, select the Use small size check box to shrink the icons in the toolbar. Also, the Show popup menu in the lower-left corner of the window enables you to have the toolbar items show icons, text, or both.

When you are finished customizing the toolbar, simply click the Done button.

Navigation bar

The AppleScript Editor's navigation bar, shown in Figure 6.4, is the bar just below the toolbar and above the body. If the navigation bar is not visible, click the View menu and choose Show Navigation Bar.

Figure 6.4

The AppleScript Editor's navigation bar

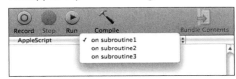

The popup menu on the far left of the navigation bar lists the script language the document is using. It will only show an AppleScript option unless you install other Open Scripting Architecture (OSA) scripting languages on your computer such as JavaScript.

The second navigation bar popup menu provides a way to quickly navigate to any property, global variable, command handler, and subroutine in your script. Just click the item you want to navigate to and the script scrolls down to the appropriate location. This is especially useful when you're editing lengthy scripts with dozens or hundreds of subroutines.

CROSS-REF

Subroutines are groups of code segregated from other code. See chapter 21 for more information.

Script text area

The script text area, shown in Figure 6.5, is the text entry area above the split view control where you write the content of your scripts. In this area, you can perform search and replace functions on a script as you would in any other text-based application.

NOTE

A *split view* is a control that exists between two interface elements that share a common space. In this case, the bar between the two text areas enables you to shrink one and enlarge the other or vice versa.

Figure 6.5

The AppleScript Editor's script text area

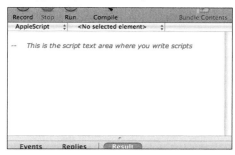

Description

The script description is the text entry area below the split view control that appears when you click the Description tab at the bottom of the window. The description text area is shown in Figure 6.6.

Figure 6.6

The AppleScript Editor's description, results, and event log tab area

The description text area gives you a rich text area to enter notes, copyright information, and other details about the script. The options in the Font and Format menus are only used when editing the script description. If you select Show Ruler while your cursor is in the description area, you will see that you can modify alignment, tabs, lists and more. You can also perform search and replace functions on the description as you would in any text-based application.

Event Log

The Event Log is the text area below the split view control that appears when you click the Event Log tab at the bottom of the window. It enables you to view results, replies, and events that occur when the script in the window is executed. Three buttons appear at the top of the event log: Events, Replies, and Result (see Figure 6.2 earlier in this chapter). These can be invaluable tools when troubleshooting bugs in a script of any size:

- **Events.** This button shows details about the commands, replies, log entries and error results that are executed or occur when the script is running. These details will be cleared each time you run the script.

- **Replies.** This button, which is selected by default when you click the Events button, adds reply information to the event log. This shows the replies from certain commands, such as which button a user clicked when presented with a dialog box.

- **Results.** This button shows the final result after the script was executed.

You can perform search functions on the text displayed in the Event Log area as you would in any text-based application.

TIP

To view the trailing history of results, click on the Window menu and choose Event Log History.

Contextual menus

Both the script text and description areas have a contextual menu. You can view these by placing the cursor over the area and pressing the Control key while clicking the mouse or by clicking the right side of your mouse.

While each text area has standard text-related menu items such as search, spelling suggestions, and lookup definition, the script text area has a very powerful, and often overlooked, feature: the contextual menu, which is shown in Figure 6.7.

The lower half of this menu contains a fully customizable set of scripts that can perform actions on the script in the document window. These include accessing, adding to, deleting, modifying, and otherwise manipulating the entire script, the selected area, or the selection point.

Menus

The AppleScript Editor menu bar has many basic features you would find in any document-based application and a few that enable you to access unique scripting features with key commands.

AppleScript Editor

The AppleScript Editor menu is consistent with those found in all Mac OS X applications. From this menu, shown in Figure 6.8, you can control and access several important application features:

- Choosing About AppleScript Editor opens a dialog box that shows the version of both the AppleScript Editor and AppleScript.
- Choosing Preferences opens the application's preferences dialog box, enabling you to edit many features of the application.
- Choosing Services provides access to various system services. This list will vary depending on the applications installed on your computer.
- Choosing Hide AppleScript Editor, Hide Others, or Show All enables you to control the visibility of the AppleScript Editor and other open applications.
- Choosing Quit AppleScript Editor enables you to quit the AppleScript Editor application.

Figure 6.7

The AppleScript Editor's script entry
area contextual menu

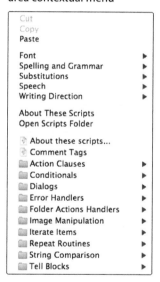

Figure 6.8

The AppleScript Editor application menu

File

The File menu works like the same menu in any other application that supports documents. You can choose Open, Open recent, Close, Save, Save As, Revert, Page Setup, and Print to manage and manipulate script documents, as shown in Figure 6.9.

Figure 6.9

The AppleScript Editor's File menu

The one item in this menu that is unique to the AppleScript Editor File menu is Open Dictionary, which enables you to browse the AppleScript dictionary of any scriptable application, or scripting addition that is installed on your computer. However, if you have a lot of applications installed on your computer, accessing a dictionary using this menu item can be a little slow because it gathers a list of every version of every application that is scriptable and asks you to choose one to browse. Using the Library command under the Windows menu (discussed later in this section) or dragging the application onto the AppleScript Editor are much faster ways to access an application's dictionary.

Edit

The Edit menu, shown in Figure 6.10, also works in a similar manner to the same menu in other document-based applications. This menu includes Undo, Redo, Cut, Copy, Paste, Paste and Match Style, Delete, Select All, Finder, Spelling, Speech, and Special Characters, which operate like they would in any application.

Unique to the AppleScript Editor, there is a Paste Reference menu item that will paste a reference to a file you copied to the clipboard. Currently, in version 2.2.1 (OS 10.5) and 2.3 (OS 10.6) of the AppleScript Editor, this feature appears to not function.

The Copy Style and Paste Style menu items will copy the style information for a highlighted piece of text and then apply (paste) that style information to another piece of highlighted text. This feature only works in the Description text area of the script window.

Figure 6.10

The AppleScript Editor's Edit menu

View

The View menu, shown in Figure 6.11, contains items unique to the AppleScript Editor. These include toggling (hide/show) the toolbar and the navigation bar.

Figure 6.11

The AppleScript Editor's
View menu

Like many Mac OS X applications, the View menu has a Customize Toolbar option that enables you to personalize the toolbar with a variety of different buttons. It also has buttons that enable you to toggle between the tab view options at the bottom of a document window. These include Show Description, Show Result, and Show Event Log.

Script

The Script menu, shown in Figure 6.12, is unique to the AppleScript Editor and enables you to control the status of a script. You can record, stop, run, and compile a script.

Figure 6.12

The AppleScript Editor's
Script menu

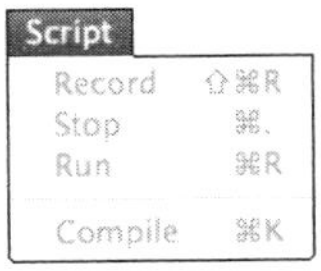

Font

Like most Mac OS X applications that feature text editing, the AppleScript Editor includes a Font
menu, which is shown in Figure 6.13. This menu includes options for setting the font, style, and
color of text. Because scripts have color and style settings that take precedence over any styles
you may apply to script text, the Font menu is only useful for styling text in the Description field
at the bottom of a script window.

Figure 6.13

The AppleScript Editor's
Font menu

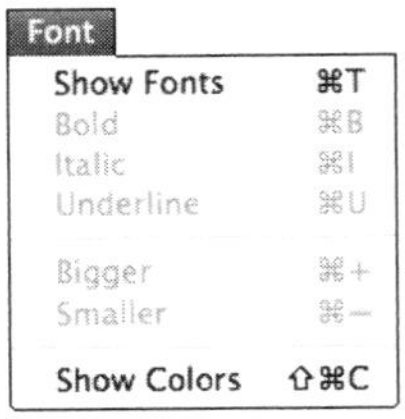

Format

The Format menu, shown in Figure 6.14, includes options for adjusting the alignment of text
and showing or hiding the ruler. However, text alignment and toggling the visibility of the ruler
are only used to edit the formatting of the script description.

Figure 6.14

The AppleScript Editor's
Format menu

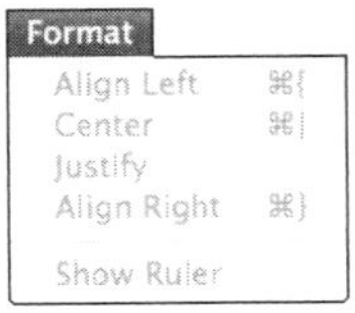

Window

Also similar to many Mac OS X applications, the Window menu enables you to manage all of your open script documents. You can minimize, zoom, bring all to front, and select a specific window that you want to bring to the front, as shown in Figure 6.15.

Figure 6.15

The AppleScript Editor's Window menu

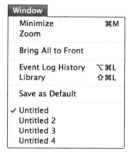

Several options in the Window menu are specific to the AppleScript Editor:

- Event Log History opens the trailing script event history window.
- Library opens the Library window, which provides access to scripting addition and application script dictionaries.
- Save as Default saves the current window size of the front script document as the default for all new windows.

Help

The Help menu, shown in Figure 6.16, is another standard Mac OS X menu. It provides quick access to AppleScript Editor Help, AppleScript Help, the online AppleScript Language Guide, and the Example Scripts folder. It also features a built-in search field that enables you to locate specific topics and locate menu items.

Figure 6.16

The AppleScript Editor's Help menu

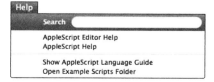

Preferences

The AppleScript Editor has several preferences that you can customize. Click on the AppleScript Editor menu and choose Preferences or type a comma while pressing the Command key. There are five preference tabs to choose from: General, Editing, Formatting, History, and Plug-ins.

General preferences

In the General preferences dialog box, shown in Figure 6.17, you can choose your preferred script editor, OSA language component, dictionary viewer, and Scripts menu.

Figure 6.17

The AppleScript Editor's General preferences dialog box

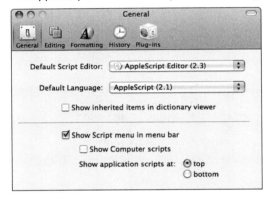

Default script editor

The Default Script Editor popup menu enables you to select your default script editor application preference. This enables you to use one of the script editing applications developed by third parties such as Late Night Software's Script Debugger or Satimage's Smile. When installed, these editors will be available in the Default Script Editor popup menu alongside the AppleScript Editor provided by Apple. The editor you select will be launched whenever you double-click a script, much the same as your preferred Web browser or e-mail software launches when you click a URL or a `mailto:` link.

Default language

The Default Language popup menu enables you to select the default script language when creating a new script document. By default, there is only one choice — AppleScript (2.1); however, if you install other OSA scripting languages, they appear in this list as well.

Show inherited items in dictionary viewer

When the Show inherited items in dictionary view check box is selected, class definitions show all the properties and elements they inherit from other classes in the dictionary viewer.

NOTE
The Show inherited items check box was added in Mac OS X 10.6.

Script menu settings

Finally, the lower portion of the General section of the preferences dialog box enables you to show or hide the Script Menu icon in the menu bar. This menu can display default scripts provided by Apple as well as custom scripts you write or download from the Internet. You can choose to show application scripts — those only visible when the application they pertain to is in the front — at the top or bottom of the overall list of scripts displayed in the menu.

CROSS-REF
See Chapter 3 for more information about the Script menu in the menu bar as a deployment option.

Editing preferences

In the Editing preferences dialog box, shown in Figure 6.18, there are five settings you can modify: Line Wrap, Tabs, Script Assistant, Escape tabs and line breaks in strings, and the Show "tell" application popup menu.

Figure 6.18

The AppleScript Editor's editing preferences dialog box

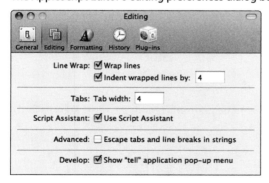

Line Wrap

When selected, the "Wrap lines" box causes lines of a script to wrap if they are too long for the current width of the script document window. Deselect this check box to make long lines disappear to the right of the window's edge. Also, you can select the "Indent wrapped lines by" check box and enter a number indicating how many spaces should be placed in front of a line that wraps.

Tabs

This preference enables you to enter a number for the width of a tab character in a script, enabling you to tighten or loosen the indentation of each level of a nested code structure.

CROSS-REF

Nested code structures are lines of code that have multiple indentations, one for each instance of a nesting statement. Both `if-then` (Chapter 13) and `repeat` loops (Chapter 14) can be nested.

Script Assistant

When selected, the Script Assistant box enables the AppleScript Editor to monitor and learn the way you name variables and subroutines in your script. Then, when you start typing, it can estimate what you might be typing and make a suggestion. If your script includes a variable called `nameCompany`, anytime you type `nameC`, you will see `ompany` appear in slightly grayed out text.

To ignore the suggestion, you can just keep typing. To accept it, press the Esc key and the full phrase will be automatically completed.

Because it only suggests names that have been used in the current script, the choices are always relevant and almost always helpful.

Escape tabs and line breaks in strings

When selected, any tabs or line breaks in a piece of text in your script will automatically convert to a markup character when the script is compiled. Tabs are converted into `\t` and line breaks are converted to `\n`.

This saves space, which can help reduce line wrapping for strings with a lot of tabs. It also keeps a string on a single line when there is a line break. For example, the following code contains a tab and a line break that pushes the last word to a second line:

```
set x to "Hello this        →      is a
string"
```

With the escape preferences checked, the same code will recompile onto a single line:

```
set x to "Hello this \tis a \nstring"
```

If you choose to not use this feature, you can also eliminate extra space and line wraps by using the verbal name of the character rather than the actual character:

```
set x to "Hello this" & tab & "is a" & return & "string"
```

Show "tell" application popup menu

This preference option is new to Mac OS 10.6. When selected, it adds a menu to the AppleScript Editor's document navigation bar. This menu lists all of the applications that are displayed in the Editor's Library dialog box. When you choose an application from the menu, the entire script targets the selected application. This means you do not need to use a `tell application` command because the entire script automatically targets the chosen application.

CROSS-REF

The `tell application` command is discussed in Chapter 17.

Formatting preferences

In the Formatting preferences dialog box, shown in Figure 6.19, there are seven code style settings you can modify, including several that are new to AppleScript Editor 2.3 that ships with Mac OS 10.6. These code settings and other options are as follows:

- New text (uncompiled)
- Operators
- Language keywords
- Application keywords
- Comments
- Values (numbers, date)
- Variables and subroutine names
- Strings (new)
- Command names (new)
- Parameter names (new)
- Classes (new)
- Properties (new)
- Enumerated values (new)

TIP

Unless you strongly dislike any of these default styles, it's probably best to just leave them alone for the sake of consistency from one computer to the next. If they have been modified, you can reset them to their defaults by clicking the Use Defaults button.

History preferences

In the History preferences dialog box, shown in Figure 6.20, there are three event log history settings you can modify. You can enable or disable the AppleScript Editor's capability to maintain a history of results and event log entries and choose between an unlimited number of entries or a preferred maximum number for both. The event log history also has an option to only log events when the event log pane is visible at the bottom of the script or the Event Log History window is open.

Figure 6.19

The AppleScript Editor's Formatting preferences dialog box

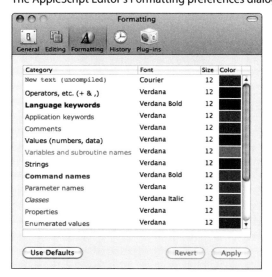

Figure 6.20

The AppleScript Editor's History preferences dialog box

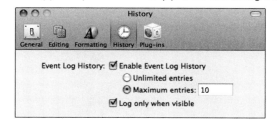

Plug-ins preferences

The AppleScript Editor's extensible plug-in architecture enables you to expand its feature set. The Plug-ins preferences dialog box, shown in Figure 6.21, provides information about third-party plug-ins and enables you to turn them on or off.

Figure 6.21

The AppleScript Editor's Plug-ins preferences dialog box

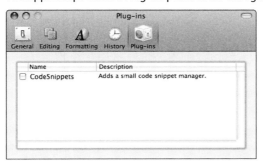

You can install plug-ins in several folders:

```
~/Library/Application Support/Apple/Script Editor/
/Applications/Utilities/AppleScript Editor.app/Contents/PlugIns/
/Library/Application Support/Apple/Script Editor/
/System/Library/Application Support/Apple/Script Editor/
```

While the AppleScript Editor will look at all four of these locations, the first option is the best choice because it is local to the user account. If you need to install plug-ins system wide for multiple user accounts, any of the remaining three choices achieve this.

NOTE

It appears that there is some buggy behavior with installing and removing plug-ins. Sometimes, they still show up in the preference window even when they are not present in all of these locations. In this event, you can open the `com.apple.ScriptEditor2.plist` preference file and remove the related entry.

Library window

Once configured, the AppleScript Editor's Library window, shown in Figure 6.22, provides quick access to script dictionaries for any scriptable application on your computer. Select Library from the Window menu to get started.

CROSS-REF

For more information about using the Library to learn about commands available in Scripting Additions, see Chapter 16. For using the Library to learn about automating applications, see Chapters 17–20.

Figure 6.22

The AppleScript Editor's Library window

Using the Library window toolbar

The Library window features a standard Mac OS X toolbar. You can hide and show the toolbar by clicking the button in the top-right corner of the window. The default toolbar, shown in Figure 6.23, is configured with four buttons:

- **Add.** This button presents a choose file dialog box and enables you to select an application that you want to add to the libraries listed.
- **Remove.** This button removes the selected application(s) from the Library window.
- **Open Dictionary.** This button opens the dictionary for the application you have selected. You can also double-click an application directly to achieve the same result.
- **New Script.** This button creates a new script containing a `tell application` command for the application you had selected.

Like most toolbars found in Mac OS X applications, the AppleScript Editor's Library toolbar is customizable. To do so, click on the View menu and choose Customize Toolbar.

Adding an application to the Library

By default, the Library window includes the dictionary of various scripting additions installed as part of Mac OS X. You can add applications to the list by dropping them onto the window or by pressing the "+" button and selecting them in the navigation dialog box.

Figure 6.23

The customize toolbar dialog box for the Library window

Removing an application from the Library

To remove any application or scripting addition from the Library list, simply select it and click the "–" button. The AppleScript Editor deletes the item without any warning. If you accidentally delete something, you can also add it back to the list as described previously.

Opening an application or scripting addition's dictionary

If you want to view an application or scripting addition's AppleScript Library, double-click it in the Library window or select it and click the Open Dictionary button.

CROSS-REF

To learn how to use an application or scripting addition's dictionary, see Chapter 17.

Creating a new script for an application in the Library

Rather than typing a `tell application` command for an application in the Library list, you can select the application and click the New Script button in the toolbar. This creates a new script document window, as shown in Figure 6.24, and automatically inserts the `tell` command for that application.

Event Log History window

The Event Log History window, shown in Figure 6.25, displays a history of the events, replies, log entries, and results of all script documents in chronological order. To open this window, click on the Window menu and choose Event Log History.

While the Event Log tab of a script document window only shows you the events, replies, and results of the last time you ran that particular script, the history window shows you all the results not only from the script you just ran but also from all scripts you have run since launching the AppleScript Editor application. They are limited by the maximum entries preference set on the history tab of the Preferences window.

Figure 6.24

An untitled new script document with an automatically added `tell application` command

Figure 6.25

The Event Log History window

NOTE

In Mac OS 10.5, the AppleScript Editor had two windows: one for event history and one for result history. These are now merged into the single Event Log History window.

Working with the history

Looking at a chronological list of results while you have several script documents open can be a little disorienting. Fortunately, the toolbar has a Show Script button. If you select any of the results and want to know which script generated that result, clicking this button brings the related script forward in front of any other script windows.

If you close a script with or without saving, select one of the results from its script and then click the Show Script button. This creates a new script document with the script, as it existed when the results were generated. While it would be foolhardy to rely on this in place of actually saving scripts and is obviously not a reliable way to navigate to scripts that you did save, it is an interesting feature for the accident-prone.

The left column showing the data for each script run displays the logged results in a hierarchical structure, enabling you to "drill down" and only display details for an individual step. You can select multiple logged items by clicking them while pressing the Command key.

Managing the results

To modify the number of entries saved or to disable or enable the history feature, click the History tab in the Preferences window.

To clear the current history, click the Clear History button in the window toolbar. The history will also be cleared when you quit the AppleScript Editor.

Customizing the toolbar

The Event Log History window has a standard Mac OS X toolbar you can customize by clicking on the View menu and choosing Customize Toolbar (see Figure 6.26).

Figure 6.26

The customize toolbar dialog box for the Event Log History window

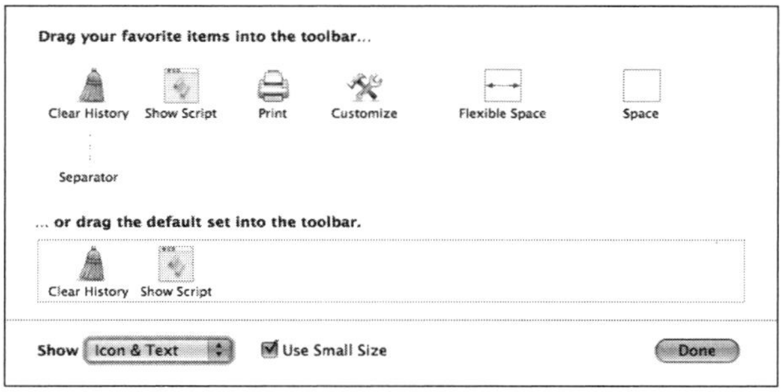

In this case, you can only add a Print and Customize button, control the size of the icons, and choose to show text only, icons only, or both icons and text.

To hide and reveal the toolbar, click the button in the top-right corner of the window.

Building the "Hello World" Script

When you're learning a new programming language, starting with the "Hello World" tutorial has become somewhat of a tradition. Writing a "Hello World" dialog script is also a perfect way to get started with AppleScript. In its most basic form, it is very easy to write and provides immediate results. When it is scaled up, it provides a well-rounded first lesson about several different topics. The short lesson in this chapter quickly covers a few specific areas; everything involved is covered in more detail in later chapters.

Your goal is to create a dialog box with the message "Hello World" and two buttons. You can achieve this with a single line of code made up of only four words.

Creating the script

The first step is to launch the AppleScript Editor application and open a new untitled script document. Then type the following into the script text area:

```
display dialog "Hello World!"
```

Compiling

To compile the code, click the Compile button in the toolbar, type **K** while pressing the Command key down or press the Enter key. You should see the code reformatted. If you see a dialog box stating a "Syntax Error," you may have typed the line incorrectly. In that case, check it carefully and make sure it is identical.

Before you run the code, click the Result tab at the bottom of the window and make sure that the lower text area is open.

Running

Now it's time to run the script. Click the Run button in the toolbar or type **R** while pressing the Command key. You should see a dialog box like the one shown in Figure 6.27.

Figure 6.27

The "Hello World" dialog box

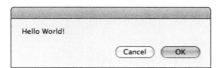

Viewing the results

Next, click OK in the dialog box. (Because it is the default button, you can also press the Enter key.) The dialog box should disappear and the result `{button returned: "OK"}` should be present in the Result text area at the bottom of the screen.

Now run the same script again and click the Cancel button. This time, there is no result, because you canceled the process.

Troubleshooting

One of the most important skills a programmer must possess is the ability to troubleshoot code errors. Take a moment to become acquainted with error messages by purposely creating some errors.

First, remove the last quote from the script so that it reads:

```
display dialog "Hello World!
```

Now try to compile the code. You should see an error dialog box appear (attached to the top of the document window), as shown in Figure 6.28.

Figure 6.28

A Syntax Error dialog box

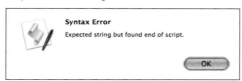

Notice how the error is worded. It is very difficult for a programming language to tell you exactly what mistake is causing the error. In this case, it is telling you that the script ended with something that was supposed to be a string. When you click OK notice where the cursor is located just after the first quote. This is AppleScript's way of telling you it sees the first quote and expects a text string but the end of the script was reached and the full string wasn't found. In other words, you are missing a quote.

Put the quote back and recompile the code. Now purposely create another typo; this time, remove the "a" from the word "display," as shown here:

```
disply dialog "Hello World!"
```

When you attempt to compile this script, you should see another error dialog box appear indicating a syntax error has occurred, as shown in Figure 6.29.

Figure 6.29

Another syntax error dialog box

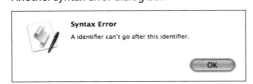

Notice that this dialog box contains a different error message. When you click OK, it highlights the words display dialog. This is AppleScript's way of telling you there is a problem with that command. A closer inspection would reveal the typo.

These are two of the most common errors that you will see with AppleScript: a typo in a command or a terminating characters missing like the quote missing in the earlier example, or a bracket or parenthesis.

Wrapping up

Before moving on, take a moment to work with the script document. Save the file to your desktop as a compiled script, close it, and then reopen it. Get the feel for how similarly the application works compared to other document-based applications like TextEdit. Modify the text "Hello World" with another phrase and take a peek at the Event Log History window to see how your interaction with the script was recorded.

Expanding the script

Many commands in AppleScript have a lot of default behavior. This enables you to shorten code when the defaults are considered acceptable.

For example, the "Hello World" dialog box has two buttons. The OK button is on the right and is blue, indicating that it is the default button. Pressing the Enter key clicks it. The Cancel button is on the left. Pressing the period key while pressing the Command key clicks the Cancel button. This is typical default behavior that you are probably already accustomed to from working with the Mac OS X.

The display dialog command has a lot more power for just such a circumstance. Next, you'll expand the script and explore some of its customization options.

Adding a title

Often you might want to add a title to a dialog box to help a user know more about the message they are seeing. Add the with title command to the script and then compile and run:

```
display dialog "Hello World!" with title "Greeting"
```

The dialog box should look the similar to the last one but with the addition of a title, as shown in Figure 6.30.

Figure 6.30

A dialog box with a title

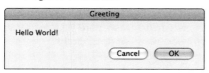

Adding an icon

Adding an icon to the dialog box is a great way to inform a user what kind of message he is reading. There are three choices you can pick: `stop`, `note`, or `caution`. Add the `with icon` parameter to the script:

```
display dialog "Hello World!" with icon stop
```

The `with title` parameter has been removed in this example to save space. You can add the new `with icon` parameter at the end of the `with title` if you want both a custom title and a custom icon. Also, notice that the word `stop` is not in quotes, because it is part of the command and not a text value.

Now compile and run the script to see the dialog box with the stop icon, as shown in Figure 6.31.

Figure 6.31

A dialog box with a stop icon

 CROSS-REF
The display dialog box command has many other features that are discussed in Chapter 16.

Summary

In this chapter the AppleScript Editor user interface was explored thoroughly. You learned about the components of the script document window, the application's menus, and preferences. You worked through the first scripting lesson of a classic "Hello World" dialog box. This introduced you to writing a line of code and generating a dialog box with the `display dialog` command, and familiarized you with a few customizable features to enhance a dialog box. Also, you purposely generated a few syntax errors to prepare yourself for a troubleshooting session as you continue to learn the language of AppleScript.

Working with Text Objects

A *text object* is an ordered series of Unicode characters. *Unicode* provides a number for each character regardless of the language, platform, or program. Starting in AppleScript 2.0 all text is Unicode-based, which preserves characters regardless of a user's language settings.

CROSS-REF
Visit www.unicode.org for more information about Unicode.

AppleScript's English-like terminology for text objects blends nicely with the use of terms that correlate to our day-to-day language use. This makes them rather easy to learn and use.

Introduction to Text Objects

Before delving into the language of text analysis and manipulation, here's a quick review of text objects and special characters.

Table 7.1 provides an overview of text objects.

Text object properties

Objects in the text class have only four properties: class, id, length, and quoted form, all of which are read-only.

Text class

The *class* of a text object is text. To determine the class of an object of an unknown type to make sure it is text, you simply write class of dataToCheck = text with the dataToCheck variable representing the unknown value. If the variable contains text, the result will be true. If not, it will be false.

In This Chapter

Looking at text objects and their properties and behavior

Counting, searching, and comparing text objects

Merging, splitting, extracting, and converting text objects

Using text item delimiters to manipulate text

Table 7.1 Overview of Text Objects

Properties	`class, id, length, quoted form`
Elements	`character, paragraph, text, word`
Coercions supported	`list` (single item), `number` (conditionally)
Constants	`space, tab, return, linefeed`
Operators	`&, =, >, ≥, <, ≤, starts with, ends with, contains, is in, does not contain, is not in, =, equals, ≠, is not equal to, is contained by, is not contained by, as`
Variable naming convention (optional)	`text«Prefix»«Type»«Description»«…»` `name«Prefix»«Type»«Description»«…»`

Text ID

The *id* of a text object is a Unicode representation of each character in the object independent of how it is rendered in a given language. You can convert a character into a numeric id and back again with a simple statement:

```
id of "A"
-- result = 65
character id 65
-- result = "A"
```

You can use this property to convert a text string consisting of more than one character. A phrase will be converted into a list of numeric values and visa-versa:

```
id of "AppleScript"
-- result = {65, 112, 112, 108, 101, 83, 99, 114, 105, 112, 116}
string id {65, 112, 112, 108, 101, 83, 99, 114, 105, 112, 116}
-- result = "AppleScript"
```

Table 7.2 contains a list of Unicode text ids for upper and lower case alphabetic characters, numbers, and commonly used symbols and punctuation marks.

Text length

The *length* of a text object contains the number of characters that make up its contents:

```
length of "AppleScript"
-- result = 11
```

Text quoted form

The *quoted form* of a text object contains a version of the text with single-quotes, which is useful when passing text to a shell script:

```
quoted form of "AppleScript"
-- result = "'AppleScript'"
```

Table 7.2 Unicode Text IDs

ID	Symbol	ID	Symbol	ID	Symbol	ID	Symbol
33	!	57	9	81	Q	105	i
34	\"	58	:	82	R	106	j
35	#	59	;	83	S	107	k
36	$	60	<	84	T	108	l
37	%	61	=	85	U	109	m
38	&	62	>	86	V	110	n
39	'	63	?	87	W	111	o
40	(	64	@	88	X	112	p
41	)	65	A	89	Y	113	q
42	*	66	B	90	Z	114	r
43	+	67	C	91	[	115	s
44	,	68	D	92	\\	116	t
45	-	69	E	93	]	117	u
46	.	70	F	94	^	118	v
47	/	71	G	95	_	119	w
48	0	72	H	96	`	120	x
49	1	73	I	97	a	121	y
50	2	74	J	98	b	122	z
51	3	75	K	99	c	123	{
52	4	76	L	100	d	124		
53	5	77	M	101	e	125	}
54	6	78	N	102	f	126	~
55	7	79	O	103	g	105	i
56	8	80	P	104	h	106	j

CROSS-REF

See Chapter 16 for more information about Shell Scripts.

Special consideration for quotes

Because characters contained within two double-quotes represent text to AppleScript, there is a special requirement if you need a text value to contain one or more double-quotes. To make a quote regarded as part of the text, instead of representing the termination of the text, you place a backslash in front of it.

If you typed the following code into the AppleScript Editor and attempted to compile it, you would receive a syntax error dialog box, as shown in Figure 7.1:

```
set textData to "He said "Hello""
```

Figure 7.1

A syntax error caused by extra double-quote in a piece of text

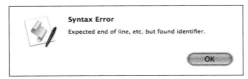

To avoid this problem, each double-quote contained within the text object needs to have a backslash in front of it like this:

```
set textData to "He said \"Hello\""
```

A character after a backslash will be considered literal text, allowing the code will compile.

Analyzing Text

There are many ways to analyze text. You can count characters, words, and paragraphs. You can search for characters, words, and phrases at the beginning, ending, or any position within the text. Text can be compared while ignoring or considering many properties, such as case, hyphens, punctuation, and more.

Counting text

Often when manipulating pieces of text, a script will need to calculate how many characters, words, or paragraphs are contained within a variable. This is not a problem when you set a variable to some static text, because you know and can see what you typed. However, it is important when a script is dynamically reading a text file, grabbing data from a field in a database, or scanning pages of a desktop publishing application. Any time text is accessed or generated without prior knowledge of what it contains, your code may have to peek in to count the number of objects waiting to be processed.

AppleScript gives you two primary methods for counting: the `count` and `number of` commands. While these commands achieve the same results and can be used interchangeably, for the sake of consistency you should pick one and stick with it. Because `count` is shorter, it is probably the best choice.

Here is an example of both methods used to count characters in a literal string of text:

```
set numCharacters to count characters of "Write Track Media"
--   result = 17
set numCharacters to number of characters of "Write Track Media"
-- result = 17
```

The basic building block of any piece of text is a character and AppleScript provides many ways to count them. Even ignoring the `number of` option, there are three other methods to count characters: `count`, `length`, and `count characters`. Here is an example of each of them all returning the same result:

```
set numCharacters to count characters of "Write Track Media"
--   result = 17
set numCharacters to count of "Write Track Media"
--   result = 17
set numCharacters to length of "Write Track Media"
--   result = 17
```

T I P
You should choose one of these methods to count characters and use it consistently.

Counting words and paragraphs work in a similar manner but each only has one choice for `count` and `number of`. Here is an example of counting the number of words in text.

```
Set numWords to count words of "Write Track Media"
--   result = 3
set numWords to number of words of "Write Track Media"
-- result = 3
```

And, finally, here is an example of counting paragraphs in text:

```
Set textData to "Paragraph 1" & return & "Paragraph 2"
set numParagraphs to count paragraphs of textData
--   result = 2
set numParagraphs to number of paragraphs of textData
-- result = 2
```

Searching text

For a script to get more information than counting alone will provide, it might be time for searching. AppleScript gives you several easy ways to scan text for a specific value. It can also tell you at which position a piece of text begins.

NOTE
By default, all text searching is not case sensitive.

CROSS-REF
Enforcing case-sensitive searches is explained later in this chapter.

Contains, is contained by, and is in

When a script needs to peek inside a piece of text to see if it contains a value, the `contains` operator can do the job. This command provides a result of `true` or `false`, indicating the presence or absence of a specific value existing within a piece of text.

The following example shows a short sentence followed by an inquiry that asks if that sentence contains the word "saves". Because it does, the result is `true`, which is a boolean.

```
set textData to "Workflow automation saves time. "
set blnFound to textData contains "saves"
-- result = true
```

CROSS-REF
Booleans are discussed in Chapter 10.

This command can be phrased in another direction: `is contained by`. This phrasing reverses the question, asking if a value is contained by a piece of text, as shown here:

```
set blnFound to "saves" is contained by textData
-- result = true
```

A third alternative, `is in`, operates `is contained by` and provides the same result:

```
set blnFound to "saves" is in textData
-- result = true
```

Both the phrase being searched and the value being searched for can be any length and can contain punctuation, numbers, and symbols. As long as the phrase you are searching for exists within the searched text, the command will produce a `true` result.

The following example shows a search phrase of two words that is in a different order as the same two words in the search text and, therefore, has a result of `false`.

```
set blnFound to textData contains "time saves"
-- result = false
```

Correct the order of the phrase to "saves time" and it works:

```
set blnFound to textData contains "saves time"
-- result = true
```

Starts/Ends with

While `contains` enables your script to discover if a phrase exists anywhere within a piece of text, `starts with` and `ends with` focus on the beginning and ending of the text being searched. This is useful if you want to add a prefix or suffix to every paragraph of a block of text or sort text by a prefix grouping. It can also be useful to ensure that a file extension exists at the end of a file name, enabling you to add it if it's missing.

The number of characters in the phrase you check for can vary just like with `contains`. This example shows part of a word being detected at the beginning of the text in `textData`:

```
set textData to "Workflow automation saves time. "
set blnResults to textData starts with "Work"
-- result = true
```

This example checks for the existence of an extension, which can be used to search for any suffix at the end of a piece of text:

```
set textData to "Production Report.txt"
set blnResults to textData ends with ".txt"
-- result = true
```

Offset

The `offset` command reveals the character position number for a given piece of text within another piece of text. It enables you to not just check for the existence of the text but also discover exactly where it exists. This example shows a script step locating the starting point of the # symbol in the file name `Production Report #8593.txt`. It correctly identifies its position as `19`.

```
set textData to "Production Report #8593.txt"
set numStart to offset of "#" in textData
-- result = 19
```

If the text you are searching for exists in more than one location within the phrase being searched, the result only provides the first instance of that text within the phrase, as shown in this example:

```
set textData to "#Production#Report#8593.txt"
set numStart to offset of "#" in textData
-- result = 1
```

The value you are searching for does not have to be a single character; it can locate phrases as well. In this example, searching for the symbol # alone would return a result of 1, which is not the location you want to acquire. If you know that the second symbol always has a space in front of it, you can change the offset request to look for the symbol with a space in front. Now, no matter how many instances of the symbol exist before the one you are looking for, the result will be the correct one because the code is requesting the phrase and not just the character:

```
set textData to "#Production Report #8593.txt"
set numStart to offset of " #" in textData
-- result = 19
```

You can use the offset command to find words, phrases, and even entire paragraphs if needed.

Continuing the previous example, suppose you need to calculate where the number ends. If the number is always a four-digit number, you can perform some simple math to figure out the character where the last number falls:

```
set numStart to offset of " #" in textData
set numEnd to numStart + 4
-- result = 23
```

However, if the number varies in length from file to file, you need a more dynamic method for calculating the last character. In this case, you again use the offset command but this time search for a different value. These two examples show code calculating the end of numbers of a different length:

```
set textData to "#Production Report #8593.txt"
set numStart to offset of " #" in textData
set numEnd to offset of ".txt" in textData
-- result = 25
set textData to "#Production Report #85936453.txt"
set numEnd to offset of ".txt" in textData
-- result = 29
```

If the value you are searching for is not found in the search string, the resulting value will be zero. Be sure you take this into account if a script will continue processing with the faulty assumption that the result was not zero:

```
set textData to "Production Report 8593.txt"
offset of "#" in textData
-- result = 0
```

NOTE
All of the examples in the previous section assume a consistent file naming structure, which may not always be what you encounter in an actual workflow. Often, you will need a combination of these techniques in order to locate the presence and location of a particular value. Also, remember that you can search for any text, including numbers, symbols, spaces, tabs, returns, and more.

Comparing text

Often, you will encounter the need to compare two or more pieces of text to determine if they are the same or not. Once again, by default, all comparisons are not case-sensitive.

CROSS-REF
Enforcing case-sensitive searches is explained later in this chapter.

Equality

You can discover if two pieces of text are the same or different using words or symbols. This example compares two variables, textData1 and textData2, each containing a different value. Therefore, the comparison of them being equal results in a false value, while a comparison of them being not equal results in a true value:

```
set textData1 to "Hello"
set textData2 to "Goodbye"
textData1 = textData2 -- result = false
textData1 is equal to textData2 -- result = false
textData1 ≠ textData2 -- result = true
textData1 is not equal to textData2 -- result = true
```

NOTE
You can type a "not equal to" symbol (≠) by pressing the Option key while typing an equal sign.

In this example, the two variables have the same word but they are in different cases, emphasizing the default "case-blindness" of AppleScript. The comparison of them being equal is still true because the same characters exist in the same order and their case is ignored:

```
set textData1 to "HELLO"
set textData2 to "Hello"
textData1 = textData2 -- result = true
textData1 is equal to textData2 -- result = true
textData1 ≠ textData2 -- result = false
textData1 is not equal to textData2 -- result = false
```

Comparisons can be made of portions of the values within a variable and do not have to compare the entire value. You can do more complex comparisons on a single line, as shown in the examples here:

```
set textData1 to "AppleScripts saves time and money"
set textData2 to "Write Track Media creates AppleScripts"
word 1 of textData1 = word 5 of textData2 -- true
word 3 of textData1 = "time" -- true
textData1 starts with word 5 of textData2 -- true
```

TIP
Using symbols for comparisons such as = and ≠ take up less space and can be typed in less time than their English-language equivalents.

Less, greater, before, and after

Sorting text can be somewhat complicated and involves `if-then` and `repeat` statements, which are discussed later in this chapter. However, AppleScript provides an easy way to compare two object's relative alphabetical positions using the `less than`, `greater than`, `comes before`, and `comes after` comparison operators:

```
set textData1 to "Apple"
set textData2 to "Pear"
textData1 < textData2 -- true
textData1 is less than textData2 -- true
textData1 > textData2 -- false
textData1 is greater than textData2 -- false
textData1 comes before textData2 -- true
textData1 comes after textData2 - false
textData1 does not come before textData2 -- false
textData1 does not come after textData2 - true
```

NOTE
You can type a "less than or equal to" symbol (≤) by pressing the Option key and typing a comma or by typing "<=," which changes to the unified symbol when you compile your code. You type the "greater than or equal to" symbol (≥) by pressing the Option key and typing a period.

Combining the `equal to` and `not equal to` operators with `less than` and `greater than` enables you to create compound comparisons:

```
textData1 ≤ textData2 -- true
textData1 ≥ textData2 -- false
textData1 is less than or equal to textData2 -- true
textData1 is greater than or equal to textData2 - false
```

TIP

Using symbols for comparisons such as > and < takes up less space and they can be typed in less time than their English-language equivalents.

CROSS-REF

To make an AppleScript–based sort routine that will handle more than two values, you would use the technique presented here in combination with `if-then` statements (Chapter 13) and `repeat` loops (Chapter 14). However, when you learn to control applications with AppleScript (Chapter 17), you might decide to find a third-party off-the-shelf application that you can simply instruct to sort text for you to save you the trouble.

Considering and ignoring text

When comparing text, AppleScript ignores case and numeric strings but pays attention to diacriticals, hyphens, punctuation, and white space — unless you tell it to do the opposite.

To do this, you use the `considering` and `ignoring` control statements. A *control statement* is a statement that wraps around one or more other statements and exerts some control over how they perform. These statements enable you to force AppleScript to act in opposition to its default inclinations.

Case

When you compare two text objects containing the same words but with different capitalization, AppleScript sees them as identical because it is ignoring case:

```
set textData1 to "Write Track Media"
set textData2 to "write track media"
textData1 = textData2
-- result = true
```

To override this behavior, place the comparison line inside of a `considering case` statement. Now, when the two pieces of text are compared, AppleScript sees their differences:

```
considering case
   textData1 = textData2
end considering
-- result = false
```

This statement also modifies AppleScript's perception when asked if text contains a value. Without the `considering case` statement, the text returns a true result because case is being ignore. With it, the result is false:

```
textData1 contains textData2
-- result = true

considering case
   textData1 contains textData2
end considering
-- result = false
```

Diacriticals

When comparing text that might contain diacriticals to text without, AppleScript recognizes they are different. For example "résumé" is considered different than "resume". If you use the ignoring diacriticals statement, they would appear to be the same.

```
set textData1 to "résumé"
set textData2 to "resume"
textData1 = textData2
-- result = false
ignoring diacriticals
    textData1 = textData2
end ignoring
-- result = true
```

When using ignoring diacriticals, the following punctuation marks are ignored: acute accent, grave accent, circumflex, umlaut, and tilde.

Hyphens

Text containing hyphens will not appear equal to identical text without the hyphens unless you use the ignoring hyphens statement, as shown here:

```
set textData1 to "Send me an e-mail"
set textData2 to "Send me an email"
textData1 = textData2
-- result = false
ignoring hyphens
    textData1 = textData2
end ignoring
-- result = true
```

Numeric strings

Text containing numeric strings will be considered greater than or less than another numeric string depending on whether or not you use of the considering numeric strings statement:

```
set textData1 to "Version 1.10"
set textData2 to "Version 1.9"
textData1 > textData2
-- result = false
considering numeric strings
    textData1 > textData2
end considering
-- result = true
```

Punctuation

Text containing punctuation marks will be considered different from identical text without those marks or with different marks depending on whether or not you use of the `ignoring punctuation` statement:

```
set textData1 to "Wow, this is amazing!!!"
set textData2 to "Wow this is amazing"
textData1 = textData2
-- result = false
ignoring punctuation
    textData1 = textData2
end ignoring
-- result = true
```

When using `ignoring punctuation`, the following punctuation marks are ignored: exclamation mark, quotation mark, opening single quote, comma, period, colon, semicolon, question mark.

White space

Using the `ignoring white space` statement makes AppleScript ignore all the spaces within both pieces of text being compared. This can be useful if there might be inconsistent double-spaced typos in one or both pieces of text:

```
set textData1 to "He scored a home run."
set textData2 to "He   scored   a   homerun."
textData1 = textData2
-- result = false
ignoring white space
    textData1 = textData2
end ignoring
-- result = true
```

Combining attributes

Using the `ignoring` and `considering` statements, you can combine attributes in any combination. For example, you can consider case and white space but ignore punctuation. Or, you can ignore case and consider hyphens, white space, and case:

```
set textData1 to "Multi-attribute TEST."
set textData2 to "Multi attribute test!"
textData1 = textData2 -- result = false
ignoring hyphens, case, punctuation and white space
    textData1 = textData2 -- result = true
end ignoring
considering case but ignoring hyphens, white space and
    punctuation
    textData1 = textData2 -- result = true
end considering
```

Manipulating Text

More than any other data class, scripts can manipulate text in a variety of ways. Strings can be merged together or split apart. Words or phrases can be located in and extracted from a larger piece of text. Pieces of text can also be converted into other data classes.

Merging text

AppleScript can merge pieces of text together with an ampersand. This works with actual text strings as well was text residing in variables. This simple example demonstrates merging five pieces of text — three words separated by two spaces — into a single variable:

```
set textData to "Write" & " " & "Track" & " " & "Media"
-- result = "Write Track Media"
```

Now try another example showing the same process but with the text contained in variables:

```
set textData1 to "Write"
set textData2 to "Track"
set textDsta3 to "Media"
set textData to textData1 & " " & textData2 & " " & textData3
-- result = "Write Track Media"
```

Text can be combined with any of AppleScript's text constants: `tab`, `space`, `return`, and `linefeed`. So, rather than typing those characters within quotes, you can refer to them by name as shown here:

```
set textData to "Write" & tab & "Track" & tab & "Media"
-- result = "Write    Track    Media"
```

This can be especially useful when you use a return or a linefeed. If you typed either of these in between quotes, it would make your line of code wrap. By using the name `return` instead, it remains on a single line.

NOTE

AppleScript also enables you to merge text lists into text using the more advanced `text item delimiters` property, which is discussed later in this chapter.

Splitting text

AppleScript enables you to split a piece of text into pieces for further processing. You can accomplish this by using the `every` command. With this command you can extract a list of every character, word, or paragraph of a given piece of text.

This example demonstrates the list of characters that result when you use the `every charac-ter` command:

```
set nameCompany to "Write Track Media"
every character of nameCompany
-- result = {"W", "r", "i", "t", "e", " ", "T", "r", "a", "c",
    "k", " ", "M", "e", "d", "i", "a"}
```

This example demonstrates the list of words that result when you use the `every word` command:

```
set nameCompany to "Write Track Media"
every word of nameCompany
-- result = {"Write", "Track", "Media"}
```

This example demonstrates the list of paragraphs that result when you use the `every para-graph` command:

```
set textData to "Paragraph 1" & return & "Paragraph 2"
every paragraph of textData
-- result = {"Paragraph 1", "Paragraph 2"}
```

CROSS-REF

AppleScript also enables you to split text into lists using the more advanced `text item delimiters` property, which is discussed later in this chapter.

Extracting text

AppleScript can extract portions of a text object in a variety of ways.

Extracting text by position

When you know, or had AppleScript dynamically calculate, the position of the part of a text object that you want to extract, the next step is to extract and place that data into a variable for future processing. You can do this a number of ways for characters, words, and paragraphs.

All of the examples for this topic assume this first line of code:

```
set nameCompany to "Write Track Media"
```

You can refer to any character, word, or paragraph by its numeric position:

```
character 1 of nameCompany -- results = "W"
character 2 of nameCompany -- results = "r"
character 10 of nameCompany -- results = "r"
character 11 of nameCompany -- results = "k"
word 1 of nameCompany -- result = "Write"
word 3 of nameCompany -- result = "Media"
paragraph 1 of nameCompany -- result = "Write Track Media"
```

If you request an object by position beyond the length of its value, you will invoke an error.

```
word 10 of nameCompany
```

The previous code is requesting the tenth word from a three-word text string, which results in the error shown in Figure 7.2.

Figure 7.2

An AppleScript error message for a request beyond the available range in the text variable

You can also use the English language equivalent for a value, but only from 1 to 10:

```
first character of nameCompany -- results = "W"
second character of nameCompany -- results = "r"
tenth character of nameCompany -- results = "r"
first word of nameCompany -- result = "Write"
last word of nameCompany -- result = "Media"
first paragraph of nameCompany -- result = "Write Track Media"
```

TIP
Using the numeric request instead of the English equivalent saves time and space.

You can also merge multiple requests on a single line:

```
first character of word 2 of nameCompany -- result = "T"
```

The `last` command enables a script to specify and extract the last character, word, or paragraph in a more efficient way than using the numeric value. Because AppleScript calculates which requested item is last, your script does not have to explicitly calculate or count which character is last:

```
last character of nameCompany -- results = "a"
```

If you were to access the last character of a text object with the numeric position, you would first have to count how many characters were present and then use that number to extract the last one, resulting in a longer piece of text, like this:

```
character (length of nameCompany) of nameCompany -- result = "a"
```

Another way to specify text based on its position, the `middle` command automatically calculates which value is in the middle and returns it as a result:

```
middle character of nameCompany
-- result = "a"
middle word of nameCompany
-- result = "Track"
```

Extracting a phrase

To extract a range of characters, a script can use the keywords `through` or `thru` and specify the desired range. Also, using the `text` property returns a result as a text string while the `character` property returns a list of each character:

```
set nameCompany to "Write Track Media"
characters 7 through 11 of nameCompany
-- result = {"T","r","a","c","k"}
text 7 thru 11 of nameCompany
-- result = "Track"
```

Often, you will not know the actual range of text that is needed for a script. In that case, you have to use the offset command to get the start and end of the desired phrase and then extract the range using the previous technique. The following example shows how to get a start and end position with the `offset` command and then use those values to extract the report number from the name of the file:

```
set textData to "#Production Report #8593.txt"
set numStart to offset of " #" in textData
set numEnd to offset of ".txt" in textData
text (numStart + 1) thru (numEnd - 1) of textData
-- result = "#8593"
```

Remember that this short example might appear overly complex when you can see the file name that is going into the `textData` variable. However, in a realistic scripting environment you would not know the name of every file or variable that your script needs to process. Therefore, you need a more dynamic methodology. You can replace the file name in the previous example with any of the following and they will still correctly locate and extract the correct number:

```
"#Production Rpt #68.txt" -- result = "#68"
"Prd Rpt #275.txt" -- result = "#275"
"####Rep Request #39542.txt" -- result = "#39542"
```

Extracting random characters

One of the more interesting extraction methods available with AppleScript is extracting a random character, word, or paragraph from a piece of text. Each time you run the script, the result will be randomized, as shown here:

```
set textData to "Workflow Automation provides huge cost savings"
some character of textData
-- result = "W"
-- result = " "
-- result = "c"
some word of textData
-- result = "cost"
-- result = "Automation"
-- result = "savings"
```

While this might appear to be an impractical command, it can be very useful when stress testing a script. While it is possible to generate random results without using `some`, it would be much more verbose.

Converting text to other data types

Text objects can be converted into a number, integer, real number, or date.

Converting text to a number

A piece of text can be converted into a number, integer, and real number as long as it is a text-based representation of a number. In other words, `"1.75"` can be converted to a number while `"$1.75"` or `"Price: 1.75"` can't because they contain textual elements.

To convert the text, simply use the `as` keyword followed by the desired class. When converting to an integer, notice that AppleScript automatically rounds the number, thereby removing its decimal part:

```
"1.75" as number -- result 1.75
"1.75" as integer -- result 2
"1.75" as real -- result 1.75
```

CROSS-REF
Numbers are discussed in more detail in Chapter 8.

Converting text to a date

Text can also be converted into a date as long as it is a text-based representation of a date. So, `"1/1/2010"` or `"August 1, 2010"` can be converted into a date object while `"Next Friday is my birthday"` can't. For example:

```
set textDate to "1/1/2010"
date textDate
-- result = date "Friday, January 1, 2010 12:00:00 AM"
set textDate to "August 1, 2010"
date textDate
-- result = date "Friday, August 1, 2010 12:00:00 AM"
set textDate to "10.1.2010"
date textDate
-- result = date "Friday, October 1, 2010 12:00:00 AM"
set textDate to "Aug 10, 1999"
date textDate
-- result = date "Tuesday, August 10, 1999 12:00:00 AM"
```

If you type a date into a script with the word "date" in front of it, the AppleScript Editor converts it into a date object when you compile the script, like this:

```
-- uncompiled
date "1/1/2010"
-- compiled
date "Friday, January 1, 2010 12:00:00 AM"
```

CROSS-REF
Dates are discussed in more detail in Chapter 9.

Using text item delimiters

Text item delimiters are a property of AppleScript used for processing text. It is a list of strings that will be used to convert text into lists and vise versa. Instead of counting, comparing, or extracting `characters`, you can extract `text items` of text with custom delimiters.

The default delimiter is an empty string, so using `character` and `text items` initially yields the same result. Every character appears as an individual piece of text in a list. When you set a custom delimiter, the pieces of text will be of a size dictated by the character(s) you choose to be the delimiter until you reset them or restart your computer.

The delimiters are case-insensitive by default, so be sure to use the `considering case` statement for case-sensitive operations.

NOTE
Currently, AppleScript only uses the first delimiter in the list. To split text at multiple delimiters, you will have to repeat each process with the next delimiter, one by one.

Accessing text item delimiters

To check the current delimiter, simply type `text item delimiters` and run the script:

```
text item delimiters
-- result = {""}
```

The result will be displayed.

Modifying the delimiters

To change the current delimiter, use the `set` command. Be sure to put a text value in quotes within two brackets. Once you run the script, the delimiter will be whatever value you specified.

This script will display the default behavior. Every character is treated as a text item:

```
set textData to "one-cent, one-nickel, one-dime"
every text item of textData
-- results = {"o", "n", "e", "-", "c", "e", "n", "t", ",", " ",
    "o", "n", "e", "-", "n", "i", "c", "k", "e", "l", ",", " ",
    "o", "n", "e", "-", "d", "i", "m", "e"}
```

If you set the text item delimiter to `{"-"}`, the results will be dramatically different:

```
set textData to "one-cent, one-nickel, one-dime"
set text item delimiters to {"-"}
every text item of textData
-- result = {"one", "cent, one", "nickel, one", "dime"}
```

You can also set the delimiter to a phrase as long as it is within the two quotes. Setting the text item delimiter to `{", "}` again changes the results:

```
set textData to "one-cent, one-nickel, one-dime"
set text item delimiters to {", "}
every text item of textData
-- result = {"one-cent", "one-nickel", "one-dime"}
```

Just as easily as the delimiter enables you to split text into a list of values, it can work in reverse, helping you merge a list of text values back into a single one. The resulting text will have each value from the list with the delimiter automatically added between them:

```
set listData to {"one", "two", "three"}
set text item delimiters to {"--"}
listData as text
-- result = "one--two--three"
set text item delimiters to {" & "}
listData as text
-- result = "one & two & three"
```

This can be useful if you need to change the delimiter of a piece of text. If you have text that is tab-delimited and you need to convert it to comma-delimited, you can do so quickly by setting the delimiter twice. First, change the delimiters to a tab and get every item into a list. Then, change the delimiter to a comma and space and convert list to text, like this:

```
--  Start with tab separated text
set textData to "one two  three  four"
--  set delimiters to tab and convert to a list
set text item delimiters to {"  "}
set listData to every text item of textData
--  set delimiters to comma-space and convert to text
set text item delimiters to {", "}
listData as text
-- result = "one, two, three, four"
```

TIP

Always change the text item delimiter back to an empty string to ensure that other scripts or other text operations operate correctly.

Summary

In this chapter you learned about the properties and behaviors of text objects, and how to analyze and manipulate them in many different ways. You learned how to count, search, and compare text as well as how to merge, split, extract, and covert text using a variety of different methods. Also, you saw how the power of text item delimiters was harnessed to facilitate manipulating text and fast text delimiter conversions.

Working with Numbers and Unit Types

A *number object* is any numeric value in the form of an integer or a real number. Technically the class, number, doesn't exist. Instead, number generically refers to either an integer or a real number that is automatically assigned to a variable based on the type of number placed within it.

Like text objects, writing scripts that work with numbers is rather easy to learn because of their similarity to your day-to-day interactions with them.

Introduction to Number Objects

Before you delve into the language of numbers, take a moment to review the difference between the two types of numbers — integers and real numbers — and a few basics.

Table 8.1 provides an overview of number objects.

Looking at types of numbers

An *integer* is a positive or negative number without a fractional part. For example, 150 is an integer, while 150.0 is not.

AppleScript limits the largest integer to a value of 536870911 in either direction, positive or negative. Any number larger than this is automatically converted to real numbers, expressed in exponential notation. For example, compiling 536870912 automatically converts it to 5.36870912E+8.

A *real number* is a number that includes a fractional part such as 19.99. This is the kind of number most people use in their daily lives.

AppleScript limits the largest real number to a value of 1.797693e+308 in either direction, positive or negative. Any real number that is greater than or equal to 10,000.0, or less than or equal to 0.0001, is automatically converted to exponential notation.

In This Chapter

Looking at number objects

Comparing and converting numbers

Performing math with AppleScript

Working with unit types

Table 8.1 Overview of Number Objects

Properties	class
Elements	N/A
Coercions supported	list (single item), real, integer, text
Constants	N/A
Operators	+, −, *, ÷ (or /), div, mod, ^, =, <, >, ≥, <, and ≤
Naming convention (optional)	num«Prefix»«Type»«Description»«…» int«Prefix»«Type»«Description»«…» real«Prefix»«Type»«Description»«…»

N O T E
All the examples of number-based variables in this section use the generic naming prefix "num" instead of "real" or "int."

In the same way AppleScript converts numbers, real or integer, to exponential notation when they fall outside the specified range, AppleScript also returns them to decimal notation when they fall within the specified range. For example, compiling 5.75E+2 automatically converts it to 575.0.

Putting a number into a variable

The set command is used to put a numeric value into a variable:

```
set numValue to 150
```

To discover the class of a number variable, use the class property as shown in the following code. Notice how the class changes automatically between integer and real depending on the value placed into the variable:

```
set numValue to 150
class of numValue
-- result = integer
set numValue to 25.75
class of numValue
-- result = real
```

Negative numbers can be placed into variables in the same way. Just put a minus symbol (–) in front of them:

```
Set numValue to -15
-- result = -15
```

Comparing numbers

Comparing numbers with AppleScript works like it does in the real world. You check if the numbers are equal, not equal, greater than, or less than some other number, performing each of these comparisons in several different ways. The result of any comparison will be a boolean value of `true` or `false`.

CROSS-REF

Booleans are discussed in Chapter 10.

Equal to, not equal to

You can check to see if two numbers are equal many ways. You can use `is equal to`, `is`, or an equal sign (=). If you type `equals`, AppleScript automatically converts it to `is equal to` when you compile your script.

All of the following examples achieve the same result:

```
1 is equal to 1 -- result = true
1 is 1 -- result = true
1 = 1 -- result = true
```

Notice that the result is a Boolean value of `true` and not a string value of "true".

This example returns a result of `false`, indicating that the numbers are not equal to one another:

```
1 = 10 -- result = false
```

You can also reverse the logic to check if numbers are not equal to one another by rephrasing the same operators:

```
1 is not equal to 1 -- result = false
1 is not 1 -- result = false
1 ≠ 1 -- result = false
1 ≠ 10 -- result = true
```

TIP

Using a symbol for comparisons takes up less space and is less visually cluttered. To create the "not equal to" symbol (≠), press the Option key while typing an equal sign.

Greater than, less than

Like `equal to` and `not equal to`, comparing the relative value of two numbers can be accomplished more than one way. You can use `comes before`, `is greater than`, or the greater than symbol (>).

All of the following examples achieve the same result:

```
1 comes before 10 -- result = true
10 is greater than 1 -- result = true
10 > 1 -- result = true
```

You can also reverse the logic to see if a value is less than another value:

```
10 comes after 1 -- result = true
1 is less than 10 -- result = true
1 < 10 -- result = true
1 ≤ 1 -- result = true
```

Combination comparisons

Combining any of the previous operators creates a compound comparison, as shown here:

```
1 is greater than or equal to 1 -- result = true
1 ≥ 1 -- result = true
1 is less than or equal to 1 -- result = true
1 ≤ 1 -- result = true
```

TIP

To create the "less than or equal to" symbol (≤), press the Option key while typing a comma. To create the "greater than or equal to" symbol (≥), press the Option key while typing a period.

Manipulating Numbers

AppleScript can perform various manipulations of numbers, including basic math calculations and rounding, and can convert numbers into either real, integer, or other data classes.

Performing calculations

Because it was designed to work with other specialized applications, AppleScript's math features are limited to the basics. AppleScript can add, subtract, multiply, and divide.

Adding

To add to numbers, use the plus symbol (+). The number to the right of the symbol will be added to the number on the left. The numbers can be actual numbers typed into a script, numbers in variables, or a combination of both, as shown here:

```
10 + 10
-- result = 20
set numX to 150
numX + 50
-- result = 200
set numX to 150
set numY to 150
numX + numY
-- result = 300
```

You can perform as many addition calculations per line of code as you like. This example shows the addition calculations of seven numbers on a single line:

```
10 + 20 + 30 + 40 + 50 + 60 + 70
-- result = 280
```

This example shows seven addition calculations of numbers in variables on a single line:

```
set numA to 10
set numB to 20
set numC to 30
set numD to 40
set numE to 50
set numF to 60
set numG to 70
numA + numB + numC + numD + numE + numF + numG
-- result = 280
```

You can use any combination of these and perform math that cascades through multiple lines of code like this:

```
set numA to 100
set numB to 10
set numC to numA + numB -- result = 110
set numD to numC + 100 -- result = 210
```

Subtracting

To subtract numbers, use the minus symbol (–). The number to the right of the symbol will be subtracted from the number on the left. The numbers can be actual numbers or values placed inside of variables, as shown here:

```
10 - 10
-- result = 0
set numX to 150
numX - 50
```

```
-- result = 100
set numX to 150
set numY to 100
numX - numY
-- result = 50
```

Like with addition, a script can perform any number of subtraction calculations on a single line of code or on separate lines using actual numbers, numbers in variables, or a combination of these.

Multiplying

To multiply numbers, use the asterisk symbol (*). The number on the left of the symbol will be multiplied by the number on the right. The numbers can be actual numbers or values placed inside of variables, as shown here:

```
10 * 10
-- result = 100
set numX to 150
numX * 10
-- result = 1500
set numX to 15
set numY to 10
numX * numY
-- result = 150
```

Like with addition and subtraction, a script can perform any number of multiplication calculations on a single line of code or on separate lines using actual numbers, numbers in variables, or a combination of these.

Dividing

To divide numbers, use the forward slash symbol (/). The number on the left of the symbol will be divided by the number on the right. The numbers can be actual numbers or values placed inside of variables, as shown here:

```
100 / 10
-- result = 100
set numX to 100
set numY to 5
numX / numY
-- result = 20
```

Again, a script can perform any number of division calculations on a single line of code or on separate lines using actual numbers, numbers in variables, or a combination of these. There are two functions that can divide numbers as well: Div and Mod.

Div

The `Div` function is an operator that divides the number to its left by the number to its right and returns an integer. For example:

```
100 / 9
-- result = 11.111111111111
100 div 9
-- result = 11
```

Mod

The `Mod` function is an operator that divides the number to its left by the number to its right and returns the remainder. For example:

```
100 / 9
-- result = 11.111111111111
100 mod 9
-- result = 1
```

Combining functions and operator precedence

Like regular math, all math operators in AppleScript can be combined into a single line of code:

```
set numValue to 5 * 20 / 4 - 8 -- result = 17.0
```

Operator precedence determines which order each step of a calculation will be evaluated. A common example is the use of parenthesis, which always evaluate the equation within, and work outward. Adding parenthesis around the subtraction portion of the equation yields a different result than the one calculated previously, as shown here:

```
set numValue to 5 * 20 / (4 - 8) -- result = -25.0
```

Converting numbers

Numbers can be rounded in several ways and can be converted into different kinds of numbers and other data classes.

Converting numbers to numbers

To convert a real number into an integer, use the `as` operator, which drops the fractional portion of the number. This example shows a real number converted to an integer:

```
set numValue to 10.3
class of numValue -- result = real
numValue as integer -- result = 10
class of numValue -- result = integer
```

To convert an integer into a real number, use the `as` operator, which adds a fractional portion to the number. This example shows an integer converted to a real number:

```
set numValue to 10
class of numValue -- result = integer
numValue as real -- result = 10.0
class of numValue -- result = real
```

Converting numbers to other data classes

AppleScript enables you to convert an integer or a real number into other data types. Both an integer and a real number value can be converted into a single item list or a text object, as shown here:

```
set numValue to 150
numValue as list -- result = {150}
numValue as text -- result = "150"
set numValue to 150.75
numValue as list -- result = {150.75}
numValue as text -- result = "150.75"
```

Rounding numbers

To round numbers, use the `round` command and, optionally, one of five command parameters. The command can be performed on positive or negative numbers. The default behavior rounds the number to the nearest even integer, as shown here:

```
round 1.5 -- result = 2
round 1.1 -- result = 1
set numValue to 25.75
round numValue -- result = 26
```

You can choose the rounding direction by choosing the optional `rounding up` or `rounding down` parameters. No matter how close to a whole number the fractional portion of the number might be, your choice will override the default behavior:

```
round 1.1 rounding up -- result = 2
round 1.9 rounding down -- result = 1
```

Using the option `rounding toward zero` parameter, sometimes called *truncation*, rounds toward zero, discarding any fractional part:

```
round 1.9 rounding toward zero -- result = 1
round -1.25 rounding toward zero -- result = -1
```

Using the optional `rounding to nearest` parameter, which is sometimes called "unbiased rounding" or "banker's rounding" rounds to the nearest integer. A fractional portion of .5 is rounded to the nearest even integer, as shown here:

```
round 1.5 rounding to nearest -- result = 2
round 0.5 rounding to nearest -- result = 0
round -1.75 rounding to nearest -- result = -2
```

Finally, using the optional `rounding as taught in school` parameter, which uses rules that are typically taught in elementary math classes, rounds .5 away from zero, as shown here:

```
round 1.5 rounding as taught in school -- result = 2
round 1.49 rounding as taught in school -- result = 1
round -1.5 rounding as taught in school -- result = -2
```

CROSS-REF

For more complex conversions, such as converting a number (1000.75) into a formatted dollar amount ($1,000.75) see Chapter 14.

Working with Measurement Unit Types

While `unit types` is a class unto itself, it is grouped with numbers because of its close relationship to numeric calculations. There are six different measurement groups, each with a list of related classes. These classes include length, area, cubic volume, liquid volume, weight, and temperature. Table 8.2 lists the classes of each.

Table 8.2 Unit Type Classes by Group	
Length	`centimeters, feet, inches, kilometers, meters, miles, yards`
Area	`square feet, square kilometers, square meters, square miles, square yards`
Cubic volume	`cubic centimeters, cubic feet, cubic inches, cubic meters, cubic yards`
Liquid volume	`gallons, liters, quarts`
Weight	`grams, kilograms, ounces, pounds`
Temperature	`degrees Celsius, degrees Fahrenheit, degrees Kelvin`

Using measurement types

Using `unit types` is rather simple. Set a variable to a numeric value and add `as «type»` to indicate your choice of measurement unit class. For example:

```
set numValue to 12 as inches
```

The variable `numValue` now contains a value of `12 inches`. You can check the class with the `class of` statement like this:

```
class of numValue -- result =  inches
```

Converting within the type group

All unit types within a related group are interchangeable. For example, to transform inches into feet, simply modify the class of the variable and AppleScript does all the work for you:

```
set numValue to 12 as inches
set numValue to numValue as feet -- result = feet 1.0
set numValue to numValue as meters -- result = meters 0.3048
```

NOTE

Only unit types within a group can be transformed in this manner for what should be obvious reasons. After all, you can't convert length units into volume units.

Here are a few examples using other unit type groups converting to related classes:

```
--  Area example
set numValue to 200 as square feet
numValue as square yards -- result = square yards 22.222222222222
--  Weight example
set numValue to 100 as ounces
numValue as pounds -- result = pounds 6.25
--  Temperature example
set numValue to 32 as degrees Fahrenheit
numValue as degrees Celsius -- result = degrees Celsius 0.0
numValue as degrees Kelvin -- result = degrees Kelvin 273.15
```

Converting to other data types

You can convert measurement units to several other classes including integer, real, or text like this:

```
set numValue to 12 as inches
numValue as number -- result = 12.0
numValue as integer -- result = 12
numValue as text -- result = "12"
```

Once the conversion occurs, the class of the object will be lost. In other words, if you convert a unit value of 12 inches to text, you will have a value of "12". If you converted it to an integer, you would have a value of 12. If you wanted to convert it to a text string of "12 inches", you would have to get both the value as text and the class as text and then merge them together, as shown here:

```
set numValue to 12 as inches
set textValue to numValue as text -- result = "12"
set textClass to class of numValue as text -- result = "inches"
textValue & " " & textClass -- result = "12 inches"
```

Summary

In this chapter you learned about numbers and how to compare and manipulate them in various ways, as well has how to perform basic mathematical calculations with AppleScript. You also learned about the powerful measurement unit type class and how you can use it.

Working with Dates and Times

A *date object* contains a specific date and time. It has many properties that can be used to perform a variety of time-based calculations.

Even when a script doesn't need to interact with date and time data, the date class can be used to calculate and log the duration of a scripted process. Knowing how long scripts might take to run is useful from a scheduling point of view, but it can also be a benefit when testing different statements that achieve the same results.

Introduction to Date Objects

A date object contains a specific date and time value. It includes day of the week, month, day, year, hour, minutes, and seconds. Table 9.1 provides an overview of date objects.

To get the current date, simply type `current date` into the AppleScript Editor and run the script:

```
current date -- result = date "Friday, July
    31, 2009 3:58:53 PM"
```

Although the date appears to be a string, it is really much more. The string that you see is a text representation of all the properties that make up the date object.

A date can be converted into a string by adding the `as text` command after it like this:

```
(current date) as string
-- result = "Friday, July 31, 2009 4:00:01
    PM"
```

To create a date object with a specific date, type `date "8/1/2009"`. Compiling that converts it to a date object: `date "Saturday, August 1, 2009 12:00:00 AM"`. When you don't provide a time, AppleScript automatically enters a time of midnight, the beginning of the day you specified. You can also include a time. For example, typing `date "8/1/2010 3 PM"` compiles into `date "Sunday, August 1, 2010 3:00:00 PM"`. This seemingly simple object has a lot more power than it might first appear.

In This Chapter

Looking at date objects and their properties and behavior

Comparing dates with other dates

Calculating time elapsed

Table 9.1 Overview of Date Objects	
Properties	`class, day, weekday, month, year, time, date string, time string`
Elements	N/A
Coercions supported	`single item list, text`
Constants	`Monday, Tuesday, Wednesday, Thursday, Friday, Saturday, Sunday, January, February, March, April, May, June, July, August, September, October, November, December, minutes, hours, days, weeks`
Operators	`&, +, −, as, div, =, equals, is equal to, ≠, is not, is not equal, comes before, does not come before, comes after, does not come after, >, is greater than, is not greater than, ≤, is greater than or equal to, is not greater than or equal to, <, is less than, is not less than, ≥, is less than or equal to, is not less than or equal to`
Naming convention (optional)	`date«Prefix»«Type»«Description»«…»`

Date object properties

Objects in the date class have eight properties. Most of these enable you to inquire about specific values relating to a date object. For example, you might need to extract the day as a number (1) or the day as a name (Saturday).

Date class

The *class* of a date object is `date`. To determine the class of an object of an unknown type to make sure it is a date with a script, write `class of dataToCheck = date` with the `dataToCheck` variable representing the unknown value. If the variable contains text, the result will be `true`. If not, it will be `false`.

Date day

The *day* of a date object contains an integer value of the day of the week for the date:

```
set dateValue to date "Saturday, August 1, 2009 2:17:10 PM"
day of dateValue -- result = 1
```

You can edit this property of a date object using the `set` command and providing an integer:

```
set dateValue to date "Saturday, August 1, 2009 2:17:10 PM"
set day of dateValue to 10
dateValue -- result = date "Monday, August 10, 2009 2:17:10 PM"
```

AppleScript calculates the correct date if you set the day to a value out of the month's range. For example, given a date of February 28, 2009, if you set the day to 29, the script correctly returns a value of March 1, 2009. This works for any day number you specify:

```
set dateValue to date "Saturday, February 28, 2009 12:00:00 AM"
set day of dateValue to 29
dateValue -- result = date "Sunday, March 1, 2009 12:00:00 AM"
```

This feature is limited to 127 days, after which the result will be calculated back in time. For example:

```
set dateValue to date "Friday, January 1, 2010 12:00:00 AM"
set day of dateValue to 127
dateValue
-- result = date "Friday, May 7, 2010 12:00:00 AM"
set day of dateValue to 128
dateValue
-- result = date "Wednesday, December 23, 2009 12:00:00 AM"
```

Date weekday

The *weekday* of a date object is a read-only property that contains the day name for that date. The possible results are Monday, Tuesday, Wednesday, Thursday, Friday, Saturday, and Sunday:

```
set dateValue to date "Saturday, August 1, 2009 2:17:10 PM"
weekday of dateValue -- result = Saturday
```

The weekday result Saturday is an AppleScript constant and is not the same as a text object "Saturday". To change the weekday into a text object, add as string after it like this:

```
set dateValue to date "Saturday, August 1, 2009 2:17:10 PM"
weekday of dateValue as string -- result = "Saturday"
```

Date month

The *month* of a date object contains the month name for the date. The possible results are January, February, March, April, May, June, July, August, September, October, November, and December:

```
set dateValue to date "Saturday, August 1, 2009 2:17:10 PM"
month of dateValue -- result = August
```

The month result August is an AppleScript constant and not the same as a text object "August". To change the weekday into a text object, add as string after it like this:

```
set dateValue to date "Saturday, August 1, 2009 2:17:10 PM"
month of dateValue as string -- result = "August"
```

You can also change the month using the `set` command, as shown here:

```
set dateValue to date "Saturday, August 1, 2009 2:17:10 PM"
set month of dateValue to September
dateValue
-- result = date "Tuesday, September 1, 2009 2:17:10 PM"
```

If you set the month to a short month like February in a date of the 31st of another month, AppleScript automatically moves the date forward by the amount of the discrepancy. This example starts with a date of July 31. When the script sets the month to `February`, AppleScript automatically changes the date to March 3 because February only has 28 days:

```
set dateValue to date "Friday, July 31, 2009 12:00:00 AM"
set month of dateValue to February
dateValue -- result = date "Tuesday, March 3, 2009 12:00:00 AM"
```

Date year

The *year* of a date object contains the year of the date as an integer:

```
set dateValue to date "Saturday, August 1, 2009 2:17:10 PM"
year of dateValue -- result = 2009
```

You can change the year using the `set` command, as shown here:

```
set dateValue to date "Saturday, August 1, 2009 2:17:10 PM"
set year of dateValue to 2010
dateValue -- result = date "Sunday, August 1, 2010 2:17:10 PM"
```

N O T E
The day name changes automatically.

AppleScript automatically adjusts for discrepancies when changing the year. For example, it handles leap years automatically, as shown here:

```
set dateValue to date "Wednesday, February 29, 2012 12:00:00 AM"
set year of dateValue to 2013
dateValue -- result = date "Friday, March 1, 2013 12:00:00 AM"
```

Date time

The *time* of a date contains an integer that represents the number of seconds since midnight of the date in question. For example, a date with a time of `12:00:00 AM` would contain a time value of 0, while `8:00:00 AM` would contain a time value of `28800`, as shown here:

```
set dateValue to date "Friday, July 31, 2009 12:00:00 AM"
time of dateValue -- result = 0
set dateValue to date "Friday, July 31, 2009 8:00:00 AM"
time of dateValue -- result = 28800
```

You can modify the time property with the `set` command:

```
set dateValue to date "Saturday, August 1, 2009 2:17:10 PM"
set time of dateValue to 86399
dateValue -- result = date "Saturday, August 1, 2009 11:59:59 PM"
```

As with other properties, if you set the time out of the range of a day, AppleScript automatically calculates the date object that is appropriate for the number of seconds you provide:

```
set dateValue to date "Saturday, August 1, 2009 2:17:10 PM"
set time of dateValue to 90000
dateValue -- result = date "Sunday, August 2, 2009 1:00:00 AM"
```

Date "date string"

The *date string* of a date is read-only property that contains a text-based representation of the date in the object without the time:

```
set dateValue to date "Saturday, August 1, 2009 2:17:10 PM"
date string of dateValue -- result = "Saturday, August 1, 2009"
```

Because the result is a text string and not a date object, it no longer processes the date properties discussed earlier. For example, if you tried to set the `year` of the date string to 2012, it would give you an error.

Date "time string"

The *time string* of a date is read-only property that contains a text-based representation of the time in the object without the date:

```
set dateValue to date "Saturday, August 1, 2009 2:17:10 PM"
set textDate to time string of dateValue -- result = "2:17:10 PM"
```

As with the date string, the resulting time string is a text value and no longer possesses the properties of the date object from which it was derived.

Manipulating Date and Time

You can compare and manipulate data objects in various ways to determine a chronological sequence, time elapsed, and more.

Comparing dates

Date objects can be compared with other date objects. You can check to see if they are equal, not equal, greater than, less than, or a combination of these.

TIP
Using symbols for comparisons such as = and ≠ takes up less space, and you can type them in less time than their English-language equivalents.

Equality

For two dates to be equal, they must have the same date and time. Because the two dates in the following example are different by one second, comparing them produces a result of `false`:

```
set dateValue1 to date "Saturday, August 1, 2009 2:17:10 PM"
set dateValue2 to date "Saturday, August 1, 2009 2:17:11 PM"
dateValue1 is equal to dateValue2 -- result = false
dateValue1 is dateValue2 -- result = false
dateValue1 = dateValue2 -- result = false
```

You can also check to see if two dates are not equal by reversing the phrasing or using the ≠ symbol, as shown here:

```
set dateValue1 to date "Saturday, August 1, 2009 2:17:10 PM"
set dateValue2 to date "Saturday, August 1, 2009 2:17:11 PM"
dateValue1 is not equal to dateValue2 -- result = true
dateValue1 is not dateValue2 -- result = true
dateValue1 ≠ dateValue2 -- result = true
```

NOTE
To type a "not equal to" symbol (≠), press the Option key and type an equal sign.

Less than, greater than, before, and after

Of more use to you than attempting to equate two dates is comparing them for chronological superiority. You do this using the `less than` and `greater than` operators, and once again, AppleScript offers several options when phrasing these comparisons.

You inquire if one date value is greater than (or chronologically occurs after) another, as shown here:

```
set dateValue1 to date "Saturday, August 1, 2009 2:17:10 PM"
set dateValue2 to date "Monday, January 12, 2201 2:17:10 PM"
dateValue2 > dateValue1 -- result = true
dateValue2 is greater than dateValue1 -- result = true
dateValue1 does not come after dateValue2 -- result = true
dateValue1 comes before dateValue2 -- result = true
```

You inquire if one date value is less than (or chronologically occurs before) another using any of the methods shown here:

```
set dateValue1 to date "Saturday, August 1, 2009 2:17:10 PM"
set dateValue2 to date "Monday, January 12, 2201 2:17:10 PM"
dateValue2 < dateValue1 -- result = false
dateValue2 is less than dateValue1 -- result = false
dateValue2 is not equal to dateValue1 -- result = false
dateValue1 does not come before dateValue2 -- result = false
dateValue1 comes after dateValue2 -- result = false
```

Combination comparisons

You can combine all of the queries described previously as needed to discover the relationship between two dates with `less than or equal to` and `greater than or equal to` or their corresponding symbols, ≤ and ≥.

Performing calculations with dates and times

You can perform various basic calculations with date objects, including adding and subtracting seconds and calculating the time elapsed between two times.

Adding and subtracting time to dates

Adding to or subtracting from a date object is easy with AppleScript. You place the number of seconds in front of a + or – symbol. The result will be a new date object that falls before or after the original date by the number of seconds you specified, as shown here:

```
set dateValue1 to date "Thursday, January 1, 2009 12:00:00 AM"
dateValue1 + 29
-- result = date "Thursday, January 1, 2009 12:00:29 AM"
```

When you need to shift the date more than a few seconds, there are a few shortcuts you can use to automatically calculate the shift in seconds without having to do the math yourself. You can do anything from minutes to weeks with a simple expression.

To add five minutes to the same date in the previous example, the equation inside the parenthesis is evaluated into seconds and the seconds are then added to the date object. So, (5 * minutes) becomes 300 seconds, which is then added to the date like this:

```
dateValue1 + (5 * minutes)
-- result = date "Thursday, January 1, 2009 12:05:00 AM"
```

NOTE

The use of the multiplication symbol to convert minutes, hours, days, and weeks into a quantity of seconds is somewhat counter-intuitive. However, AppleScript automatically converts these keywords to the number of seconds they represent. For example, `minutes` is converted to `60` and hours is converted to `3600`. Therefore, `5 * minutes` is the equivalent of `5 * 60`.

These examples show each of the other options used to manipulate the date object into the future:

```
dateValue1 + (3 * hours)
-- result = date "Thursday, January 1, 2009 3:00:00 AM"
dateValue1 + (10 * days)
-- result = date "Sunday, January 11, 2009 12:00:00 AM"
dateValue1 + (4 * weeks)
-- result = date "Thursday, January 29, 2009 12:00:00 AM"
```

Subtracting time from a date works exactly the same way.

TIP

To dynamically calculate the last day of a month, subtract 1 from the first day of the following month. AppleScript will automatically calculate how many days there are in the previous month.

Calculating time elapsed

To determine how much time has elapsed between two date objects, simply subtract them from one another. The result will be the number of seconds elapsed:

```
set dateValue1 to date "Thursday, January 1, 2009 12:00:00 AM"
set dateValue2 to date "Saturday, August 1, 2009 5:24:19 PM"
set numElapsedSeconds to dateValue2 - dateValue1
-- result = 18379459
```

You could manually convert that result into minutes, hours, days, or weeks, as shown in the first line of the following code, or you can have AppleScript do the work for you with the simple statement shown on the second line:

```
numElapsedSeconds / 60 / 60 / 24 -- result = 212.725219907407
numElapsedSeconds / days -- result = 212.725219907407
```

This works for each time constant:

```
numElapsedSeconds / minutes -- result = 3.06324316666667E+5
numElapsedSeconds / hours -- result = 5105.40527777778
numElapsedSeconds / days -- result = 212.725219907407
numElapsedSeconds / weeks -- result = 30.38931712963
```

You can also use the Div function to calculate the integral result:

```
numElapsedSeconds div minutes -- result = 306324
numElapsedSeconds div hours -- result = 5105
numElapsedSeconds div days -- result = 212
numElapsedSeconds div weeks -- result = 30
```

CROSS-REF

For more information about the Div function, see Chapter 8.

Summary

In this chapter you learned all about dates and their extensive properties, many of which are editable. You learned how to add and subtract time from a date object, and how to calculate the amount of time elapsed between two dates and to convert that into more human friendly units of time.

Other AppleScript Data Classes

This chapter covers five additional data classes: boolean, RGB color, alias, file, and reference. Although they are relatively simple and do not require a lot of introduction, they can be quite useful and should not be overlooked.

Working with Booleans

A *boolean* is a true or false value. Don't let the simplicity of this class obscure its incredible usefulness, which increases exponentially as a script grows beyond a simple linear set of commands.

Booleans are the result of any value comparison that enables a script to compare data values and to use these comparisons to determine a course of action. They are the "toll booths" of every if-then statement and certain repeat statements, determining which set of statements should be executed and for how long.

CROSS-REF
If-then and repeat statements are discussed in Chapters 13 and 14, respectively.

A boolean's value will always be one of two AppleScript keywords: true or false. It is important to understand the distinction between the keywords true and false and the text values "true" and "false". The former are booleans while the latter are text. It is possible to convert a boolean into a string, as shown in the following example:

```
true as string -- result = "true"
```

After this conversion is complete, the text value "true" will no longer be usable as a boolean.

A *boolean expression* is a statement that results in a boolean value. The following example shows six boolean expressions, each involving a comparison involving two numeric variables:

```
set num1 to 100
set num2 to 50
num1 is equal to num2 -- result = false
```

```
num1 = num2 -- result = false
num1 ≠ num2 -- result = true
num1 > num2 -- result = true
class of num1 = text -- result = false
class of num2 = boolean - result = true
```

T I P

Using symbols for comparisons such as = and ≠ takes up less space, and they can be typed in less time than their English language equivalents.

N O T E

Typing a "not equal to" symbol (≠) is accomplished by holding down the Option key while typing an equal sign.

The `class` of a variable that contains a boolean is, of course, `boolean`. To determine the class of an object of an unknown type to make sure it is a boolean, use the boolean expression: `class of dataToCheck = boolean` with the `dataToCheck` variable representing the unknown value. If the variable contains a boolean, the result will be `true`. If not, it will be `false`.

Table 10.1 provides an overview of boolean objects.

Table 10.1 Overview of Boolean Objects	
Properties	`class`
Elements	N/A
Coercions supported	`list` (single item), `text`
Constants	`true, false`
Operators	`=, equals, is equal to,` `≠, is not, is not equal to`
Variable naming convention (optional)	`bln«Prefix»«Type»«Description»«…»`

Working with RGB Colors

An *RGB color object* is a three-item list of integers ranging from 0 to 65535, which together specify a color object by its red, green, and blue values.

```
set rgbBlack to {0, 0, 0} -- Black
set rgbWhite to {65535, 65535, 65535} -- White
set rgbWTMLogo to {21845, 31097, 28527} -- Write Track Media's
    logo color
```

You can define a color by hard-coding the list of values or enable your users to choose a color using the Mac OS X color dialog box. Because this class is really a list, it has all the properties, characteristics, coercions, and comparisons of a list.

CROSS-REF
The choose color dialog box is discussed in Chapter 16.

Table 10.2 provides an overview of RGB color objects.

Table 10.2 Overview of RGB Color Objects	
Properties	class
Elements	N/A
Coercions supported	N/A
Constants	N/A
Operators	=, is equal to
	≠, is not equal to
Variable naming convention (optional)	rgb«Type»«Description»«…»

Working with Aliases

An *alias* is a dynamic reference to an existing disk, file, or folder accessible to or located anywhere on a computer. It is signified by the keyword alias, which precedes a string representation of the file or folder it points to. The following example shows an alias pointing to a folder named Test Folder, which is located on the current user's desktop:

```
alias "Macintosh HD:Users:mmunro-wtm:Desktop:Test Folder:"
```

There are two properties of an alias: class and POSIX path.

The class property of an alias will always be alias. To determine the class of an object of an unknown type to make sure it is an alias, use the boolean expression class of dataToCheck = alias where dataToCheck represents the unknown value. If the variable contains an alias, the result will be true. If not, it will be false.

The POSIX path property of an alias will be a reference to the item expressed as a POSIX-style path. POSIX, which stands for Portable Operating System Interface for Unix, is a path delimited by forward slashes (/). You can convert an alias into a POSIX path like this:

```
POSIX path of alias "Macintosh HD:Users:mmunro-wtm:Desktop:"
-- result = "/Users/mmunro-wtm/Desktop/"
```

NOTE
Unlike an alias, the hard drive name is not required when specifying a POSIX path. For example, an item contained within the user folder can start with `/Users/`, while a reference to applications can begin with `/Applications/`. Neither includes the name of the hard drive upon which it resides.

A script can convert a text-based path into an alias like this:

```
set pathToFolder to "Macintosh HD:Users:mmunro-wtm:Desktop:"
pathToFolder as alias
-- result = alias "Macintosh HD:Users:mmunro-wtm:Desktop:"
```

An alias is the result of many of the choose dialogs available in the Standard scripting additions package. For example, the `choose folder` dialog will result in an alias pointing to the folder the user selected.

CROSS-REF
Standard Additions are discussed in Chapter 16.

NOTE
As of AppleScript 2.0, an alias will not attempt to resolve the path until the script is run. Previously you could not compile a script containing a hard-coded alias for a file or folder that did not exist; instead, you had to use a text-based path and convert it into an alias at a time when it does exist. This change means that you can now hard-code an alias to a file that does not yet exist. However, when the script runs, if the file is still missing, it will cause an error.

AppleScript enables you to convert an alias into a single item list or a text object, as shown here:

```
set pathToFolder to alias "Macintosh HD:Users:mmunro-
   wtm:Desktop:"
pathToFolder as list
-- result = {alias "Macintosh HD:Users:mmunro-wtm:Desktop:"}
pathToFolder as text
-- result = "Macintosh HD:Users:mmunro-wtm:Desktop:"
```

While it may lack a practical application, aliases can be compared to other aliases. This example shows two variables, each containing an alias being compared to each other:

```
set path1 to alias "Macintosh HD:Users:mmunro-wtm:Desktop:"
set path2 to alias "Macintosh HD:Users:mmunro-wtm:Documents:"
path1 = path2 -- result = false
path1 ≠ path2 -- result = true
```

On its own, an alias isn't very useful. However, when used by applications to open and save documents and by the Finder to perform various functions on files and folders, it becomes a vital command in an AppleScript developer's toolkit.

Table 10.3 provides an overview of alias objects.

Table 10.3 Overview of Alias Objects	
Properties	`class`, `POSIX path`
Elements	N/A
Coercions supported	`list` (single item), `text`
Constants	`alias`
Operators	`=`, `is equal to`
	`≠`, `is not equal to`
Variable naming convention (optional)	`alias«Type»«Description»«...»`

Working with Files

A *file* is essentially the same as an alias. It refers to a file located anywhere on a user's computer or an accessible network volume.

A file object can only be used with a command that requires a file, such as those that read and write to text files, or within a `tell application` command for a document-based application. For example, the following script will compile, but when executed it will generate an error because AppleScript can't directly work with a file:

```
set pathToFile to file "Macintosh HD:Users:mmunro-
    wtm:Desktop:Catalog Data.txt"
```

CROSS-REF

Learn about controlling applications with scripts and the `tell application` command in Chapter 17. Learn about manipulating text files in Chapter 16.

Surprisingly, AppleScript can convert a file object into an alias as shown here:

```
file "Macintosh HD:Users:mmunro-wtm:Desktop:Catalog Data.txt" as
    alias
-- result = alias "Macintosh HD:Users:mmunro-wtm:Desktop:Catalog
    Data.txt"
```

Table 10.4 provides an overview of file objects.

Table 10.4 Overview of File Objects

Properties	`class`
Elements	N/A
Coercions supported	`list` (single item), `text`
Constants	`file`
Operators	`=`, is equal to
	`≠`, is not equal to
Variable naming convention (optional)	`pathTo«Type»«Description»«…»`

Working with References

A *reference* is a value that points to an object or group of objects within an application. The object(s) referred to can be within a container within the application. For example, a document of any document-based application can typically be referred to as:

```
document 1 of application "«name application»"
```

So, using the Pages application, a reference to the document in front would be:

```
document 1 of application "Pages"
```

CROSS-REF
Learn more about controlling applications and referring to their objects in Chapter 17.

Depending on the application, references can point to any object, including a document, page, text box, record, field, cell, script, menu, menu item, window, folder, or file.

NOTE
A reference typically must refer to an object that exists or a script error may occur; however, the Finder will allow you to refer to files and folders that do not exist yet.

A reference can be placed into a variable to shorten repetitive instances of the object to which it refers. Subsequent uses can refer to the object with the variable rather than the entire object specified, resulting in less code clutter. The following example shows a variable called `ref-Document` being initialized to contain a reference to the first document of the Pages application. Then, the next line needs to state only the variable to route instructions to the document.

```
set refDocument to a reference to document 1 of application
  "Pages"
tell refDocument
  -- instructions here
end
```

The real advantage is multiplied when referring to an object that is contained deep within an object hierarchy. For example, putting a reference to a paragraph of some text that is contained within a text box on a specific page within a document will save an enormous amount of clutter if it can be referred to with a single variable.

The class of a reference varies from one reference to another because it refers to the class of the object being referred to rather than the reference itself. The following example shows four references, each referring to a different object type. Notice the consistency between Pages and Microsoft Word when referring to a document. This kind of happy coincidence occurs a lot with AppleScript and gives a sense of continuity between well-designed application dictionaries.

```
tell application "Finder"
    set refFile to a reference to file "Macintosh
    HD:Users:mmunro:Desktop:Catalog Data.txt"
end tell
class of refFile -- result = document file
tell application "Pages"
    set refDocument to a reference to document 1
end tell
class of refDocument -- result = document
tell application "Microsoft Word"
    set refDocument to a reference to document 1
end tell
class of refDocument -- result = document
tell application "Pages"
    set refPage to a reference to page 1 of document 1
end tell
class of refPage -- result = page
```

A reference can be converted into a single item list as shown in this example:

```
tell application "Pages"
    set refPage to a reference to page 1 of document 1
    refPage as list
    -- result {page 1 of document 1 of application "Pages"}
end tell
```

A reference can sometimes be converted into text but not always. The previous Pages example will return an error if you attempt to convert `refPage` to text. When a reference to an object in the Finder refers to a file or folder path, it can be converted into text as shown here:

```
tell application "Finder"
    set refFile to a reference to file "Macintosh
    HD:Users:mmunro:Desktop:Catalog Data.txt"
    return refFile as string
    -- result = "Macintosh HD:Users:mmunro:Desktop:Catalog Data.
    txt"
end tell
```

Because a reference refers to an object within an application, it may cause errors if you try to use it outside of a `tell application` command or inside one for a different application. For example, trying to set the contents of a text box in a desktop publishing application must occur within a `tell application` command to that application.

A reference can also be compared to another reference to determine if they contain the same information. This example shows a reference to a file and a reference to a folder being compared a few different ways:

```
tell application "Finder"
    set refFile to a reference to file "Macintosh
    HD:Users:mmunro:Desktop:Catalog Data.txt"
    set refFolder to a reference to folder "Macintosh
    HD:Users:mmunro:Desktop:Catalog Folder:"
    refFile = refFile -- result = true
    refFile = refFolder -- result = false
    refFile is equal to refFolder -- result = false
end tell
```

Table 10.5 provides an overview of reference objects.

Table 10.5 Overview of Reference Objects

Properties	`class`
Elements	N/A
Coercions supported	`list`, `text (sometimes)`
Constants	N/A
Operators	`=`, `is equal to`
	`≠`, `is not equal to`
Variable naming convention (optional)	`ref«Type»«Description»«…»`

Summary

In this chapter you learned about the five additional data classes: boolean, RBG color, alias, file, and reference.

Working with Lists

A *list object* is a collection of values grouped in a specific order and contained within a set of brackets ({ }). Lists provide a convenient way of storing and managing groups of related data. When values are grouped into a list, they can be used and transmitted as a single entity, which is represented by a single variable.

Lists are common among scripts that work with batches of information. Whether a group of files or folders, a found set of database records, or each page of a document, lists allow a script to easily iterate through each item.

Introduction to Lists

A list can contain hard-coded data and data contained in variables. For example:

```
{"Apples", "Oranges", "Pears"}
{nameCompany, textURL}
{2, 4, 6, 8}
```

A list can contain any and all AppleScript data classes in any combination. This example has two text strings and two numbers for a total of four items:

```
{"Saturday", "August", 2, 2009}
```

A list can even contain other lists, which, in turn, can contain lists forming a nested list of lists. Each list within the nested structure is contained within one set of two brackets.

The following example has two items, the second of which is a list containing three items:

```
{"Fruit", {"Apples", "Oranges", "Pears"}}
```

Table 11.1 provides an overview of list objects.

In This Chapter

Looking at list objects, their properties, and their behavior

Counting and comparing lists and list items

Converting, extracting, adding, replacing, and removing list items

Table 11.1 Overview of List Objects

Properties	`class, length, rest, reverse`
Elements	`item, indexed item`
Coercions supported	`varies by classes of data within`
Constants	`pending`
Operators	`&, =, ≠, is equal to, is not equal to, starts with, ends with, contains, and is contained by`
Naming convention (optional)	`list«Prefix»«Type»«Description»«…»`

Looking at list properties

Objects in the list class have four properties: `class`, `length`, `rest`, and `reverse`.

Class

The `class` property of a list is a read-only value that will always be `list`. To determine the class of an object of an unknown type to make sure it is a list, you simply write `class of dataToCheck = list` with `dataToCheck` representing the unknown value. If the variable contains a list, the result will be `true`. If not, it will be `false`.

Length

The `length` property of a list is a read-only value that contains an integer specifying the number of items contained with the list. For example:

```
length of {1, 2, 3, 4} -- result = 4
length of {7, 8, 9} -- result = 3
length of {"Hello", 15, 200} -- result = 3
```

This property will only return the number of items found in the first level of items. So, a list of lists, like the one that follows, has only two items even though those items, which are lists, contain additional values:

```
length of {{1,2,3},{4,5,6}} -- result = 2
length of {{"Hello","Goodbye"},{"Hi","Bye"}} -- result = 2
```

Rest

The `rest` property of a list is a read-only value that contains all of the items in the list, except the first item. For example:

```
rest of {1, 2, 3, 4} -- result = {2, 3, 4}
rest of {"Hello", 15, 200} -- result = {15, 200}
```

Reverse

The `reverse` property of a list is a read-only value that contains all of the items in the list in reverse order. For example:

```
reverse of {1, 2, 3, 4} -- result = {4, 3, 2, 1}
reverse of {"Hello", 15, 200} -- result = {200, 15, "Hello"}
```

Looking at specialty lists

Text-based record lists and synchronized lists are somewhat unconventional types of lists that occasionally come in handy and are worth noting.

Text-based record list

A *text-based record list* contains a two-item list. The first item represents a field name; the second item contains the actual value. Unlike a record, which has field names, a text-based record list allows for more flexibility when adding, searching, or using values.

The following is an example of a text-based record list:

```
{{"«fieldname»","«fieldValue»"}}
{{"Name","Mark Munro"},{"Company","Write Track Media"}}
```

CROSS-REF

Learn more about records in Chapter 12.

Synchronized list

A *synchronized list* is two or more lists that all have the same number of items in the same order, so that a value in any position in one list corresponds to a value in the same position in every list. This can be useful when processing related data points such as names, addresses, and phone numbers or product names, prices, and categories. Each entity represented by the three lists in these examples has one value in the same position in each list.

In the following example, the first value from `listNames` corresponds to the first value from `listQuotes`:

```
set listNames to {"John Galt", "Howard Roark"}
set listQuotes to {"A is A", "Form Follows Function"}
```

NOTE

When dealing with any position in one list, you can use the same numeric placeholder to access the corresponding values in any other synchronized list.

Analyzing Lists

You can analyze lists several different ways. You can count all the items in a list or just those of a particular data class. Also, you can check a list to see if it starts with, ends with, or contains a given value.

Counting list items

When you are using a list to contain dynamic data, which can change from one process to the next, your script will need to count the number of items contained within. To do this, use the `count`, `length`, or `number of` command.

The result will be the total number of items at the first level of the list. In other words, if the list contains one or more nested list, the nested list will be seen and treated as a single item — a list — and not count the individual items it contains.

In the following example, a variable called `list1` is set to a string, a number, a list, another number, and another list:

```
set list1 to {"AppleScript", 15, {1, 3, 5}, 200, {2, 4, 6}}
```

AppleScript will see this as a list of five items. Even though the third item is a list of three values and the fifth item is a list of three values, each is viewed as a single item at the first level of the list.

```
count items of list1 -- result = 5
length of list1 -- result = 5
number of items of list1 -- result = 5
```

Because the primary element of a list is an item, you do not need to specify that you are counting items:

```
count of list1 -- result = 5
```

You can use the `count` and `number of` commands to count specific classes of data within the list. You can count how may of the items are text, dates, numbers, or any AppleScript class of data. You can also count how many of the items are lists. For example:

```
count text of list1 -- result = 1
count integer of list1 -- result = 2
count list of list1 -- result = 2
count dates of list1 -- result = 0
number of text of list1 -- result = 1
number of integers of list1 -- result = 2
number of lists of list1 -- result = 2
number of dates of list1 -- result = 0
```

Comparing lists

Lists can be compared to other lists to determine if they are equal or if they contain, start with, or end with a particular value.

Equality

Two lists are considered equal if they contain the same values in the same order. To determine whether two lists are equal, you can use three different operators: =, is, or is equal to, as shown here:

```
set list1 to {1, 2, 3}
set list2 to {1, 2, 3}
list1 = list2 -- true
list1 is list2 -- true
list1 is equal to list2 -- true
```

TIP

Using symbols for comparisons such as = and ≠ takes up less space and they can be typed in less time than their English language equivalents.

Even one minor difference or the slightest change in order will make the lists unequal. For example:

```
set list1 to {1, 2, 3}
set list2 to {3, 2, 1}
list1 = list2 – false
```

You can compare a specific value in a list to some other value in two ways. First, put the list value that you want to compare into a variable. Then compare that variable to the other value, like this:

```
set list1 to {3, 4, 6, 8}
set dataValue to item 3 of list1
dataValue = 6 -- result = true
```

The other method requires only one line. By referencing the value in the list, you can compare it directly without having to remove it from the list, like this:

```
set list1 to {3, 4, 6, 8}
item 3 of list1 = 6 -- result = true
```

Using the same single line method, you can check for the existence of a list of values of a given type. The values in the list you are checking must have the values you are comparing in the same order, but not necessarily together in the list. The following example shows a list of three integers in `list1` and those same integers in `list2` separated by text values, but in the same order as `list1`. Because the line doing the comparing compares `list1` to `every integer of list2`, instead of `every item of list2`, the comparison result is `true`.

```
set list1 to {1, 2, 3}
set list2 to {"A", 1, "B", 2, "C", 3}
every item of list2 = list1 -- result = false
every integer of list2 = list1 -- result = true
```

This same technique works no matter what position the integers are, as long as they are in the same order. Following are two examples. The first shows the numeric values in different position but still in the same order and with a result of `true`. The second shows the numeric values in a different order of `{2, 1, 3}` and, therefore, the result s are `false`.

```
set list2 to {1, 2, "A", "B", "C", 3}
every integer of list2 = list1 -- result = true
set list2 to {"A", "B", 2, 1, 3, "C"}
every integer of list2 = list1 -- result = false
```

To compare lists to see if they are not equal, you use all of the same techniques described previously but invert the wording toward the negative. You can use three different operators: ≠, `is not`, or `is not equal to` as shown in these examples:

```
set list1 to {4, 5, 6}
set list2 to {1, 2, 3}
list1 ≠ list2 -- true
list1 is not list2 -- true
list1 is not equal to list2 -- true
```

NOTE

Typing a "not equal to" symbol (≠) is accomplished by holding down the Option key while typing an equal sign.

Contains, is contained by, and is in

You can check lists to see if a list contains a given value using the `contains, is contained by,` and `is in` operators. The value you search for can be any AppleScript class, including other lists. The result of the process will return a boolean value of `true` or `false`.

The following example shows a list with three numeric values. Checking for the value `2` returns a result of `true`:

```
set list1 to {1, 2, 3}
list1 contains 2 -- result = true
```

If you search the same list for a value of `"2"`, it will return `false`. Although the list contains the integer 2, it does not contain the text string `"2"`.

```
list1 contains "2" -- result = false
```

Searching for the existence of a list within a second list works in much the same way. The following example sets two variables, each with a list, and then checks to see if the longer list contains the shorter list. The result is true because the items in `list1` exist as items within `list2` and they are in the same order:

```
set list1 to {1, 2, 3}
set list2 to {"A", "B", "C", 1, 2, 3}
list2 contains list1 - true
```

In this example, even though the second list contains the values from the first list and they appear in the same order, because they are not together, the result is `false`:

```
set list1 to {1, 2, 3}
set list2 to {"A", 1, "B", 2, "C", 3}
list2 contains list1 -- false
```

Keep in mind that the difference between numeric values and text values may cause values that you might think are similar to return a `false` value. This example shows `list2` with text-based versions of the numeric values in `list1` and the resulting `false` value when they are compared:

```
set list1 to {1, 2, 3}
set list2 to {"A", "B", "C", "1", "2", "3"}
list2 contains list1 - false
```

Another similar mistake can be demonstrated with a date in a list. Because the date object is made up of quoted data, it is not a text object. Checking to see if a list contains a portion of the text that you see within the date will return a result of `false`. The following examples show that the date in the list does not contain the text "August" or the short date as a text string:

```
set list1 to {date "Saturday, August 1, 2009 12:00:00 AM"}
list1 contains "August" -- result = false
list1 contains "8/1/2009" -- result = false
```

To get a positive result, you need to use an entire date object for comparison:

```
list1 contains date "Saturday, August 1, 2009 12:00:00 AM"
-- result = true
```

You can also parse the date object and compare an individual component:

```
set list1 to {date "Saturday, August 1, 2009 12:00:00 AM"}
set nameMonth to month of item 1 of list1
nameMonth contains August -- result = true
```

You can check to see if a portion of a list specified by a data class contains another list. For example, because every integer of `list2` results in a value of `{1, 2, 3}`, it contains `list1` and will return a value of `true`:

```
set list1 to {1, 2, 3}
set list2 to {"A", 1, "B", 2, "C", 3}
every integer of list2 contains list1 - true
```

This command can be phrased in the opposite direction: `is contained by`. This phrasing reverses the question, asking if a value is contained by a list, as shown here:

```
set list1 to {1, 2, 3}
1 is contained by list1 -- result = true
```

The `is in` operator works similarly to `is contained by` and offers the same results:

```
set list1 to {1, 2, 3}
1 is in list1 -- result = true
```

Starts with, ends with

While `contains` enables your script to discover if one or more items exists within a list, `starts with` and `ends with` focus on the beginning and ending of the list. The value you search for can be a single value or a list of values, as shown in the following example:

```
set list1 to {1, 2, 3, 4, 5, 6}
list1 starts with 1 -- result = true
list1 starts with {1, 2} -- result = true
list1 ends with 6 -- result = true
list1 ends with {5, 6} -- result = true
```

Here are two examples of checking for text values:

```
set list1 to {"Indiana", "Ohio", "New York", "Pennsylvania"}
list1 starts with "Indiana" -- result = true
list1 starts with {"Indiana", "Ohio"} -- result = true
set list1 to {"Cent", 1857, 1858, "Flying Eagle"}
list1 starts with "Cent" -- result = true
list1 starts with {"Cent", 1857} -- result = true
```

Considering and ignoring text properties

When comparing text in lists, AppleScript ignores case and numeric strings but pays attention to diacriticals, hyphens, punctuation, and white space — unless you tell it to do the opposite.

You can accomplish this by using the `considering` and `ignoring` control statements. These statements enable you to force AppleScript to act in opposition to its default inclinations. For example:

```
set list1 to {"AppleScript"}
considering case
   list1 starts with "applescript" -- false
end considering
list1 starts with "applescript" -- true
```

CROSS-REF
Chapter 7 contains more details about the options for these control statements used with text objects. The same options and techniques can be applied to text within lists.

Searching in lists

You can find the position of a specific value in a list or in a list of lists by using a `repeat` loop. The following example checks every item contained in the list to see if one of the items matches the value in the variable `numToFind`. When the script finds a match, it will exit the loop and the variable `numPostiion` will contain the positional location of the value in the list, which in this case is 4:

```
set listData to {1, 3, 5, 7, 9}
set numToFind to 7
set numPosition to 0
repeat with a from 1 to count items of listData
    set numPosition to a
    if item a of listData = numToFind then exit repeat
end repeat
return numPosition -- result = 4
```

CROSS-REF
Learn more about `repeat` loops in Chapter 14.

Manipulating Lists

Lists can be manipulated in many different ways. They can be converted into other data types. List items can be extracted by position, by type, or randomly. They can also have values added, replaced, or removed.

Converting lists to other data types

A list can be converted into a single text string. When you do this, all of the items of the list will be converted to text and then merged together into a single text item with no delimiter, unless a custom text item delimiter has been selected. For example:

```
set list1 to {"Text1", "Text2"}
list1 as text -- result = "Text1Text2"
set list1 to {1, 2, 3, 4, 5, 6}
list1 as text -- result = "123456"
set list1 to {true, false, true}
list1 as text -- result = "truefalsetrue"
```

If you set a custom text item delimiter, that delimiter will be placed between each value in the list when converting it to text, like this:

```
set text item delimiters to {"-"}
set list1 to {"Text1", "Text2"}
list1 as text -- result = "Text1-Text2"
set text item delimiters to {"..."}
set list1 to {"Text1", "Text2"}
list1 as text -- result = "Text1...Text2"
```

CAUTION

Be sure to change the text item delimiters back to an empty string when your script is finished to avoid unexpected behavior later:

```
set text item delimiters to {""}
```

CROSS-REF

Read more about text item delimiters in Chapter 7.

Extracting list items

If you know, or had AppleScript dynamically calculate, the position of a specific list item that you want to extract, the next step is to extract and place that data into a variable for future processing. You can extract by position, by type, or randomly. You can also extract a range of items.

All of the following examples assume this first line of code:

```
set list1 to {"AppleScript", 15, {1, 3, 5}, 200, {2, 4, 6}}
```

Extracting items by position

In much the same way as extracting characters or words from a text object, extracting a list item can refer to an item in the list by its position:

```
item 1 of list1 -- result = "AppleScript"
item 2 of list1 -- result = 15
item 5 of list1 -- result = {2, 4, 6}
```

If you request an object by position beyond the number of items in the list, you will invoke an error:

```
item 10 of list1
```

The previous code is requesting the tenth item from a five-word list, which will result in the error shown in Figure 11.1.

Figure 11.1

An AppleScript error message for a request
beyond the available range in the list variable

You can also use the English language equivalent for a value but only from 1 to 10. For example:

```
first item of list1 -- result = "AppleScript"
second item of list1 -- result = 15
fifth item of list1 -- result = {2, 4, 6}
```

One useful English language positional specifier enables you to extract the last item in a more efficient way than using the numeric value. Because AppleScript calculates which requested item is last, your code remains short:

```
last item of list1 -- results = {2, 4, 6}
```

If you were to access the last item of a list with the numeric specifier, you would first have to count how many items were present and then use that number to extract the last one, resulting in a longer piece of text:

```
item (count items of list1) of list1 -- results = {2, 4, 6}
```

Another English language positional specifier, `middle`, automatically calculates which value is in the middle and returns it as a result. For example:

```
middle item of list1 -- result = {1, 3, 5}
```

If the number of items in the list is an even number, this command rounds down. So, in a list of four items, the second item would be considered the middle one.

Extracting a range of items

When you need to extract a range of items, you can do so by adding the `through` or `thru` keywords and specifying the desired range. The result will always be a list of the requested items. For example:

```
items 1 thru 2 of list1 -- result = {"AppleScript", 15}
items 3 thru 4 of list1 -- result = {{1, 3, 5}, 200}
```

Extracting random items

As with extraction of text, you can ask for a random item from a list. Each time you run the script, the result will be randomized:

```
some item of list1 -- "AppleScript"
some item of list1 -- 200
some item of list1 -- {1, 3, 5}
```

Extracting items by class

Items in a list can be extracted by their class type all at once or based on their position within the list. When you extract by position, is it important to know how many items are in the list of the particular class you are attempting to extract:

```
set list1 to {"AppleScript", 15, {1, 3, 5}, 200, {2, 4, 6}}
```

For example, `item 2` and `item 4` of the list are integers. You can extract the first one from the list using `item`, `integer`, or `number`. The only difference between these is the position you specify. Because 15 is the second item in the list, you would extract it using that position.

```
item 2 of list1 -- result = 15
```

However, to extract an item by type you would refer to the items position based on the items of that type only. So, while 15 is the second item in the list, it is the first integer in the list. If you refer to it by type, it is in position one. The second integer in the list is item four, or 200.

```
Integer 1 of list1 -- result = 15
integer 2 of list1 -- result = 200
```

If you are not distinguishing between real numbers and integers, you can also use `number` instead, like this:

```
number 1 of list1 -- result = 15
number 2 of list1 -- result = 200
```

This technique will work with any AppleScript data classes, including `list`. The variable `list1` has a list at item 3 and item 5:

```
item 3 of list1 -- result = {1, 3, 5}
item 5 of list1 -- result = {2, 4, 6}
```

Again, you can refer to these by their position based on class and get the same result:

```
list 1 of list1 -- result = {1, 3, 5}
list 2 of list1 -- result = {2, 4, 6}
```

AppleScript also enables you to extract a list of items of a certain class into a new list with the `every` reference form as shown here:

```
every integer of list1 -- result = {15, 200}
```

Adding items to a list

You can add additional items to a list in a variety of places. You can add to the beginning, end, or middle.

To add a value to the beginning of a list, use the `copy to beginning` command:

```
set list1 to {1, 2, 3, 4}
copy 5 to beginning of list1
list1 -- result = {5, 1, 2, 3, 4}
```

To add a value to the end of a list, use the `copy to end` command:

```
set list1 to {1, 2, 3, 4}
copy 0 to end of list1
list1 -- result = {1, 2, 3, 4, 0}
```

Both commands can be used to copy any data class to the end of a list. When copying another list to the end of a list, the list will be added as a single item in the original list. If you want o actually merge the list, use the `&` operator, as shown in the following example:

```
-- Copy a list to the end of a list
set list1 to {1, 2, 3, 4, 5}
set list2 to {10, 11, 12, 13, 14}
copy list2 to end of list1
```

```
list1 -- result = {1, 2, 3, 4, 5, {10, 11, 12, 13, 14}}
--  Merge a list to the end of a list
set list1 to {1, 2, 3, 4, 5}
set list2 to {10, 11, 12, 13, 14}
set list1 to list1 & list2
list1 -- result = {1, 2, 3, 4, 5, 10, 11, 12, 13, 14}
```

Replacing items in a list

To replace an item in a list, use the `set` command and specify the item by position:

```
set list1 to {1, 2, 3, 4, 5}
set item 3 of list1 to 100
list1 -- result = {1, 2, 100, 4, 5}
```

You can also specify the item to replace using its class type and position. In other words, if the fifth item in a list were text and the other items were numbers, you could set the first text item in the list like this:

```
set list1 to {1, 2, 3, 4, "Text1"}
set text 1 of list1 to 100
list1 -- results = {1, 2, 3, 4, 100}
```

Removing items from a list

There are several ways to remove an item from a list.

The first method is to use the `rest of` property of the list. Using this property, you can instantly access the list without the first item:

```
set list1 to {1, 2, 3, 4, 5, 6, 7, 8, 9}
set list1 to rest of list1
list1 -- result = {2, 3, 4, 5, 6, 7, 8, 9}
```

You can also extract a range of values from a list by position and the `through` or `thru` keywords:

```
set list1 to {1, 2, 3, 4, 5, 6, 7, 8, 9}
set list1 to items 2 thru 5 of list1
list1 -- result = {2, 3, 4, 5}
```

There are a couple ways to get all the items of a list except for the last item. If you know how many items are in the list, or have your script use the `length of` property to determine this, you can extract a range from 1 to one less than the number of items in the list. Here are two examples:

```
-- hard-coded numeric range
set list1 to {1, 2, 3, 4, 5, 6, 7, 8, 9}
set list1 to items 1 thru 8 of list1
list1 -- result = {1, 2, 3, 4, 5, 6, 7, 8}

-- using the length of property, less 1
set list1 to {1, 2, 3, 4, 5, 6, 7, 8, 9}
set list1 to items 1 thru ((length of list1) - 1) of list1
list1 -- result = {1, 2, 3, 4, 5, 6, 7, 8}
```

Finally, using the `reverse of` property twice, you can achieve the same result with fewer characters of code:

```
set list1 to {1, 2, 3, 4, 5, 6, 7, 8, 9}
set list1 to (reverse of (rest of (reverse of list1)))
list1 -- result = {1, 2, 3, 4, 5, 6, 7, 8}
```

Summary

In this chapter you learned about the properties and behaviors of lists and list items, and how to analyze and manipulate them in many different ways. You learned how to count, compare, merge, extract, and covert lists and their items using a variety of different methods.

Working with Records

A *record object* is an unordered list of labeled values contained within a set of brackets ({ }). Records are useful when managing data that is too large or complex for lists. They are also convenient because of the ease of modifying and accessing the values they store.

Records and script objects are the only two AppleScript classes that allow user definable properties. This means you can define the name or label of each field value in the record.

Introduction to Records

Like lists, records are built inside braces; however, each value has a label to its left separated by a colon. A comma separates each field in a record.

Here is a simple formula for a record with one field:

```
{«field»:«value»}
```

A comma separates other fields in the same record:

```
{«field»:«value», «field»:«value»}
```

The «field» portion of a record, sometimes called the "label" or "name," can be assigned any name you desire. The same rules for naming variables apply to record field labels. You can add as many fields to a record as needed, but any given name can only be used once in a single record. For example, although the following record will compile, the resulting script will only have the first instance of nameContact because that field is used twice:

```
{nameContact:"John Galt", nameContact:"Dagny
    Taggart"}
```

The «value» portion of a record can contain hard-coded data and data contained in variables:

```
{nameContact:"John Galt",
    nameLocation:"Colorado"}
{nameContact:name1, nameLocation:location1}
```

In This Chapter

Looking at record objects and their properties and behavior

Counting and comparing records and values

Converting, extracting, adding, replacing, and removing record labels and values

The «value» portion of a record can contain any and all AppleScript data classes, including records. The following example has two fields. The first field value is text and the second field value is a record with two fields, one text and one numeric:

```
{title:"Atlas Shrugged", data:{author:"Ayn Rand", year:1957}}
```

Table 12.1 provides an overview of record objects.

Table 12.1 Overview of Record Objects	
Properties	class, length
Elements	N/A
Coercions supported	pending
Constants	pending
Operators	&, -, contains, is contained by
Naming convention (optional)	«Prefix»rec«Description»«…»

Comparing an AppleScript record to a database record

The collection of field/value combinations is aptly called a "record" for a good reason. For those familiar with databases, it helps to compare an AppleScript record to a record in a database. Each labeled field and its corresponding value is just like a field in a database field.

To extend the comparison and create the equivalent of a "database" with AppleScript records, one might place a sequence of records with identical field labels into a list. The duplication of the same field label is allowed because it is used in two separate records, which are then joined into a list:

```
{{nameContact:"John Galt"}, {nameContact:"Dagny Taggart"}}
```

When putting records into lists to form a "database," the class of the result will be a list. The class of each item in the list continues to be a record.

Looking at record properties

Records have two default properties: class and length. In addition, records can have any number of developer-defied custom properties in the form of field/value combinations.

Class

The default class of a record is record. To determine the class of an object of an unknown type to make sure it is a record, simply write class of dataToCheck = record where dataToCheck represents the unknown value. If the variable contains a record, the result will be true. If not, it will be false.

An unusual feature of AppleScript records is their capability to possess a custom class value by simply adding a label of `class` and then specifying the class. Surprisingly, the custom class can be any data type, including a date, a file alias, and even a script object. However, for practical purposes, you should probably limit yourself to text, as shown here:

```
set recData to {class:"Company", nameCompany:"Write Track Media"}
class of recData -- result = "Company"
```

A custom class would be practical in a script that manipulates multiple record formats. You could create custom classes like `Report Data` or `Contact Data` to allow the script to route any given record to the correct subroutine for further processing.

Length

The length property of a record is a read-only value that contains an integer specifying the number of values contained by the record:

```
length of {num1:1, num2:100, num3:50} -- result = 3
```

Each labeled value counts as a single value, so a list of four items is counted as a single item:

```
length of {text1:"WTM", list1:{1, 3, 5, 7}} -- result = 2
```

Creating a Record

To create a record, simply write a `set variable` line and type the record, including the number of fields you need. You can name the field labels however you want as long as they are not the same as some AppleScript reserved word or command.

Following are three simple examples, each with one field more than the last and with label names consisting of single alphabetic characters. All of the values are text based:

```
set recData to {a:""}
set recData to {a:"", b:""}
set recData to {a:"", b:"", c:""}
```

This example has more clearly named labels, a mix of text and integer values, and default values:

```
set recData to {textName:"Month", numGross:25000, numNet:20000}
```

Here is the same example except the two numeric values are now part of a nested record, `recData`:

```
set recData to {textName:"Month", recData:{numGross:25000,
    numNet:20000}}
```

You can have as many nested records as you need and each one can have as many or as few of the same or unique labels as needed.

Analyzing Records

There are a few ways that you can analyze the contents of a record. You can count the number of fields a record contains and compare one record to another in a variety of ways.

Counting records

You can count records by using the length property or the count command. Both will return an integer representing the number of labeled properties within the record:

```
length of {num1:1, num2:100, num3:50} -- result = 3
count of {num1:1, num2:100, num3:50} -- result = 3
```

You can also count specific data classes within a record, similar to the method used for lists. By placing the class name after the count command, the results will isolate the count to the type of data you specify:

```
count text of {num1:1, num2:100, num3:50} -- result = 0
count numbers of {num1:1, num2:100, num3:50} -- result = 3
```

Comparing records

You can compare two records and determine if they are identical and determine if a record contains a specific value.

Equality

Two records are considered equal if they contain the same values with the same labels. The fields can be in a different order; as long as the label names and corresponding values remain the same, the records will be considered the same.

To compare records, you can use three different operators: =, is, or is equal to:

```
set rec1 to {num1:150, num2:3500, num3:10}
set rec2 to {num2:3500, num1:150, num3:10}
rec1 = rec2 -- results = true
rec1 is rec2 -- results = true
rec1 is equal to rec2 -- results = true
```

TIP
Using symbols for comparisons such as = and ≠ takes up less space, and they can be typed in less time than their English language equivalents.

NOTE
Typing a "not equal to" symbol (≠) is accomplished by holding down the Option key while typing an equal sign.

To compare records to see if they are not equal, use all of the same techniques described earlier but invert the wording toward the negative. You can use three different operators: ≠, is not, or is not equal to, as shown in these examples:

```
set rec1 to {num1:150, num2:3500, num3:10}
set rec2 to {num1:150, num2:0, num3:10}
rec1 ≠ rec2 -- results = true
rec1 is not rec2 -- results = true
rec1 is not equal to rec2 -- results = true
```

This example shows a comparison where the three values are the same, but the records are not equal because the first field labels in each are different:

```
set rec1 to {num1:150, num2:3500, num3:10}
set rec2 to {numX:150, num2:3500, num3:10}
rec1 ≠ rec2 -- results = true
```

Contains, is contained by, and is in

You can check to see if a record contains a given value using the contains and is in operators. The value you search for must be a record with at least one label and one value. The result of the process will return a boolean value of true or false.

The following code shows two examples: one searching for a text string that is false and the other searching for the text string as a labeled value, which is true:

```
set rec1 to {text1:"Hello", text2:"Goodbye"}
rec1 contains "Hello" -- result = false
rec1 contains {text1:"Hello"} -- result = true
{text1:"Hello"} is in rec1 -- result = true
```

Just like when you compare records for equality, when you confirm that a record contains more than a single value, the labels don't have to be in the same order. As long as the labels and their corresponding values are the same, the result will be true.

These examples show several different arrangements for the comparison data, which all return a result of true:

```
set rec1 to {num1:150, num2:3500, num3:10}
rec1 contains {num1:150} -- result = true
rec1 contains {num1:150, num2:3500} -- result = true
rec1 contains {num1:150, num3:10} -- result = true
rec1 contains {num3:10, num1:150} -- result = true
```

If you invert the comparison language to the negative, you can check whether a value is not contained by a record using the does not contain and is not in operators, like this:

```
{text1:"Hello"} is not in rec1 -- result = false
rec1 does not contain {text1:"Hello"} -- result = false
```

Considering and ignoring text properties

When comparing text in records, AppleScript ignores case and numeric strings but pays attention to diacriticals, hyphens, punctuation, and white space — unless you tell it to do the opposite.

You do this by using the `considering` and `ignoring` control statements. These statements enable you to force AppleScript to act in opposition to its default inclinations:

```
set rec1 to {text1:"Hello", text2:"Goodbye"}
considering case
    rec1 contains {text1:"HELLO"} -- result = false
end considering
rec1 contains {text1:"HELLO"} -- result = true
```

CROSS-REF

Chapter 7 contains more details about the options for the `considering` and `ignoring` control statements used with text objects. The same options and techniques can be applied to text within lists.

Manipulating Records

Records can be manipulated in a variety of different ways. You can add or remove specific fields from a record and modify a field's value with another value. Records can also be converted into a list.

Converting records to other data types

As a whole, a record can only be converted into a list. When you do so, all of the value labels will be permanently removed from the record, but you can keep the original record in a separate variable if needed. There are two ways to convert the record to a list:

```
set rec1 to {text1:"Hello", text2:"Goodbye"}
rec1 as list -- result = {"Hello", "Goodbye"}
every item of rec1-- result = {"Hello", "Goodbye"}
```

Extracting data from a record

You can extract values from a record one by one or as all values of a single type all at once.

To extract a single field, you need to know the name of the field. Using that and specifying the record that contains the data, you can extract the value for immediate use or place it into a variable for future use. Here is an example:

```
set rec1 to {text1:"Hello", text2:"Goodbye"}
text1 of rec1 -- result = "Hello"
```

You can also extract all values of a data class using the `every «class» of` command, as shown here:

```
set rec1 to {text1:"Hello", text2:"Goodbye"}
every text of rec1-- result = {"Hello", "Goodbye"}
every number of rec1 -- result = {}
```

Adding something to a record

There is no way to dynamically create new record value labels. Each record's label must be typed and compiled by a developer, thereby creating that placeholder for data to be added, accessed, and manipulated.

Before you start creating unusually large records to contain every possible combination of value placeholders you might ever need, it is possible to merge two records within a script. While you need to type and compile both of them, they can be programmatically merged with the `&` operator. The following example demonstrates two records, each with a single field being merged into a single record:

```
set rec1 to {text1:"Hello"}
set rec2 to {num1:15}
set rec3 to rec1 & rec2 -- result = {text1:"Hello", num1:15}
```

Once this code is executed, you will have three variables, each containing a record. The original two record variables `rec1` and `rec2` still exist with their original value. The new variable, `rec3`, contains the combined values of the other two.

Replacing a value in a record

To set or replace a value in a record, use the `set` command and specify the label for the value you want to modify. The existing value for that label will be replaced with the new value. For example:

```
set rec1 to {data1:"Hello", num1:100}
set data1 of rec1 to "Goodbye"
rec1 -- result = {data1:"Goodbye", num1:100}
```

If you set a value to a different class from the original value, the class of that record value will change to reflect the class of the new data. This example shows the class of `data1` changing from `text` to `integer` after the value is set to `500`:

```
set rec1 to {data1:"Hello", num1:100}
class of data1 of rec1 -- result = text
set data1 of rec1 to 500
class of data1 of rec1 -- result = integer
```

Removing a value from a record

Just as you can't programmatically add a new labeled value to a record, you can't directly remove one, either. However, you can achieve the same result by rebuilding the record to contain just the values you want.

To do this, set a new variable to just the fields you want. Type the field label, a colon, and a reference to the value in the record. The following examples show this process, reducing a three value record into a one and two value records:

```
set rec1 to {num1:150, num2:3500, num3:10}
set rec2 to {num1:num1 of rec1} -- result = {num1:150}
set rec2 to {num2:num2 of rec1, num3:num3 of rec1}
-- result = {num2:3500, num3:10}
```

NOTE

While this method achieves the desired result, it still requires you to type the reduced fields into a new variable and can't be called a programmatic change.

Summary

In this chapter you learned about the properties and behaviors of records. I discussed how to analyze and manipulate them in a variety of different ways. You learned how to count, compare, merge, extract, and covert record values using a variety of different methods.

Logical Branching

Scripts that execute code in a strictly linear fashion are only practical when automating simple and very consistent work-flows. Real-world situations often require more flexibility. When a script needs to diverge between two or more courses of action depending on one or more conditions, it is time to take the first step toward non-linear programming.

Logical branching, the programmatic choice of one out of multiple batches of code, is achieved with an `if-then` control statement. It determines which code will execute and which will be skipped, based on an evaluative expression.

AppleScript's `if-then` statement enables a script to "skip ahead" depending on the result of an equation. In this chapter you'll explore the anatomy of the statement, create a simple conditional "Hello World" script, and discover the branching capabilities this powerful piece of the language allows.

Looking at the Anatomy of an if-then Statement

There are two custom portions within the structure of the basic `if-then` statement: the equation and the conditional code. Verbally, you could describe this kind of statement as: "If this equation is true, then run this code." For example:

```
if «equation» then
    «conditional code»
end if
```

The *equation* must contain one or more expressions that evaluate to a boolean value of `true` or `false`. The equation can be made up of multiple expressions that work together or separately to determine if the conditional portion of the statement should be executed.

The *conditional code* is one or more lines of AppleScript code that will run only if the conditions expressed by the equation are true.

Figure 13.1 illustrates a basic `if-then` control statement in AppleScript.

Figure 13.1

A basic if-then statement
as a flow chart

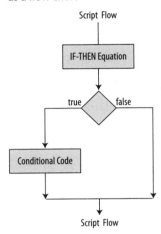

Building a conditional "Hello World" dialog

To illustrate the use of conditional code further, you will modify the "Hello World" dialog box example from Chapter 6 to only display under certain conditions. First, type the dialog code, compile it, and run it to make sure that it's working:

```
display dialog "Hello World"
```

Next, add a variable above the dialog line called blnX and give it a value of true. Then, wrap an if-then statement around the dialog so that it looks like this:

```
set blnX to true
if blnX = true then
    display dialog "Hello World"
end if
```

If you run the script, you should see the dialog appear as before. Now, if you change the first line to set blnX to false and run the script, the dialog will not appear. This is because the false value in blnX causes AppleScript to skip the dialog line altogether.

NOTE
AppleScript automatically indents the lines of code between the **if** and **end if** lines to create a visual cue of which lines are enclosed within the statement.

A simple, one line `if-then` statement like this can be expressed on a single line, which saves space and reduces visual clutter. When the conditional code follows the equation portion on the same line, the `end if` is dropped altogether, leaving you with this formula:

```
if «equation» then «conditional code»
```

You can rewrite the previous conditional dialog script on a single line using this formula like this:

```
set blnX to true
if blnX = true then display dialog "Hello World"
```

Running this script should perform exactly like the multi-line one shown previously.

TIP

Because the equation portion of the statement automatically evaluates if it is `true`, you don't have to include "`= true`" in the equation. So, `if blnX then display dialog "Hello World"` works exactly the same as the example shown.

Expanding the equation

The equation portion of the statement can be as complex as a script requires.

Using the AND operator

You can use multiple equations but they must all be true in order for the code to execute. The formula for an `if-then` statement with two equations that must both be true looks like this:

```
if «equation» and «equation» then
   «conditional code»
end if
```

Each equation is first evaluated independently and then the results are compared for the final decision. If either of them results in a false value, the conditional code will not execute.

Using the conditional dialog script with multiple equations, you would create a dual equation with an `and` operator like this:

```
set bln1 to true
set bln2 to true
if bln1 = true and bln2 = true then
   display dialog "Hello World"
end if
```

NOTE

Changing either of the variables in the equation to false causes the dialog line to be skipped.

Using the OR operator

You can set up multiple equations so that the code will execute if any one of them is true. The formula for an if-then statement with two equations that will execute if at least one of them is true looks like this:

```
if «equation1» or «equation2» then
   «conditional code»
end if
```

Using the conditional dialog script, you can create a dual equation with an or operator. If one or both of the variables is true, the dialog will appear. For example:

```
set bln1 to true
set bln2 to true
if bln1 = true or bln2 = true then
   display dialog "Hello World"
end if
```

Using both AND and OR operators

The equation portion of the statement includes a combination of both the and and or operators. Here is an example of a formula with four equations:

```
if «equation1» and «equation2» or «equation3» or «equation4» then
   «conditional code»
end if
```

These can be as complex as you need, although once you have three to five conditions with a mix of and and or operators, it can become increasingly difficult to predict what will or will not execute the code. To help reduce this difficulty and to reduce horizontal wrapping, you can pre-calculate the choices in variables prior to using the if-then statement.

This formula shows the same logical setup to the previous example, but with the values recalculated to save clutter:

```
set bln1 to («equation1») and («equation2»)
set bln2 to («equation3») or («equation4»)
if bln1 or bln2 then
   «conditional code»
end if
```

Here is the conditional dialog based on this new formula:

```
set blnA to true
set blnB to true
```

```
set blnC to true
set blnD to true
set bln1 to (blnA = true) and (blnB = true)
set bln2 to (blnC = true) or (blnD = true)
if bln1 or bln2 then
   display dialog "Hello World"
end if
```

The previous examples use booleans in the equation portion of the statement for illustrative clarity. However, it is important to remember that this part of the statement can include comparisons of any type of data. The following examples show four if-then statements, each with a different data class in the equation:

```
if numPages < 10 then
   display dialog "Hello World"
end if
if textMessage contains "Hello" then
   display dialog "Hello World"
end if
if listOfNames contains "Mark Munro" then
   display dialog "Hello World"
end if
if (weekday of (current date)) = Thursday then
   display dialog "Hello World"
end if
```

Creating a Multiple Condition Statement

So far, you have seen a single logical branch — conditional code that is either skipped or executed. Statements can be made much more powerful by adding the else portion to an if-then statement. This creates a two-alternative situation. If the equation is true, the first conditional code is used. If the equation is false, the second conditional code is used. Verbally, you could describe this kind of statement as: "If something is true then run this code, else run that code."

Figure 13.2 illustrates a basic if-then-else statement in AppleScript.

The formula for an if-then-else statement has an else line followed by a second conditional code, as shown here:

```
if «equation» then
  «conditional code»
else
  «conditional code2»
end if
```

Figure 13.2

A basic `if-then-else` statement as a flow chart

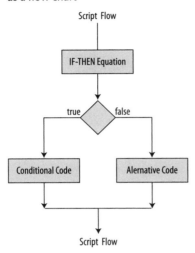

Using this new formula, you can expand the "Hello World" conditional dialog script to include an alternative dialog. First, duplicate the display dialog portion of the script and place an `else` between the two lines. Then, modify the text of the dialogs so that you can distinguish between them. Finally, run the code once with `blnX` set to `true` and once with it set to `false` to see the difference. For example:

```
set blnX to true
if blnX = true then
  display dialog "Hello World #1"
else
  display dialog "Hello World #2"
end if
```

When writing scripts, you should always watch for opportunities to compress the code. Rather than having two `display dialog` lines, you can place the actual messages into variables and the dialog statement is only stated once outside the `if-then` statement like this:

```
set blnX to true
if blnX = true then
  set textMessage to "Hello World #1"
else
  set textMessage to "Hello World #2"
end if
display dialog textMessage
```

At first glance this might seem like a waste because the code is actually longer. However, in this case, where you have only two choices and the messages are placed in variables, you can further compress the code as shown here:

```
set blnX to true
set textMessage to "Hello World #2"
if blnX = true then set textMessage to "Hello World #1"
display dialog textMessage
```

Because the message will be one or the other, placing one message in the variable and then replacing it if the equation is true enables you to significantly reduce the size of the code. This would not have been possible with two dialog calls.

Also, using variables allows the code to be more flexible over time as you add additional conditions to the if-then statement.

Adding Additional Conditions

A *compound* if-then statement has more than two alternatives and uses an else if statement to add equations for each additional code condition.

Often your scripts will have to deal with more than a binary true/false situation. You might have ten different reports to build or a dozen different naming conventions for photographs. Any number of situations will arise where you need more than two alternatives. When this happens, you use a compound if-then statement.

Verbally, you could describe this kind of statement as: "If this is true, then run this code; else if that is true, run this code; else if these are true…and so on."

Figure 13.3 illustrates a compound if-then statement in AppleScript.

Modifying the conditional dialog to have three messages is easy. For now, you will use the first version of the compressed code from the last section, modifying it slightly to allow for three possible dialogs depending on the value of numX:

```
set numX to 1
if numX = 1 then
    set textMessage to "Hello World #1"
else if numX = 2 then
    set textMessage to "Hello World #2"
else if numX = 3 then
    set textMessage to "Hello World #3"
end if
display dialog textMessage
```

Figure 13.3

A compound `if-then` statement as a flow chart

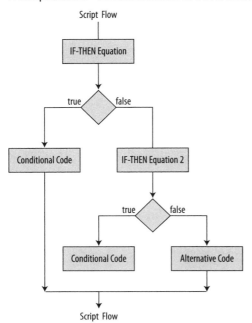

Once you have tested this script with numX containing a value of 1, 2, and 3, try it with a value of 4. This results in an error stating that the variable textMessage is not defined. This is a preview of a common error of a conditionally undefined variable (which is discussed later in this chapter). For now, the best way to solve this problem is to make sure that there is a "catch-all" for any value that falls outside the range specified in the explicit equations. You can do this by adding a final else to the statement. This provides a fourth conditional safety net of code that will be executed for any other situation. So, if numX equals 4, 5, 10, 300, or any number except those contained in the statement, the code after the final else will be executed.

This example shows the same code shown previously, with the final else setting the variable to "Hello World #4":

```
set numX to 1
if numX = 1 then
    set textMessage to "Hello World #1"
else if numX = 2 then
    set textMessage to "Hello World #2"
else if numX = 3 then
    set textMessage to "Hello World #3"
else
    set textMessage to "Hello World #4"
```

```
    end if
display dialog textMessage
```

NOTE

As an example, this is a fine alternative. If your code requires that the variable controlling the action must be in the range of 1 to 3, then any other value should create an error message.

CROSS-REF

Learn more about handling and generating errors in Chapter 15.

Using Nested Statements

A *nested statement* is any control statement that is repeated within a control statement of the same type. A nested if-then statement is a secondary if-then statement that will only be evaluated if the first "parent" statement results in a specified value. This can be verbalized as "If a is true and if b is true, then execute this code."

Figure 13.4 illustrates a nested if-then statement in AppleScript.

In Figure 13.4, the first, overriding if-then evaluates a choice between one of the nested if-then statements, each of which chooses from one of two message values. If the first equation is true, the second equation determines a choice of code 1 or 2. If the first equation is false, the third equation determines a choice of code 3 or 4.

Here is an example of this logic. The variable blnA is used to determine which nested (inner) if-then statement will be evaluated. Then, blnB is used to determine which of the two messages will be used. So, if blnA is true, blnB chooses between message 1 or 2. If blnA is false, blnB chooses between message 3 and 4.

```
set blnA to true
set blnB to true
if blnA = true then
   if blnB = true then
      set textMessage to "Hello World #1"
   else
      set textMessage to "Hello World #2"
   end if
else
   if blnB = true then
      set textMessage to "Hello World #3"
   else
      set textMessage to "Hello World #4"
   end if
end if
display dialog textMessage
```

Figure 13.4

A nested `if-then` statement as a flow chart

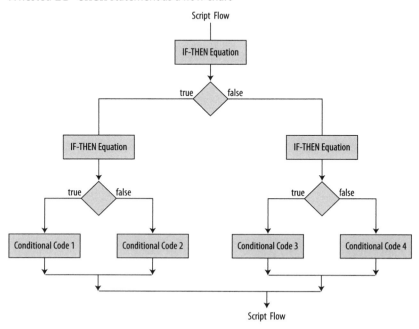

The inner nested `if-then` statements can be compressed because they only offer one of two choices like this:

```
set blnA to true
set blnB to true
if blnA = true then
    set textMessage to "Hello World #2"
    if blnB = true then set textMessage to "Hello World #1"
else
    set textMessage to "Hello World #3"
    if blnB = true then set textMessage to "Hello World #3"
end if
display dialog textMessage
```

Understanding Common Mistakes

Those new to AppleScript coding often fall victim to several common mistakes when adding logical branching to a script. Being familiar with these can be a valuable asset.

Missing parenthesis

When including mathematical equations as part of the `if-then` evaluation, the lack of paren-thesis can sometimes be an issue. The following example illustrates this problem:

```
set num1 to 10
set num2 to 5
set num3 to 2
if num1 + num2 / num3 = 7.5 then
    display dialog "Hello World #1!"
end if
if (num1 + num2) / num3 = 7.5 then
    display dialog "Hello World #2!"
end if
```

The first equation will evaluate `false` because AppleScript calculates `num1 + num2 / num3` to 12.5. The second equation will be `true` because AppleScript calculates `(num1 + num2) / num3` to 7.5.

Missing conditions

A *missing condition* is a situation in which none of the equations in a compound `if-then` statement result in a true value and, therefore, do not execute any of the conditional code seg-ments. Once you move from a binary `true-false` statement and introduce multiple condi-tions, it becomes more difficult to anticipate all possible outcomes. When a developer loses track of one or more conditions, the script ends up being improperly tested and can cause problems when a user encounters those lost conditions.

This example demonstrates such a situation:

```
set bln1 to false
set bln2 to true
set bln3 to false
if bln1 = true and bln2 = true then
    display dialog "Hello World #1!"
else if bln3 = true then
    display dialog "Hello World #2!"
end if
```

With the three variables current values, no dialog box will appear. Modify any of the variables and dialog boxes will begin appearing.

There are a few methods you can use to avoid missing a condition. Keeping your equations as simple as possible will make it easier to see what might be missing. If the equations require added complexity, try pre-evaluating them into one or more variables prior to the `if-then` statement. Finally, for very complex logic, you might consider making a table that cross-refer-ences all the possible conditions.

Table 13.1 shows every possible combination for the previous script.

Table 13.1	Missing Condition Analysis		
bln1	bln2	bln3	Dialog Displayed
true	true	true	#1
true	true	false	#1
true	false	false	None
false	false	false	None
false	false	true	#2
false	true	false	None
false	false	true	#2

Under two conditions, each dialog will appear. However, there are three conditions missing where no dialog will appear. This kind of analysis can help you avoid missing conditions and spare the script's users the errors and confusion that would accompany this oversight.

NOTE
You need to be sure that you anticipate and test all possible outcomes of your logical statements.

Conditionally undefined variables

A *conditionally undefined variable* is a variable that is only declared within an if-then state-ment that never evaluates as true. Because the code that declares and sets the variable never executes under one or more conditions, in those instances, it will generate an error.

In this example, with numX set to 3, none of the if-then statement's set textMessage lines will execute, and the variable textMessage is undefined:

```
set numX to 3
if numX = 1 then
    set textMessage to "Hello World #1"
else if numX = 2 then
    set textMessage to "Hello World #2"
end if
display dialog textMessage
```

The if-then as written is only able to handle a value of 1 or 2 so any other value will cause an error message, as shown in Figure 13.5.

Figure 13.5

A conditionally undefined variable will generate this error message.

You can use or combine several methods to overcome this dilemma. These include:

- Make sure your if-then statement is set up to handle every logical condition.
- Define the variable to some default value before the if-then statement. That will ensure that the variable is never undefined.
- Add a final else condition to capture all unanticipated logical conditions.
- Add a second if-then statement around the display dialog line that ensures that it only attempts to execute if the anticipated conditions are true or a default value is not present in the variable.
- Add error protection around the display dialog line to capture the error.

CROSS-REF
Learn how to create, capture, and work around script errors in Chapter 15.

Summary

In this chapter you learned about logical branching code with the if-then statement. You built a conditional "Hello World" dialog and learned about multiple equations and compound and nested if-then statements.

Looping

A *repeat loop* is a control statement that executes one or more statements multiple times. It is used to save space by repeatedly executing statements that are only stated once within the script.

Without a repeat loop, any code that needs to be run more than once will have to be included multiple times within the script, as shown in Figure 14.1.

This repetition causes a script to be unnecessarily lengthened and more complex to modify. Far worse than this obvious inefficiency, which is contradictory to the very nature of workflow optimization promised by AppleScript, is an inherent practical failure. Each time a script is used, the number of times the code in question must be run will vary. Without a repeat loop, a developer must predict the number of times the code might be repeated and then duplicate the code that many times, placing each instance within an if-then statement, which will skip the unnecessary repetitions. When you consider that a user might want a script to manipulate a dozen, a hundred, or even thousands of files at a time, the impracticality of non-repeating code becomes all too obvious.

With a repeat loop, the code that needs to be repeated only exists once, as shown in Figure 14.2. The script simply reruns that block of code over and over until it has performed the required number of loops.

The repeat loop can be hardcoded to run a specific number of times or the script can dynamically calculate the number of loops required and run it that number of times. For example, if a user drops ten files onto the script for processing, the loop will run ten times. The next time, the same user might drop three dozen files and the loop will run once for each file.

In This Chapter

Looking at the `repeat` command

A review of each type of repeat statement

Nesting and creating `repeat` loops

Modifying and extracting data with `repeat` loops

Figure 14.1

A flow chart showing one block of "repetitive code" being stated four times without a repeat loop

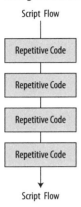

Figure 14.2

A flow chart showing one block of "repetitive code" stated once within a repeat loop

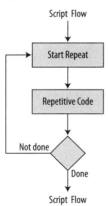

Looking at the Anatomy of a Repeat Statement

A repeat statement begins with the `repeat` keyword. There may be optional parameters included on the same line. The statement ends when the `end repeat` keywords are used. Any code between these two will be executed continuously until the loop is terminated. For example:

```
repeat «optional control parameters»
  «repeated code»
end repeat
```

A repeat loop can wrap around one or more lines of code. It may contain optional control parameters indicating how many times to run the repeated code or to specify what conditions should sustain the loop. It can also contain an exit repeat line, which, under specified circumstances, will exit the loop immediately and resume running the remaining portion of the script.

NOTE

AppleScript automatically indents the lines of code between the `repeat` and `end repeat` lines to create a visual cue of which lines are enclosed within the statement.

Defining the Types of Repeat Loops

There are many types of repeat loops, each offering features to accommodate specific needs. These include `repeat`, `repeat x times`, `repeat while`, `repeat until`, `repeat with a from x to y {by z}`, and `repeat with a in list`.

Repeat (until exit)

The simplest type of a repeat statement will continue repeating forever until it is stopped either by a code condition or the user typing a period while holding the Command key.

Here is the formula:

```
repeat
  «repeated code»
  if «equation» then exit repeat
end repeat
```

The `repeat` and `end repeat` lines wrap around one or more lines of repeated code. The code will be executed continuously until an `exit repeat` command is executed, which is shown in the previous example as part of an `if-then` equation. When the equation produces a true result, the repeat loop will be stopped and any remaining statements in the script will continue executing.

In the following example, a random item from a list of five numbers is copied to the end of the `listValues` variable each time through the loop. Once this list contains ten values, the repeat is exited. The result will be a list of the ten randomly selected numbers.

```
set listValues to {}
repeat
  copy (some item of {1, 2, 3, 4, 5}) to end of listValues
  if ((count listValues) = 10) then exit repeat
end repeat
listValues -- result = {1, 3, 4, 3, 1, 2, 2, 2, 3, 2}
```

The first line initializes a variable called `listValues` to an empty list. This is where the randomly selected values will be placed, one per loop. The first line within the repeat statement copies a randomly selected number to the end of `listValues`. The next line counts the number of items in that list and exits the repeat if that count equals 10.

NOTE
While this type of repeat loop can occasionally satisfy a practical need, all of the other types offer better control of when the repeat should be terminated.

Repeat x times

The `repeat x times` command enables a script to specify how many times the repeated code should be executed. An `exit repeat` command is not required unless the repeat loop should stop early under specific circumstances. The formula requires an integer between the `repeat` and `times` keywords, indicating the number of items the code should be repeated. For example:

```
Repeat «integer» times
   «repeated code»
end repeat
```

Like the example in the previous section, this example builds a list of ten randomly selected numbers without an `exit repeat` command. The loop automatically stops after the specified number of repeats:

```
set listValues to {}
repeat 10 times
   copy (some item of {1, 2, 3, 4, 5}) to end of listValues
end repeat
listValues -- result = {5, 3, 3, 2, 1, 5, 2, 4, 5, 3}
```

Repeat while

The `repeat while` command continues to execute the repeated code as long as the equation portion of the `repeat` results in a `true` value. Once the equation result is false, the script exits the repeat and continues executing any remaining code. For example:

```
Repeat while «equation»
   «repeated code»
end repeat
```

This example performs the same function as the previous two examples except it uses the `repeat while` command. As long as the equation — in this case `blnX = true` — is true, the repeated code will be executed over and over like this:

```
set listValues to {}
set blnX to true
```

```
repeat while blnX = true
   copy (some item of {1, 2, 3, 4, 5}) to end of listValues
   set blnX to ((count listValues) > 10)
end repeat
listValues -- result = {5, 4, 1, 3, 5, 5, 2, 3, 1, 2}
```

Repeat until

Similar to `repeat while`, but using the opposite logic, the `repeat until` command executes the repeated code until the equation returns a true result. It repeats until the equation is true instead of while an equation is true. For example:

```
Repeat until «equation»
   «repeated code»
end repeat
```

This example performs the same function as the previous three examples but uses the repeat until command:

```
set listValues to {}
set blnX to true
repeat until blnX = false
   copy (some item of {1, 2, 3, 4, 5}) to end of listValues
   set blnX to ((count listValues) < 10)
end repeat
listValues -- result = {2, 1, 3, 5, 3, 3, 4, 5, 4, 5}
```

Repeat with a from x to y {by z}

When a script needs to process a list of files, folders, text items, or other lists of multiple objects, a `repeat with` command can be enormously beneficial. It uses an *index variable* to automatically store the current loop number, which controls the number of loops and can be used to manipulate the corresponding item in a list. For example:

```
Repeat with «variable» from «integer» to «integer»
   «repeated code»
end repeat
```

To use this type of repeat, you first must choose a variable name. This can be as descriptive as you need it to be, or can be a single character. Traditionally, the most commonly used character is "i", which stands for "index". However, when you begin using nested repeat loops (discussed later in this chapter), it makes more sense to use characters that clearly denote which repeat statement in the nest each piece of code is within. The best way to do this is to name the first loop "a", the second "b", and so on. This keeps the index variable short and reduces clutter, while still denoting which level you are on.

Next, you need to assign a start and end integer, which instructs the repeat loop to repeat the code while the index variable is within the range specified.

The following example shows a list of numbers that are added to one another to result in a single number, which is the sum of all numbers in the list. Using a list of ten numbers, the `repeat` command is instructed to run with the index variable `a` starting at 1 and stopping at the number representing the count of items in the list:

```
set listValues to {2, 1, 3, 5, 3, 3, 4, 5, 4, 5}
set numTotal to 0
repeat with a from 1 to count listValues
    set numTotal to numTotal + (item a of listValues)
end repeat
numTotal -- result = 35
```

NOTE
Each time through the loop, the item added to the running total is extracted from the list based on its position relative to the current value of the index variable. Because AppleScript automatically sets the index to one more than the last time through the loop, you can dynamically extract the next value.

To really grasp the power of this type of repeat, try changing the number of values in the `listValues` variable. It will continue to create a total of all the numbers in the list, whether there are two or two hundred.

Although the index variable typically starts with 1, it is not a requirement. Unique circumstances might require starting somewhere in the middle of a list. For example, consider a hypothetical list of Adobe PDF files that need to be merged into a single PDF file. The script might open the first one and then add each remaining file into that file. Therefore, the merging action applies to all but the first file. So, you might use `repeat with a from 2 to count listFiles` to accomplish this.

The repeat with command enables you to add an *increment parameter*, which specifies how much the index variable should increment per loop. This formula shows the expanded repeat clause with the additional `by «integer»` clause:

```
Repeat with «variable» from «integer» to «integer» by «integer»
   «repeated code»
end repeat
```

Whatever value is placed in the increment integer, the index variable will increment that many times for every one loop. The following example is identical to the previous example except that it has an increment integer value of 2, which means adds the numbers in the list skipping every other number:

```
set listValues to {2, 1, 3, 5, 3, 3, 4, 5, 4, 5}
set numTotal to 0
repeat with a from 1 to count listValues by 2
    set numTotal to numTotal + (item a of listValues)
end repeat
numTotal -- result = 16
```

The previous script starts with the first item in the list on the first loop and then adds the third, fifth, seventh, and ninth items for a total of 16.

The increment integer also enables a repeat loop to work backwards through a list of items. Reversing the range of integers and setting the increment integer to a negative number accomplishes this feat. The following example creates a new list that contains the values of the list-Values variable in reverse order:

```
set listValues to {1, 2, 3, 4, 5, 6, 7, 8, 9, 10}
set listResults to {}
repeat with a from (count listValues) to 1 by -1
   copy (item a of listValues) to end of listResults
end repeat
listResults -- result = {10, 9, 8, 7, 6, 5, 4, 3, 2, 1}
```

Repeat with a in list

Similar to the repeat with command, the repeat with a in list command makes it even easier to process a list of items. The only difference is that the index variable contains the actual item from the corresponding location in the list rather a numeric value. For example:

```
repeat with «variable» in «list»
   «repeated code»
end repeat
```

This example adds each number in a list. However, there is no need to extract the current item from the list on each loop because the current value will automatically be placed into the index variable, which, in this case, is numX.

```
set listValues to {2, 1, 3, 5, 3, 3, 4, 5, 4, 5}
set numTotal to 0
repeat with numX in listValues
   set numTotal to numTotal + numX
end repeat
numTotal -- result = 35
```

Nesting Repeat Loops

A *nested statement* is any control statement that is repeated within a control statement of the same type. A *nested repeat statement* contains one or more other repeat statements, as shown in Figure 14.3.

The formula for one repeat loop nested inside of another repeat loop looks like this:

```
repeat «optional control parameters»
 repeat «optional control parameters»
    «repeated code»
  end repeat
end repeat
```

Figure 14.3

A flow chart showing a repeat loop "nested" within another repeat loop

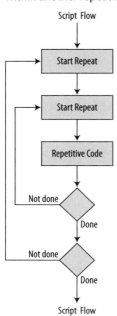

A script can contain as many nested control statements required for any task. Each can have different control parameters because they are distinct statements. The repeated code does not have to be limited to the innermost repeat. So, the code between each `repeat` command can have any other code, including but not limited to a nested repeat. The formula that follows demonstrates this by showing repeated code for the first "outer" repeat before and after the "inner" repeat, which has its own repeated code:

```
repeat «optional control parameters»
  «repeated code for level 1»
  repeat «optional control parameters»
    «repeated code for level 2»
  end repeat
  «repeated code for level 1»
end repeat
```

Nested repeat loops are useful when a script needs to manipulate a list of lists. They are also helpful when breaking down and manipulating multilevel data such as text whose characters make up words, which make up sentences and paragraphs. The first level would repeat through each paragraph, while the second, nested repeat would loop through each sentence of the current paragraph, and so on.

NOTE
When using a repeat type with an index variable, be sure to use a different variable for each successive nested state-ment or you will get some very interesting results. The best approach to avoid confusion is to use an "a" for the first level, "b" for the next level, and so on.

This example shows a nested repeat loop processing a list of lists. It adds each sub-list within the list into a total, which is then placed into the `listResults` variable. The result is a list of totals summarizing the values of each sub-list.

```
set listToProcess to {{1, 2, 3}, {4, 5, 6, 7}, {8, 9, 10, 11,
    12}}
set listResults to {}
repeat with a from 1 to count items of listToProcess
    set listCurrent to item a of listToProcess
    set numTotalCurrent to 0
    repeat with b from 1 to count items of listCurrent
        set numCurrent to item b of listCurrent
        set numTotalCurrent to numTotalCurrent + numCurrent
    end repeat
    copy numTotalCurrent to end of listResults
end repeat
return listResults -- result = {6, 22, 50}
```

TIP
Avoid using lengthy nested **repeat** commands, which can become visually distracting and difficult to follow. A script containing five nested repeats, each with one or two lines of repeated code is easy to read because it is vertically short. In a single glance you can see which line of code falls between a particular level of the nest. However, if the repeated code for each level were several dozen or hundreds of lines long, the script would span many pages and it would be much more difficult to follow visually. On page three, you might not be able to tell which level a particular line of code falls within. Try using subroutines to break the structure into separate pieces.

CROSS-REF
Using subroutines to break code into smaller and more manageable parts is discussed in Chapter 21.

Using Repeat Loops

Repeat loops can be used to create, analyze, or manipulate multiple pieces of data in a uniform way.

Creating with repeat loops

Repeat loops can be used to create lists of any kind of data for various purposes, such as a list of random numbers or a range of dates.

Creating a list of random numbers

This simple example uses a repeat loop to create a list of random numbers:

```
set listData to {}
repeat 10 times
    copy (random number 100) to end of listData
end repeat
return listData
-- result = {70, 26, 32, 81, 55, 33, 61, 91, 74, 39}
```

Creating a range of dates

A more complex example creates a list of dates starting from the current date and spanning five days. The starting date and number of days are placed into variables, dateStart and numDays, and can be customized.

```
--   Setup control variables
set dateStart to current date
set numDays to 5
--   Setup result variable
set dateCurrent to dateStart
set listDatesInRange to {dateCurrent}
repeat numDays times
    set dateCurrent to dateCurrent + (1 * days)
    copy dateCurrent to end of listDatesInRange
end repeat
return listDatesInRange
--   result = {date "Sunday, September 20, 2009 2:09:43 PM", date
    "Monday, September 21, 2009 2:09:43 PM", date "Tuesday,
    September 22, 2009 2:09:43 PM", date "Wednesday, September 23,
    2009 2:09:43 PM", date "Thursday, September 24, 2009 2:09:43
    PM", date "Friday, September 25, 2009 2:09:43 PM"}
```

N O T E
Once a list of dates within the range has been created, a script might check to see if a date exists in the list and, therefore, falls within the date range.

Modifying with repeat loops

It is common to use repeat loops to manipulate data. Each item of a list might be modified in a uniform manner or a single piece of data might be manipulated until it reaches a certain length, divisibility, or value.

Adding prefixes and suffixes to a text list of values

A repeat loop makes it easy to add prefixes or suffixes to a list of values. The script shown in Listing 14.1 demonstrates this using a simple nested repeat loop.

Listing 14.1

Adding a prefix and suffix to a list of values

```
Adding a prefix and suffix to a list of text values
--  Setup the control variables
set listToProcess to {"$100", "49.5", "26.25", "133"}
set numDecimalPlaces to 2
repeat with a from 1 to count items of listToProcess
    --  Isolate the current item and add a prefix and decimal if needed
    set textCurrentItem to item a of listToProcess
    if textCurrentItem does not start with "$" then set textCurrentItem
    to "$" & textCurrentItem
    if textCurrentItem does not contain "." then set textCurrentItem to
    textCurrentItem & ".00"
    --  Separate the whole number and decimal portion
    set AppleScript's text item delimiters to {"."}
    set listNumParts to every text item of textCurrentItem
    set AppleScript's text item delimiters to {""}
    set textWhole to item 1 of listNumParts as string
    set textDecimals to item 2 of listNumParts as string
    -- Add decimal places as needed
    repeat while (count textDecimals) < numDecimalPlaces
        set textDecimals to textDecimals & "0" as string
    end repeat
    --  Assemble the new value and replace it in the list
    set item a of listToProcess to textWhole & "." & textDecimals
end repeat
return listToProcess
-- result = {"$100.00", "$49.50", "$26.25", "$133.00"}
```

NOTE

The code in Listing 14.1 is available for download from the book's Web site at www.wileydevreference.com.

The variable listToProcess contains several text-based, numeric values that need to be formatted into dollar amounts. In their raw form, they are inconsistently formatted. The script will add a dollar sign unless one is already present. Then, it adds a decimal and two zeros to those values that have no decimal place. Next, it uses text item delimiters to split the text into two parts along the decimal place so that the nested repeat loop can add zeros to the end until the value has the number of decimal places specified in the numDecimalPlaces variable. Finally, it unites the two parts into a single dollar formatted text-based number and puts it back into the list before moving on to the next value in the list. When finished, the list will contain properly formatted dollar amounts.

N O T E
The currency formatting examples in this section can't handle numbers expressed in exponential notation.

Converting a number to a formatted dollar amount

Similar to the example in the previous section, the script shown in Listing 14.2 uses `if-then` and `repeat` statements to convert a real number into a text-based dollar formatted value, complete with appropriately located commas.

Listing 14.2

Converting a number into a text-based, formatted dollar amount

```
--  Setup the control variables
set numToFormat to 1628.49
set numDecimalPlaces to 2
set textPrefix to "$"
--  Separate the whole number and decimal portion
set numToFormat to numToFormat as string
if numToFormat does not contain "." then
   set numWhole to numToFormat as string
   set textDecimals to "00"
else
   set numToFormat to numToFormat as string
   set AppleScript's text item delimiters to {"."}
   set listNumParts to every text item of numToFormat
   set AppleScript's text item delimiters to {""}
   set numWhole to item 1 of listNumParts as string
   set textDecimals to item 2 of listNumParts as string
end if
--  Modify the number of decimal places if required
repeat while (count textDecimals) < numDecimalPlaces
   set textDecimals to textDecimals & "0" as string
end repeat
if numDecimalPlaces ≠ 0 then
   set textDecimals to "." & (text 1 thru numDecimalPlaces of
   textDecimals) as string
else
   set textDecimals to ""
end if
--  Format the whole number
set textFormattedNumber to ""
set numValCharacterCount to count of characters of numWhole
repeat with a from 1 to numValCharacterCount
```

```
    set textFormattedNumber to textFormattedNumber & character a of
    numWhole
    set numCommaDetector to (numValCharacterCount - a)
    if (numCommaDetector / 3) = (round numCommaDetector / 3) and
    numCommaDetector ≠ 0 then set textFormattedNumber to
    textFormattedNumber & ","
end repeat
--  Assemble the formatted number
set textFormatedNumber to textPrefix & textFormattedNumber &
    textDecimals as string
return textFormatedNumber
--  result = "$1,628.49"
```

NOTE

The code in Listing 14.2 is available for download from the book's Web site at `www.wileydevreference.com`.

The first repeat loop ensures that the number of decimal places is specified in the `numDecimalPlaces` variable while the second loop inserts a comma between every three numbers.

Converting some text to uppercase

The following example converts any piece of text into uppercase. It only modifies alphabetic characters a–z, so it will not disturb punctuation, numbers, or any other characters that might be contained within the text. The repeat loop processes each character, using the id text property to identify characters in the range of lowercase letters (97–122), and subtracts 32 to arrive at the ID of the corresponding uppercase letter, which is then placed into the `textResult` variable.

```
set textToProcess to "This iS a TeSt. it should maKe this text
    aLL upPerCaSE!"
set textResult to ""
repeat with a from 1 to count of textToProcess
    set textCharacter to character a of textToProcess
    set textID to id of textCharacter
    if textID < 123 and textID > 96 then
        set textCharacter to character id (textID - 32)
    end if
    set textResult to textResult & textCharacter
end repeat
return textResult
--  result = "THIS IS A TEST. IT SHOULD MAKE THIS TEXT ALL
    UPPERCASE!"
```

CROSS-REF
The id property of text is discussed in Chapter 7.

Extracting with repeat loops

Repeating code makes repeatedly extracting values from data easy.

Extracting specific columns of data from a tab-delimited text file

A repeat loop can be helpful in extracting a subset of data from a database export. Given a hypothetical tab-delimited product text file, shown in Figure 14.4, the following script extracts only the product name and price and creates a new tab-separated file with only those values shown in Figure 14.5:

```
set pathToFile to (choose file) as string
set textData to read file pathToFile
set textResults to ""
set text item delimiters to {tab}
repeat with a from 1 to count paragraphs of textData
    set textCurrentParagraph to (paragraph a of textData)
    if textCurrentParagraph is not "" then
        set listData to every text item of textCurrentParagraph
        set listData to {item 2 of listData, item 4 of listData}
        set textNew to listData as text
        set textResults to textResults & textNew & return as string
    end if
end repeat
set text item delimiters to {""}
set pathToSave to (choose file name) as string
open for access file pathToSave with write permission
write textResults to file pathToSave
close access file pathToSave
```

Figure 14.4

A tab-separated product text file with more data
than is required for a specific task

01	Widget A	10oz	15.99	Kitchen
02	Widget B	13oz	12.99	Garage
03	Widget C	8oz	18.50	Kitchen
04	Widget D	11oz	13.99	Bedroom
05	Widget E	3oz	8.99	Office
06	Widget F	32oz	40.00	Kitchen
07	Widget G	14oz	12.75	Bedroom
08	Widget H	12oz	12.99	Bedroom

The script uses text item delimiters to break each paragraph into separate fields. Then it extracts the second and fourth fields and merges them back into a tab-delimited paragraph added to the `textResults` variable. This process is repeated for every paragraph of the source file, after which the user is asked to specify a location and name into which the results are saved.

Figure 14.5

A tab-separated product text file pared down to include only the product name and price

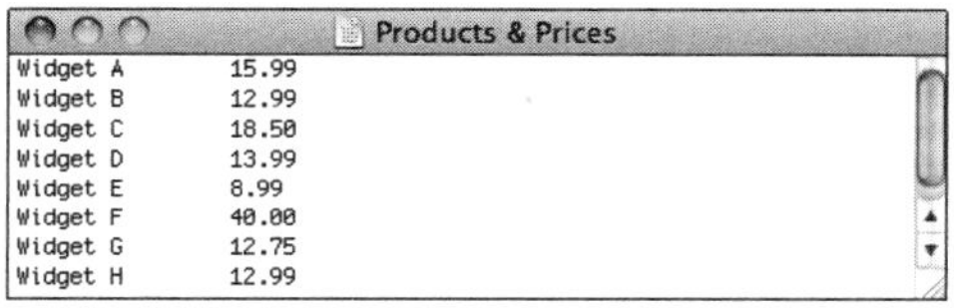

Products & Prices	
Widget A	15.99
Widget B	12.99
Widget C	18.50
Widget D	13.99
Widget E	8.99
Widget F	40.00
Widget G	12.75
Widget H	12.99

CROSS-REF

Learn how to use text item delimiters to parse and merge text in Chapter 7. Learn more about the `choose file name` command in Chapter 16.

Extracting specific rows of data from a tab-delimited text file

Using the same source file from the previous example (shown earlier in Figure 14.4), the following script uses the `repeat` command to extract only product records of a specific category:

```
set nameCategory to "Kitchen"
set pathToFile to (choose file) as string
set textData to read file pathToFile
set textResults to ""
set text item delimiters to {tab}
repeat with a from 1 to count paragraphs of textData
    set textCurrentParagraph to (paragraph a of textData)
    if textCurrentParagraph is not "" then
        set listData to every text item of textCurrentParagraph
        if item 5 of listData = nameCategory then
            set textResults to textResults & textCurrentParagraph &
return as string
        end if
    end if
end repeat
```

```
set text item delimiters to {""}
set pathToSave to (choose file name) as string
open for access file pathToSave with write permission
write textResults to file pathToSave
close access file pathToSave
```

The resulting data, shown in Figure 14.6, is saved in a file of the user's choosing.

Figure 14.6

The resulting file of items from the "Kitchen" category

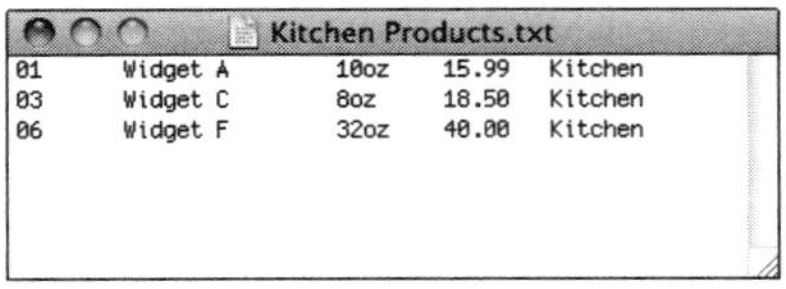

Processing files with repeat loops

One of the most common uses of AppleScript is to provide a user with a drop script application upon which he can drop a batch of files for processing.

CROSS-REF

Drop script applications are discussed in Chapter 3 and Chapter 21.

The following code shows a formula for an `on open` subroutine with a `repeat` statement ready to receive file manipulation code that will be executed on each file the user drops:

```
on open listFiles
    repeat with a from 1 to count items of listFiles
        set pathToFile to item a of listFiles as string
        «file manipulation code»
    end repeat
end open
```

CROSS-REF

Subroutines, including **on open**, are discussed in Chapter 21.

When the user drops items onto the script application, they are automatically placed into the `listFiles` variable. The script then executes the `repeat` command once for every item in the list. Each file is placed into the `pathToFile` variable after which any file manipulation code that needs to be performed can be added.

The `repeat` command is not only helpful for processing batches of files, but also for processing multiple items within files. Many text processing and desktop publishing application files have multiple pages. If the script functions are applied to each page, a nested repeat statement might be added to the script. The script might also have additional nested repeat statements to process every paragraph or text box of each page.

CROSS-REF
Because file manipulations require controlling a specific application, more detailed examples of using repeat loops can be found in Chapters 17–24.

Summary

In this chapter you learned about the `repeat` command and its six varieties. I also discussed using the command to create, modify, extract, and process various types of data.

Dealing with Script Errors

Any errors encountered when a script fails to compile can be referred to as *compile-time errors*. These are not "script errors" in the strictest sense, as they do not affect the actual execution of the script by a user.

By contrast, a *runtime-script error* occurs whenever a line of code cannot be successfully executed. Unlike errors during development, some runtime errors can occur through no fault of the code or the developer who wrote it. However, it is important to understand how errors affect the user of a script and to use this knowledge to build defenses against them. One might successfully argue that the quality of a script's design can be judged simply by how well it manages errors.

AppleScript provides a simple, yet powerful, command that can capture errors and provide information about the situation that caused them. However, this is only the first step. What a script does with the information and how it manages erroneous activity is completely up to you, the developer.

While the exact approach to error management will vary from script to script, it should attempt to communicate the error to the user and either offer an alternative or stop the script. Ideally, it should also provide enough information in a log or dialog box to assist in the process of tracking down the cause of the problem.

This may sound easy at first, but as scripts become more complex, error management can quickly become a daunting task. A poorly designed error management system can hinder the entire process by replacing one cryptic error dialog box with dozens of them as the error cascades through the remaining groups of protected code.

If left unprotected or poorly managed, errors can ruin a user's experience and bias her opinion of automation with AppleScript and of your ability to improve her workflow.

15 ▸ In This Chapter

Defining script errors

Managing errors with the `try` command

Using errors to your advantage

Recording errors in a log for further review

Introduction to Script Errors

Many factors can cause a script to generate an error. While only some might be considered "development errors," caused directly by faulty use of the AppleScript language, many are beyond your control. It is important to be aware of the troublesome situations a script may encounter and attempt to manage their impact on the user.

Defining programming errors

A *programming error* occurs because of a faulty use of the AppleScript language. It can occur even when a script compiles successfully. Ideally, programming errors will be discovered and corrected during a quality testing process, prior to being deployed to users.

Runtime syntax errors

A *runtime syntax error* occurs due to faulty code that compiles successfully but fails in some way when the script is executed. Unlike *compile-time syntax errors*, which can only occur when editing a script, runtime syntax errors can occur even after a script has been successfully compiled.

Here are a few examples of the more frequently encountered runtime syntax errors:

- **The wrong variable class is used.** Examples include attempting to perform mathematical calculations with variables that do not contain numeric values or trying to manipulate a text-based date as if it were a `date` object.

- **The script includes faulty subroutine calls.** If a subroutine being called doesn't exist in the script or if the name used in the call doesn't match the actual subroutine name, an error will occur because the subroutine can't be located and executed. If you add, rename, or remove subroutine parameters and forget to reflect this change in the calls to the subroutine, an error will occur. (Subroutines are discussed in Chapter 21.)

- **Read-only AppleScript keywords are modified.** If you use a reserved keyword as a variable and try to change its contents, your script will generate an error because keywords are read only. This can be avoided by using two or more words for every variable you create.

Conditionally undefined variables

A *conditionally undefined variable* occurs when a variable is initialized with a value in some but not all parts of a logical branch. Given the right circumstances, the variable will not be defined and a script assuming it is will create an error.

Commonly, this error occurs when you are expanding a binary `if-then` statement to contain three or more branches. Once you move from `true/false` to `one/two/three`, the chances of incurring this error increase.

The following code demonstrates the simplest formula of a conditionally undefined variable. The variable `textMessage` is only defined if the variable `numX` equals 1. When `numX` is set to a value that is not 1, the last line of the script will fail when it attempts to use the undefined variable as the message in a dialog box:

```
set numX to 2
if numX = 1 then
    set textMessage to "Hello World 1"
end if
display dialog textMessage
-- result - error "The variable textMessage is not defined."
    number -2753 from "textMessage"
```

The following code contains a more realistic example that works when you are converting a binary `if-then` statement to include a third option. Code that would work fine if the only options were `true` and `false` will then break when the variable contains any number greater than two.

```
set numX to 3
if numX = 1 then
    set textMessage to "Hello World 1"
else if numX = 2 then
    set textMessage to " Hello World 2"
end if
display dialog textMessage
-- result - error "The variable textMessage is not defined."
    number -2753 from "textMessage"
```

Even binary `true`/`false` values can get a little confusing when there are two or more of them within a single `if-then` statement. As a result of an oversight in the possible combinations, this example will fail when both `blnX` and `blnY` are false:

```
set blnX to false
set blnY to false
if blnX = true and blnY = true then
    set textMessage to "Hello World 1"
else if blnX = false and blnY = true then
    set textMessage to "Hello World 2"
else if blnY = false and blnX = true then
    set textMessage to "Hello World 3"
end if
display dialog textMessage
-- result = error "The variable textMessage is not defined."
    number -2753 from "textMessage"
```

The dilemma becomes even more complex when there are more than two possible values for a combination of two or more variables, all merged into a single `if-then` statement.

Being aware of this issue is the first step to early detection of problems before they are deployed. There are a couple of ways you can avoid these types of confusion. First, try to keep logical choices as simple as possible. You might condense each option into a single boolean value prior to the `if-then` statement so there are less variables in play within a single statement. Another way to avoid undefined variables is to simply define the variable prior to the `if-then` statement, which will create a dialog box with the default value. For example:

```
set numX to 2
set textMessage to "Default Value"
if numX = 1 then
    set textMessage to "Hello World 1"
end if
display dialog textMessage
```

Entering a default value enables the script to continue without an error. For sensitive situations, the script can check the variable after the `if-then` statement and stop in an orderly fashion if it contains the default value.

Finally, the best way to ensure you have taken into account every possible combination is to draw a table showing the intersection for every possible value and then test them one by one.

CROSS-REF
See how to use a value intersection table in a complex `if-then` statement in Chapter 13.

Range accessing errors

A *range accessing error* occurs when a script tries to access or manipulate one of a group of objects that falls outside the available range. Within lists and records are the most common places this error occurs, but they can also occur when a script is manipulating text and other data classes.

When working with lists and records that contain a range of values or fields, a script should always access data dynamically. If your code assumes a list will always contain ten items and some unforeseen circumstance arises where there are only nine items, an error will occur when it tries to access the non-existent tenth item. To avoid this, scripts should always count the number of items before attempting to manipulate or access them.

CROSS-REF
Lists are discussed in Chapter 11.

The same problem can arise when a script assumes that a group of records all have the same fields. If one suddenly doesn't, an error will occur. The best way to avoid this is to construct a template of the record, including all the required fields with default values, and copy this into variables for each required instance of the record. The following example shows a single, two-field record being copied into three variables to ensure that each of them has both of the required fields:

```
set recTemplate to {namePerson:"", txtAddress:""}
copy recTemplate to recOne
copy recTemplate to recTwo
copy recTemplate to recThree
```

CROSS-REF
Records are discussed in Chapter 12.

A similar issue can arise when a script manipulates text. A script that assumes there are a static number of characters, words, sentences, or paragraphs in a given piece of text is at risk. Simply counting the number of objects prior to accessing them eliminates the chances of a problem.

Range-accessing errors can also occur when working with third-party applications. For example, if a script attempts to put text on page 10 of an eight-page document, an error will occur. The same error will occur if a script tries to access data on database record twenty in a found set that only has ten. Once again, to avoid these problems, simply have the script count the number of objects rather than presume what the situation is.

Intentional errors

AppleScript allows a developer to intentionally generate an error. Doing so enables a script to preemptively detect a problem and create an intentional error that provides more useful information than a generic default error message. For example, a developer-generated error might inform a user that "the catalog image folder could not be found on the company file server" instead of generically stating, "folder not found."

Defining situational errors

A *situational error* is an error that is caused by any problem the script encounters while attempting to interact with an external resource. Understanding how to detect these kinds of situations before they generate an error is what separates a novice from a professional.

Missing network resources

While many scripts may only access resources that are local to the user's computer, in an office environment, resources are often accessed across a network. A *network resource* can include any file, image, or database server. It can also include a specialized automation server, resources on another user's computer, or Internet resources such as Web and file transfer servers. When any of these systems crash or go offline due to network traffic issues or scheduled maintenance, a script that relies on them will become vulnerable to errors.

CROSS-REF
Learn about mount server volumes in Chapter 16.

Even when the network resources are online and accessible, errors can occur. When a server is shared with other users, there is always the risk that someone will rename or move a resource that is required for a script to function. To avoid such an error, it is advisable that a script check if the network resource exists before attempting to access them. Also, whenever possible, automation-related materials should always be kept in a reserved folder on a server that is clearly named in a way that warns people that it is used by a script and should not be moved or renamed.

Missing application components

An *application component* is any object contained within an application or a document, such as menus, windows, preferences, buttons, style sheets, text frames, page numbers, records, scripts, fields, toolbars, and more. When AppleScript interacts with third-party software, errors can occur when a required component of the application or a document is missing or improperly named. This can happen when a software title is upgraded, a desktop publishing template is redesigned, a database file structure is modified, or when any object is renamed.

To avoid disruption to a workflow, test any new software upgrades or redesigned resources that are used by scripts thoroughly before they are deployed. Also, name named objects in a way to remind everyone that they are used by a script and should not be renamed. You can do this by clearly communicating to anyone who might modify resources the importance of maintaining a functioning automated workflow.

TIP

Scripts should also be written to expect the worse case situation. In many cases, a script can check to see if a require component is missing and warn the user before generating a bunch of errors. While it may be impractical to include code to check every resource, a script can check for the existence of a folder, style sheet, or master page before sending dozens of commands as if they exist. For more complex solutions with multiple page layout templates, you can create a small script tool separate from the main solution that checks each file for the required resources before they are placed into the live workflow.

Crashing applications

Although significantly more uncommon than it was years ago, third-party applications may crash during the execution of a script. When a crash occurs, a script will begin experiencing errors as it continues to try to access features of the application as if it was still running. Even though the application will reopen when the first post-crash command is sent to it, any documents that were being manipulated will typically not reopen and, therefore, create errors. Some applications, upon a post-crash relaunch, will present a dialog box offering to open documents that were closed. While such a message can be helpful for humans, is not beneficial to a script that is not designed to detect and dismiss such a dialog box.

Application crashes are difficult to protect against. You can easily check and confirm the existence of a network resource with one line of code. Configuring a script to confirm that an application is still running before each command is sent to the application just isn't practical, especially when a script performs dozens or hundreds of interactions with applications. Therefore, scripts must play defense by capturing and reporting the rare crashes that do occur and halting the automated process in a controlled fashion. Some applications create a specific error code that, if detected, might help a script identify the problem as a crash and take control of the process before an error cascade begins.

Obstructive application user interaction

Application user interaction is any method by which an application interacts with a user. This typically takes the form of a dialog message that must be manually dismissed. Such dialog boxes may report font issues, missing images, and more. When this occurs during an automated process, any commands being sent to the application will not be able to execute until the dialog box is dismissed. Eventually the script will timeout, give up, and encounter an error.

Well-designed applications, such as many components of Adobe's Creative Suite, include a command that enables scripts to specify the amount of user interaction that should occur. A script can turn off all interactions, silencing dialogs while it is performing automated tasks. Then, when finished, it can simply turn them back on.

CROSS-REF
Learn more about controlling applications in Chapter 17.

If an application does not provide this type of scriptable control, dialog messages that may appear when opening documents or performing certain tasks can typically be automated with the user-interface scripting capabilities made possible by System Events. This amazing application, which is part of the standard Mac OS X installation, allows direct user-like control over applications by performing menu selections, clicking interface elements, and even typing words and key commands. Once a particular dialog has been identified, a few lines of code enable a script to check for its existence during a process and, if detected, dismiss it just as a user would.

CROSS-REF
Learn more about controlling unscriptable applications with System Events in Chapter 20.

Searching database failures
When performing an AppleScript-driven search in a database like FileMaker Pro, if no records are found, an "Object not found" error will be generated.

You can easily avoid this one of two ways. First, you can wrap the search process inside of a `try` statement, which is discussed later in this chapter. Then, if an error is detected, you can check the error description or number to determine that no records were found.

Another way to avoid this error is to have the actual find process performed by a FileMaker Pro script, which includes a command to suppress errors. The AppleScript will perform the database script and then count the records in the found set. As long as the database script is set to capture errors, this will work fine and the found set will be reported as contain zero records. One added benefit of this approach is that the database script will automatically be updated if a related field, table, or layout name changes. However, if the name of the database script changes, it will cause the script to fail unless it is synced with the new name.

Exploring Error Management

With AppleScript, error management is handled with the `try` command. The `try` command is a control command that contains one or more other statements that it will protect. A script will attempt to execute the protected statements and will capture any errors that might occur. This enables a script to recover from the error and continue processing or to stop executing the code in a controlled fashion.

There are several steps required to manage script errors. First, the error must be detected and captured. The script must be able to identify the error number, description, and other key information about the cause of the problem. It needs to record the details of the error in a log file for developer troubleshooting. Finally, if the error has a catastrophic effect on the workflow, it needs to notify the user about the issues at hand and abort the script in a controlled manner. The `try` statement provides the means for a script to perform all of these functions.

Looking at the anatomy of a try command

The basic formula for a `try` statement is:

```
try
    -- protected code
end try
```

Any number of lines of code can be placed between the `try` and `end try` statements. If any part of that code causes an error, it will not create a dialog error message or any interruption to other parts of the script that are outside of the statement.

NOTE

AppleScript automatically indents the lines of code between the `try` and `end try` lines to create a visual cue of which lines are enclosed within the statement.

The following example shows a display dialog statement wrapped inside of a `try` statement. The dialog box will fail because the `textMessage` variable has not yet been initialized to contain a value. If it were not in the protected statement, it would produce a dialog box stating, "The variable `textMessage` is not defined". However, due to the error protection, the script will run and finish without any indication that an error occurred.

```
try
    display dialog textMessage
end try
```

Taking action when errors occur

By adding an `on error` clause, the `try` statement becomes significantly more useful. Rather than simply suppressing errors, it enables you to include code that will only execute when an error occurs. The statement formula expands to:

```
try
    -- protected code
on error
    -- error code
end try
```

If an error occurs within the protected code, the script immediately skips any remaining code in the statement and jumps to the error code. The error code might display an error dialog box informing a user of a problem or logging the fact that an error has occurred. Using the undefined variable from the previous example, the following code includes an error display dialog line that will inform the user of the error by presenting the dialog box shown in Figure 15.1.

```
try
    display dialog textMessage
on error
    display dialog "Custom Error message here"
end try
```

Figure 15.1

A sample error dialog box with a custom error message

Remember, the error code will only execute if an error occurs within the protected code. Replacing the undefined variable with literal text, shown in the following example, you will see the "Hello World" dialog text but not the error dialog text. When the protected code executes without an error, the error code will be skipped completely.

```
try
    display dialog "Hello World"
on error
    display dialog "Custom Error message here"
end try
```

Accessing the text description of an error

For situations in which a batch of protected code can experience more than one error, hardcoding an error message like the error dialog text shown previously is not advisable. The on error clause can include an optional parameter into which the text description of the error will be placed. The statement formula expands to include the description:

```
try
    -- protected code
on error textError
    -- error code
end try
```

When an error occurs, the text description of the error is automatically placed into the variable that immediately follows the `on error` statement. In this case, the variable is named `textError`. This example will again cause an error because of an undefined variable. However, this time it will now display the default error description, shown in Figure 15.2, in a dialog box rather than a custom description.

```
try
display dialog textMessage
on error textError
    display dialog textError
end try
```

Figure 15.2

A sample error dialog box with the actual error description of whatever error occurred

The same error code will produce a different dialog box if the protected code generates a different error. To help illustrate the point, in the following example the error dialog text will inform you that "hello" cannot be made into a number:

```
try
    5 + "hello"
on error textError
    display dialog textError
end try
```

Accessing the number of an error

An *error number* is a unique numeric value, defined by the application generating the error, which helps a developer identify an error more precisely than the text description allows. Adding the keyword `number` followed by a variable into which the error number will be placed, the formula becomes:

```
try
    -- protected code
on error textError number numError
    -- error code
end try
```

This example shows how the `numError` variable will, upon the occurrence of an error, contain the error number. The error number –2753 appears in the dialog box, as shown in Figure 15.3, which indicates a variable is not defined.

```
try
   display dialog textMessage
on error textError number numError
   set textErrorDetails to numError & ": " & textError as string
   display dialog textErrorDetails
end try
```

While this error's description is clear enough to make the number superfluous, often that is not the case. Including the numeric value of the error in dialog boxes and logs can go a long way toward helping you track down the error's cause.

Figure 15.3

A custom error dialog box showing the number
and description of the error that occurred
in the protected code

Accessing the object that caused an error

The *error object* is the name of the object that is responsible for the error. Adding the keyword `from` followed by a variable into which the name of the object will be placed, the formula becomes:

```
try
   -- protected code
on error from nameObject
   -- error code
end try
```

N O T E
All of the parameters of the `on error` clause can be used with the `from` parameter. They have been omitted from the remaining examples for clarity.

This example shows how the `nameObject` variable after the `from` parameter will, upon the occurrence of an error, contain the name of the object responsible for the error. The dialog box message shown in Figure 15.4 will be displayed.

```
try
    display dialog textMessage
on error from nameObject
    set textErrorDetails to "Error caused by: " & nameObject as
    string
    display dialog textErrorDetails -- result = "Error caused by:
    textMessage"
end try
```

Figure 15.4

A custom error dialog box showing the name
of the object causing the error

Most of the time, the error description will contain the object that caused the error. However, for circumstances where it does not or for situations were your code creates custom error messages, identifying the object responsible for the failure can be a valuable asset.

Accessing the expected type

The *expected type* is an AppleScript data class that was expected to be in the offending object. Adding the keyword `to` followed by a variable into which the expected type of the object will be placed, the formula becomes:

```
try
    -- protected code
on error to refExpectedType
    -- error code
end try
```

The following example contains one protected statement that is attempting to add the number 10 with the word "Hello World," which will obviously fail. With the expected type parameter included in the `on error` clause, the expected class will be placed into the `textType` variable. In this case the result is `number`.

```
try
    set numRecords to 10 + "Hello World"
on error to refExpectedType
    return refExpectedType -- result = number
end try
```

Accessing the partial result

The *partial result* is so rare that there isn't an example of it, even in Apple's AppleScript documentation. It is available for an application that returns multiple results to use when it experiences an error prior to completion. Adding the keyword `partial result` followed by a variable into which the partial result list will be placed, the formula becomes:

```
try
    -- protected code
on error partial result listPartialResult
    -- error code
end try
```

Applications supporting this feature are impossible to find. Adding this feature to your intentionally created error is easy if you can find a practical use for it. Usually, if a process results in an error, getting the description, number, and object for the error far outweighs a partial result of data. However, sometimes knowing which of a list of items were successfully processed before the error can be a crucial piece of information when troubleshooting an error prone batch of data.

The following example demonstrates a simple repeat loop that adds together each number in a list. Each time through the loop, it copies the current item from the list to the end of a variable named `listPartialResult` and then tries to add that item to the `numResults` variable. The `try` statement captures the error and then re-creates it so that it includes the partial result. The error is then sent to the parent subroutine or the script containing the code, where it should be handled by error management (not shown). Because the third item in the list of data is the word "Hello", an error will occur when the code attempts to add that as a number. The resulting error will include the partial result, which helps point to the fact that the script failed on the third item, which is the last item in the partial result.

```
set listData to {5, 10, "Hello", 15}
set numResult to 0
try
    set listPartialResult to {}
    repeat with a from 1 to count items of listData
        set dataCurrent to item a of listData
        copy dataCurrent to end of listPartialResult
        set numResult to numResult + dataCurrent
    end repeat
on error textError number numError
    error textError number numError partial result
    listPartialResult
end try
return numResult
-- result = error "Can't make \"Hello\" into type number." number
    -1700 partial result {5, 10, "Hello"} from «script» to item
```

NOTE

The partial result variable in this example is only used for tracking the progress of the script. If there is no error, this "result" is ignored in favor of the real result in the **numResults** variable.

Understanding More Realistic Error Scenarios

Most of the examples in this chapter have included only one line of protected code that contains an obvious programming error. While this simplistic approach helps to clearly demonstrate the feature of the moment, they are not practical in real-world situations.

Typically, a single `try` statement would contain a handful of statements although it might encompass an entire subroutine or an entire script. It is difficult to provide guidelines for the exact location and features of error protection as they may vary from one script to another. As a developer, you need to consider the available options, the needs of the script before you, and draw on your own experience and preferences for how best to manage errors.

Mixing optional error parameters

While the spatial limitations of the printed page make it difficult to show examples with multiple error parameters in a single statement, it is important to understand that they can all be used at once if desired. The following example includes four of them: description, number, object, and expected type:

```
try
    set numRecords to 10 + "Hello World"
on error textError number numError from nameObject to nameClass
    return {numError, textError, nameObject, nameClass}
    -- result = {-1700, "Can't make \"Hello World\" into type
    number.", "Hello World", number}
end try
```

Handling multiple errors

When a `try` command surrounds multiple lines of code that might experience a variety of anticipated errors, a single error message or error action just isn't enough. In this case, the error code can include an `if-then` statement that will carry out a separate set of commands depending on the specific error.

This formula demonstrates three error handling options: two for specific error codes and a final one to handle any other error that may occur.

```
try
    --  protected code
on error textError number numError from nameObject to nameClass
    if numError = -1700 then
        --   Error code for -1700
    else if numError = -2763 then
        --   Error code for -2763
    else
        --  Error code for any other error
    end if
end try
```

Generally, it is better to reduce the protected code into smaller batches rather than increase the error code with dozens of different error-handling branches. This is especially true when a script grows to several pages in length. When protecting smaller scripts, a single `try` command wrapped around the entire script with several conditional error actions can sometimes be justified.

Generating your own errors

As mentioned earlier in this chapter, AppleScript allows a script to intentionally generate errors. This occurs when a script has automatically detected a problem and needs to generate an error containing customized information instead of the more generic error message. While this feature may not be very useful for smaller scripts, complex solutions often benefit greatly from script-generated errors in response to script-detected issues.

You can do this with the `error` command followed by literal text or a variable containing a description of the error:

```
error «description»
```

This example will generate an error dialog box, as shown in Figure 15.5:

```
set textMessage to "This is an error description"
error textMessage
-- result = error "This is an error description" number -2700
   from «script» to item
```

T I P

If a script displays an error or any other material in a dialog box, the script should be written in a friendly and non-technical way, especially if the user is not a developer.

Figure 15.5

An example of an error dialog box with a custom description

Notice in the previous example that the result of the error line includes an error number and indicates the `from` and `to` parameters. These are default values inserted automatically when you generate an error. However, you can also replace these with custom values, making your script-generated errors more informative, as shown here:

```
set textMessage to "This is an error description"
error textMessage number 123 from "Catalog" to "ID"
error "This is an error description" number 123 from "Catalog" to
   text
```

While the dialog box for this code remains the same as the one shown earlier in Figure 15.5, the result displays the custom error number and other parameters.

NOTE
Unlike the previous examples, which are unprotected, intentionally generated errors should be managed just like "real" errors.

Understanding cascading errors

A *cascading error* is a sequence of errors set in motion by an error that occurred in a previous group of protected code. An error cascade can only occur in a script in which there are multiple successive groups of protected code, as shown in Figure 15.6. One group fails, resulting in an undefined variable or some other issue, which causes another group to fail. This process continues for the remaining groups of protected code until the end of the script is reached. Depending on the method of error management, a user might be bombarded with a dialog box for each failed code group. If the script records errors to a log file, each error would create a new entry.

Figure 15.6

A flow chart illustrating a linear succession of six batches of protected code

It is ironic that a thorough web of error protection with a cascade of errors can be even worse than completely unprotected code, especially if each error produces a dialog box for the user. Code that is unprotected or encased in a single `try` statement is immune from this phenomenon because an error halts the entire process, thereby skipping any remaining code. However, this should not discourage you from using multiple groups of error-protected code. Larger scripts with subroutines or multiple modules benefit greatly from, and typically require, multiple try statements.

CROSS-REF
Learn more about subroutines in Chapter 21 and multi-module solutions in Chapter 24.

Recording Errors Into a Log File

Displaying an error dialog box is an important method of communicating information to a user. However, dialog boxes can only display a limited amount of information and aren't the best option for communicating detailed error messages, especially for complex solutions. Also, for scripts running constantly on a server with no one watching and dismissing them, error dialog boxes can be disastrous. Writing error information to a log file can solve both of these problems.

As your skills develop and your scripts become more complex, you will find these logging techniques to be invaluable aids to identifying and tracking problems as they occur.

Writing information to the event log

In addition to displaying script events and replies, the AppleScript Editor's Results text area can display custom messages by using the `log` command. The following line of code will log "Hello World" into the result area shown in Figure 15.7:

```
log "Hello World"
```

This command can be a useful tool when troubleshooting a script problem as it enables you to insert code that will write data to the log. You can use it to peek inside variables at a specific point within a script and see that data logged in-line with other result data from the script. However, as an "error recording" mechanism, the command isn't very practical. Deployed scripts are almost never open in the AppleScript Editor and, therefore, are not writing to the AppleScript Editor's event log.

Figure 15.7

A custom message written to the event log and visible in the AppleScript Editor's window

Writing errors to text files

Recording errors in a text file is the best way to preserve valuable details about the failed events. A good log file can assist in identifying bugs and problems that occur during the development, testing, and deployment of a script. While the exact location and format of the log file will vary dramatically based on the complexity and users of a particular script, the following examples provide some basic subroutines for logging errors.

```
on logWrite(textOfError)
    -- Establish the name and location of the log file
    set nameLogFile to "Script Log.txt"
    set pathToLog to (path to desktop folder as string) &
    nameLogFile
    -- Format the error data and save it to the log file
    set textToLog to date string of (current date) & tab &
    textOfError & return & return
    open for access file pathToLog with write permission
    write textToLog to file pathToLog starting at eof
    close access file pathToLog
end logWrite
```

When an error occurs in a script, the error message and any other data about the error that you want to send can be included in a call to the subroutine. The subroutine will open the log file and add the new error data to anything already written. This example shows a statement whose error will be captured and routed to the previous subroutine, where it will be written to an error log, as shown in Figure 15.8:

```
try
    set numTotal to 10 + "Hello World"
on error textError number numError
    logWrite(numError & " " & textError)
end try
```

Figure 15.8

An error written to a script log file

```
●○○                      Script Log.txt
Wednesday, October 28, 2009    -1700 Can't make "Hello World" into type number.
```

CROSS-REF
Learn about subroutines in Chapter 21 and how to create and write to a text file in Chapter 16.

Looking at the AppleScript and Mac OS X Errors

Table 15.1 contains a list of the AppleScript errors that a script might encounter while executing code.

Table 15.1 AppleScript Error Codes	
Code	**Description**
-2700	Unknown error.
-2701	Can't divide <number> by zero.
-2702	The result of a numeric operation was too large.
-2703	«reference» can't be launched because it is not an application.
-2704	«reference» isn't scriptable.
-2705	The application has a corrupted dictionary.
-2706	Stack overflow.
-2707	Internal table overflow.
-2708	Attempt to create a value larger than the allowable size.
-2709	Can't get the event dictionary.
-2720	Can't both consider and ignore <attribute>.
-2721	Can't perform operation on text longer than 32K bytes.
-2729	Message size too large for the 7.0 Finder.
-2740	A <language element> can't go after this <language element>.

continued

Table 15.1 Continued

Code	Description
-2741	Expected <language element> but found <language element>.
-2750	The <name> parameter is specified more than once.
-2751	The <name> property is specified more than once.
-2752	The <name> handler is specified more than once.
-2753	The variable <name> is not defined.
-2754	Can't declare <name> as both a local and global variable.
-2755	Exit statement was not in a repeat loop.
-2760	Tell statements are nested too deeply.
-2761	<name> is illegal as a formal parameter.
-2762	<name> is not a parameter name for the event <event>.
-2763	No result was returned for some argument of this expression.

Table 15.2 contains a list of the Mac OS X errors that a script might encounter when sending commands to the Finder or other scriptable portions of the operating system.

Table 15.2 Macintosh OS Error Codes

Code	Description
-34	Disk <name> full.
-35	Disk <name> wasn't found.
-37	Bad name for file.
-38	File <name> wasn't open.
-39	End of file error.
-42	Too many files open.
-43	File <name> wasn't found.
-44	Disk <name> is write protected.
-45	File <name> is locked.
-46	Disk <name> is locked.
-47	File <name> is busy.
-48	Duplicate file name.
-49	File <name> is already open.
-50	Parameter error.

Code	Description
-51	File reference number error.
-61	File not open with write permission.
-108	Out of memory.
-120	Folder <name> wasn't found.
-124	Disk <name> is disconnected.
-128	User cancelled.
-192	A resource wasn't found.
-600	Application isn't running.
-601	Not enough room to launch application with special requirements.
-602	Application is not 32.
-605	More memory needed than is specified in the size resource.
-606	Application is background.
-607	Buffer is too small.
-608	No outstanding high.
-609	Connection is invalid.
-904	Not enough system memory to connect to remote application.
-905	Remote access is not allowed.
-906	<name> isn't running or program linking isn't enabled.
-915	Can't find remote machine.
-30720	Invalid date and time <date string>.

Summary

In this chapter you learned about script errors, and I presented an overview of their most popular causes. I discussed the `try` statement as the ideal method for capturing and getting information about errors. I also discussed the methods for managing and logging errors.

Getting Started with Scripting Additions

A *scripting addition* is a file that extends the AppleScript language by providing a set of additional commands. When installed, the commands it contains can be used if they are part of the core language.

As part of the Mac OS X install, Apple provides several bundles of scripting additions: Standard Additions, System Events, URL Access Scripting, Image Events, Digital Hub Scripting, Keychain Scripting, and ColorSyncScripting.

Third-party developers can create and distribute their own scripting additions.

CROSS-REF
See the Appendix for AppleScript resources on the Internet.

Finding Scripting Additions

Scripting additions can be installed in several different locations on your computer: the `System Library` folder, the `Library` folder, and the `Library` folder inside the user's `Home` folder.

System Library folder

The `System Library` folder contains all the scripting additions provided by Apple as part of the default system install. It is located at:

    /System/Library/ScriptingAdditions

If the Library window in the AppleScript Editor does not list all of the default additions within this folder, you should add them now. You can either choose the "+" button on the library window and then navigate to this folder or open the folder and then drag and drop all the additions onto the library window.

Typically, you should not add or remove files in the `System Library` folder. The Mac OS provides two other, more suitable locations for installing other, third-party scripting additions: the `Library` folder and the `Library` folder within the user's `Home` folder.

In This Chapter

Finding and using
Scripting Additions

Reviewing the nine
suites of the Standard
Additions package

Library folder

The `Library` folder is typically used by third-party software's scripting additions. Companies such as Adobe Systems and QuarkXPress install their additions in this folder, which is located at:

```
/Library/ScriptingAdditions
```

Depending on the software installed on your computer, you may have these additions installed: `Unit Types`, `Adobe Unit Types.osax`, or `QXPScriptingAdditions.osax`. You can add other third-party additions to this folder if you need them to be available to all user accounts. If not, the best place to install them is in the `Library` folder within the user's `Home` folder, as discussed in the next section.

User's Home Library folder

Within a user's `Library` folder you will find a folder for scripting additions that will be available only to the user who installs them. It is located at:

```
~/Library/ScriptingAdditions/
```

To install third-party additions, you simply copy them into this folder. Then, drag and drop the file onto the AppleScript Editor's Library window to make their dictionary available when writing scripts.

Embedding Scripting Additions

It is possible to embed third-party scripting additions within a script application bundle. This enables the script user to run a script that uses the additions without having to install them on her computer.

To embed a scripting additions file, follow these steps:

1. **Save the script as an Application Bundle.**

2. **Click the application in the Finder while pressing the Ctrl key and select show package contents.**

3. **Open the** `Contents/Resources/` **folder found within the application package folder.**

4. **Create a folder named** `Scripting Additions` **in the** `Resources` **folder.**

5. **Copy the addition file(s) into the new folder.**

Because the AppleScript Editor does not look within an application bundle when running a script, during development the additions must be installed in one of the three folders listed earlier. Also, there is no need to embed any of the default scripting additions as they are installed on every Mac computer as part of the OS.

Scripting Addition Call Restrictions Introduced in Mac OS 10.6

In Mac OS 10.6, a new security feature has been added that affects scripting additions. If a call to a scripting addition is nested into a `tell application` command, it will return a `-10004 privilege violation` error. This avoids situations where malicious code might attempt to instruct an application to perform certain destructive commands. In order to enable existing scripts to continue running without generating an error, AppleScript will automatically contain the error and re-run the scripting addition code outside of the `tell application` command. You can see this behavior in the event log history.

For example, if your script is using the current date scripting addition command within a `tell application` `"Finder"` command, the following event history will show that the date command is performed twice. The first attempt within the `tell` command results in an error that is automatically absorbed. The second attempt is outside of the `tell` command and successfully accesses the date.

```
tell application "Finder"
    current date
        --> error number -10004
end tell
tell current application
    current date
        --> date "Monday,
    September 7, 2009 12:37:43
    PM"
end tell
-- result = "Monday, September
    7, 2009"
```

To avoid this, you should access scripting additions outside of any `tell application` command.

Working with Standard Additions

The Standard Additions package contains dozens of very useful commands. To get started, open the AppleScript Editor and choose Library ⇨ Window from the menu. Then, double-click Standard Additions to see the library of commands shown in Figure 16.1.

Figure 16.1

The Standard Additions library of commands

User Interaction

The User Interaction suite of the Standard Additions package provides basic commands for interacting with a user. These enable you to ask a user to choose a file, folder, and other items as well as provide feedback to users or ask a question.

Beep

Perhaps the simplest command in AppleScript, beep enables you to make a script user's computer beep. The sound he hears varies based on which sound he chose in his System Preferences. To use this command, simply place it at the appropriate position of the script, typically before an error dialog box or some other event that you want to be sure they take notice of.

If you want the script to beep more than once, put an integer after the command causing it to beep that many times. For example:

```
beep 2
```

Typically, you shouldn't have too many beeps in your script, and when you do, one to three is usually enough at any single location. Use a single beep before a dialog box appears that requires the user's attention. Reserve two or three beeps for notifying the user of a serious error or issue that demands more attention than a simple dialog message.

Choose application

The choose application command enables a script to prompt the user to select one or more applications that are installed on the computer or on the network. This command is useful when a script needs to send a command to one of several applications, depending on the user's choice. The basic command, choose application, displays a dialog box containing all of the available applications, as shown in Figure 16.2.

When the user selects an application, the result is an application object:

```
application "Adobe Photoshop CS4"
```

Figure 16.2

The Choose Application dialog box

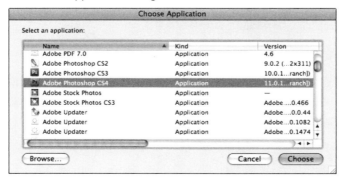

Several optional command parameters give you more control over the dialog box:

- **with title «text»** adds a custom title to the dialog box.
- **with prompt «text»** includes the text as a prompt, giving the user a little more information about why he is being asked to make a choice.
- **multiple selections allowed «Boolean»** enables the user to select multiple options if set to true. In this case, the result will be a list of application objects.
- **as «class»** can be set to return the application object (the default) or an alias to the application.

The following example uses some of these optional parameters to create a more informative dialog box. Figure 16.3 shows the results.

```
choose application with title "Build Catalog with..." with prompt "Please choose
    an application to use when building the catalog:" as alias
```

Once the selection has been made, the result is now an alias:

```
alias "Macintosh HD:Applications:Adobe Photoshop CS4:Adobe Photoshop CS4.app:"
```

The user has the option to click the Browse button in the dialog box. If she does, she will be presented with a Mac OS X standard choose dialog box with the same title and prompt as the Choose Application dialog box. This enables her to choose an application that resides elsewhere on their computer or on a network volume.

Figure 16.3

The Choose Application dialog box with optional elements

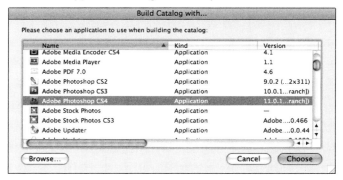

Choose color

The choose color command enables a script to prompt the user to select a color from the standard MacOS X color chooser dialog box. The basic command is choose color. Figure 16.4 shows the Colors dialog box.

Figure 16.4

The Colors dialog box

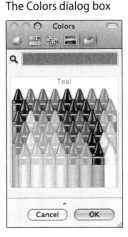

Once the selection has been made, the result is a list of the RGB (red, green, blue) color values:

```
-- result = {0, 32896, 32896}
```

If a user clicks the Cancel button, the script assumes the user is stopping the entire scripted process and stops the script without returning a value.

The `choose color` command can have a specified default color that will be selected when the dialog box appears. You do this with the «`list`» parameter with RGB color values as shown here:

```
choose color default color {0, 0, 0}
```

Choose file

The `choose file` command gives the user a chance to select a file located on her computer or on an accessible network volume. The `choose file` command will present the Choose a File dialog box shown in Figure 16.5.

Once the selection has been made, the result is an alias to the location of the selected file:

```
-- result = alias "File Server:Catalogs:Product Data.txt"
```

NOTE

All of the `choose file` and `choose folder` style dialog boxes enable the user to create new folders like any Mac OS X file dialog will.

Figure 16.5

The default file selection dialog box

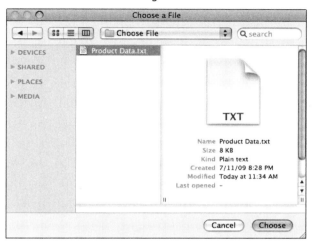

If a user clicks the Cancel button, the script assumes the user is stopping the entire scripted process and stops the script without returning a value.

Several optional command parameters give you more control over the dialog box:

- **with prompt «text»** includes the text as a prompt, giving the user a little more information about why she is being asked to make a choice.

- **of type «list»** enables you to specify one or more file types as selectable. Only file types listed will be accessible to the user.

- **default location «alias»** enables you to specify the folder that is visible when the dialog box is presented to the user. This can help a user remember where she should be saving or opening items for specific tasks.

- **invisibles «boolean»** enables you to specify if the user should see and be able to select invisible files. The default for this option is `true`.

- **multiple selections allowed «boolean»** controls if user is able to select multiple files. If `true`, the result will be a list of file paths rather than a single text-based path. The default for this option is `false`.

- **showing package contents «boolean»** controls if a user is able to navigate inside packages, such as application bundles, as if they were regular folders. The default for this option is `false`.

The following example uses some of these optional parameters to create a more informative dialog box. Figure 16.6 shows the resulting dialog box.

```
set pathToDefault to "File Server:Catalog Data:"
choose file with prompt "Choose a product data file" default location file
    pathToDefault with multiple selections allowed without invisibles
```

Figure 16.6

The Choose a File dialog box with optional elements

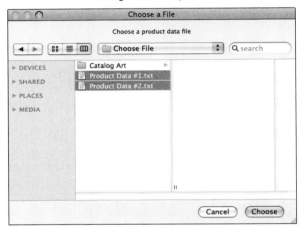

In this case, the result of the dialog box shown in Figure 16.6 will be a list of aliases to each file:

```
Result = {alias "File Server:Catalog Data:Product Data #1.txt", alias "File
    Server:Catalog Data:Product Data #2.txt"}
```

Choose file name

The `choose file name` command is used to allow a user to select a folder and file name for a new item the script will create. This process is similar to the `save` or `save as` commands in most document-based applications, such as TextEdit.

The basic command is `choose file name`. Figure 16.7 shows the Choose File Name dialog box.

Once the selection has been made, the result is an alias to the new file that should be created:

```
-- result = alias "File Server:Catalog Data:New File Name"
```

If a user clicks the Cancel button, the script assumes the user is stopping the entire scripted process and stops the script without returning a value.

Figure 16.7

The Choose File Name dialog box

Several optional command parameters give you more control over the dialog box:

- **with prompt «text»** includes the text as a prompt, giving the user a little more information about why she is being asked to make a choice.
- **default name «text»** enables you to specify the default name that should appear in the dialog box. The default is "untitled" but you can use this option to provide more guidance to the user by including a default name.
- **default location «alias»** enables you to specify the folder that should be visible when the dialog box is presented to the user. This help the user remember where he should be saving or opening items for specific tasks.

The following example uses some of these optional parameters to create a more informative dialog box. Figure 16.8 shows the resulting dialog box.

```
choose file name with prompt "Save new catalog file as" default name "Untitled
    Catalog File
```

Figure 16.8

The Choose File Name dialog box with optional elements

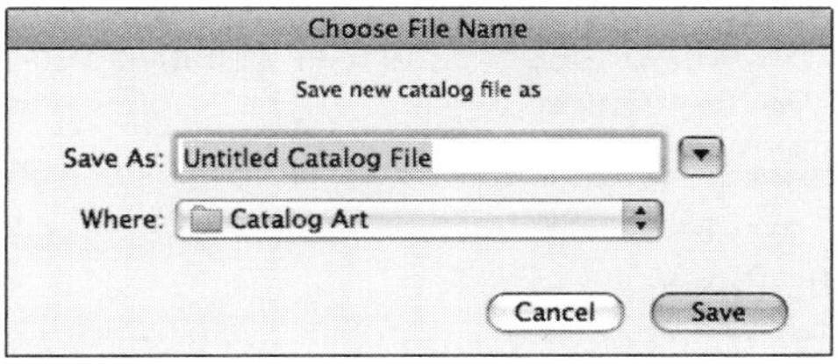

Choose folder

The `choose folder` command enables the user to select a folder anywhere on her computer or accessible network volume. The basic command is `choose folder`. Figure 16.9 shows the standard folder selection dialog box.

Figure 16.9

The Choose a Folder dialog box

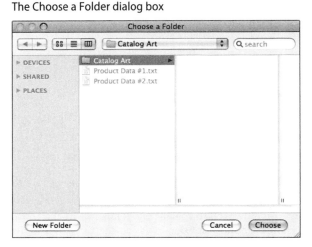

Once the selection has been made, the result is an alias to the selected folder:

```
-- result = alias "File Server:Catalog Data:Catalog Art:"
```

If a user clicks the Cancel button, the script assumes the user is stopping the entire scripted process and stops the script without returning a value.

Several optional command parameters give you more control over the dialog box:

- **with prompt «text»** includes the text as a prompt, giving the user a little more information about why he is being asked to make a choice.
- **default location «alias»** enables you to specify the folder that should be visible when the dialog box is presented to the user. This can help a user remember where he should be saving or opening items for specific tasks.
- **invisibles «boolean»** enables you to specify if the user should see and be able to select invisible files. The default for this option is `true`.
- **multiple selections allowed «boolean»** controls if the user is able to select multiple files. If `true`, the result will be a list of file paths rather than a single text-based path. The default for this option is `false`.
- **showing package contents «boolean»** controls if a user is able to navigate inside packages, such as application bundles, as if they were regular folders. The default for this option is `false`.

The following example uses some of these optional parameters to create a more informative dialog box. Figure 16.10 shows the resulting dialog box.

```
choose folder with prompt "Select a folder to the new art file:"
```

Figure 16.10

The Choose a Folder dialog box with optional elements

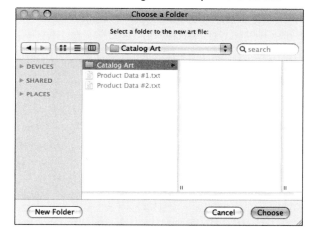

Choose from list

The `choose from list` command will display a dialog box with a list of custom values for the user to choose from. This is useful when there are more than two or three options that need to be presented to the user for selection.

The basic command is shown here with a list of three choices:

```
choose from list {"Choice 1", "Choice 2", "Choice 3"}
```

This list can contain any number of options for the user to choose. Figure 16.11 shows the list selection dialog box.

Figure 16.11

The list selection dialog box

Once the selection has been made, the result is a list of the selected item(s):

```
-- result = {"Choice 2"}
```

If a user clicked the Cancel button, the result will be `false`.

Several optional command parameters give you more control over the dialog box:

- **with title «text»** adds a title to the top of the window.
- with prompt «text» overrides the default prompt "Please make your selection," enabling you to provide your users with a little more information about what they are selecting.
- **default items «data»** enables you to specify which item(s) will be selected when the dialog box is presented. The «data» portion of this parameter should be a list of items or numbers specifying the item(s) on the list to be selected by default.
- **OK button name «text»** enables you to customize the name of the OK button for circumstances where OK is too ambiguous.
- **Cancel button name «text»** enables you to customize the name of the Cancel button. Regardless of the name, if a user clicks the button on the left side of the dialog box, the results will be `false`.
- **multiple selections allowed «boolean»** controls if a user is able to select multiple items from the list. If `true`, the result will be a list of the selected items. The default for this option is `false`.
- **empty selection allowed «boolean»** enables the user to click the OK button without selecting an item. If `true` the user will be able to click the "OK" button without selecting any of the list of choices. If they do, the result will be an empty list. The default for this option is `false`.

The following example uses some of these optional parameters to create a more informative dialog box. Figure 16.12 shows the resulting dialog box.

```
set listValues to {"Adobe InDesign", "QuarkXPress"}
choose from list listValues with title "Catalog Choice" with prompt "Build
    catalog with:" default items "Adobe InDesign" OK button name "Begin" cancel
    button name "Stop"
```

Figure 16.12

The choose from list dialog box
with optional elements

Choose remote application

The `choose remote application` command enables you to select an application that is running on a remote machine. In order to connect, the remote computer must be configured to allow Remote Apple Events and must be visible on the same network as the computer running the script.

CROSS-REF
For more on controlling applications on a remote computer, see Chapter 17.

The basic command is `choose remote application`. Figure 16.13 shows the Choose Remote Application dialog box.

Once the selection has been made, the result is an application object with a machine specifier:

```
-- result = application "FileMaker Pro" of machine "eppc://10.0.1.5/?uid=501&
   pid=238"
```

If a user clicks the Cancel button, the script assumes the user is stopping the entire scripted process and stops the script without returning a value.

Figure 16.13

The default Choose Remote Application dialog box

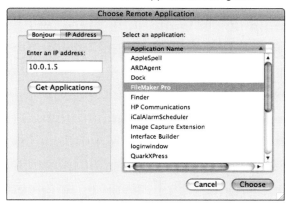

Several optional command parameters give you more control over the dialog box:

- **with title «text»** overrides the default title "Chose Remote Application".
- **with prompt «text»** enables you to provide your users with a little more information about what they are selecting.

The following example uses some of these optional parameters to create a more informative dialog box. Figure 16.14 shows the resulting dialog box.

```
choose remote application with title "Choose Catalog Application" with prompt
    "Choose a remote application to build the catalog:"
```

Figure 16.14

The remote application selection dialog box
with optional elements

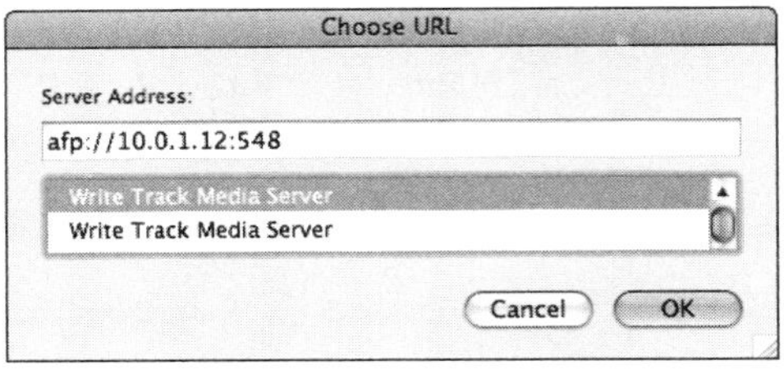

Choose URL

The `choose URL` command will present the user with a dialog box of available servers. When the user selects one, it returns the URL (uniform resource locator) for the selected server. The servers can be files servers, mail servers, Web servers, and so on.

The basic command is `choose URL`. Figure 16.15 shows the URL selection dialog box.

Figure 16.15

The Choose URL dialog box

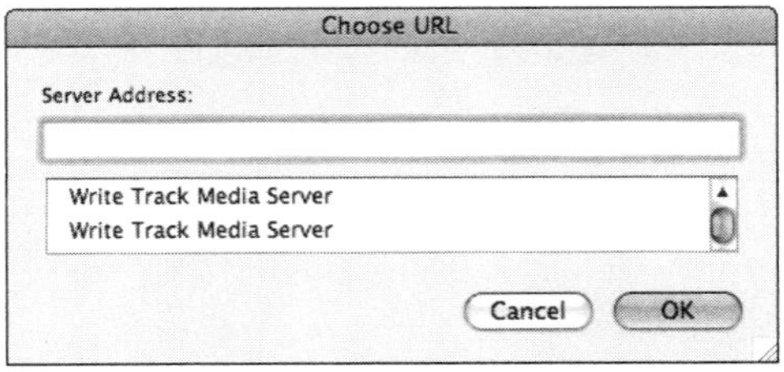

Once the selection has been made, the result is a URL to the service the user selected:

```
-- result = "afp://10.0.1.12:548"
```

If a user clicks the Cancel button, the script assumes the user is stopping the entire scripted process and stops the script without returning a value.

Several optional command parameters give you more control over the dialog box:

- **showing «list»** enables you to specify a list of which services are available to the user. These can include Web servers, FTP (File Transfer Protocol) servers, Telnet hosts, File servers, News servers, Directory services, Media servers, and Remote applications.

- **editable URL «boolean»** enables you to specify if the user should be able to type a URL into the field or not. The default for this parameter is true.

The following example uses some of these optional parameters to create a more informative dialog box. Figure 16.16 shows the dialog box.

```
choose URL {Directory services} without editable URL
```

Figure 16.16

The Mac OS X 10.6 Choose URL dialog box
with optional elements

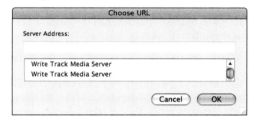

Delay

The delay command instructs a script to pause execution at a selected point for a specific period of time. This can be useful if you want your script to wait for some action to complete. To specify how many seconds the script should pause, place an integer after the word delay. This example will create a five-second pause before the script continues:

```
delay 5
```

You can create a delayed "Hello World!" dialog box to experience how long the delay will feel to your users, like this:

```
delay 5
display dialog "Hello World!"
```

Display alert

The display alert command enables you to provide feedback to your user. It presents the user with a dialog box; however, it is only able to notify a user and can't accept user input beyond button choices:

```
display alert «text» -- result = {button returned:"«name»"}
```

The «text» portion of the formula is the alert title. This example will display the "Hello World" alert dialog box. Figure 16.17 shows the resulting dialog box.

```
display alert "Hello World!" -- result = {button returned:"OK"}
```

Figure 16.17

The standard alert dialog box

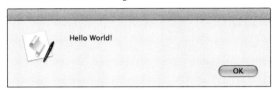

Several optional command parameters give you more control over the alert dialog box:

- **message «text»** adds an explanatory message below the alert text. This parameter can be used to provide additional information that might not fit the main alert text. For example, an alert text might be "Script Error" and the message text would be a longer explanation of the error that occurred.
- **as critical/informational/warning** enables you to specify the type of alert being displayed to the user. In the past each option (critical, informational, and warning) would each display a unique icon, making it visually clear what kind of an alert was occurring. As of this writing, only warning has a unique icon: a yellow exclamation triangle. The other two alerts both display the AppleScript icon.
- **buttons «list»** enables you to control how many buttons are included in the dialog box and their names. The list can have up to three buttons, which will be displayed in the reverse of the order in the list.
- **default button «text or integer»** enables you to control which button is the default button that will be clicked if the user presses Enter or Return.
- **cancel button «text»** enables you to control which button will be clicked if the user types a period while holding down the ⌘ key.
- **giving up after «integer»** enables you to specify the number of seconds before the alert should be dismissed. If this option is used and the time elapses, the result will be {button returned:"", gave up:true}; so be sure to program an if-then statement to test for this result and have your script react accordingly.

The following example uses some of these optional parameters to create a more informative dialog box. Figure 16.18 shows the dialog box.

```
set textMessage to "The catalog product data file you selected has not yet been
    approved. Are you sure you want to continue?"
display alert "Product Data Warning" message textMessage buttons {"Cancel",
    "Continue"} as warning
```

Figure 16.18

The alert dialog box with optional elements

Display dialog

The `display dialog` command enables you to provide feedback to, and request information from, your user:

```
display dialog «text» -- result = {button returned:"«name»"}
```

The `«text»` portion of the formula is the dialog message. This example will display the "Hello World" alert dialog box. Figure 16.19 shows the resulting dialog box.

```
display dialog "Hello World!" -- result = {button returned:"OK"}
```

Figure 16.19

The standard display dialog box

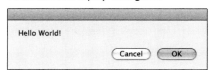

Several optional command parameters give you more control over the dialog box:

- **default answer** `«text»` allows a user to enter text input into a field in the dialog box. For this dialog box to appear, you must either include default text or an empty string.
- **hidden answer** `«boolean»` makes the default answer field obscured with bullets to hide sensitive information such as passwords.
- **buttons** `«list»` enables you to control how many buttons are included in the dialog box and their names. The list can have up to three buttons, which will be displayed in the reverse of the order in the list.
- **default button** `«data»` enables you to control which button will be clicked if the user presses Enter or Return.
- **cancel button** `«data»` enables you to control which button will be clicked if the user types a period while holding down the ⌘ key.

- **with title «text»** adds a title to the top of the dialog box.
- **with icon «text»** adds the icon specified by its name or ID to the dialog box.
- **with icon stop/note/caution** adds the selected MacOX icon to the dialog box.
- **with icon «file»** adds the specified alias or file path to the dialog box.
- **giving up after «integer»** enables you to specify the number of seconds before the dialog box should be dismissed. If this option is used and the time elapses, the result will be {button returned:"", gave up:true}; so be sure to program an if-then statement to test for this result and have your script react accordingly.

The following example uses some of these optional parameters to create a more informative dialog box. Figure 16.20 shows the resulting dialog box.

```
set textMessage to "Workflow Automation with AppleScript can be addicting!"
display dialog textMessage with title "Hello World!" with icon stop buttons
    {"Stop", "OK"} default button 2 cancel button 1\
```

Figure 16.20

The Hello World dialog box with optional elements

This example uses the default message option to capture user input. Figure 16.21 shows the dialog box.

```
set textMessage to "How are you today?"
display dialog textMessage with title "Hello World!" default answer "" with icon
    stop buttons {"Stop", "OK"} default button 2 cancel button 1
```

Figure 16.21

The Hello World dialog box with a user feedback field

When the default message option is used, the feedback will include the text the user typed with the button name:

```
{text returned:"Just fine", button returned:"OK"}
```

Say

The `say` command enables a script to speak a specified text phrase as long as the computer's speaker is not muted. It can also be used to generate audio files.

While some might find it unnerving to have a computer suddenly talk to them, a quick verbal queue, like the word "done," at the end of a scripted process can be helpful. It clearly indicates to the user that the script has finished and they can take control and get on with their work.

The basic `say` command formula is:

```
Say «text»
```

To create a "Hello Word" say command, simply add the text into the placeholder of the formula:

```
Say "Hello World!"
```

Several optional command parameters give you more control over the `say` command:

- **displaying «text»** displays the specified text in the feedback window if Speech Recognition is on.
- **using «text»** enables you to control which voice is used for the command, overriding the user's speech preferences.
- **waiting until completion «boolean»** enables you to control if the script will wait until the speech is completed before continuing. The default is `true` and this is ignored if Speech Recognition is not on.
- **saving to «data»** enables you to have the spoken phrase saved as an audio file to the alias, file reference, or path you provide.

File Commands

The File Commands suite of Standard Additions extends AppleScript's capabilities to locate folders and files and to mount server volumes.

Mount volume

The `mount volume` command enables a script to log onto a file server volume by specifying the server name or IP (Internet Protocol) address and the volume name or URL path, which are both shown here:

```
mount volume "WTM Server" on server "10.0.1.12"
mount volume "afp://10.0.1.12/WTM Server/"
```

NOTE

Notice that when specifying a URL path for the volume, the `on server` portion is dropped because the path includes this information.

If the user is already connected to another drive on the same server, the volume will be mounted. If not, the user will need to provide a user name and password in a standard Mac OS X server login dialog box, as shown in Figure 16.22.

Figure 16.22

The Mac OS X server login dialog box

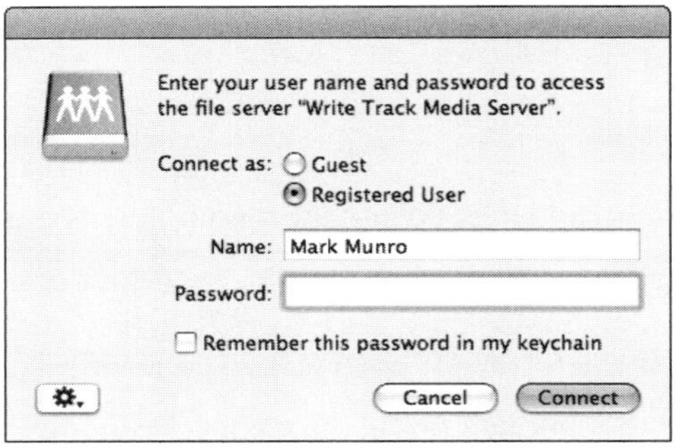

Optionally, you can hardcode a user name and password in your script so the user doesn't have to provide this information. Obviously, this should only be done for servers that are considered "public" within the user's network because it could give unauthorized users access to sensitive files.

```
mount volume "WTM Server" on server "10.0.1.12" as user name
    "Mark Munro" with password "Fake Password"
```

To include the user name and password when using a URL path for the volume, you would do this:

```
mount volume "afp://Mark Munro:Fake Password@10.0.1.12/WTM
    Server/"
```

Path to (application)

The `path to (application)` command enables you to get the path of an application or, in the case of scripts saved as documents, the path to the saved file. In its default state without any parameters, this command will return the path to the application being referenced.

If you place this command in a script that has not been saved, it will return the path of the AppleScript Editor:

```
path to
-- result = alias "Macintosh HD:Applications:AppleScript:Script
    Editor.app:"
```

If the script has been saved, it will return the path to the script document:

```
path to
-- result = alias "Macintosh HD:Users:mmunro-wtm:Desktop:test.
    scpt"
```

If the command is placed within a `tell application` control statement, the path to the application being referenced will be returned:

```
tell application "Mail"
    path to
end tell
-- result = alias "Macintosh HD:Applications:Mail.app:"
```

CROSS-REF

See Chapter 17 for more information about controlling applications with the `tell application` command.

The `path to` command includes several parameters that can be used to specify which application path to return. These include `current application`, `frontmost application`, `application «name»`, `me`, or `it`. Here are a few examples:

```
path to current application
-- result = alias "Macintosh HD:Applications:AppleScript:Script
    Editor.app:"
path to application "FileMaker Pro Advanced"
-- result = alias "Macintosh HD:Applications:FileMaker Pro 10
    Advanced:FileMaker Pro Advanced.app:"
```

The parameters `it` and `me` act very much like the parameter-less `path to` command and they both return the same information depending on the saved status and file type of the script file.

Path to (folder)

The `path to (folder)` command enables you to dynamically access the location of various standard folders, regardless of the variable parts of the path, such as the startup disk name or the user folder name.

There are dozens of standard Mac OS X folders that can be accessed with this command. They are shown in Table 16.1. Here are a few examples:

```
path to applications folder
-- result = alias "Macintosh HD:Applications:"
path to users folder
-- result = alias "Macintosh HD:Users:"
path to desktop folder
-- result = alias "Macintosh HD:Users:mmunro-wtm:Desktop:"
```

Table 16.1 Folders Accessible to the Path to (Folder) Command

application support	applications	desktop
desktop pictures	documents	downloads
favorites	Folder Action scripts	fonts
help	home	internet plugins
keychain	library	modem scripts
movies	music	pictures
preferences	printer descriptions	public
scripting additions	scripts	shared documents
shared libraries	sites	startup disk
startup items	system	system preferences
temporary items	trash	users
utilities	workflows	

For folders that exist in several different locations in Mac OS X but have the same name, you can specify the domain parameter for the path to command. Table 16.2 shows all of the available options. For example, accessing the path to the applications folder from the user domain is different from the system domain:

```
path to applications folder from system domain
-- result = alias "Macintosh HD:Applications:"
path to applications folder from user domain
-- result = alias "Macintosh HD:Users:mmunro-wtm:Applications:"
```

Table 16.2 Domains Accessible to the Path to (Folder) Command

system	/System
local	/Library
network	/Network
user	~ (Folders in the user home folder)
classic	This domain is used when locating folders in the classic Mac OS, such as extensions, apple menu, and control panels.

By default, the path to command automatically creates any folder that is missing. However you can force the opposite with the optional without folder creation parameter:

```
path to applications folder without folder creation
```

Path to resource

The `path to resource` command is used to locate a specified resource from a file or application bundle. This example locates the application icon file within the Mail application:

```
path to resource "app.icns" in bundle (path to application
    "Mail")
-- result = alias "Macintosh HD:Applications:Mail.
    app:Contents:Resources:app.icns"
```

This command can also locate a resource within the script or application bundle being executed. This means you don't have to worry about were the file is located within a script; the bundle will automatically scan its interior and return the exact path to the resource:

```
path to resource "Catalog Image.png"
-- result = alias "Macintosh HD:Users:mmunro-wtm:Desktop:Path To
    Temp.scptd:Contents:Resources:Summer:Catalog Image.png"
```

If your script bundle has more than one file with the same name but in different folders, you can specify which one should be used by adding the `in directory` parameter:

```
path to resource "Catalog Image.png" in directory "Summer"
-- result = alias "Macintosh HD:Users:mmunro-wtm:Desktop:Path To
    Temp.scptd:Contents:Resources:Summer:Catalog Image.png"
```

If the file you are searching for is in a different bundle than the script or application being executed, you can specify an external bundle file using the `in bundle` parameter:

```
set pathToBundle to (path to desktop folder) & "Catalog Resource
    Bundle.scptd" as string
path to resource "Catalog Image.png" in bundle file pathToBundle
    in directory "Summer"
-- result = alias "Macintosh HD:Users:mmunro-wtm:Desktop:Catalog
    Resource Bundle.scptd:Contents:Resources:Summer:Catalog Image.
    png"
```

String Commands

The String Commands suite enables a script to perform additional text manipulations.

Localized string

The `localized string` command allows a script to access a particular piece of text in a localized "strings file" contained within a script or application bundle. This enables you to create a script for use with a user's choice of language in the same way the Mac OS does. So, when a user has her preferred language set to "French," the text in dialog boxes and such will be in French instead of English. This enables you to deliver a single file, multi-language script solution.

NOTE
The files for the Localized String Example described in this section are available for download from the book's Web site at www.wileydevreference.com.

Before using this command, the script must be saved as a bundle and has at least one strings file set up within it. Follow these steps to set up an English language strings file:

1. **Save the script as a script bundle.**

2. **Click the file in the Finder while holding the Ctrl key.**

3. **Select Show Package Contents, which will open a folder showing you the internal contents of the script bundle.**

4. **Open the** Contents **folder.** (This should be the only folder.)

5. **Open the** Resources **folder.**

6. **Create a folder in the** Resources **folder named** English.lproj.

7. **Create a plain text document named** Localizable.strings **and place it into the new** English.lproj **folder.** You may need to create this file on the desktop and then drag it into the English.lproj folder.

8. **Within this file, create a test "key" = "value" entry.** For example: "Hello" = "Howdy".

The following script will pull the value ("Howdy") for the specified key ("Hello"):

```
localized string "Hello"
-- result = "Howdy"
```

Next, repeat these steps to create a similar folder for other languages, such as French.lproj. Using a duplicate of the Localizable.strings file with the same keys, change the values to their French equivalent. Change your language system preference to French, and run the script; you will see the alternate value shown here:

```
localized string "Hello"
-- result = "Bonjour"
```

Offset
The offset command reveals the character number for a given piece of text within another piece of text.

CROSS-REF
The offset command is discussed at length in Chapter 8.

Summarize

The `summarize` command enables a script to process a piece of text to create a summary of its content. You can even specify how many sentences the summary should contain. Copying Thomas Jefferson's first inaugural address to the clipboard, this script generated the resulting text below it.

```
set textToProcess to the clipboard
summarize textToProcess
-- result = "Equal and exact justice to all men, of whatever
   state or persuasion, religious or political; peace, commerce,
   and honest friendship with all nations, entangling alliances
   with none; the support of the State governments in all their
   rights, as the most competent administrations for our domestic
   concerns and the surest bulwarks against antirepublican
   tendencies; the preservation of the General Government in its
   whole constitutional vigor, as the sheet anchor of our peace
   at home and safety abroad; a jealous care of the right of
   election by the people -- a mild and safe corrective of abuses
   which are lopped by the sword of revolution where peaceable
   remedies are unprovided; absolute acquiescence in the
   decisions of the majority, the vital principle of republics,
   from which is no appeal but to force, the vital principle and
   immediate parent of despotism; a well-disciplined militia, our
   best reliance in peace and for the first moments of war till
   regulars may relieve them; the supremacy of the civil over the
   military authority; economy in the public expense, that labor
   may be lightly burthened; the honest payment of our debts and
   sacred preservation of the public faith; encouragement of
   agriculture, and of commerce as its handmaid; the diffusion of
   information and arraignment of all abuses at the bar of the
   public reason; freedom of religion; freedom of the press, and
   freedom of person under the protection of the habeas corpus,
   and trial by juries impartially selected. "
```

By adding an integer after the command, you can control how many sentences the summary should contain:

```
summarize textToProcess 3
```

Clipboard Commands

The Clipboard Commands suite provides access to the clipboard. A script can get and set the current value of the clipboard and inquire about its contents.

Set the clipboard to

The `set the clipboard to` command enables you to change the contents of the clipboard:

```
Set the clipboard to «data»
```

The `«data»` portion of the previous formula can be any AppleScript data class. Here are a few examples:

```
set textMessage to "Write Track Media provides professional
    workflow automation services."
set the clipboard to textMessage
set listServices to {"AppleScript", "FileMaker Pro"}
set the clipboard to listServices
set dateFounded to date "Thursday, August 4, 1994 3:00:00 PM"
set the clipboard to dateFounded
```

NOTE

If a script will modify the clipboard, you should be sure whoever will use it knows this before using the script.

The clipboard

This command enables you to access the contents of the clipboard. Once the script below runs, the variable `dataToProcess` will contain whatever was in the user's clipboard:

```
set dataToProcess to the clipboard
```

Clipboard info

The `clipboard info` command will provide detailed information about the contents of the clipboard. Copying the phrase "This is a test." to the clipboard generated the following result:

```
clipboard info
-- result = {{«class RTF », 277}, {«class utf8», 15}, {«class
    ut16», 32}, {uniform styles, 144}, {string, 15}, {scrap
    styles, 22}, {Unicode text, 30}}
```

Copying a file from the finder to the clipboard generated the following result:

```
clipboard info
-- result = {{«class furl», 152}, {«class icns», 166766},
    {picture, 42}, {«class ut16», 28}, {«class utf8», 13}, {«class
    hfs », 80}, {string, 13}}
```

File Read/Write

The File Read/Write suite enables a script to create, read, and write files.

Open for access

The `open for access` command enables a script to create a file anywhere on a user's computer or any accessible network volume. If the script will need to write to the file, you must include the optional `write permission` parameter like this:

```
open for access «file»
open for access «file» with write permission
```

The «file» portion of the formula is a path or alias of the file to open or create.

The result of this command will be a file reference number, which is interchangeable with the path for use by other commands in the File suite.

You must be sure to close the file when finished, even if an error occurs; otherwise no other script or process will be able to open the file.

CROSS-REF
Capturing and handling script errors is discussed in Chapter 15.

Close access

The `close access` command closes access to a file that a script has opened:

```
Close access «data»
```

The «data» portion of the formula can be an alias or path to the file or a reference number provided by the `open for access` command. The following code shows an example of each:

```
set pathToData to ((path to desktop folder) as string) & "Data.
   txt"
set numFile to open for access file pathToData
```

To close the file with the file reference number, use:

```
close access numFile
```

To close the file with a file path, use:

```
close access file pathToData
```

To close the file opened previously with a file alias, use:

```
close access alias pathToData
```

Read

The `read` command enables a script to read data from a file opened with the open for access command.

```
Read «data»
```

The «data» portion of the formula can be an alias or path to the file or a reference number provided by the `open for access` command.

If you create a text file on the desktop named `product data.txt`, as shown in Figure 16.23, you can then read the data from that file with the `read` command:

```
set pathToData to ((path to desktop folder) as string) & "product
    data.txt"
set textData to read file pathToData
every paragraph of textData
-- result = {"0001 MacBook", "0002 MacBook Pro", "0003 MacBook
    Air"}
```

Figure 16.23

The contents of a text file located
on the desktop

There are several optional command parameters that give you more control over what the script reads from the file. These include:

- **from «integer»** enables the script to start reading from a specified position within the file. The `read` command defaults from the last position you read from. If this parameter is not specified, it will read the entire data file.

- **for «integer»** enables you to specify the number of bytes to read from the current position. The `read` command reads to the end of the file by default. This parameter can't be used in combination with `to`, `before`, or `until`.

- **to «integer»** enables you to specify at what position to stop reading within the file. This parameter can't be used in combination with `for`, `before`, or `until`.

- **before «text»** indicates the script should read up to but not including the character(s) provided. This parameter can't be used in combination with `for`, `to`, or `until`.

- **until «text»** indicates the script should read up to, including the character(s) provided. This parameter can't be used in combination with `for`, `to`, or `before`.

- **using delimiter «text»** enables you to specify a delimiter to be used when reading. This returns a list of values based on the delimiter you provide.
- **using delimiters «list of text»** enables you to specify more than one delimiter to be used when reading.
- **as «class»** enables you to specify the class the data should be returned as.

The following example uses some of these optional parameters:

```
set pathToData to ((path to desktop folder) as string) & "product
    data.txt"
read file pathToData for 10
-- result = "0001    MacB"
read file pathToData until "k"
-- result = "0001    MacBook"
read file pathToData using delimiter {linefeed, tab}
-- result = {"0001", "MacBook", "0002", "MacBook Pro", "0003",
    "MacBook Air"}
```

Write

The `write` command enables a script to write data to a file that has been opened for access:

```
write «data» to «file»
```

The «data» portion of the formula is the data that will be written to the file while «file» should be an alias or path to the file or a reference number provided by the `open for access` command:

```
set pathToData to ((path to desktop folder) as string) & "hello
    world.txt"
set textToWrite to "Hello World!"
open for access file pathToData with write permission
write textToWrite to file pathToData
close access file pathToData
read file pathToData
-- result = "Hello World!"
```

Several optional command parameters provide more control over what the script writes to the file. These include:

- **starting at «integer»** specifies at what position the new data should be written. The default position when this parameter is not specified varies. When the script writes additional data to a file that has been previously written to, the default starting position will be the end of the file. When the script writes data to a newly opened file, the default will be the beginning of the file. This parameter allows you to modify this default behavior if needed.
- **for «integer»** specifies the number of bytes to write. If this parameter is omitted, the script will write all the data provided.

● **as «class»** specifies the class to use when writing the data. This enables you to read/write other data classes such as lists, records, and more. You must use the same class that was written into the file or the script might generate an error.

This example demonstrates how to write and read an AppleScript list using the `as list` parameter on both commands (it works with any data class):

```
set pathToData to ((path to desktop folder) as string) & "hello
   world.txt"
set textToWrite to {"Hello World!", "Hello World!"}
open for access file pathToData with write permission
write textToWrite to file pathToData as list
close access file pathToData
read file pathToData as list
-- result = {"Hello World!", "Hello World!"}
```

This example shows writing to a file with the `starting at` and `for` parameters used:

```
set pathToData to ((path to desktop folder) as string) & "Hello
   World.txt"
set textToWrite to "Hello World!"
open for access file pathToData with write permission
write textToWrite to file pathToData
close access file pathToData
open for access file pathToData with write permission
write textToWrite to file pathToData starting at 7 for 11
close access file pathToData
read file pathToData
-- result = "Hello Hello World"
```

Get end of file (eof)

The `get eof` command enables a script to read the length of the file in bytes. This allows you to write a script that processes smaller chunks of data from a large file:

```
get eof «data»
```

The «data» portion of the formula is an alias or path to the file or a reference number provided by the `open for access` command:

```
set pathToData to ((path to desktop folder) as string) & "Hello
   World.txt"
set textToWrite to "Hello World!"
open for access file pathToData with write permission
write textToWrite to file pathToData
close access file pathToData
get eof file pathToData
-- result = 12
```

Set end of file (eof)

The `set eof` command enables a script to set the end of file for a file. Any data that exists in the file beyond the newly specified end of file will be lost:

```
set eof «data» to «integer»
```

The «data» portion of the formula is an alias or path to the file or a reference number provided by the `open for access` command. The «integer» portion of the formula should contain the new location of the end of file:

```
set pathToData to ((path to desktop folder) as string) & "Hello
    World.txt"
set textToWrite to "Hello World!"
open for access file pathToData with write permission
write textToWrite to file pathToData
set eof file pathToData to 5
close access file pathToData
read file pathToData
-- result = "Hello"
```

Scripting Commands

The Scripting Commands suite enables a script to load another script into a variable. Once a script is loaded, you can read and edit its properties, run it, or store it into a new or existing script file. This simple suite of commands makes possible developing large multi-module solutions possible.

CROSS-REF

See Chapter 24 for more information about loading, running, and storing external scripts and creating multi-module solutions.

Load script

The `load script` command enables a script to load a second script file and place it into a variable:

```
load script «file»
```

The «file» portion of the command is a file path or alias. Here is an example script that loads a script named "External Script" from the desktop and places it into a variable:

```
set pathToScriptFile to ((path to desktop folder) as string) &
    "External Script.scpt"
set scriptExample to load script file pathToScriptFile
-- result = «script»
```

Once a script is loaded, you can get or set property values and run the script or subroutines contained within.

Store script

Once you have a script in a variable, you can write that script to a new or existing file using the store script command:

```
store script «script» in «file»
```

The «script» portion is a script loaded into a variable while the «file» portion of the command is a file path or alias specifying where the script file will be saved:

```
set pathToScriptFile to ((path to desktop folder) as string) &
    "External Script.scpt"
set scriptExample to load script file pathToScriptFile
set pathToScriptFile to ((path to desktop folder) as string) &
    "New Script.scpt"
store script scriptExample in file pathToScriptFile
```

Run script

When a script is loaded into a variable, you can run the entire script or an individual subroutine contained within using the run script command.

CROSS-REF
Subroutines are discussed at length in Chapter 24.

To see this capability in action, follow these steps:

1. **Save the script shown in Figure 16.24 in a file named** New Script.scpt **on the desktop.**

Figure 16.24

A script that will be loaded and run by another script

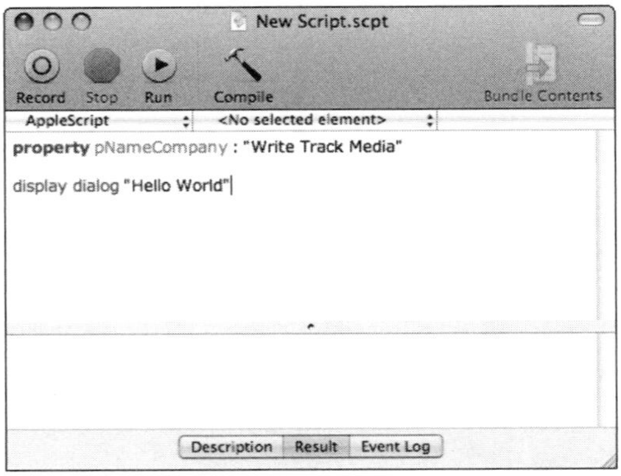

```
● ● ○                    New Script.scpt
  ○       ●      ▶      🔧                              ↗
Record  Stop   Run   Compile                    Bundle Contents
AppleScript        ⬍   <No selected element>    ⬍
property pNameCompany : "Write Track Media"

display dialog "Hello World"|




                             ·


             Description  Result  Event Log
```

2. **Run the following script:**

```
set pathToScriptFile to ((path to desktop folder) as string) &
   "New Script.scpt"
set scriptExample to load script file pathToScriptFile
run scriptExample
```

The script will be loaded from the desktop and run, generating the dialog box shown in Figure 16.25.

Figure 16.25

A "hello world" dialog box generated from a loaded script

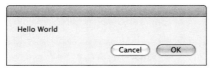

Scripting components

The `scripting components` command will return a list of all the scripting components installed on the computer it is run on. By default, only one component is installed: AppleScript. If a script is written in another language and will be used by others who may not have additional script components installed, you can use this command to determine if the script can run on a specific computer:

```
scripting components
-- result {"AppleScript"}
```

If you install the JavaScript extension, the results will be:

```
-- result {"JavaScript", "AppleScript"}
```

To check if a specific OSA (Open Scripting Architecture) language component other than AppleScript is installed, place the following code at the beginning of the script. It will check for the component and, if it is not found, will notify the user of the missing required component and then stop the script using the `return` command:

```
if (scripting components) does not contain "JavaScript" then
   set textMessage to "This script requires the JavaScript
  scirpting component. Please install it and try again"
   display alert "JavaScript Component Missing" message
  textMessage
   return -- << exit the script after the dialog
end if
```

Miscellaneous Commands

Ten commands are grouped into the `Miscellaneous Commands` suite.

Current date

The `current date` command gives you access to the current date and time:

```
current date
-- result = date "Friday, August 14, 2009 12:05:20 PM"
```

CROSS-REF

See Chapter 10 for more information about manipulating date objects.

Do shell script

The `do shell script` command gives AppleScript the capability to run shell scripts:

```
do shell script «text»
```

The `«text»` portion of the formula is the command or shell script that will be executed.

This example gets the current date as a "short date" using this command:

```
set textShortDate to do shell script "date '+%m.%d.%y'"
-- result = "08.14.09"
```

Several optional command parameters provide more control over the `do shell script` command. These include:

- **as «class»** specifies class type the result should be. The default is text.
- **administrator privleges «boolean»** enables the script to run the shell script as an administrator.
- **user name «text»** enables a script to run the shell script without a password dialog by providing a hard-coded user name. If this parameter is specified, the `password` parameter must also be specified.
- **password «text»** enables a script to run the shell script without a password dialog box by providing a hard-coded password. If this parameter is specified the `user name`, the parameter must also be specified.
- **altering line endings «boolean»** changes all line endings to Mac-style and will trim any trailing line endings. The default is `true`.

Get volume settings

The `get volume settings` command returns information regarding a computer's current volume settings:

```
get volume settings
-- result = {output volume:100, input volume:53, alert
   volume:100, output muted:false}
```

The result of this command contains four values:

- Output volume is the sound output volume as a percentage (0–100%).
- Input volume is the sound input volume as a percentage (0–100%).
- Alert volume is a percentage of the output volume.
- Output muted indicates if the output sound is muted or not.

Set volume

The `sound output` command enables a script to modify any of the four volume settings discussed in the previous section: output volume, input volume, alert volume, and output muted. The following example modifies some volume settings and then uses the `get volume settings` command to show that the settings have changed:

```
set volume output volume 50 input volume 45 alert volume 75
   without output muted
get volume settings
-- result {output volume:50, input volume:47, alert volume:75,
   output muted:false}
```

Random number

The `random number` command generates a random number. The default upper limit for this command is 1.0. Each time you run the script, a random number between 0 and 1.0 will be generated:

```
random number
-- result = 0.526353332949
-- result = 0.723015174814
```

To specify a custom upper limit, simply place that number after the command. Each time you run the script, a random number will be generated from 0 and the number you specify:

```
random number 100
-- result = 41
-- result = 90
-- result = 38
```

There are several optional command parameters that provide more control over the `random number` command. These include:

- `from «number»` enables you to specify a starting number other than 0.0.
- `to «number»` enables you to specify an upper limit of any number.
- `with seed «number»` instructs the random number generator to initialize a pseudorandom number. This can be useful in computer security, encryption, and other synchronized remote systems such as GPS (Global Positioning System) satellites and receivers or randomized algorithms. Once this is called with a specific value, it will generate the same sequence of numbers.

Round

The `round` command enables you to round numbers in a variety of ways:

```
round 175.75
-- result = 176
```

CROSS-REF
See Chapter 9 for more information about rounding numbers.

System attribute

The `system attribute` command returns a list of the names of all environmental variables on a computer:

```
system attribute
-- result = {"PATH", "TMPDIR", "SHELL", "HOME", "USER",
    "LOGNAME", "DISPLAY", "SSH_AUTH_SOCK", "Apple_PubSub_Socket_
    Render", "__CF_USER_TEXT_ENCODING", "SECURITYSESSIONID",
    "COMMAND_MODE"}
```

This command can also handle a specified attribute to provide additional information. To get the current shell, you would add "SHELL" as the attribute like this:

```
system attribute "SHELL"
-- result = "/bin/bash"
```

System info

The `system info` command returns a record of information about a computer and its current user, such as various addresses for the machine and the versions of AppleScript, AppleScript Studio, and operating system. It also contains useful information about the current user's name, home directory, and more:

```
system info
-- result = {AppleScript version:"2.0.1", AppleScript Studio
   version:"1.5", system version:"10.5.8", short user
   name:"mmunro-wtm", long user name:"Mark Munro", user ID:503,
   user locale:"en_US", home directory:alias "Macintosh
   HD:Users:mmunro-wtm:", boot volume:"Macintosh HD", computer
   name:"Mark Munro's MacBook Pro", host name:"Macintosh.local",
   IPv4 address:"10.0.1.4", primary Ethernet
   address:"00:17:f2:c3:83:aa", CPU type:"Intel 80486", CPU
   speed:2330, physical memory:2048}
```

If a script uses commands or language elements that are unique to AppleScript version 2.0, you might consider using this command to confirm that a user is not running an older version:

```
if (AppleScript version of (system info)) < 2.0 then
   display dialog "This script requires AppleScript 2.0 or
   later"
end if
```

You may also do the same with the operating system version. This example will display a dialog box if the Mac OS X version is less than 10.5:

```
if (system version of (system info)) < 10.5 then
   display dialog "This script requires MacOS 10.5 or later"
end if
```

Time to GMT

The `time to GMT` returns the difference between local time and Greenwich Mean Time (GMT), or Universal Time, in seconds:

```
time to GMT
-- result = -14400
```

POSIX file

A POSIX file path is a file object formatted with a slash-style path name. The `POSIX file` command enables a script to convert a path to a POSIX path and vise versa:

```
set pathToFile to "Macintosh HD:Users:mmunro-wtm:Desktop:Hello
   World.txt"
set pathToFile to POSIX path of pathToFile
-- result = "/Users/mmunro-wtm/Desktop/Hello World.txt"
POSIX file pathToFile
-- result = file "Macintosh HD:Users:mmunro-wtm:Desktop:Hello
   World.txt"
```

Folder Actions

A Folder Action is a script that can be linked to one or more folders to perform custom tasks in response to a user's actions. Scripts that will be assigned to folder actions must be installed in one of two `Folder Action Scripts` folders. One exists in the Library folder and contains default Folder Action scripts included in the Mac OS X install. It is located here:

```
/Library/Scripts/Folder Action Scripts/
```

The other `Folder Actions Scripts` folder is inside the user's Library folder, which is located here:

```
~/Library/Scripts/Folder Action Scripts/
```

NOTE
The Folder Action Example script file that contains all five of the subroutines described in this section is available for download from the book's Web site at www.wileydevreference.com.

Before reviewing the commands available, follow these steps to set up a folder with a linked script:

1. **Create a folder on the desktop called** `Folder Action Test Folder.`

2. **Create a script called Folder Action Example and store it in** `~/Library/Scripts/Folder Action Scripts/.`

3. **Open the Folder Actions Setup application located in** `/Applications/AppleScript/.`

4. **Add the folder created in Step 1 by clicking the plus (+) button in the lower-left corner.** A dialog box will appear attached to the application's window.

5. **Choose the script created in Step 2.** The application's window should appear as shown in Figure 16.26.

Figure 16.26

The Folder Actions Setup window

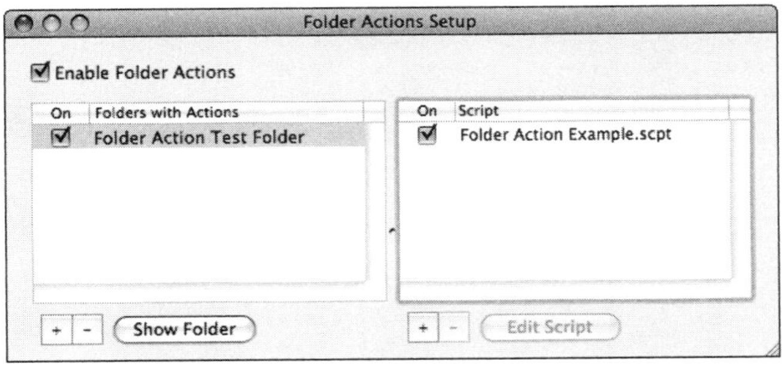

From the interface, you can add and delete additional folders and link them to one or more scripts. You can also disable the folder actions feature or individual folders or scripts as needed. To edit a script, select it in the window and click the Edit Script button.

CROSS-REF
Each item in the Folder Actions suite is a subroutine. Learn more about subroutines in Chapter 21.

Opening folder

The `opening folder` subroutine will be called within a folder's action script(s) each time a user opens it.

Click the script in the Setup application and then click the Edit button. Add this code into the script and then save and close it:

```
on opening folder
    display alert "You just opened this folder"
end opening folder
```

Now, if you open the folder on your desktop, you should see a dialog box with a message of "You just opened this folder".

If a folder action script will need to perform different tasks depending on which folder is opened, your script will need an extra parameter added to the command. This is useful if you want to use a single script any time a user opens one of multiple folders. The new variable `pathToFolder` after the `on opening folder` statement will contain an alias to the folder being opened:

```
on opening folder pathToFolder
    display alert "You just opened this folder:" & pathToFolder
end opening folder
```

After saving the script, if you open the folder the dialog message will include the path to the folder that you opened, as shown in Figure 16.27.

Figure 16.27

The dialog box created by the `opening folder` subroutine in the Folder Action Example script

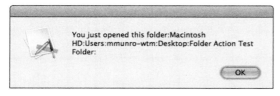

You can use this command to perform any sequence of scripted tasks each time a user opens the folder.

Closing folder window for

The `closing folder window for` subroutine will be called within a folder's linked script(s) each time a user closes the folder.

Open the example script again, and add this code beneath the `opening folder` subroutine, then save and close the script:

```
on closing folder window for
    display alert "You just closed that window"
end closing folder window for
```

Now, you will see both the open and close alert dialog boxes when you open and close the folder. A single script can respond to one or more of the folder action subroutines.

Like the opening folder subroutine, this one can also receive the alias to the folder being closed. This code will include the path to the folder in the dialog box, as shown in Figure 16.28:

```
on closing folder window for pathToFolder
    display alert "You just closed that window for " &
    pathToFolder
end closing folder window for
```

Figure 16.28

The dialog box created by the `closing folder window for` subroutine in the Folder Action Example script

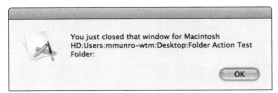

Moving folder window for

The `moving folder window for` subroutine will be called within a folder's linked script(s) each time a user moves the open window for the folder with the script attached.

Open the example script again and add this code beneath other two subroutines then save and close the script:

```
on moving folder window for
    display alert "You just moved that window"
end closing folder window for
```

Now you will see the alert dialog box each time you move the window.

NOTE
If you have both a moving folder window for subroutine and a closing folder window for subroutine, the latter will be ignored when you close the window in favor of the former.

Like the other subroutines in this suite, this one can receive additional information with the aid of optional parameters and variables. The script that follows adds the `pathToFolder` variable and the `from listBounds` parameter variable. When run, these variables will contain the alias to the folder moved and the bounds of the window it was moved from. The bounds are converted into text and added to the alert message:

```
on moving folder window for pathToFolder from listBounds
    set text item delimiters to ", "
    set textData to listBounds as text
    set text item delimiters to ""
    display alert "You just moved that window from" & return &
"{" & textData & "}"
end moving folder window for
```

This code will include the path to the folder in the dialog box shown in Figure 16.29.

Figure 16.29

The dialog box created by the `moving folder window for` subroutine in the Folder Action Example script

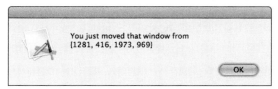

Adding folder items to

The `adding folder items to` subroutine will be called within a folder's linked script(s) each time a user adds an item to a folder with the script attached.

Open the example script again and add this code beneath other subroutines; then save and close the script:

```
on adding folder items to
    display alert "You just added an item!"
end closing folder window for
```

Like the other subroutines in this suite, this one can receive additional information with the aid of optional parameters and variables. The script that follows adds the `pathToFolder` variable and the `after recieving listItems` parameter variable. When run, these variables will contain the alias to the folder moved and the bounds of the window it was moved from. The bounds are converted into text and added to the alert message, as shown in Figure 16.30:

```
on adding folder items to pathToFolder after receiving listItems
    set numItems to count items of listItems
    display alert "Item(s) added to '" & pathToFolder & "' — " &
    numItems
end adding folder items to
```

Figure 16.30

The dialog box created by the `adding folder items to` subroutine in the Folder Action Example script

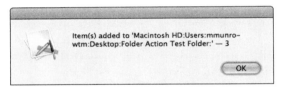

Item(s) added to 'Macintosh HD:Users:mmunro-wtm:Desktop:Folder Action Test Folder:' — 3

OK

Removing folder items from

The `removing folder items from` subroutine will be called within a folder's linked script(s) each time a user removes an item from a folder with the script attached.

Open the example script again and add this code beneath other subroutines; then save and close the script:

```
on removing folder items to
    display alert "You just added an item "
end closing folder window for
```

Like the other subroutines in this suite, this one can receive additional information with the aid of optional parameters and variables. The script that follows adds the `pathToFolder` variable and the `after recieving listItems` parameter variable. When run, these variables will contain the alias to the folder moved and the bounds of the window it was moved from. The bounds are converted into text and added to the alert message, as shown in Figure 16.31:

```
on removing folder items from pathToFolder after losing listItems
    set numItems to count items of listItems
    display alert "Item(s) removed from '" & pathToFolder & "' —
    " & numItems
end removing folder items from
```

Figure 16.31

The dialog box created by the `removing folder items from` subroutine in the Folder Action Example script

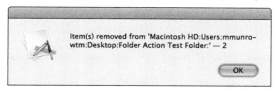

Internet

The Internet suite gives a script the capability to open and access information about URLs.

Open location

The `open location` command will open a URL in a user's default Web browser:

```
open location "http://www.wtmedia.com/"
```

This command has one optional parameter that enables you to specify if the script should report errors in a dialog box:

```
open location "http://www.wtmedia.com/" with error reporting
```

URL

The `URL` command enables a script to convert a text-based URL into a record of information about the URL, such as the scheme, domain name server, dotted decimal form of the address, and more.

This example converts a text-based Web address into a URL:

```
set textURL to "http://www.wtmedia.com/index.html"
textURL as URL
-- result = {class:URL, scheme:http URL, path:"http://www.
   wtmedia.com/index.html", host:{class:Internet address, DNS
   form:"www.wtmedia.com", port:80, dotted decimal
   form:"204.186.93.31"}}
```

This example converts a text-based FTP address into a URL:

```
set textURL to "ftp://www.wtmedia.com/"
textURL as URL
-- result = {class:URL, scheme:ftp URL, path:"ftp://www.wtmedia.
   com/", user name:"", password:"", host:{class:Internet
   address, DNS form:"www.wtmedia.com", port:21, dotted decimal
   form:"204.186.93.31"}}
```

Summary

In this chapter you learned about AppleScript Scripting Additions, where they are installed, and how they expand the AppleScript language. Each of the nine Standard Additions suites was introduced with details on each of their commands.

Using Scripts to Control Applications

Controlling Applications with Scripts

AppleScript's true power is realized when it is used to control applications. When AppleScript was released, only a handful of third-party applications were scriptable, even those created by Apple. For example, the Finder wasn't immediately scriptable without an extension when AppleScript was first released. However, within a relatively short period of time, the Finder became natively scriptable and other software makers began to follow suit. Today, almost all Apple-branded software and most third-party applications have at least some support for AppleScript.

While the extent of this support varies from one software title to the next, you can typically automate most popular functions of an application. Scripts can instruct applications to create, delete, duplicate, edit, and search documents, windows, pages, text boxes, picture boxes, records, and a variety of other objects. They can perform application functions such as opening, closing, saving, or printing a file as well as getting and setting properties of objects such as height, width, location, color, font, size, contents, count of, and more.

As wonderful as controlling one application can be, using scripts to coordinate activity and data manipulation between multiple applications reveals how AppleScript can automate a *workflow*. A script can extract data from a database, locate images from a folder structure, use these to construct a desktop publishing document, save the document in a portable document format (PDF) file, and then uploaded the file to a server for final approval. This is just one example of the enormous potential when AppleScript is used to control applications.

In This Chapter

Understanding application automation

Reading an application's script dictionary

Looking at multi-application workflows

Controlling remote applications with AppleScript

Introduction to Application Automation

There are a few control statements that help route and manage commands sent to an application. Applications can possess various levels of "scriptablity," which determines what tasks scripts can instruct the application to perform and how an application's automation capabilities can be learned.

Looking at the "tell application" statement

Applications are controlled by AppleScript with the `tell application` control command. It begins with the `tell application` keywords followed by the name of the application that is to receive and handle the commands that follow. The statement ends with the `end tell` keywords. Any code between these two lines of code will be sent to the application where it will be executed.

Following is the formula for the `tell application` control command statement:

```
tell application "«application name»"
  -- application commands
end tell
```

NOTE

AppleScript automatically indents the lines of code between the `tell application` and `end tell` lines to create a visual cue of which lines are enclosed within the statement.

This example shows a simple activate command being sent to the Finder:

```
tell application "Finder"
    activate
end tell
```

More than one command can be placed within a single `tell application` statement. This example brings the Finder to the front and opens the startup disk:

```
tell application "Finder"
  activate
  open folder "Macintosh HD:"
end tell
```

When the statement contains a single command, the statement can be converted into a single line with the addition of the `to` keyword, as shown here:

```
tell application "Finder" to open folder "Macintosh HD:"
```

Managing timeouts

If a command sent to an application does not generate a response after two minutes, a timeout error occurs. Typically this two-minute default is more than enough, especially on modern computers with fast processing cores. However, for the occasional command that might take longer than two minutes, a `with timeout` control statement can avert a timeout error by lengthening the amount of patience the script will possess.

Understanding the timeout statement

The timeout statement enables you to explicitly state the number of seconds you consider a tolerable duration for a specific command. For example:

```
with timeout of «number» seconds
    -- protected command here
end timeout
```

The `timeout` statement can be placed within a `tell application` statement or vice versa, as demonstrated by the following two examples:

```
tell application "«application name»"
  with timeout of «number» seconds
    -- protected command here
  end timeout
end tell

with timeout of «number» seconds
  tell application "«application name»"
  -- protected command here
  end tell
end timeout
```

Protecting multiple lines of code

Although the `timeout` statement can be wrapped around more than one line of code, the protection applies to each line of code and is not affected by the duration of the entire block of code. So, if two-dozen lines of code are protected inside of a single statement, a timeout will only occur if any one of those lines takes longer than the specified amount of time.

To illustrate, the following script contains three `display dialog` statements inside of a `timeout` statement that will timeout after three seconds. The script automatically dismisses each dialog after two seconds. Although the combined total of the dialog's presence is six seconds, each lasts only two seconds so no timeout error will occur:

```
with timeout of 3 seconds
  display dialog "Hello World" giving up after 2
  display dialog "Hello World" giving up after 2
  display dialog "Hello World" giving up after 2
end timeout
```

By contrast, this script contains a single dialog that will be dismissed after four seconds. Because the timeout protection only lasts three seconds, a timeout error will occur:

```
with timeout of 3 seconds
  display dialog "Hello World" giving up after 4
end timeout
```

Situations Prone to Timeouts

Any line of code can experience a timeout under the right circumstances. However, some functions are more prone to timeouts. Two of the most common are creating a PDF file of a huge image-laden page layout document and running a lengthy FileMaker Pro database script. Also, when an application presents an unexpected dialog box, which must be dismissed before continuing, a timeout will occur on the next statement the script tries to send to that application unless the dialog box is dismissed.

Avoiding excessive timeout protection

Timeout statements are great for protecting functions that might take too long to complete due to false errors. However, they shouldn't be overused. In cases were an actual problem exists, a script error is preferable. If a file server a script relies on is offline, forcing the script to try to connect for two hours is pointless. No matter how large the timeout protection you add, the script will fail because there is an actual problem. The extra delay from the timeout will only serve to frustrate your troubleshooting process.

Finding a balance of reasonable caution is a good practice where timeouts are concerned.

Ignoring an application response

When a command is sent to an application, the script issuing the command will wait for a response before moving forward. This response can be a simple acknowledgement that the requested command has been successfully performed or that some actual data that was requested. To force the script to not wait for a response, the `ignoring application responses` control statement is used.

Any commands within the statement will be executed and immediately released so the script can continue executing any remaining code. As with the timeout clause, the ingoing clause can be nested within a `tell application` command or around it, like this:

```
ignoring application responses
  tell application "«application name»"
    -- command here
  end tell
end ignoring
```

A simple example of this command can be seen when a script instructs the Finder to empty the trash. If a particularly large number of files are waiting to be deleted, the script will wait until they are all removed before resuming the rest of the script. However, add the `ignoring` command and the script will send the command and immediately continue processing:

```
ignoring application responses
   tell application "Finder"
      empty trash
   end tell
end ignoring
```

CAUTION

When using the `ignoring` command, be sure that a script doesn't trip over itself. For example, if the script ignores responses for a lengthy command and then tries to send another command to the same application, you run the risk of a timeout. Also, any command that expects a response, such as reading a property or getting data from a field or text box, will cause errors if it is told to ignore responses.

Respecting hierarchy when nesting disparate control commands

When nesting multiple control commands, such as `if-then`, `repeat`, and `tell application` commands, you need to terminate the current command before ending a command that surrounds it. This is required to maintain the hierarchy of commands, which are indicated by successive indentation. This example shows a command to the finder conditional based on an `if-then` statement:

```
if blnActive = true then
   tell application "Finder"
      activate
   end tell
end if
```

Notice in the previous example that the `tell application` command is contained within an `if-then` command and will only be executed if the variable `blnActive` is true. If you want to send a command to the Finder when `blnActive` is `false`, you can't interweave the commands as shown in the following code, because it will not compile:

```
if blnActive = true then
   tell application "Finder"
      activate
   else
         beep
   end tell
end if
```

The `else` statement in the previous example is within the `tell application` command rather than the `if-then` command so it will not compile. To add an alternative action if the variable is `false`, you must either create another `tell application` command or move the `if-then` statement inside of the `tell` statement.

The following example uses an additional a `tell application` statement after the `else` statement. Because the `tell` command is terminated and then repeated after the `else` condition of the `if-then` statement, this code will compile and achieve the desired results:

```
if blnActive = true then
  tell application "Finder"
    activate
  end tell
else
  tell application "Finder"
    beep
  end tell
end if
```

The next example moves the `if-then` statement within the `tell application` statement. Again, because the hierarchy is respected, it will compile and work as expected:

```
tell application "Finder"
  if blnActive = true then
    activate
  else
    beep
  end if
end tell
```

Defining different types of AppleScript support

Applications can possess several types of behavior. These include scriptable, recordable, attachable, embeddable, and customizable behaviors.

Scriptable applications

A *scriptable application* is any application that can send and receive Apple Events. When an application is scriptable, it will have a script dictionary embedded that can be viewed in the AppleScript Editor by either dropping the application onto the Editor application or by adding it to the Script Library window and double-clicking it. Being scriptable is required for an application to possess any other type of AppleScript support.

CROSS-REF
The AppleScript Editor interface is discussed in Chapter 6.

For example, the System Events application can check to see if an open application process has scripting terminology, as shown here:

```
tell application "System Events"
  tell process "Finder"
    has scripting terminology -- result = true
  end tell
end tell

tell application "System Events"
  tell process "Preview"
    has scripting terminology -- result = false
  end tell
end tell
```

NOTE

When an application has scripting terminology, there is no guarantee of a usable object model and command set. Xcode enables a developer to make an application "scriptable" by adding a property to the `Info.plist` file, which automatically creates a default script library. However, in such a case, the commands are not at all helpful to an AppleScript developer trying to automate the application.

Recordable applications

A *recordable application* is any application that uses Apple Events to capture actions performed by a user in a form that can be converted into a script. While recorded scripts can be a great help when learning a new feature of an application, they tend to be too specific for use in a dynamic workflow and require a lot of modification. The most popular recordable application is the Finder.

To record a script, open a new script document and click the Record button. Then create a folder on your desktop and give it a name. Then click the Stop button to cease recording. Your script might look something like this one:

```
tell application "Finder"
  activate
  make new folder at folder "Desktop" of folder "mmunro" of
    folder "Users" of startup disk with properties {name:"untitled
    folder"}
  set name of folder "untitled folder" of folder "Desktop" of
    folder "mmunro" of folder "Users" of startup disk to "Test"
end tell
```

Notice how the creation and the renaming of the folder are recorded as two steps. Also, all paths are "verbal" references rather than references as a path or alias. By contrast, the following script will perform the same action with a single line of code and substantially less clutter:

```
tell application "Finder"
  activate
  make new folder at (path to desktop folder) with properties
    {name:"Test"}
end tell
```

Recorded scripts are very helpful when you are learning a new application. However, it is more desirable to view them as suggestions or guides to performing a sequence of tasks, rather than a deployable script ready for practical use.

Attachable applications

An *attachable application* is any application that provides a menu, palette, toolbar, or some other interface mechanism into which a user can place scripts.

The best example of an attachable application is the Finder, which allows scripts to be placed into window toolbars and in an optional script menu, as well as in pop-up lists for various system preferences. Other examples include the Adobe InDesign CS Scripts palette, and the Microsoft Office and QuarkXPress Scripts menus.

CROSS-REF
Many locations accepting attached scripts are discussed in Chapter 3.

Using an attachment point to deploy scripts is a great way to give users convenient access to the scripts they need within the context of the application in which they are working. Also, attaching scripts directly to applications reduces clutter in other areas, such as the desktop and dock.

Embeddable applications

An *embeddable application* is any application that allows scripts to be copied and pasted within its application or document interface. While somewhat rare, the best example is found in FileMaker Pro where AppleScript code can be placed into a database "Perform AppleScript" script step, as shown in Figure 17.1.

Figure 17.1

An embedded "Hello World" dialog AppleScript inside of a FileMaker Pro script

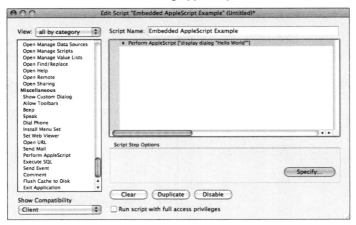

AppleScript-based customizable applications

An *AppleScript-based customizable application* is any application that provides a method for a script to run in addition to or in place of a built-in command. Applications exhibiting this feature are colloquially referred to as being "tinkerable" because they let you tinker with the internal workings of the applications. The point of access were a subroutine can override default behavior are usually called *event handlers* because they provide a method to customize the response of an application to specific user or automatic events.

 Retrospect, the popular backup software package, included a file called the `Retrospect Event Handler`, which contains a group of commented out subroutines. When the application begins a key function, it first looks at this file and, if a corresponding subroutine is not commented out, it executes any custom code placed in the event handler. For example, you can add code that will send you an e-mail when a server backup begins or place errors into a FileMaker Pro database. While the recent rewrite of Retrospect Version 8 is missing this feature, it is planned to reappear in the next version.

NOTE
You can learn more about Retrospect at www.retrospect.com.

Apple's Mail software enables you to use a script as a rule. While this might qualify as customization, it is a meager implementation. Likewise, a FileMaker Pro custom menu can point to a FileMaker Pro script containing a Perform AppleScript step, which sort of qualifies as script-driven customization.

Beyond these, AppleScript-based customization of this kind is not common, although it should be.

Savable as script applications

A *savable as script application* is any application that enables a document to be saved as an AppleScript. This rare feature is similar to recording a script based on user interaction but, instead, it creates a script that will re-create the current document on command. Like recordable applications, the resulting code may need to be modified for a more open-ended use. However, it is a wonderful way to learn how to script a new application.

 The best example of a savable application is Create, the page layout application from Stone Design. Along with Save and Save As, the software has a Save [as] AppleScript menu item, shown in Figure 17.2, that enables a user to save a document as a script.

NOTE
Visit Stone Design's Web site at www.stone.com for more information about Create.

Figure 17.2

The Save AppleScript menu item in the Create application

Exploring an Application's Dictionary

A *script dictionary* is a resource embedded within scriptable applications that contains vital information about the commands to which the application will respond and the object classes it contains and their related properties.

Opening a dictionary

There are two ways to access an application's dictionary: double-clicking the application's library listed in the AppleScript Editor's Library window, or dragging and dropping the application onto the AppleScript Editor's icon.

If the application is listed in the Library window of the AppleScript Editor, you can simply double-click it to open its dictionary. If the application is not in the library, you can add it by clicking the Add button or by dragging the application to the window. Opening an application's dictionary through the AppleScript Library window is the most desirable method because it keeps the dictionary of all the applications you use at your fingertips. In addition, you can quickly use it to create `tell application` statements for any of them.

CROSS-REF
The AppleScript Editor interface is discussed in Chapter 6.

The second method is to drag and drop the application onto the AppleScript Editor's icon. This opens the dictionary directly without adding it to the library and can be useful for a quick look at its dictionary.

The Finder's dictionary, shown in Figure 17.3, is a great place to get started, as most of your scripts will probably involve at least some manipulation of files and folders.

Figure 17.3

The Finder's AppleScript dictionary open in the AppleScript Editor

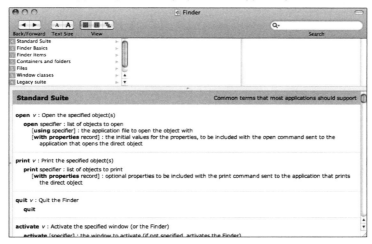

Exploring the dictionary interface

The dictionary user interface offers multiple viewing styles. The top of the horizontal split view and the left of the vertical split view both show the hierarchical list of commands, classes, and properties while the remaining area shows the details for the selected command or class. The toolbar offers three viewing options for the top portion of this view. The default view was shown earlier in Figure 17.3.

Using the iTunes-like left-hand list of items and completely hiding the top of the split view, as shown in Figure 17.4, might be tempting. However, the search results will continue to be displayed in the hidden top portion of the split view and will need to be opened to be seen and navigated. Keeping both the left and the top portions open at the same time creates a visually cluttered and non-friendly experience because it shows the same information in two places. Also, the left list only drills down two levels whereas the upper list provides an endless hierarchical navigation experience.

Figure 17.4

The Finder's dictionary viewed with the item chooser on the left only

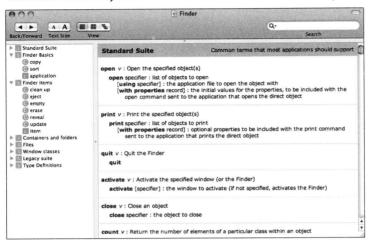

Exploring an application's dictionary content

An application's script library contains commands, classes, properties, and elements organized into suites.

Suites

A *command suite* is a group of commands and classes grouped in logical order within an application's AppleScript library. Suites are identified with a small orange square with an "s" located to the left of the suite name.

NOTE

The Standard Suite of most applications contains commands such as activate, close, count, delete, duplicate, exists, get, make, move, open, print, save, set, select, and quit with some variation depending on the application's functionality. While other suite names and contents typically vary, occasionally you will find some similarities as well.

While some suites will be similar in many applications, such as the Standard Suite, most vary greatly from one application to the next. Each application has different commands and classes as required based on their unique functionality. These are grouped according to the logical sensibilities of the developers of the application, which can be very different, even between similar applications such as page layout or database programs. The Finder's script library is divided into eight suites, shown in Figure 17.5.

Figure 17.5

The eight suites of the Finder's
script dictionary

CAUTION

Be on the lookout for important indicators of a library entry's status. Things labeled "Deprecated" will eventually be removed. Things labeled "Legacy" are there to support backward compatibility but may eventually become deprecated or disappear. These situations are frequently found in applications by Apple, which has also included "NOT AVAILABLE YET" as a status in the Finder dictionary and in the past, have indicated cgi commands as "not supported."

Commands

A *command* is a function that the application can perform. Commands are identified by a small blue circle with a C, located to the left of the command name.

You may already be familiar with the commands in the dictionary from your own experience using the application. For example, the Finder has commands that will empty the trash, reveal an item, eject a disk, clean up a folder window, create folders, and more. Likewise, page layout programs have commands that will create a page, textbox, and picture box and place text and images within them. Databases can perform commands such as creating and deleting records, setting and getting the value of fields, and more.

When you select a command, its properties and commands are displayed in the lower-right portion of the split view. The Finder's empty command, shown in Figure 17.6, explains that the command empty and empty trash can be used interchangeably. Any optional elements of the command will be in square brackets. So, you can add the optional security clause with a boolean to indicate whether the trash should be securely deleted or not.

Figure 17.6

The Finder's empty command

```
empty  v : Empty the trash
   empty [specifier] : "empty" and "empty trash" both do the same thing
      [security boolean] : Specifies whether or not to empty the trash securely
```

All six possible combinations of the Finder's `empty` command are shown here:

```
tell application "Finder"
   empty
   empty with security
   empty without security
   empty trash
   empty trash with security
   empty trash without security
end tell
```

NOTE

When compiling a script, AppleScript automatically changes `empty trash security true` to `empty trash with security`.

Classes

A *class* is an object or item that the application can create, modify, delete, or in some way manage. Classes are identified by a small purple square with a C, located to the left of the class name.

While some classes might be similar from one application to another, their properties and capabilities will vary greatly because they represent objects that the application uses in its own unique way. For example, many applications have documents but the contents of those documents are almost never the same except in applications within similar categories. Also, the Finder has windows instead of documents, but most applications can refer to their documents as a window because they essentially are the same thing. The differences become more profound when you explore the properties and elements of the class objects.

Properties

A *property* is an attribute of a class object, such as its name, color, size, location, or status. Properties are identified with a small purple square with a P, located to the left of the property name.

Most properties may be familiar to anyone who has uses a given program while others may not. A Finder window has many familiar properties such as name, bounds (size and position), current view (list, column, icon), toolbar visible (true/false), and more. Other, less familiar properties of a folder include the id, index, floating, modal, zoomed, and more.

Classes can be part of an object hierarchy and, therefore, inherit properties from a parent class. For example, in the Finder both a `folder` and a `file` are `items` and, therefore, inherit the majority of their properties from their parent. By sharing a single batch of properties between similar classes, only the differences between the two need to be defined. Figure 17.7 shows the benefit of this approach by highlighting the list of properties inherited from `item`, leaving only a small group of five properties that are unique to the `file` class.

Figure 17.7

The properties of a Finder file include a large group, which are inherited from the `item` class.

```
file n [inh. item] : A file

ELEMENTS INHERITED FROM ITEM
contained by application, containers, disks, folders, desktop-objects, trash-objects.

PROPERTIES
file type (type) : the OSType identifying the type of data contained in the item
creator type (type) : the OSType identifying the application that created the item
stationery (boolean) : Is the file a stationery pad?
product version (text, r/o) : the version of the product (visible at the top of the "Get
    Info" window)
version (text, r/o) : the version of the file (visible at the bottom of the "Get Info"
    window)

PROPERTIES INHERITED FROM ITEM
name (text) : the name of the item
displayed name (text, r/o) : the user-visible name of the item
name extension (text) : the name extension of the item (such as "txt")
extension hidden (boolean) : Is the item's extension hidden from the user?
index (integer, r/o) : the index in the front-to-back ordering within its container
container (specifier, r/o) : the container of the item
disk (specifier, r/o) : the disk on which the item is stored
position (point) : the position of the item within its parent window (can only be set for
    an item in a window viewed as icons or buttons)
desktop position (point) : the position of the item on the desktop
bounds (rectangle) : the bounding rectangle of the item (can only be set for an item in a
    window viewed as icons or buttons)
label index (integer) : the label of the item
locked (boolean) : Is the file locked?
kind (text, r/o) : the kind of the item
description (text, r/o) : a description of the item
comment (text) : the comment of the item, displayed in the "Get Info" window
size (double integer, r/o) : the logical size of the item
physical size (double integer, r/o) : the actual space used by the item on disk
creation date (date, r/o) : the date on which the item was created
modification date (date) : the date on which the item was last modified
icon (icon family) : the icon bitmap of the item
URL (text, r/o) : the URL of the item
owner (text) : the user that owns the container
group (text) : the user or group that has special access to the container
owner privileges (read only/read write/write only/none)
group privileges (read only/read write/write only/none)
everyones privileges (read only/read write/write only/none)
information window (specifier, r/o) : the information window for the item
properties (record) : every property of an item
class (type, r/o) : the class of the item
```

NOTE

The dictionary only shows inherited items if the corresponding preference is checked in general preferences. After setting this preference, you will need to quit and relaunch the AppleScript Editor.

The following example shows that the term `item` can be used interchangeably with `file` while scripting the Finder when manipulating the properties that they have in common. Both lines will achieve the same result because of these interchangeable terms:

```
tell application "Finder"
   set the name of file pathToFile to "test.jpg"
   set the name of item pathToFile to "test.jpg"
end tell
```

In the library window, the information in parenthesis to the right of the property name indicates the data class of the property. So, the `name` of a `file` is `text` while its `label index` is an `integer`. Properties that are read-only and, therefore, can't be modified by a script, include "r/o" in the parenthesis to indicate this limitation.

Elements

An *element* is a class object that is contained within another class object. Its presence in the dictionary helps to communicate the hierarchy of classes. Elements are identified with a small orange square with an E, located to the left of the element name.

The `folder` class in the Finder script dictionary, shown in Figure 17.8, has ten elements, which are classes of objects that a folder can contain. The hierarchy can go both ways. Sometimes an element of a class can also have that class as an element of itself. For example, a container class can be an element in a `folder` class while a folder is also an element of the container class. By contrast, the `file` class has no elements due to the fact that no Finder objects can go inside of a file.

Figure 17.8

The `folder` class in the Finder script dictionary

Using AppleScript to Control Applications

Now that you have an understanding of the basic statements used to control applications, it is time to move on to learning how to control applications with scripts.

Activating, launching, and quitting applications

Applications automatically launch when they are first asked to execute a line of code. However, you can explicitly send a `launch` command at the beginning of a `tell application` statement. Similarly, the `activate` command will launch the application if needed and then bring it to the front, like this:

```
tell application "Pages"
  activate
end tell
```

To ask an application to quit, you send the `quit` command, as shown here:

```
tell application "Pages"
  quit
end tell
```

TIP

When quitting a document-based application, a script should first check to see if there are any open unsaved documents that should be managed before closing the application to avoid an error causing dialog box.

A script can check if any application is currently running by checking the active processes as shown in the following script:

```
tell application "Finder"
  "«application name»" is in (the name of every process)
end tell
```

The result will be a `true` or `false` value, indicating the open status of the specified application.

This approach is preferable as any command sent directly to the application will cause that application to launch and therefore render the query mute. When a script is trying to quit an application, it becomes especially useless to cause it to launch prior to quitting it.

Manipulating the Finder with scripts

Scripts can instruct the Finder to perform a variety of automated activities and gather information about files and folders. In this section, I discuss a few key commands, including the `make`, `open`, and `move` commands, and show you how to read and write properties of items.

Using the make command

A script can create a folder anywhere on an accessible disk by using the `make` command, which is located in the Standard Suite of commands. The `make` command's library entry, shown in Figure 17.9, shows two required parameters: the `type` and `location` of the object to be created. The description for the type indicates that it should specify the class of the new object being created. The location needs to specify a path, alias, or reference to the folder in which the new object will be created. This gives you a script formula for the `make` command that looks like this:

```
tell application "Finder"
  make new «class» at «folder path»
end tell
```

NOTE

Not every class in the Finder dictionary can be created with a script. Although there is no indication of this in the dictionary, most cases are common sense. For example, a script can't create a disk drive, because that is a piece of hardware. The most common classes to create with a script are files, folders, aliases, and finder windows.

Figure 17.9

The `make` command from the Finder's dictionary

```
make  v : Make a new element
    make
        new type : the class of the new element
        at location specifier : the location at which to insert the element
        [to specifier] : when creating an alias file, the original item to create an alias to or when creating a file viewer window, the
            target of the window
        [with properties record] : the initial values for the properties of the element
        → specifier : to the new object(s)
```

The `folder` class in the Finder script dictionary To create a new folder on the desktop, specify the class and the path in which the new folder will be created, like this:

```
set refDesktop to (path to desktop folder)
tell application "Finder"
  make new folder at refDesktop
end tell
```

While a script could name the new folder on separate lines, the `make` command's optional `with parameters` clause enables you to specify properties of the new folder within a single command. Not only does this reduce the number of lines of code, but also it eliminates some juggling that would be required after a name change. The following example creates a folder, changes its name to "Hello World!", resets the reference to the folder based on the new name, and then changes the color of the folder to blue which is a label index of 4:

```
set refDesktop to (path to desktop folder)
tell application "Finder"
  set refFolder to make new folder at refDesktop
  set name of refFolder to "Hello World!"
  set refFolder to folder "Hello World!" of refDesktop
  set label index of refFolder to 4
end tell
```

By contrast, the following script creates the folder with the name "Hello World!" in one line of code. As a result of this, the `refFolder` variable already contains a reference to the newly named folder, eliminating the extra steps:

```
set refDesktop to (path to desktop folder)
tell application "Finder"
  set refFolder to make new folder at refDesktop with properties
    {name:"Hello World!"}
  set label index of refFolder to 4
end tell
```

NOTE

As of Mac OS 10.6.2, attempting to set certain properties of a folder, such as the label index, in the `with properties` clause will be ignored. Therefore, you must set these properties on a separate line.

Using the open command

A script can open files and folders by using the `open` command, which is located in the Standard Suite of commands. The command's library entry, shown in Figure 17.10, requires a "specifier" indicating which object(s) should be opened. The specifier can be a path or reference to any alias, file, or folder, or a list thereof. This gives you a script formula for the `open` command that looks like this:

```
tell application "Finder"
  open «path»
end tell
```

Figure 17.10

The `open` command from the Finder's dictionary

```
open v : Open the specified object(s)
  open specifier : list of objects to open
    [using specifier] : the application file to open the object with
    [with properties record] : the initial values for the properties, to be included with the open command sent to the
      application that opens the direct object
```

When opening a folder, a script needs only to specify the path to a folder. The following script instructs the Finder to open the previously created "Hello World!" folder that is on the desktop:

```
set pathToFolder to (path to desktop folder) & "Hello World!" as
  string
tell application "Finder"
  open folder pathToHelloFolder
end tell
```

Once the folder window is open, you can change the size, location, toolbar visibility, view type, and more. This script shows a variety of examples of these types of settings:

```
set pathToFolder to (path to desktop folder) & "Hello World!" as
  string
tell application "Finder"
  open folder pathToFolder

  -- Change the view
  tell window 1
    set current view to icon view
    set current view to column view
    set current view to flow view
```

```
    set current view to list view

    -- Toggle the toolbar
    set toolbar visible to true
    set toolbar visible to false

    -- Change the position
    set the position to {0, 0}

    -- zoom the window to its minimum size
    set the zoomed to true

  end tell
end tell
```

NOTE

As of Mac OS 10.6.2, attempting to set certain properties of the window of a folder, such as the view, location, or size, in the with properties clause of the open command will be ignored. For now, you must explicitly set these settings in a separate statement.

When opening a file, the Finder automatically opens the file with its default application unless an application specifier is included with the using clause. When opening a PDF file created by Adobe Acrobat, the first open file line of the following script opens the file in Acrobat while the second opens it in Preview:

```
set pathToFile to "Macintosh HD:Users:mmunro:Desktop:Hello.pdf"
tell application "Finder"
  open file pathToFile
  open file pathToFile using (path to application "Preview")
end tell
```

Using the move command

The move command enables a script to instruct the Finder to move a file or folder to any other accessible folder. The following script shows a PDF file on the desktop being moved inside the Documents folder:

```
set pathToFile to "Macintosh HD:Users:mmunro:Desktop:Hello.pdf"
set pathToFolder to "Macintosh HD:Users:mmunro:Documents:"
tell application "Finder"
  move file pathToFile to folder pathToFolder
end tell
```

If the destination folder already contains a file with the same name and extension, the script will generate an error. To avoid this, a script can first check the destination folder to see if such a situation exists and either delete, move, or rename it, or rename the file to be moved. A replacing clause can also be added to the move command to instruct the script to automatically replace a file if one exists with the same name, as shown here:

```
tell application "Finder"
  move file pathToFile to folder pathToFolder replacing true
end tell
```

The result of the command will be a reference to the file in its new location. This can be placed into a variable so that future command can be sent to the file without having to reformulate the path. This script will move the same file to the `Documents` folder and then open it:

```
tell application "Finder"
  set refFile to move file pathToFile to folder pathToFolder
  open refFile
end tell
```

Reading properties of folders and files

A script can read any of the properties of a folder, including those inherited from the `item` class. The following script shows several examples, including the capability of a script to get the path to the file as a URL that can be placed into an e-mail or other documents as a clickable hyperlink:

```
set pathToFolder to (path to desktop folder) & "Hello World!" as
   string
tell application "Finder"
  creation date of folder pathToFolder
  -- result = date "Friday, December 4, 2009 3:50:28 PM"

  modification date of folder pathToFolder
  -- result = date "Friday, December 4, 2009 3:58:43 PM"

  URL of folder pathToFolder
  -- result = "file://localhost/Users/mmunro/Desktop/Hello%20
   World!/"

  desktop position of folder pathToFolder
  -- result = {1641, 605}
end tell
```

TIP

If you are having difficulty figuring out how to get a script to create an object or change a property based on the application dictionary, try getting the properties of the object with a script. Often, a reverse approach like that will provide a clue to the required syntax.

Filtering content

AppleScript's `whose` clause is used to filter application content based on specified criteria. For example, a script can get a list of items inside of a folder whose name contains some text or whose extension is `txt`, as shown in these examples:

```
set pathToFolder to "Macintosh HD:Users:mmunro:Desktop:Stuff:"
tell application "Finder"
  the name of every file of folder pathToFolder whose name
   contains "Hello"
  -- {"Hello World.scpt", "Hello.pdf"}

  the name of every file of folder pathToFolder whose name
   extension = "txt"
  -- {"United States Data.txt"}
end tell
```

Many applications support this powerful command, making it easier to get information about a subset of a larger group of content.

TIP

The keywords `that`, `where`, and `whose` can be used interchangeably. However, it is best to choose one and use it consistently.

Controlling Inter-Application Communication

Inter-application communication is achieved when a script sends commands to and exchanges data with more than one application to perform a given task. AppleScript's intended purpose is to exploit the feature sets of mass marketed applications. Acting as the "glue" between them, scripts make narrowly focused, custom solutions possible that are too specialized to warrant mass production.

There is no limit to the kinds of scripted solutions you can build. Any application on your computer can provide, process, or present data of any kind. Any repetitive steps you manually perform from one application to the next to complete a task, however small or large, can be developed into a script that will perform them automatically.

Figure 17.11 shows a hypothetical inter-application solution. A FileMaker Pro database or data exported from a mainframe can be searched, sorted, and exported by a script. The appropriate images (stored in a folder structure on a server) are located and opened with Adobe Photoshop, which converts them to the appropriate file type and size. An Adobe InDesign template is opened and the data and converted images are place on pages. Text is placed and styled, images are placed and sized, all based on the business rules that are embedded in the script. This process is repeated for dozens, hundreds, or perhaps thousands of products.

Once the catalog file is built and saved, a PDF is created, which is then uploaded to a corporate FTP site using Panic's Transmit application. Finally, an e-mail is sent to the appropriate staff members, informing them that the file is ready for review. All this activity is performed with two clicks on a script application that acts as the conductor guiding the various applications in a performance, not unlike a skillfully performed symphony.

Figure 17.11

A hypothetical workflow controlled by a script

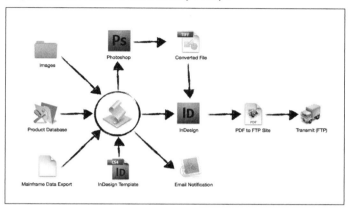

Controlling Remote Applications

In addition to controlling applications on a local computer, scripts can also reach across a network to send Apple Events to applications installed on another computer. This is called *Remote Apple Events* and it is surprisingly easy to do with a minor change to the `tell application` command: the addition of a reference to the remote computer, which is the target of the commands to follow:

```
tell application "«application name»" of machine «eppc specifier»
   -- application commands
end tell
```

Of course, there is a bit of software preparation and other considerations that must be attended to prior to sending remote events.

Configuring Remote Apple Events

In order for a computer to receive remote event commands, Remote Apple Events must be enabled in the Sharing panel of system preferences, as shown in Figure 17.12. The default setting for who has access to send remote events to the computer is All users. However, you can specify a select list of user accounts who will have access by clicking the + button and selecting user accounts, network users, or network groups, or creating a new account for anyone, including people listed in your address book.

Once configured, any running application can receive Apple Events from any other computer with an authorized user name and password, including script applications that are configured to stay open.

Figure 17.12

The Remote Apple Events portion of the system preferences Sharing panel

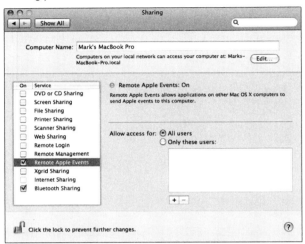

CROSS-REF
Saving scripts as applications is discussed in Chapter 3.

Understanding eppc computer specifiers

Once a remote computer is configured to receive remote events, a script that sends events must establish an *eppc specifier* to a computer and authenticate with a user name and password.

An eppc specifier is a URL style path to a computer that facilitates process-to-process communication. It specifies the computer address that will be targeted with remote events and optionally can include authentication information. The formula for the specifier is shown here:

```
"eppc://[user[:password]@]IP_address"
```

In its simplest form, without the optional user name and password, an eppc specifier includes only the address of the remote computer. The address can be the host name, Internet Protocol (IP) address, or server address of the computer, all shown here:

```
"eppc://Server.local"
"eppc://10.0.1.20"
"eppc://writetrackmedia-server"
```

NOTE
If there are any spaces in any part of the eppc specifier, they must be replaced with %20 in order to function correctly.

To save a user some time, the user name can be included. In that case, they will only be required to enter a password. The name can be hard-coded into the script or be entered based on the user's local account name. Both techniques are shown here:

```
"eppc://mmunro@10.0.1.20"
tell application "System Events"
  set nameUser to name of current user
end tell
"eppc://" & nameUser & "@10.0.1.20"
```

When a human will use a script, requiring her to authentic the connection is a good security measure. However, for situations were a script will run autonomously, there is only one user of the script, or to help save the user's time, the eppc specifier can include a user name and password. For example:

```
"eppc://mmunro:fakepassword@10.0.1.20"
```

CROSS-REF
The `choose remote application` command in the Standard scripting additions package (Chapter 16), makes it possible for a script to allow a user to select an application from a remote computer and authenticate all in one dialog.

Sending commands to a remote application

An eppc machine specifier does not establish a connection to the remote computer, even when a name and password are included. All it does is refer to a computer and optionally contain authentication information. During the first attempt to send a command to a remote application with a successful authentication, a connection will be opened. The local computer can freely send instructions to applications on the remote computer.

With a successful authentication, the following script will instruct the Finder to say the words "Hello World!":

```
set refComputer to "eppc://mmunro:fakepassword@10.0.1.20"
tell application "Finder" of machine refComputer
  say "Hello World!"
end tell
```

Compiling a script using terms from a local application

Each time you compile a script, any commands within a `tell application` statement must be compiled based on the terminology of that application. If the application is located on a remote computer, and that computer may not be available when the script is to be compiled, there is still a way to compile the script.

The `using terms from` control statement enables you to specify a local application that provides the terminology required for compilation while preserving the remote application as the command target. The statement formula is:

```
using terms from application "«local app»"
   tell application "«remote app»" of machine «eppc specifier»
      -- commands for remote application
   end tell
end using terms from
```

The application is typically the same for the local and remote computer except in rare cases when an application on the remote computer has a different name. This happens with applications that might have a "lite" version and a "pro" version. For example, FileMaker Pro might be installed on the remote computer while locally you might use FileMaker Pro Advanced.

This version of the "Hello World" script will compile without making a connection to the remote computer, even if that computer is offline:

```
using terms from application "Finder"
   set refComputer to "eppc://mmunro:fakepassword@10.0.1.20"
   tell application "Finder" of machine refComputer
      say "Hello World!"
   end tell
end using terms from
```

Summary

In this chapter you learned how to control applications with scripts. You learned how to use the `tell application` command to build several scripts using information gleaned from the script dictionary of the Finder. You also learned about creating multi-application workflows and sending script commands to applications on remote computers.

Working with Image Events

I*mage Events* is a faceless, background application that enables scripts to access the image processing functions of the Core Image framework, which was added in Mac OS X 10.4. It enables a script to directly get information about image files, perform various manipulations, and save the files in a variety of formats. It is not intended to replace interface-driven image processing applications such as Adobe Photoshop. However, Image Events provides an ideal format for script-managed batch processing of image files.

Introduction to Image Events

Image Events enable a script to quickly open a file, read various properties, modify those properties, and then save the updated image back into a file. Because Image Events is an application, all commands sent to it must be placed within a `tell application` statement, like this:

```
tell application "Image Events"
  -- image commands here
end tell
```

To get started with Image Events, open the AppleScript Editor and select Library from the Window menu. Double-click Image Events to see the library of Image Events commands shown in Figure 18.1. If Image Events is not in the Library list, click the Add button and select the application to add it to the list. It is located in `System/Library/CoreServices/Image Events.app`.

NOTE

The Image Events script dictionary includes some suites of commands, which are present in most scriptable applications. However, because it is a background application and does not support text classes, many of these suites are not useful. Also, some suites provide an easy way for the application to directly access key folders of the user and computer from within a `tell application` command. Most of these commands exist in the Standard Additions scripting addition or in the System Events application.

Figure 18.1

The Image Events library of commands

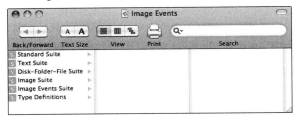

Getting started with basic functionality

Before an image can be manipulated, it must be opened by the Image Events application. Unlike a user-interface driven application, such has iPhoto or Adobe Photoshop, when Image Events opens a file, it does not display the image in a window because it is a faceless background application.

Launching the Image Events application

Image Events automatically launches whenever a command is sent to it with the `tell application` command. However, like any other MacOS X application, it can be launched explicitly with either the `activate` or the `launch` command. For example:

```
tell application "Image Events"
   activate
end tell
```

When issued, these commands will launch the Image Events application, but there will be no visible indication of their success. Because Image Events does not have an interface, it does not actually come forward like other applications.

A script can confirm if the application is currently running by checking the active processes as shown in the following script:

```
tell application "Finder"
   "Image Events" is in (the name of every process)
end tell
```

The result will be a `true` or `false` value, indicating the status of the application.

Opening an image

To open an image with Image Events, use the `open file` command. The following script uses the `open file` command to open the `Pache.jpg` file, which is shown in Figure 18.2 and specified in the `pathToImage` variable:

```
set pathToImage to "Macintosh HD:Users:mmunro:Desktop:Pache.jpg"
tell application "Image Events"
  open file pathToImage
end tell
```

Figure 18.2

The source image manipulated throughout
this section

Image © Mark Conway Munro

NOTE

To save space, most of the examples in this chapter assume the `Pache.jpg` image has already been opened with
the following code:

```
set pathToImage to "Macintosh HD:Users:mmunro:Desktop:Pache.jpg"
tell application "Image Events"
  open file pathToImage
end tell
```

To allow a user to select an image, use the `choose file` command. Be sure to place this
command outside of the `tell application` statement, as shown in the following code:

```
set pathToImage to (choose file) as string
tell application "Image Events"
  open file pathToImage
end tell
```

NOTE

Because the command is part of the Standard scripting additions package, starting in Mac OS X 10.6, it can no longer be called from within a `tell application` statement for security reasons.

Referring to an open image

Like any interface-driven application, Image Events can open more than one image at a time. When doing so, any commands directed at an image must refer to that image either by name, number, or reference to the open image. The latter is the preferred method.

The result from the `open file` command is a reference to the opened image and can easily be placed into a variable for use when sending commands to the image. The variable can be reused for each successive image; for example, used in a `repeat` loop. For more complex multi-image processing scripts, a separate reference variable can be used for each image.

The following script shows a single image being opened by the application and a reference to it being placed into a variable named `refImage`:

```
tell application "Image Events"
   set refImage to open file pathToImage
end tell
```

Any commands sent to an image can be directed in a single line or hierarchical structure, both shown in Listing 18.1. If more than one command will be sent to the same image, the hierarchical `tell` statement creates a script with less text and, therefore, less visual clutter.

Listing 18.1

An example of single line reference and hierarchical reference to an image

```
--  Single line command reference
tell application "Image Events"
  «command» of refImage1
end tell
--  Hierarchical command reference
tell application "Image Events"
  tell refImage
    «command»
  end tell
end tell
```

Counting and indentifying open images

A script can calculate the number of open image files with the `count` command, as shown here:

```
tell application "Image Events"
  count images -- result = 0
end tell
```

Using the `name of every image` command, a script can also get a list of all the open images. The following script demonstrates how to get a conditional list of every open image's name:

```
tell application "Image Events"
  set numImagesOpen to count images
  if numImagesOpen > 0 then
    name of every image -- result = {"Pache.jpg"}
  end if
end tell
```

CAUTION

The **name of every image** command should be inside of an **if-then** statement to avoid an error if there are no open images.

Closing an image

Image Events is quite forgiving about images left open. An image left open can be reopened without causing a problem. However, it is a good idea to close images once a script is finished manipulating them to avoid any potential problems, especially when the script might be opening batches of hundreds or thousands of images a day.

With a reference to an image stored in a variable, a script can easily instruct the application to close the file using the `close` command, as shown here:

```
tell application "Image Events"
  close refImage1
end tell
```

To ensure that there are no images left open, a script can ask Image Events to close all images with the `close every image` command, as shown here:

```
tell application "Image Events"
  close every image
end tell
```

Saving an image

By default, when the script closes an image, changes will be not be saved. An image can be saved with the `close` command adding a `saving` clause. Adding `yes` instructs the script to save changes while `no` discards changes. Add `ask` to have the script ask the user if changes should be saved:

```
tell application "Image Events"
  close refImage saving «yes/no/ask»
end tell
```

This example closes an image and saves changes:

```
tell application "Image Events"
   close refImage saving yes
end tell
```

TIP
Because Image Events does not have a user interface, you should refrain from asking the user if he wants to save changes to an image. He will not be able to see the image in question and, therefore, will have no context to aid him in the decision.

You can also save an image separately from the `close` command by using the `save` command, as shown here:

```
tell application "Image Events"
   save refImage
end tell
```

Saving an image as a new file

When an image has been modified, a script can save it into a new file. This can be accomplished with an optional parameter of both the `save` command. Adding the phrase `in file «path»` to the `save` command instructs the script to save the image to the file path specified. The following example demonstrates an image being saved as a JPEG into a new file:

```
set pathToImage to "Macintosh HD:Users:mmunro:Desktop:Pache.jpg"
set pathToSave to "Macintosh HD:Users:mmunro:Desktop:Pache2.jpg"
tell application "Image Events"
   set refImage to open file pathToImage
   save refImage as JPEG in file pathToSave
   close file refImage
end tell
```

When saving an image into a new file, you can choose from eight different file types. These include:

- BMP
- JPEG
- JPEG2
- PICT
- PNG
- PSD
- QuickTime Image
- TIFF

NOTE
Although the script dictionary lists the file type as an optional parameter, in Mac OS X 10.6, you must specify a file type in order for the file to be saved.

Other optional parameters of the `save` command include adding an icon, compressing packets in a TIFF file, and a compression level for JPEG files. This code provides an example of each:

```
tell application "Image Events"
  save refImage as JPEG in file pathToSave with compression level
    high with icon
  save refImage as TIFF in file pathToSave with PackBits
end tell
```

Quitting the Image Events application

While there is no harm in keeping Image Events running, it is a good practice to close the application when a script is finished unless it will be accessed continuously. As with any other application, this is achieved with the `quit` command, like this:

```
tell application "Image Events"
  quit
end tell
```

Reading properties of an image file

The `properties` record of an image file contains many pieces of information about it, as shown here:

```
tell application "Image Events"
  set recProperties to properties of refImage
end tell
-- result = {color space:RGB, image file:file "Macintosh
  HD:Users:mmunro:Desktop:Pache.jpg" of application "Image
  Events", bit depth:millions of colors, dimensions:{2224,
  2780}, location:folder "Macintosh HD:Users:mmunro:Desktop:" of
  application "Image Events", embedded profile:profile "sRGB
  IEC61966-2.1" of image "Pache.jpg" of application "Image
  Events", resolution:{600.0, 600.0}, class:image, file
  type:JPEG, name:"Pache.jpg"}
```

Viewing the entire record is useful when you are troubleshooting a problem file or are learning what information is contained within. However, a script can access each property directly in a single line of code like the rest of the examples in this section.

Bit depth

The `bit depth` property of an image file can be accessed as shown here:

```
tell application "Image Events"
  bit depth of refImage
  -- result = millions of colors
end tell
```

The possible values for the bit depth of an image are: best, black & white, color, four colors, four grays, grayscale, millions of colors, millions of colors plus, sixteen colors, sixteen grays, thousands of colors, two hundred fifty six colors, and two hundred fifty six grays. Because each of these values is an application term and not text, quotes should not be used when comparing the bit depth value of an image to any of the available values. Using quotes produces a false result, while using the keyword term produces a true result, as demonstrated in this example:

```
tell application "Image Events"
  set dataBitDepth to bit depth of refImage
  dataBitDepth = "millions of colors" -- result = false
  dataBitDepth = millions of colors -- result = true
end tell
```

Color space

The color space property of an image file can be accessed as shown here:

```
tell application "Image Events"
  color space of refImage
  -- result = RGB
end tell
```

The available values are: CMYK, Eight channel, Eight color, Five channel, Five color, Gray, Lab, Named, RGB, Seven channel, Seven color, Six channel, Six color, and XYZ. As with the bit depth property, the color space values are application terms and not text. Using quotes when comparing an image's color space to one of the values above will fail to detect a match.

Dimensions

The dimensions property of an image file can be accessed as shown here:

```
tell application "Image Events"
  dimensions of refImage
  -- result = {2224, 2780}
end tell
```

The result is a list containing the height and width of the image file in pixels: {2224, 2780}.

Embedded profile

The embedded profile property of an image file can be accessed as shown here:

```
tell application "Image Events"
  embedded profile of refImage
  -- result = profile "sRGB IEC61966-2.1" of image "Pache.jpg" of
   application "Image Events"
end tell
```

The result of the previous query is a reference to the profile within the image. To access the name of the profile, use the `name of` keywords shown here:

```
name of embedded profile of refImage
-- result = "sRGB IEC61966-2.1"
```

File type
The `file type` property of an image file can be accessed as shown here:

```
tell application "Image Events"
  file type of refImage
  -- result = JPEG
end tell
```

The available file types are: BMP, GIF, JPEG, JPEG2, MacPaint, PDF, Photoshop, PICT, PNG, PSD, QuickTime Image, SGI, Text, TGA, and TIFF. As with the bit depth and color space properties, the file type values are application terms and not text. Using quotes when comparing an image's file type to one of the previous values will fail to detect a match.

Image file
The `image file` property of an image file can be accessed as shown here:

```
tell application "Image Events"
  image file of refImage
  -- result = file "Macintosh HD:Users:mmunro:Desktop:Pache.jpg"
   of application "Image Events"

  path of image file of refImage
  -- result = "Macintosh HD:Users:mmunro:Desktop:Pache.jpg"
end tell
```

Image Events returns a file reference that can't be converted to a text-based path with the `as string` clause. The second example shows how to get the `path of` the image file of the image, which returns a string.

Locations
The `location` property of an image file contains the folder path or disk in which the file resides. For example:

```
tell application "Image Events"
  location of refImage
  -- result = folder "Macintosh HD:Users:mmunro:Desktop:" of
   application "Image Events"

  path of location of refImage
  -- result = "Macintosh HD:Users:mmunro:Desktop:"
end tell
```

Image Events returns a folder reference that can't be converted to a text-based path with the `as string` clause. The second example shows how to get the path of the image file's parent folder, which returns a string.

Name

The `name` property of an image contains the name of the actual image file, including the extension if the file contains one. This property can be accessed as shown here:

```
tell application "Image Events"
  name of refImage
  -- result = "Pache.jpg"
end tell
```

Resolution

The `resolution` property of an image contains the horizontal and vertical pixel density of the image in a list. This property can be accessed as shown here:

```
tell application "Image Events"
  resolution of refImage
  -- result = {600.0, 600.0}
end tell
```

Manipulating an image

Image Events allows substantial image manipulation with easy-to-use commands, including `crop`, `embed`, `flip`, `pad`, `rotate`, and `scale`.

NOTE

To save space, most of the examples in this section assume a source and output file path has been placed into variables, as shown here:

```
set pathToImage to "Macintosh HD:Users:mmunro:Desktop:Pache.
  jpg"
set pathToSave to "Macintosh HD:Users:mmunro:Desktop:Pache2.
  jpg"
```

Cropping

The `crop` command enables a script to crop an image to a specific height and width dimension. The following script opens an image, crops it, and saves it to a new file on the desktop:

```
tell application "Image Events"
  set refImage to open file pathToImage
  crop refImage to dimensions {150, 375}
  save refImage as JPEG in file pathToSave
end tell
```

The new image will now be cropped, as shown in Figure 18.3.

Figure 18.3

The result of using the crop command

If the new dimensions are larger than the source image being cropped, the resulting image will increase in size with a background color filling the new area. This behavior results in the same output as the `pad` command, which is discussed later in this chapter.

Embedding

The `embed` command enables a script to embed a ColorSync profile into an image. The available profiles can be found in the ColorSync Utility, shown in Figure 18.4, which is installed in `/Applications/Utilities/`.

NOTE

ColorSync is a technology pioneered by Apple to help synchronize colors between scanners, printers, and displays.

```
tell application "Image Events"
  embed refImage with source profile "Apple Cinema HD Display
  Calibrated"
  save refImage as JPEG in file pathToSave
end tell
```

Figure 18.4

The ColorSync Utility application

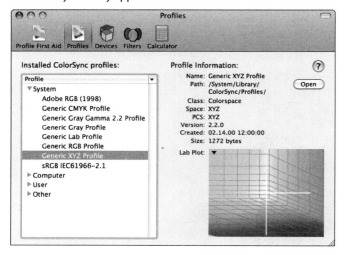

Flipping

The `flip` command enables a script to flip an image horizontally, vertically, or both. The following script flips an image horizontally, as shown in Figure 18.5:

```
tell application "Image Events"
  flip refImage with vertical and horizontal
  save refImage as JPEG in file pathToSave
end tell
```

Figure 18.5

The result of using the flip command

Padding

The pad command resizes an image to the height and width pixel dimensions specified. If the dimensions specified are smaller than the current dimensions, the image will be cropped. If the dimensions are larger than the current dimensions, space will be added around the image. This example shows the command modifying an image's dimensions to 3,000 pixels, squared:

```
tell application "Image Events"
  set refImage to open file pathToImage
  pad refImage to dimensions {3000, 3000}
  save refImage as JPEG in file pathToSave
end tell
```

By default, any extra space added around the image will be black. However, the script can include a `with pad color «RGB Color»` clause to specify a replacement color by including a list containing an RGB (red, green, or blue) color value.

Rotating

The `rotate` command enables a script to rotate an image to any angle. The following script rotates an image 90 degrees, as shown in Figure 18.6:

```
tell application "Image Events"
  rotate refImage to angle 90
  save refImage as JPEG in file pathToSave
end tell
```

Figure 18.6

The result of rotating the image 90 degrees

The image can be rotated from 0 to 360 degrees and can include factional amounts. The following script rotates the image 42.5 degrees, resulting in the image shown in Figure 18.7:

```
tell application "Image Events"
  rotate refImage to angle 42.5
  save refImage as JPEG in file pathToSave
end tell
```

Figure 18.7

The result of rotating the image 42.5 degrees

Scaling

The scale command will proportionally increase or decrease the size of an image. The command must be accompanied by one of the two optional parameters: to size or by factor. Resizing will not change the resolution of the image.

To resize an image to a specific size, the integer provided will become the new size for the longest dimension, either height or width. The other dimension will be adjusted to maintain the original proportion. The following script reduces the height of the test image to 200 and results in the image shown in Figure 18.8:

```
tell application "Image Events"
  scale refImage to size 200
  save refImage as JPEG in file pathToSave
end tell
```

Figure 18.8

The result of using the scale command

When resizing an image by a factor, the number you specify indicates the percentage of the original size that should be applied. For example, a value of .5 will decrease the image by 50 percent while a value of 1.5 will increase the image by 150 percent. As when scaling to size, the number you specify will be applied to the longest dimension, height, or width, with the other number being adjusted to maintain the original proportion. This script will decrease the image by 75 percent:

```
tell application "Image Events"
  scale refImage by factor .75
  save refImage as JPEG in file pathToSave
end tell
```

Creating an Image Batch Processor

Typically, scripts are used to perform a sequence of tasks on batches of images. In this section, you will learn how to create an image batch processing script that integrates many topics covered in earlier chapters of this book. The script, shown in Figure 18.9, will get a list of files in a folder, open each file, make sure the image is an image file, flip the image horizontally, scale the image by a factor of 25 percent, and then save the image into an output folder. When it is finished modifying every image in the batch, the script will return a list of successfully modified images and images that encountered errors.

NOTE

The Image Batch Processor script described in this section is available for download from the book's Web site at www.wileydevreference.com.

Figure 18.9

The Image Batch Processor script

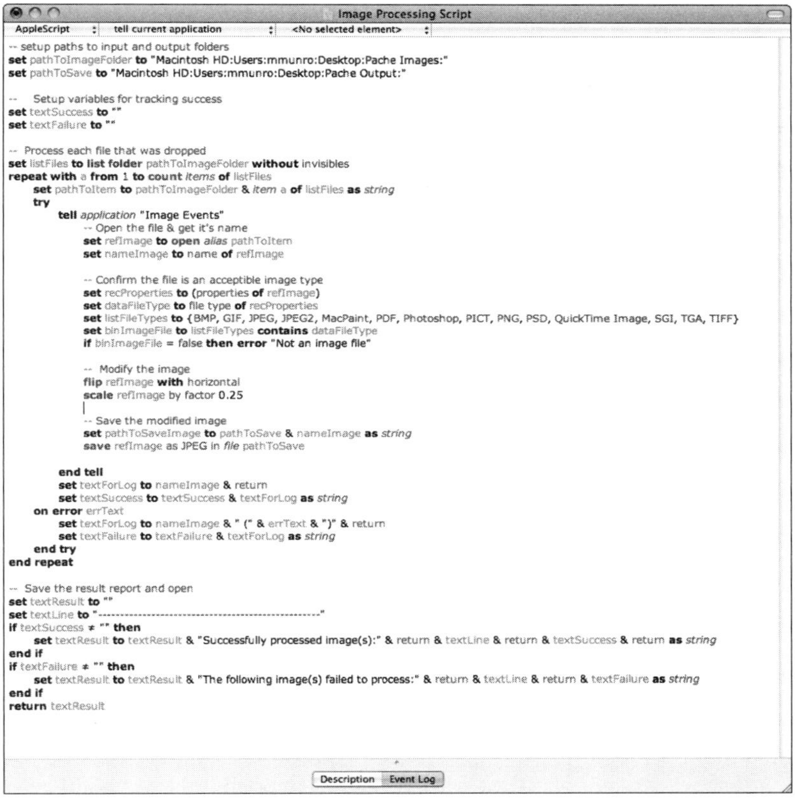

The script assumes that there are two folders on the desktop. The source folder is named `Pache Images` and the other is `Pache Output`. The output folder is empty while the images folder, shown in Figure 18.10, has only a single JPEG file of Pache and a few non-image items that will help illustrate the error reporting of the script.

Listing 18.2 shows the first four lines of the script. First, the paths to both folders are placed into variables. Then variables are initialized to contain an empty string to list the files that were successfully processed and those that were not.

Figure 18.10

The Pache Images folder on the desktop

Listing 18.2

The beginning of the script defining the input and output folders and initializing variables for session reporting

```
set pathToImageFolder to "Macintosh HD:Users:mmunro:Desktop:Pache
  Images:"
set pathToSave to "Macintosh HD:Users:mmunro:Desktop:Pache Output:"
set textSuccess to ""
set textFailure to ""
```

Next, the script can begin the process, as shown in Listing 18.3. First, it gets a list of the items in the source images folder using the `list folder` command. A repeat loop begins, which will process each item in the list, and the path to the current item from the list is placed into a variable. A `try` statement is started to protect the code responsible for processing images. Finally, a `tell application` statement instructs Image Events to open the current image.

Listing 18.3

Code that gets a list of files to process and begins a repeat statement that will step through the list

```
set listFiles to list folder pathToImageFolder without invisibles
repeat with a from 1 to count items of listFiles
 set pathToItem to pathToImageFolder & item a of listFiles as string
 try
   tell application "Image Events"
     -- Open the file & get it's name
     set refImage to open alias pathToItem
```

With the image open, Image Events is ready to begin processing images, as shown in Listing 18.4. It puts the name of the image file into a variable. This will be used later to save the image with the same name in the output folder. The properties of the current image file are placed into the `recProperties` variable. Then, before attempting to process the current item, its file type is compared to a list of acceptable image formats. If the list does not contain the current item's type, an error is generated, causing the script to skip all the code between the last line of Listing 18.4 and the forthcoming `on error` clause, where it will be added to the list of files that failed to process.

Listing 18.4

Code that checks the image file type and rejects those not compatible with Image Events

```
set nameImage to name of refImage

-- Confirm the file is an acceptable image type
set recProperties to (properties of refImage)
set dataFileType to file type of recProperties
set listFileTypes to {BMP, GIF, JPEG, JPEG2, MacPaint, PDF, Photoshop,
   PICT, PNG, PSD, QuickTime Image, SGI, TGA, TIFF}
set blnImageFile to listFileTypes contains dataFileType
if blnImageFile = false then error "Not an image file"
```

Listing 18.5 shows the heart of the script. The image is flipped horizontally and scaled by a factor of 25 percent. Then a new path in the output folder is established for the image and it is saved as a JPEG into that folder.

Listing 18.5

Code that modifies the image and saves it as a JPEG

```
--  Modify the image
flip refImage with horizontal
scale refImage by factor 0.25

-- Save the modified image
set pathToSaveImage to pathToSave & nameImage as string
save refImage as JPEG in file pathToSaveImage
```

At this point the script, shown in Listing 18.6, closes the `tell` statement and adds the current image to the list of those successfully processed. Then the error statement is terminated with an `on error` clause that places the current item on a list of unsuccessfully processed items and includes the description of the error. Because an error would cause the code to skip the steps in Listing 18.5 and go straight to the `on error` clause, each item will go onto only one of these two lists. Finally, the `repeat` loop is terminated once all the items in the folder have been processed.

Listing 18.6

Code that terminates the tell application, try, and repeat commands

```
  end tell
    set textForLog to nameImage & return
    set textSuccess to textSuccess & textForLog as string
  on error errText
    set textForLog to nameImage & " (" & errText & ")" & return
    set textFailure to textFailure & textForLog as string
  end try
end repeat
```

In the final step, shown in Listing 18.7, a report is generated listing all the items that successfully processed and all those that did not. The headings for these sections are only included if there is at least one item that qualifies for inclusion. In other words, if there are no files failing the process, the "failed" heading will not be included. The result of the script is a formatted text report, shown in Figure 18.11.

Listing 18.7

Code that reports the results of the session, listing files processed and errors

```
  set textResult to ""
set textLine to "-------------------------------------------------"
if textSuccess ≠ "" then
 set textResult to textResult & "Successfully processed image(s):" &
  return & textLine & return & textSuccess & return as string
end if
if textFailure ≠ "" then
 set textResult to textResult & "The following image(s) failed to
  process:" & return & textLine & return & textFailure as string
end if
return textResult
```

Figure 18.11

The formatted report of items that were and were not successfully processed

CROSS-REF
Learn to make this image batch processor more open-ended in Chapter 22.

Summary

In this chapter you learned about using the Image Events application to tap into the power of the Core Image framework to analyze and manipulate image files with scripts. The batch processing script gives you a real-world example of using Image Events.

Working with Database Events

D*atabase Events* is a faceless, background application that enables scripts to create, manipulate, and search databases. In complex workflows, the Database Events application is not intended to replace interface-driven database applications, such as FileMaker Pro. However, it provides an ideal format for script-managed data storage and retrieval that far exceeds the capabilities of data stored in a text file or in the properties of a script. Once a database is created, a script can search, extract, delete, modify, and create as many records and fields as are required for a specific task.

Introduction to Database Events

Database Events enables a script to quickly create and open a database as well as enter and search records. Because Database Events is an application, all commands sent to it must be placed within a `tell application` statement, like this:

```
tell application "Database Events"
  -- database commands here
end tell
```

To get started with Database Events, open the Script Editor and select Library from the Window menu. Double-click Database Events to see the library of commands shown in Figure 19.1. If it is not available in the Library window, click the Add button and navigate to the application, which is located in the `/System/Library/CoreServices/` folder.

In This Chapter

Building and manipulating databases with Database Events

Searching databases for text, numeric, and date values

Importing tab-separated data into a Database Events database

NOTE

The Database Events script dictionary includes some suites of commands, which are present in most scriptable applications. However, because it is a background application, many of these suites are not useful.

Figure 19.1

The Database Events library of commands

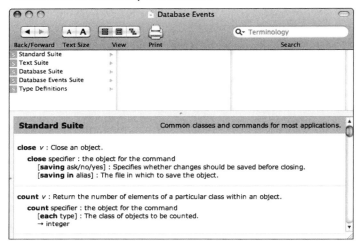

Getting started with basic functionality

You should review some basic functions of the Database Events application before creating and searching records.

Launching the Database Events application

Database Events automatically launches whenever a command is sent to it with the `tell` `application` command. However, like any other Mac OS X application, it can be launched explicitly with either the `activate` or the `launch` command. For example:

```
tell application "Database Events"
   activate
end tell
```

When issued, these commands launch the application, but there will be no visible indication of their success. Because Database Events do not have an interface, it doesn't come forward like other applications.

A script can check if the application is currently running by checking the active processes as shown in the following script:

```
tell application "Finder"
   "Database Events" is in (the name of every process)
end tell
```

The result will be a `true` or `false` value, indicating the status of Database Events.

Creating a database file

A script can easily create a database with Database Events by simply specifying a name for the file and creating at least one record. Databases are automatically created in `~/Documents/Databases/` and have an extension of `.dbev`.

```
set nameDatabase to "United States"
tell application "Database Events"
  set refDatabase to make new database with properties
   {name:nameDatabase }
  tell refDatabase
    make new record with properties {name:""}
  end tell
end tell
```

Opening a database file

Being forced to keep databases located in `~/Documents/Databases/` has one advantage: A database can be opened by specifying only its name, as shown here:

```
tell application "Database Events"
  open database "United States"
end tell
```

Database Location Restriction

Although there is a `location` property of a database that compiles if included, due to a bug, as of Mac OS X 10.6.2, databases must be located in `~/Documents/Databases/` to function properly. If a database will exist elsewhere, such as on a server, the script can move the file into the `Databases` folder prior to opening it.

This script example checks for the existence of the database folder, creates it if missing, and copies a specified database file into the folder:

```
set pathToDatabase to "«path to database here»"
set pathToDocuments to path to documents folder
tell application "Finder"
  set pathToDBFolder to pathToDocuments & "Databases:" as string
  if (folder pathToDBFolder exists) is false then
    make new folder at pathToDocuments with properties
   {name:"Databases"}
  end if
  move file pathToDatabase to folder pathToDBFolder
end tell
```

The `open database` command returns a reference to the opened database, which can be placed into a variable to route future commands directly to the database. This script shows how a `tell database` command can use the reference to the opened file:

```
tell application "Database Events"
  set refDatabase to open database "United States"
  tell database refDatabase
    -- commands here
  end tell
end tell
```

To specify the full path of a database that is not in the databases folder, a script must use a POSIX (Portable Operating System Interface for Unix) path, as shown here:

```
set pathToDatabase to "Macintosh HD:Users:mmunro:Documents:Databa
  ses:United States.dbev"
set pathToDatabase to POSIX path of pathToDatabase
tell application "Database Events"
  open database pathToDatabase
end tell
```

CROSS-REF

POSIX paths are discussed in Chapter 10.

Counting open databases

A script can get a count of open databases with the `count` command. The result will be an integer. This example shows a count of 1 open database:

```
tell application "Database Events"
  count of databases
  -- result = 1
end tell
```

Listing every open database

A script can get a list of references to and the name of every open database. It does this using the `every` command, which returns a list of the specified information. If no databases are open, the result will be an empty list. This script gets a list of database references and a list of names of all open database files:

```
tell application "Database Events"
  every database
  -- result = {database "United States" of application "Database
  Events"}
  name of every database
  -- result = {"United States"}
end tell
```

Using the `every` command, a script can quickly ascertain if a specific database is currently open by checking the list of all database names. The result will be a `true` or `false` value, indicating if the specified database is open. This script checks to see if the sample "United States" database is open:

```
tell application "Database Events"
  "United States" is in (name of every database)
  -- result = true
end tell
```

Closing a database

You can close a database with the `close` command and by specifying either its name or number. Both are shown in the following example. When the script closes a database, any changes to the database data will be saved.

```
tell application "Database Events"
  close database "United States"
end tell

tell application "Database Events"
  close database 1
end tell
```

NOTE

If the specified database is not open, an error will occur, so it is important that a script first check if the database is open before attempting to close it.

For situations were multiple databases are open simultaneously, you can instruct Database Events to close them all at once with the `close every database` command:

```
tell application "Database Events"
  close every database
end tell
```

Quitting the Database Events application

While there is no harm in keeping Database Events running, it is a good practice to close the application when a script is finished unless it will be accessed continuously. As with any other application, you achieve this with the `quit` command, shown here:

```
tell application "Database Events"
  quit
end tell
```

NOTE

When the Database Events application quits, any changes to an open database will be lost as the database is closed.

Working with database records

A *database record*, the primary objects that exist within a database, is a collection of fields of information. A record might represent one of any number of possible entities, depending on what the database is used for. It might be a contact, company, project, product, location, or task. Database Events enables a script to create, count, list, modify, and delete records.

Records have two properties: ID and name. The ID property is a read-only value that creates a unique identifier for the record. The name property is a default field that is created when a record is created.

NOTE

As of MacOS X 10.6.2, the Database Events dictionary lists the record name property as read only, but it is currently editable.

Creating records

To have a script create a record in an open database, use the make command and specify new record as the object to create. The command requires the inclusion of a properties clause, as shown here:

```
tell application "Database Events"
  set refDatabase to open database "United States"
  tell refDatabase
    make new record with properties {name:""}
  end tell
end tell
```

The required name property is automatically created as a field. It can be given a value if desired, but can also be left blank. Assigning a unique name enables a script to refer to the record by name instead of by its ID property or its location in a sequence of records. (Assigning a unique name to a record is discussed in more detail later in this chapter.)

Because the Database Events application does not contain a user interface, it may be difficult for a developer to confirm that the new record was created. Adding code to count the records contained in the database before and after the make new record command solves this problem and provides visible proof that the command is working. This technique, shown in the following example, is helpful when learning to manipulate databases with Database Events:

```
tell application "Database Events"
  set refDatabase to open database "United States"
  tell refDatabase
    set numRecordsBefore to count records
    make new record with properties {name:""}
    set numRecordsAfter to count records
  end tell
end tell
return {numRecordsBefore, numRecordsAfter}
-- results = {0, 1}
```

You can create multiple records in a batch by using a `repeat` statement. This example creates ten blank records:

```
tell application "Database Events"
  set refDatabase to open database "United States"
  tell refDatabase
    repeat 10 times
      make new record with properties {name:""}
    end repeat
  end tell
end tell
```

CROSS-REF
The `repeat` statement is discussed in Chapter 14.

Counting records

The `count` command enables a script to determine the number of records contained within a database. In the following example, this script opens a database and counts the records:

```
tell application "Database Events"
  set refDatabase to open database "United States"
  tell refDatabase
    count records -- result = 11
  end tell
end tell
```

NOTE
The result of the `count` command is an integer.

Listing records

Scripts can obtain a list of records in two forms: a list of references to each record and a list of record names. The following script obtains a list of records organized by record name:

```
tell application "Database Events"
  set refDatabase to open database "United States"
  tell refDatabase
    the name of every record
    -- result = {"New York", "Ohio", "Indiana", "Pennsylvania",
    "Missouri"}
  end tell
end tell
```

Referring to records

In order to easily create fields, access or modify their values, and delete records, you can have a script create a reference to a specific record. Once a reference is placed into a variable, it can be used to route commands to the related record with ease. The reference can use the record ID, name, or sequential location of the record. Each of these approaches is shown here:

```
tell application "Database Events"
  tell database "United States"
    set refRecord2 to record id 280714104
    set refRecord3 to record "Pennsylvania"
    set refRecord1 to record 1
  end tell
end tell
```

If records have names, referring to a record by its name field is definitely the best choice. Using the ID or sequential location of the record is not practical for complex workflows as a script would be overwhelmed with a multitude of variables tracking these values for every record.

Deleting records

Scripts can delete records by referring to the record by its ID, name, or sequential location. Each of these approaches is shown here:

```
tell application "Database Events"
  tell database "United States"
    delete record id 280714104
    delete record "Pennsylvania"
    delete record 1
  end tell
end tell
```

NOTE
Once a record is deleted, the database must be closed before quitting the Database Events application in order to save the change.

Working with fields

A *database field* is one piece of information grouped with other fields to form a record. Fields have three properties: ID, name, and value. Though the ID property is read-only, the name and value properties can be modified.

The data class of a field's value will be whatever class of data is placed within it. If a text string is placed within it, the class will be text. If a date is placed into the same field, the class will be a date. While this behavior conveniently handles field classes for you, it inadvertently creates a situation that could be prone to errors. If your code assumes the value of a given field is a date but it contains a text-based date, the script will generate an error when it attempts to use the date in a calculation. If the script checks the value before placing it into a field or immediately after extracting it from a field, this type of situation will not occur.

Database Events' Unique Approach to Fields

Typically, an interface-driven database like FileMaker Pro allows fields to be set up for a table, which is then shared for every record. Database Events has a rather quirky approach to fields, requiring a script to create each field for every record. Complicating matters more, each record can then have a different set of fields. Database Events also allows a record to have more than one field with the same name.

There might be situations where this unique approach is justifiable, such as for a script that stores different types of data, each with various fields of information in a single database file. However, in general, you should always keep the record's field list consistent to avoid serious confusion.

Creating fields

To create a field, a script must use the `make` command and specify `new field` as the object to create. The script must also specify the name of the field and its value in a `with properties` clause.

The following script assumes that a record named Pennsylvania exists and then creates a field named Abbreviation with a value of "PA":

```
tell application "Database Events"
  set refDatabase to open database "United States"
  tell refDatabase
    tell record "Pennsylvania"
      make new field with properties {name:"Abbreviation",
 value:"PA"}
    end tell
  end tell
end tell
```

Because Database Events allows a record to have more than one field with the same name, it is wise to have your script check whether a field already exists before creating one that will possibly be a duplicate. The following example uses an `if-then` statement to conditionally create the field only if it is not already present:

```
tell application "Database Events"
  set refDatabase to open database "United States"
  tell refDatabase
    tell record "Pennsylvania"
      if (field "State Name" exists) = false then
        make new field with properties {name:"State Name",
 value:"Pennsylvania"}
      end if
    end tell
  end tell
end tell
```

Counting fields

The `count` command enables a script to access the number of fields attached to a specific record. In this example, a record named Pennsylvania is found to contain two fields:

```
tell application "Database Events"
  set refDatabase to open database "United States"
  tell refDatabase
      tell record "Pennsylvania"
        count fields -- result = 2
      end tell
  end tell
end tell
```

Getting a list of fields

Scripts can get a list of every field that exists for a particular record. The resulting list can contain field references, field names, or field values. This script will return the name of every field in the Pennsylvania record:

```
tell application "Database Events"
  set refDatabase to open database "United States"
  tell refDatabase
    tell record "Pennsylvania"
      name of every field
      -- result = {"name", "State Name", "State Abbreviation"}
    end tell
  end tell
end tell
```

NOTE

The first field in a record will always be the name field, which is the record name. The name field must be created when a record is created. Any other fields are custom fields created by a script.

Referring to fields

When accessing or modifying field values, a script can create a reference to the appropriate field. Once a reference is placed into a variable, it can be used to route commands to that field. The reference can use the ID, name, or sequential location of the field. Each of these approaches is shown here:

```
tell application "Database Events"
  tell database "United States"
    tell record "Pennsylvania"
      set refField2 to field id 282517956
      set refField3 to field "Population"
      set refField1 to field 1
    end tell
  end tell
end tell
```

Referring to a field by its name field is definitely the best choice. Using the ID or sequential location of the field is not practical for complex workflows, as a script would be overwhelmed with a multitude of variables tracking these values for every record.

 CAUTION

Field names are case sensitive. A reference to the field "state name" will cause an error if the field name is "State Name."

Extracting data from fields

A script can extract data from a field and place it into a variable for later use within the workflow. The following example gets the value of the Pennsylvania record's Population field:

```
tell application "Database Events"
  tell database "United States"
    tell record "Pennsylvania"
      set numPopulation to value of field "Population"
    end tell
  end tell
end tell
return numPopulation -- result = 12448279
```

Modifying field values

A script can set the value of a field to any value. Putting a value into a field replaces any prior value that field may have contained. This example changes the value of the Pennsylvania record's Population field to 1:

```
tell application "Database Events"
  tell database "United States"
    tell record "Pennsylvania"
      set value of field "Population" to 1
    end tell
  end tell
end tell
```

Deleting fields

A script can delete a field by referring to the file by its ID, name, or sequential location. Each of these is shown here:

```
tell application "Database Events"
  tell database "United States"
    tell record "Pennsylvania"
      delete field id 280714107
      delete field "State Name"
      delete field 1
    end tell
  end tell
end tell
```

NOTE
Once a field is deleted, the database must be closed before quitting the Database Events application in order to save the change.

TIP
Keeping fields synchronized across all records in a database is a good habit to be in. Don't delete a field from one record without deleting it from all records.

Searching a Database

A script can search the contents of a database and extract field values for records that match the search criteria using a `whose` command filter. The default result of a search is a list of references to the records that match the search criteria. However, a script can extract the record name or the values of a field within the same statement.

CROSS-REF
The `whose` clause is discussed in Chapter 17.

Searching for text values

A script can search for records that contain a specific textual value in a specified field using a filter statement. To search for records that contain fields with specific textual values, use the `equals`, `contains`, `starts with`, and `ends with` operators.

Equals

You can use the `=` and `equals` keywords interchangeably. This example shows a simple search for records with a value of "New York" in the State Name field:

```
tell application "Database Events"
  tell database "United States"
    every record whose value of field "State Name" = "New York"
    -- result = {record id 281145770 of database "United States"
    of application "Database Events"}
  end tell
end tell
```

The result of the previous query is a list of the one reference to the record that matched the search criteria. The reference can then be used to extract additional information from specific fields from the record being referenced.

If no records match the criteria, the result is an empty list.

Depending on the data required for the remainder of a script, the search can extract the desired field values directly as part of the search criteria, thus eliminating additional steps. By modifying the query, the result can be a list of every field value of each record matching the specified search criteria, as shown in this example:

```
tell application "Database Events"
  tell database "United States"
    value of every field of (every record whose value of field
    "State Name" = "New York")
    -- result = {{"New York", "New York", "NY", 1788, "Albany",
    19490297}}
  end tell
end tell
```

Likewise, this example extracts the value of the State Abbreviation field for the record that matches the criteria:

```
tell application "Database Events"
  tell database "United States"
    value of field "State Abbreviation" of (every record whose
    value of field "State Name" = "New York")
    -- result = {"NY"}
  end tell
end tell
```

Reversing the logic, a script can search for records whose value in a specific field does not equal the value specified. You can use the ≠ and is not equal to keywords interchangeably to do so.

N O T E

To type a not equal to symbol (≠), hold down the Option key while typing an equal sign.

Contains

To search for values that contain instead of equal a specified criteria, replace the = keyword with contains as the operator. This example shows a simple search for any records with a value containing the word "New" in the State Name field:

```
tell application "Database Events"
  tell database "United States"
    value of field "State Abbreviation" of (every record whose
    value of field "State Name" contains "New")
    -- result = {"NH", "NJ", "NM", "NY"}
  end tell
end tell
```

The search returns four states: New Hampshire, New Jersey, New Mexico, and New York.

Reversing the logic to use the `does not contain` operator, a script can search for records whose field value doesn't contain a specified value. This example shows a search for records with a value that does not contain the word "New" in the State Name field:

```
tell application "Database Events"
  tell database "United States"
    value of field "State Abbreviation" of (every record whose
    value of field "State Name" does not contain "New")
    -- result = {"AL", "AK", "AZ", "AR", "CA", "CO", "CT", "DE",
    "FL", "GA", "HI", "ID", "IL", "IN", "IA", "KS", "KY", "LA",
    "ME", "MD", "MA", "MI", "MN", "MS", "MO", "MT", "NE", "NV",
    "NC", "ND", "OH", "OK", "OR", "PA", "RI", "SC", "SD", "TN",
    "TX", "UT", "VT", "VA", "WA", "WV", "WI", "WY"}
  end tell
end tell
```

This search returns forty-six states.

Starts with

To search for records where a specific field starts with a given value, use the `starts with` operator. This example shows a search for records whose "State Name" starts with "A":

```
tell application "Database Events"
  tell database "United States"
    value of field "State Abbreviation" of (every record whose
    value of field "State Name" starts with "A")
    -- result = {"AL", "AK", "AZ", "AR"}
  end tell
end tell
```

The search returns four states: Alabama, Alaska, Arizona, and Arkansas.

To reverse this query to find records where the specified field value does not start with a given value, use the `does not start with` operator.

Ends with

Like `starts with`, to search for records where a field ends with a given value, use the `ends with` operator. This example finds records where "State Name" ends with "Y":

```
tell application "Database Events"
  tell database "United States"
    value of field "State Abbreviation" of (every record whose
    value of field "State Name" ends with "Y")
    -- result = {"KY", "NY"}
  end tell
end tell
```

Here, two states are found: Kentucky and New York.

Again, to reverse this search to find records where the specified field value does not end with a given value, use the `does not end with` operator.

Searching for numeric values

A script can search for records that contain a specific numeric value in a specified field using a filter statement. To search for records that contain fields with specified numeric values, use the `equals`, `greater than`, and `less than` operators.

Equals

As with text-based searches, you can use the `=` and `equals` keywords interchangeably. This example shows a simple search for records with a value of 19490297 in the Population field:

```
tell application "Database Events"
  tell database "United States"
    value of field "State Abbreviation" of (every record whose
    value of field "Population" = 19490297)
    -- result = {"NY"}
  end tell
end tell
```

To reverse this search and find records where the value does not equal the given value, use the ≠ and `not equal to` keywords.

Greater than

To search for values that are greater than a specified criteria, the `>` keyword replaces the `=` as the operator. You can use the `>` and `is greater than` keywords interchangeably. This example shows a simple search for any records with a value that is greater than 9000000 in the Population field:

```
tell application "Database Events"
  tell database "United States"
    value of field "State Abbreviation" of (every record whose
    value of field "Population" > 9000000)
    -- result = {"CA", "FL", "GA", "HI", "IL", "MI", "NY", "NC",
    "OH", "PA", "TX"}
  end tell
end tell
```

The search returns eleven states: California, Florida, Georgia, Hawaii, Illinois, Michigan, New York, North Carolina, Ohio, Pennsylvania, and Texas.

NOTE

The phrase `not less than` will return the same results.

Less than

You can reverse the logic to use the < operator, to have a script search for records whose value in a specific field is less than the value specified. You can use the < and is less than keywords interchangeably. This example shows a simple search for any records with a value that is less than 800000 in the Population field:

```
tell application "Database Events"
  tell database "United States"
    value of field "State Abbreviation" of (every record whose
    value of field "Population" < 800000)
    -- result = {"AK", "ND", "VT", "WY"}
  end tell
end tell
```

Here, four states are found: Alaska, North Dakota, Vermont, and Wyoming.

NOTE

The phrase not greater than will return the same results.

Searching for date values

A script can search for records that contain a specific date value in a specified field using a filter statement. To search for records that contain fields with specified date value, use the equals, greater than, and less than operators.

Equals

As with text and number based searches, you can use the = and equals keywords interchangeably. This example shows a simple search for records with a value of "December 12, 1787" in the Date Joined field and returns the one state that joined the Union on that day:

```
set dateToCheck to date "December 12, 1787"
tell application "Database Events"
  tell database "United States"
    value of field "State Abbreviation" of (every record whose
    value of field "Date Joined" = dateToCheck)
    -- result = {"PA"}
  end tell
end tell
```

You can reverse the logic, to have a script search for records whose value in a specific field does not equal the value specified. You can use the ≠ and `is not equal to` keywords interchangeably.

Greater than

To search for records that have a date that is newer than a given date, use the greater than (>) operator. You can use the > and `is greater than` keywords interchangeably. This example shows a simple search for records with a value newer than "January 1, 1899" in the Date Joined field and returns the five states that joined the Union after that date:

```
set dateToCheck to date "January 1, 1899"
tell application "Database Events"
  tell database "United States"
    value of field "State Abbreviation" of(every record whose
    value of field "Date Joined" > dateToCheck)
    -- result = {"AK", "AZ", "HI", "NM", "OK"}
  end tell
end tell
```

Similarly, a script can use `is greater than or equal to` or the corresponding symbol, ≥. Also, the logic for all of these operators can be reversed to search of values that are `not greater than` a given value.

NOTE

To type a greater than or equal to symbol (≥), hold down the Option key while typing a greater than symbol.

Less than

To search for records that have a date that is older than a given date, use the less than (<) operator. The < symbol and `is less than` keywords can be used interchangeably. This example shows a simple search for records with a value older than "January 1, 1789" in the Date Joined field and returns eleven states that joined the union prior to that date:

```
set dateToCheck to date "January 1, 1789"
tell application "Database Events"
  tell database "United States"
    value of field "State Abbreviation" of(every record whose
    value of field "Date Joined" < dateToCheck)
    -- result = {"CT", "DE", "GA", "MD", "MA", "NH", "NJ", "NY",
    "PA", "SC", "VA"}
  end tell
end tell
```

Similarly, a script can use `is less than or equal to` or the corresponding symbol, ≤. Also, the logic for all of these operators can be reversed to `not less than`.

NOTE
To type a less than or equal to symbol (≤), hold down the Option key while typing a less than symbol.

Searching for multiple values

Searching for records in a database often requires more complex criteria. These situations are aided by the `and` keyword, the `or` keyword, or a combination of both.

And

Scripts can search for records that match both of two or more different criteria with the `and` operator. Each side of the equation must result in a `true` value for a record to qualify. The following example searches for records of states that joined the Union before the year 1800 and have a current population that is less than one million people:

```
tell application "Database Events"
  tell database "United States"
    value of field "State Abbreviation" of (every record whose
    value of field "Year Joined" < 1800 and value of field
    "Population" < 1000000)
    -- result = {"DE", "VT"}
  end tell
end tell
```

Because states only qualify if they match both criteria, the resulting list contains only two states: Delaware and Vermont.

Or

To search for records that match at least one of two or more different criteria, use the `or` operator. To find a match, at least one side of the equation must result in a `true` value. The following example searches for records for states that joined the union before the year 1800 *or* have a population that is less than one million people:

```
tell application "Database Events"
  tell database "United States"
    value of field "State Abbreviation" of (every record whose
    value of field "Year Joined" < 1800 or value of field
    "Population" < 1000000)
    -- result = {"AK", "CT", "DE", "GA", "KY", "MD", "MA", "MT",
    "NH", "NJ", "NY", "NC", "ND", "PA", "RI", "SC", "SD", "TN",
    "VT", "VA", "WY"}
  end tell
end tell
```

Because states can qualify even if they match only one of the two criteria, the resulting list contains twenty-one states.

Combinations

A script can use any combination of the and/or operators to create complex multi-criteria search requests. When doing so, be sure to use parenthesis to keep precedence executing in the order you expect.

Importing Records from Tab-Separated Files

To build a database, you need data. When using a user-interface driven database application, data might be manually entered or imported through the interface. With Database Events, everything has to be created and entered with a script. In this section, I demonstrate how to build a script that will create a database and import data from a tab-delimited text file.

NOTE
The Import Records script described in this section is available for download from the book's Web site at www.wileydevreference.com.

The script, shown in Figure 19.2, assumes that there is a file on the desktop named United States Data.txt, shown in Figure 19.3, with six fields of information: the name of the state, its abbreviation, the date that it joined the union, the year that it joined the union, the name of its capital city, and the population of the state.

Figure 19.2

The Import Records script example

Figure 19.3

The United States Data.txt file that must be on the desktop when running the import records script

The first part of the script, shown in Listing 19.1, is responsible for preparing the database for import. It instructs the Database Events application to check if there is an existing database called "United States". If it does not exist, it is automatically created. Then, as a safety precaution in case the database does exist, it deletes all records to eliminate the possibility of duplicate records being created which, in this case, would be undesirable.

Listing 19.1

The first section of the script confirms or creates a database and deletes any existing records

```
--  Create the database if necessary
tell application "Database Events"
  if (database "United States" exists) = false then
    make new database with properties {name:"United States"}
  end if
end tell
--  Delete existing record if any exist
tell application "Database Events"
  tell database "United States"
    delete every record
  end tell
end tell
```

The next section of the script, shown in Listing 19.2, establishes the path to the tab-delimited text file on the desktop and loads its contents into a variable named `listData`. The data is parsed so that each paragraph is a separate item in a list.

Listing 19.2

Establish a path to a text file and load its data into a variable

```
--  Load the data from the tab separated file
set pathToDataFile to ((path to desktop folder) as string) & "United
 States Data.txt"
set listData to every paragraph of (read file pathToDataFile)
```

The script then initializes two variables, shown in Listing 19.3, to contain a list of field names, in the same order as the data file, and corresponding field types, so the script knows how to treat each field. To facilitate parsing the tab-delimited paragraphs into fields, the `text item delimiter` is change to a `tab` character.

CROSS-REF
Parsing text with text item delimiters is discussed in Chapter 7.

Listing 19.3

Establishes a list of field names and types and sets the text item delimiters to tab

```
--   Setup field names and text item delimiters
set listFieldNames to {"State Name", "State Abbreviation", "Date
 Joined", "Year Joined", "Capital City", "Population"}
set listFieldTypes to {"text", "text", "date", "number", "text",
 "number"}
set text item delimiters to {tab}
```

The script begins a `repeat` statement to process each paragraph of the data that is now contained in the `listData` variable. The first line within the statement parses the current item into a new list of separate fields called `listRecordValues`, as shown in Listing 19.4. These are the six fields for the current state record of data that is being imported.

Listing 19.4

Begin a repeat loop and parse the current line of data into a list of field values

```
  --   Process each paragraph of the data file
repeat with a from 1 to count items of listData

   --   Parse the current paragraph into a list of values
   set listRecordValues to every text item of item a of listData
```

Because the incoming data is contained in a text file, the script treats everything like text unless it is instructed to do otherwise. Fields in the database are automatically the same class as the data being placed within them. In order to have numbers and dates be searchable as their intended class, rather than text, they need to be converted to the appropriate class.

To accomplish this, the script uses the `listFieldTypes` variable, which lists the appropriate class for each field in the same order as the `listFieldNames` variable. The code in Listing 19.5 repeats through each field in `listRecordValues` and converts it to `number` or `date` as needed.

Finally, the code in Listing 19.6 creates a new record and places a reference to it in a variable called `refRecord`. Then it creates each field and places the appropriate piece of information into it. This will be repeated for each line of data in the source file. Then the database is closed to save the imported records and the `text item delimiter` is reset to an empty string.

Listing 19.5

Loop through the current row's fields and convert numbers and dates from text to native values

```
--  Convert numbers and dates so they are not text
repeat with b from 1 to the count of listRecordValues
  set dataField to item b of listRecordValues
  if item b of listFieldTypes = "number" then set dataField to
dataField as number
  if item b of listFieldTypes = "date" then set dataField to (date
dataField)
  set item b of listRecordValues to dataField
end repeat
```

Listing 19.6

Create the new record, enter data into the fields, and terminate the repeat loop

```
tell application "Database Events"
  tell database "United States"

    --  Create a new record
    set refRecord to make new record with properties {name:item 1 of
listRecordValues}
    tell refRecord

      --  Create each field and place the value into it
      repeat with b from 1 to the count of listRecordValues
        set nameField to item b of listFieldNames
        set dataField to item b of listRecordValues
        make new field with properties {name:nameField,
value:dataField}
      end repeat
    end tell
    close
  end tell
end tell

end repeat
--  reset text item delimiters
set text item delimiters to {"" }
```

Summary

In this chapter you learned about the Database Events application and how it enables AppleScript to create and manipulate robust databases of information. Also, you learned how to create a script to import a tab-delimited text file into a newly constructed database.

Working with System Events

*S*ystem Events is a faceless, background application that makes many Macintosh Operating System (Mac OS) X features scriptable. It contains 23 suites of commands that extend AppleScript's reach into many system preference settings. System Events also enables a developer to access the user interface elements of any application, including those that do not provide any scriptable dictionary of commands.

Introduction to System Events

System Events is an application; thus all commands sent to it must be placed within a `tell application` statement, like this:

```
tell application "System Events"
  -- custom commands here
end tell
```

To get started with System Events, open the Script Editor and select Library from the Window menu. Double-click System Events to see the library of commands shown in Figure 20.1. If it is not available in the Library window, click the Add button and navigate to the application, which is located in the `/System/Library/CoreServices/` folder.

NOTE

Many of the suites of commands provided by the System Events application are not practical from a business automation point of view and are not covered extensively in this chapter. The most practical suite is the Process suite, which enables a script to send commands directly to interface elements of applications that do not possess an AppleScript dictionary.

Figure 20.1

The System Events library of commands

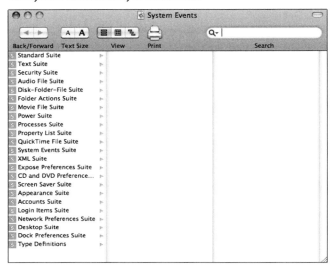

Getting started with basic functionality

Before you begin working with the suite of commands available, it's a good idea to review some basic functions of the System Events application.

Launching the System Events application

System Events automatically launches whenever a command is sent to it with the `tell application` command. However, like any other Mac OS X application, it can be launched explicitly with either the `activate` or the `launch` command. For example:

```
tell application "System Events"
   activate
end tell
```

When issued, these commands launch the application, but there is no visible indication of their success. Because System Events does not have an interface, it does not come forward like other applications.

A script can check if the application is currently running by checking the active processes, as shown in the following script:

```
tell application "Finder"
   "System Events" is in (the name of every process)
end tell
```

The result will be a `true` or `false` value, indicating the status of System Events.

Quitting the System Events application

While there is no harm in keeping System Events running, it is a good practice to close the application when a script is finished unless it will be accessed continuously. As with any other application, you do this with the `quit` command, as shown here:

```
tell application "System Events"
  quit
end tell
```

Exploring the suites of commands

System Events includes a wide range of command suites, ranging from "neat" to "useful." These commands enable a script to manipulate user accounts, the system's appearance, dock preferences, login items, property list files, computer power, and screen saver options, to name a few.

Accounts suite

The Accounts suite of commands enables AppleScript to access values for the user accounts installed a computer. A script can get a list of the name of every user account on a computer, as shown in this example:

```
tell application "System Events"
  return name of every user
  --  results = {"mm-home", "mm-work"}
end tell
```

A script can also get the name of the current user, as shown in this example:

```
tell application "System Events"
  name of current user
  --  results = "mm-work"
end tell
```

Each user account has several accessible properties. This includes the name, full name, home directory path, and picture path of the user's image. This script shows how to access each of these properties:

```
tell application "System Events"
  tell current user
    name -- result = "mmunro"
    full name -- result = "Mark Munro"
    home directory -- result = file "Macintosh HD:Users:mmunro:"
    picture path -- result = file "Macintosh HD:Library:User
   Pictures:Nature:Lightning.tif"
  end tell
end tell
```

Of these preferences, only the picture path is editable. You can set it to any image path of your choice, as shown here:

```
tell application "System Events"
  tell current user
    set picture path to file "Macintosh HD:Library:User
    Pictures:Nature:Lightning.tif"
  end tell
end tell
```

Appearance suite

The Appearance suite of commands enables AppleScript to get and set values that are available in the Appearance preferences panel.

This example shows how to access the current setting of several available values in the Appearance suite:

```
tell application "System Events"
  tell appearance preferences
    appearance -- result = blue
    double click minimizes -- result = true
    recent applications limit -- result = 10
    recent documents limit -- result = 10
    recent servers limit -- result = 10
    scroll arrow placement -- result = top and bottom
  end tell
end tell
```

Each of these properties can be modified, as shown here:

```
tell application "System Events"
  tell appearance preferences
    set recent documents limit to 100
  end tell
end tell
```

Dock Preferences suite

The Dock Preferences suite of commands provides a script with access to dock preferences. This example demonstrates how to get the current settings of the dock preferences:

```
tell application "System Events"
  minimize effect of dock preferences
  -- result = genie

  magnification size of dock preferences
  -- result = 1.017857193947

  dock size of dock preferences
  -- result = 0.296296298504
```

```
   autohide of dock preferences
   -- result = true

   animate of dock preferences
   -- result = false

   magnification of dock preferences
   -- result = false

   screen edge of dock preferences
   -- result = bottom
end tell
```

Each of these properties can be modified with a script. This example demonstrates how to change three properties:

```
tell application "System Events"
  tell dock preferences
    set animate to true
    set dock size to 0.8
    set screen edge to right
  end tell
end tell
```

Login Items suite

The Login Items suite of commands enables a script to access, create, and delete login items. A script can get a list of the names of every login item, as shown here:

```
tell application "System Events"
  name of every login item
  -- result = {"AirPort Base Station Agent", "iTunesHelper"}
end tell
```

This example shows how a script can get the properties of a specific login item:

```
tell application "System Events"
  properties of login item "iTunesHelper"
  -- result = {name:"iTunesHelper", path:"/Applications/iTunes.
   app/Contents/Resources/iTunesHelper.app", class:login item,
   kind:"Application", hidden:true}
end tell
```

Before creating a new login item, a script should check to see if it is already a login item. This example checks to see if the Calculator is currently a login item:

```
tell application "System Events"
  login item "Calculator" exists -- false
end tell
```

To create a login item, a script must first convert the path to the item to a POSIX (Portable Operating System Interface for Unix) path. Then it can use the `make` command to create the new login item, as shown here:

```
set pathToItem to (choose file) as string -- choose the
   calculator
set pathToItem to POSIX path of pathToItem
tell application "System Events"
  make new login item at end with properties {path:pathToItem,
  hidden:false}
  the name of every login item
  -- result = {"AirPort Base Station Agent", "iTunesHelper",
  "Calculator"}
end tell
```

CROSS-REF

See Chapter 10 for more information about POSIX paths.

To delete an item, a script uses the `delete` command:

```
tell application "System Events"
  delete login item "Calculator"
  the name of every login item
  -- result = {"AirPort Base Station Agent", "iTunesHelper"}
end tell
```

Property List suite

The Property List suite of commands enables a script to read any property list file on a computer. A property list file is an XML file (Mac OS 10.3.9 and earlier) or binary file (Mac OS 10.4 and later) that is used to store preferences, application information, and other data in a quick and easy-to-read format. They carry a filename extension of `plist` and are often referred to as *plist files*.

Property lists are made up of key-value relationships in which a key, or field name, is associated with a value. A script can get the name of every property list item in the file, as shown here:

```
set pathToFile to "Macintosh HD:Library:Preferences:com.apple.
   SoftwareUpdate.plist"
tell application "System Events"
  tell property list file pathToFile
    return name of every property list item
    -- result = {"LastSuccessfulDate", "LastAttemptDate",
    "LastResultCode"}
  end tell
end tell
```

The previous example returns the three items in the Software Update application's preference property list file. Using the names of the entries, the script can read the value stored relative to a field. In this example, the value in the field named `LastSuccessfulDate` is accessed:

```
tell application "System Events"
  tell property list file pathToFile
    value of property list item "LastSuccessfulDate"
    -- result = date "Friday, October 9, 2009 9:21:14 AM"
  end tell
end tell
```

Reading property lists enables scripts to directly access data relating to other applications without having to launch the application. Some preference information may not be accessible directly through the application, so this suite provides a method to access information that many not be otherwise accessible.

Power suite

The Power suite of commands enables AppleScript to control the fundamental state of a computer. It can log out the current user, put the system into sleep mode, and restart and shut down the computer.

This example shows how to restart a computer with a script:

```
tell application "System Events"
  restart
end tell
```

CAUTION

The Power suite of commands can be useful if you have an automation server that runs constantly and you want to restart it periodically as a preventative measure. However, be sure your scripts can launch and process correctly after an unmanned reboot. Also, a script should always take care to check and close documents that might have unsaved changes or you may find your script timed out while waiting for a "Do you want to save changes" dialog.

Screen Saver suite

One of the more impractical but fun suites of commands, the Screen Saver suite gives AppleScript direct control the screen saver preferences of Mac OS X. It enables a script to start and stop a specific screen saver as well as access and control preference settings.

This example demonstrates how to get a list of the names of every available screen saver:

```
tell application "System Events"
  the name of every screen saver
  -- result = {"Cosmos", "Flurry", "FloatingMessage", "Abstract",
   "Arabesque", "Forest", "iTunes Artwork", "Computer Name",
   "Nature Patterns", "RSS Visualizer", "Beach", "Shell",
   "Spectrum", "Word of the Day", "Paper Shadow", "Random",
   "screensaver.shuffle"}
end tell
```

Each screen saver has five properties, which can be accessed as follows:

```
tell application "System Events"
  return properties of screen saver "Forest"
  -- result = {path:file "Macintosh HD:System:Library:Screen
   Savers:Forest.slideSaver:", displayed name:"Forest",
   class:screen saver, picture display style:missing value,
   name:"Forest"}
end tell
```

Only the `picture display style` property is editable. It can be set to `slideshow`, `collage`, or `mosaic`. For example:

```
tell application "System Events"
  set the picture display style of screen saver "Forest" to
   slideshow
end tell
```

Four settings in the Screen Saver preference panel can be accessed and modified with AppleScript. These include `show clock`, `running`, `main screen only`, and `delay interval`. The following example shows how to access the current settings of each preference:

```
tell application "System Events"
  tell screen saver preferences
    show clock -- result = false
    running -- result = false
    main screen only -- result = false
    delay interval -- result = 1200
  end tell
end tell
```

N O T E
The `running` property is a read-only setting that indicates if the screen saver in question is currently running or not.

To modify the settings, use the `set` command as shown in this example:

```
tell application "System Events"
  tell screen saver preferences
    set show clock to true
    set main screen only to false
    set delay interval to 1500
  end tell
end tell
```

You can start and stop any installed screen saver using the `start` and `stop` commands. After starting one screen saver, you have to stop it before another one will start. This example will run the "Cosmos" screen saver for five seconds and then stop it to run the Beach screen saver for five seconds:

```
tell application "System Events"
  tell screen saver "Cosmos" to start
  delay 5
  tell screen saver "Cosmos" to stop
  tell screen saver "Beach" to start
  delay 5
  tell screen saver "Beach" to stop
end tell
```

Controlling Non-Scriptable Applications

In spite of AppleScript's pervasive existence throughout Mac OS X and virtually every popular third-party application, there will always be some function in some application that is not directly scriptable. Eventually, you will encounter a need to automate a task that does not have a scriptable class or command available. The Process suite of commands in the System Events application solves this problem by enabling a script to simulate mouse clicks and keyboard activity as well as access any interface object in any application. Essentially, User Interface (UI) Scripting makes non-scriptable applications scriptable.

 UI Scripting is based on the Mac OS X accessibility framework. It was introduced with Mac OS X 10.2 and is intended to make Mac computers accessible to users with disabilities. While it can only interact with applications that include support for this framework, most applications today are able to respond to UI Scripting commands.

 CAUTION

Use UI Scripting as a last resort after exhausting all other automation possibilities. Although it is usually a stable and useful method of automating an application, UI Scripting can be quirky in some cases. Take extra care to thoroughly test a solution with realistic workloads.

Enabling User Interface Scripting

To use UI Scripting, it is important that the Enable access for assistive devices check box in the Universal Access preferences panel is selected, as shown in Figure 20.2. A script can check the status of this preference by accessing the UI elements enabled setting of System Events as shown in the following code:

```
tell application "System Events"
  UI elements enabled — result = true
end tell
```

If result of this script is `true`, UI Scripting is enabled. If it is `false`, any attempt to automate the UI will result in an error.

Figure 20.2

The Enable access for assistive devices check box is selected, which makes UI Scripting possible.

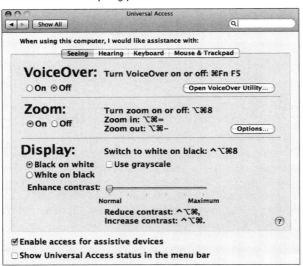

Any script that uses UI Scripting should check that the preference is enabled immediately at launch. While it is possible to enable the setting with a script, this change will require administrative privileges, and the context in which the script will be used must be taken into account. Often, it is safer and less confusing to have the script simply notify the user that the setting needs to be enabled and, perhaps, ask the user if he wants to automatically enable it. The script shown in Listing 20.1 demonstrates code that can be used at the beginning of any script that requires UI Scripting.

Listing 20.1

Enabling UI Scripting automatically

```
tell application "System Events"
  set blnEnabled to UI elements enabled
end tell
if blnEnabled = false then
  set textMessage to "Assistive devices are disabled in the Universal
  Access preference and are required by this script. Would you like to
  automatically enable this feature?"
  set dataResults to (display alert "UI Scripting Disabled" message
  textMessage as critical buttons {"Cancel", "Enable"} default button 2
  cancel button 1)
```

```
  if button returned of dataResults = "Cancel" then return
  tell application "System Events"
    set UI elements enabled to true
  end tell
end if
```

NOTE

The code in Listing 20.1 is available for download from the book's Web site at www.wileydevreference.com.

Activating and targeting applications

The application that will be the target of the UI commands must be brought to the front. Once there, all statements must be contained inside of a `tell process "«application»"` command inside of a `tell application "System Events"` command as shown here:

```
tell application "Generic Application"
  activate
end tell
tell application "System Events"
  tell process "Generic Application"
    -- UI commands
  end tell
end tell
```

In this way, commands are routed to the desired application by the System Events application. Any UI Scripting commands outside of the two nested `tell` statements will not properly reference the target application's interface and will cause an error and may not compile.

NOTE

The Generic Application is a non-functional, non-scriptable application with several interface widgets to help demonstrate UI Scripting. Although the application has three command suites (Standard, Text, and Type Definitions), they are default commands that appear in all application. No custom AppleScript support has been added.

Most of the examples in this section use the Generic Application to demonstrate various features of UI Scripting. To save space, the activation code that follows is not included in every example, but is required for the application to function:

```
tell application "Generic Application"
  activate
end tell
```

Referencing objects in an application's interface

When working with UI Scripting, the most important step is to correctly identify and refer to objects within an application's user interface. Unfortunately, unlike learning to work with a new scriptable application, there is no dictionary or user guide to help you. Figuring out how objects relate to each other and how to refer to them can be a challenge. The System Events dictionary contains information about the commands it can perform, not the various applications that might contain objects being targeted.

For example, suppose a script needs to select a Print menu item of the File menu in an application. Using the `click menu item` command from the System Events dictionary, you might expect to be able to click the menu like this:

```
tell application "System Events"
  tell process "Generic Application"
    click menu item "Print" of menu "File"
  end tell
end tell
```

Often, however, the correct method of selecting a menu requires referencing one or more unseen objects in the hierarchy, as shown here:

```
tell application "System Events"
  tell process "Generic Application"
    click menu item "Print…" of menu 1 of menu bar item "File" of
  menu bar 1
  end tell
end tell
```

This issue becomes more pronounced when a script references objects in a complex multilayer or dynamically generated interface. You may see a button in a window, but the script must have foreknowledge of the entire interface structure and include every item in an object's hierarchy as this relatively simple example shows:

```
tell application "System Events"
  tell process "Generic Application"
    click button "Hello"  of splitter group 1 of window "Generic
  Application"
  end tell
end tell
```

Trying to dig into the application's package might shed light on the hierarchical confusion, but it can often add to your frustration and can be rather tedious. Fortunately there is a solution: UI

Browser from PreFab Software. This application can help you identify and build references to an object within any application's interface.

Using PreFab Software's UI Browser application

The UI Browser application, shown in Figure 20.3, provides a simple interface that enables you to visually explore and identify interface elements within any open application. It will even build a line of code for you, which you can often use with little or no modifications.

Figure 20.3

The UI Browser window

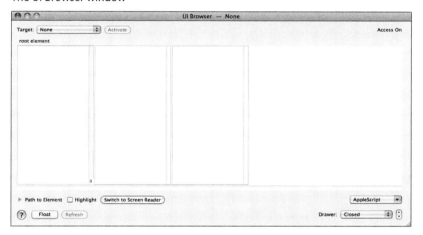

Once you launch the UI Browser, you can select a target application from the popup menu in the upper-left corner. You can then browse the object hierarchy of any application object contained within documents, dialog boxes, menus, and windows. Selecting the Highlight check box in the lower left of the interface superimposes a yellow highlight box around the object you are selecting, making it impossible to choose the wrong item. Figure 20.4 shows a text field from the Generic Application's interface selected in the UI Browser.

To instruct the browser to write a piece of code that will manipulate or access the selected object, choose an option from the AppleScript popup menu in the lower right of the UI Browser's interface. The AppleScript popup menu is shown in Figure 20.5. Choosing Set Value of Selected Element from this menu opens a window with the line of code shown in Figure 20.6.

Figure 20.4

The UI Browser window with an interface object in the Generic Application's interface selected

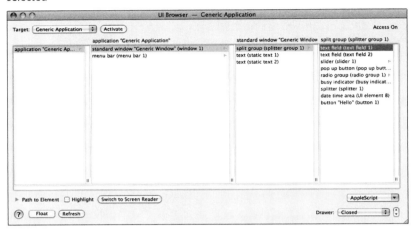

Figure 20.5

The UI Browser's AppleScript popup menu offers options for automatically generating code to perform UI actions.

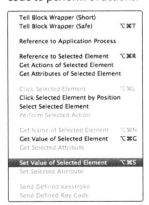

Figure 20.6

The code suggested by the UI Browser for setting the value of a text field in the interface of the Generic Application

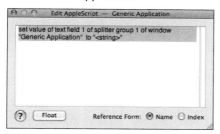

Place the suggested code into the `tell application` statement targeting the Generic Application and replace the "`<string>`" placeholder with "`Hello World`", as shown here:

```
tell application "Generic Application"
  activate
end tell
tell application "System Events"
  tell process "Generic Window"
    set value of text field 1 of splitter group 1 of window
    "Generic Application" to "Hello World!"
  end tell
end tell
```

Running this script should enter the text "Hello World!" into the text field in the Generic Application's interface, as shown in Figure 20.7.

NOTE

If an interface object has a name, that name can be used in place of a numeric reference.

When sending several commands to the same window or split view, you can convert the single line of code to a hierarchical structure, as shown here:

```
tell application "System Events"
  tell process "Generic Application"
    tell window "Generic Window"
      tell splitter group 1
```

```
        set value of text field 1 to "Hello World!"
        -- additional commands here
      end tell
    end tell
  end tell
end tell
```

NOTE

Visit PreFab Software's Web site to learn more about the UI Browser application at
`http://prefabsoftware.com`.

Figure 20.7

The phrase Hello World! entered into the Generic
Application's interface

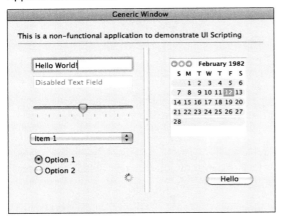

Accessing information from an interface

UI Scripting enables a script to access various information about an object, including its value,
its enabled or disabled status, whether it exists, and its name.

Value of interface elements

A script can get the value of various interface elements including fields, pop-up menus, date
time areas, and more. The class of the result will depend on the class of data contained by the
specified object. This example shows a script accessing the values of three different interface
object types:

```
tell application "System Events"
  tell process "Generic Application"
    tell window "Generic Window"
      tell splitter group 1
        get value of text field 1
        -- result = "Hello World!"

        get value of pop up button 1
        -- result = "Item 1"

        get value of UI element 8
        -- result = date "Friday, February 12, 1982 11:00:00 AM"
      end tell
    end tell
  end tell
end tell
```

Scripts can also modify the value of objects in the interface of an application. The class of the new value must be appropriate for the object whose value is being modified. This example illustrates a script that sets a date time object's value to January 1, 2010. The result of this command is shown in Figure 20.8.

```
set dateToSet to date "Friday, January 1, 2010 12:00:00 AM"
tell application "System Events"
  tell process "Generic Application"
    tell window "Generic Window"
      tell splitter group 1
        set value of UI element 8 to dateToSet
      end tell
    end tell
  end tell
end tell
```

Figure 20.8

The Generic Application's date time object after the date was set to January 1, 2010, by a script

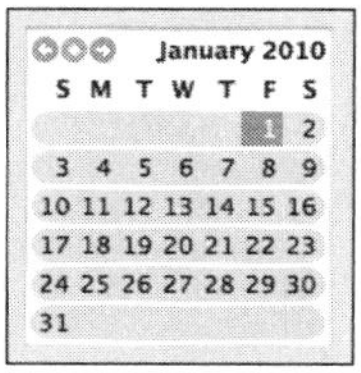

Remember that any UI object a user can modify should be modifiable with System Events. This example shows how to change the value of the slider object in the Generic Application's interface:

```
tell application "System Events"
  tell process "Generic Application"
    tell window "Generic Window"
      set value of value indicator 1 of slider 1 to 15
    end tell
  end tell
end tell
```

Enabled status

Clicking a disabled button, or simulating keystrokes within a disabled object, in an interface generates an error. To avoid this, System Events allows a script to check the enabled status of any object. The result of the inquiry will be a boolean value indicating if the object is enabled or not. This portion of a script shows an example, checking to see if a text field in enabled before modifying its value:

```
if enabled of text field 1 is true then
  set value of text field 1 to "Hello World!"
end if
```

The enabled property applies to every object, including menu items. This example shows how to check the status of the Save As menu of the Generic Application:

```
tell application "System Events"
  tell process "Generic Application"
    tell menu bar 1
      tell menu bar item "File"
        tell menu 1
          get enabled of menu item "Save As…"
          -- result = false
        end tell
      end tell
    end tell
  end tell
end tell
```

The existence of interface elements

Checking for the existence of interface elements can help a script detect and dismiss an unwelcome dialog box or determine when a progress window disappears indicating that a vital process has finished. The result of the inquiry will be a boolean value indicating whether the object exists. This example checks to see if a window named "Generic Window" exists:

```
tell application "System Events"
  tell process "Generic Application"
    window "Generic Window" exists
    -- result = true
  end tell
end tell
```

When a window can't be identified by name, your script can check for the existence of a button by name to help identify the window and, therefore, conditionally decide which button to click. This example checks for the existence of a button named "Hello" on the window in the Generic Application:

```
tell application "System Events"
  tell process "Generic Application"
    tell window "Generic Window"
      tell splitter group 1
        button "Hello" exists
        -- result = true
      end tell
    end tell
  end tell
end tell
```

Object name

When a script determines the name of an object, such as a window, it gains vital information when more than one interface option is available. This script demonstrates how to get the name of a window:

```
tell application "System Events"
  tell process "Generic Application"
    name of window 1
    -- result = "Generic Window"
  end tell
end tell
```

A button's name will be the same as the text displayed within it, as shown in this script:

```
tell application "System Events"
  tell process "Generic Application"
    name of button 1 of splitter group 1 of window 1
    -- result = "Hello"
  end tell
end tell
```

The name of a label or static piece of text will also be the text content it contains. For example, UI element 2 of the Generic Application's window is the text running across the top:

```
tell application "System Events"
  tell process "Generic Application"
    name of UI element 2 of window 1
    -- result = "This is a non-functional application to
  demonstrate UI Scripting"
  end tell
end tell
```

Performing User Interface Scripting actions

The full power of UI Scripting is discovered when performing actions in the interface of an application. Four commands are available: `click`, `keystroke`, `perform`, and `select`.

Click command

The `click` command enables a script to simulate a mouse click on interface elements as if the user were performing them. This is useful when dismissing errant dialog boxes, saving or cancelling a Save dialog box, and selecting a specific radio button. This script demonstrates a click-based selection of the second option of the radio button and a click on the (non-functional) "Hello" button:

```
tell application "System Events"
  tell process "Generic Application"
    tell window "Generic Window"
      tell splitter group 1
        click radio button "Option 2" of radio group 1
        click button "Hello"
      end tell
    end tell
  end tell
end tell
```

TIP

Don't use the `click` command to change object's value if those values can be changed directly, as shown in the previous section.

You can use the `click` command to select menu items. To print the Generic Application's window, this script clicks the Print menu item from the File menu:

```
tell application "System Events"
  tell process "Generic Application"
    tell menu bar 1
      tell menu bar item "File"
        tell menu 1
          click menu item "Print…"
        end tell
      end tell
```

```
        end tell
      end tell
    end tell
```

NOTE

The `click` command can click an item based on its position by specifying x, y coordinates after the command like this: `click at {numX, numY}`. This feature has elevated levels of risk associated with it and you should only use it for desperate situations where it is impossible to click the value by name or ID.

Keystroke command

The `keystroke` command enables a script to simulate keystrokes in an interface as if a user were typing. This includes both "regular" typing and key command combinations. Often, when scripting Save dialog boxes, the entire process can be performed with only the `keystroke` command although, in some cases, it can be used in combination with other commands.

This script types the phrase "Hello World!" into the first text field in the window of the Generic Application:

```
tell application "System Events"
  tell process "Generic Application"
    tell window 1
      keystroke "Hello World!"
    end tell
  end tell
end tell
```

NOTE

The split view and text field are not included in the hierarchy of the previous script because it is the only field capable of keyboard input and is, therefore, automatically selected. If more fields were available, the script would need to specify which one is to receive the input.

To perform key commands, a `using` clause is included after the `keystroke` command. The clause must "use" at least one key but can include any combination of `command`, `control`, `option`, and `shift`. This statement opens the Print dialog box much the same as selecting Print from the File menu or typing P while holding down the command key:

```
keystroke "P" using command down
```

When a script is combining multiple keys, they are placed in a list. This statement will select the Paste and match Style command from the Edit menu by key command:

```
keystroke "V" using {command down, option down, shift down}
```

Preview is a very useful application, but it is not scriptable. The script in Listing 20.2 saves an open document using five keystroke commands. The `delay` commands are not always required, but are a good way to insure that the script doesn't move faster than the interface.

Listing 20.2

Saving a document to the desktop named "Hello World"

```
tell application "Preview"
  activate
end tell
tell application "System Events"
  tell process "Preview"
    keystroke "S" using {command down, shift down}
    delay 0.5
    keystroke "D" using command down
    delay 0.5
    keystroke "Hello World"
    delay 0.5
    keystroke return
    delay 0.5
    keystroke "W" using command down
  end tell
end tell
```

NOTE

The code in Listing 20.2 is available for download from the book's Web site at www.wileydevreference.com.

TIP

When you use the keystroke command to save files, the desktop is a good temporary location because it can be navigated to with a key command (press D while holding the Command key down). The script can then use the tell application command to instruct the Finder to move the item to its appropriate location. To avoid file-naming conflicts with other items on the desktop, add an obscure prefix to the name or convert portions of the date and time to formulate a temporary name for the file while it resides on the desktop.

Perform command

The perform command enables a script to perform any function that is connected to an interface object. When a user manually selects a pop-up menu item, a corresponding action is performed. However, when a script sets the current value of that same pop-up menu, the action is not performed unless the perform command is explicitly issued.

Select command

The select command enables a script to select an interface item as it would if a user had made a selection. For example, a script might select a text field before using the keystroke command.

Creating a Zipped Archive File with System Events

Using the System Events Process suite to create a zipped archive of a file or folder is a great real-world example of the value of UI Scripting. The script in Listing 20.3 assumes the desktop contains a folder called Hello World. It starts by setting up variables for the path to the desktop folder, the name of the folder, and a path to the folder. These variables can be modified to point to any file or folder on the computer. However, the selection must be moved to the desktop (by a human or the script) in order for it to be compressed with the remaining portion of the script.

Next, it activates the Archive Utility, which is located in /System/Library/ CoreServices/. Then System Events takes over and uses UI Scripting to instruct the Archive Utility application to create an archive of that folder and its contents.

Then the script selects the Create Archive menu item from the File menu. This opens a dialog box asking for a selection. The key command for the desktop is typed using the keystroke command, which refreshes the folder displayed in the dialog box. The next step again uses the keystroke command to select the file from the list of items residing on the desktop. This is much the same as you might skip down a long list of files by typing the first few characters of the desired item.

Finally, the script types the return keystroke, which presses the default Archive button. The script uses a repeat loop to wait until the progress window called Archive Utility disappears, indicating that the archive is complete. Then it builds a path to the new archive file on the desktop and instructs the Finder to reveal it.

Listing 20.3

Creating a zipped archive of a folder named "Hello World"

```
-- Get the path and name of an item on the desktop
set pathToDesktop to path to desktop folder as string
set nameItem to "Hello World"
set pathToArchive to pathToDesktop & nameItem & ":" as string
--  Activate the Archive Utility application
tell application "Archive Utility"
  activate
end tell
--  Zip the folder using UI Scripting
tell application "System Events"
  tell process "Archive Utility"
    delay 1
    click menu item "Create Archive…" of menu 1 of menu bar item "File"
  of menu bar 1
    delay 1
```

continued

Listing 20.3   *(continued)*

```
    keystroke "D" using command down
    delay 1
    keystroke nameItem
    delay 1
    keystroke return
    repeat while (window "Archive Utility" exists)
      delay 1
    end repeat
  end tell
end tell
set pathToZipFile to pathToDesktop & nameItem & ".cpgz" as string
tell application "Finder"
  reveal file pathToZipFile
end tell
-- result = "Macintosh HD:Users:mmunro:Desktop:Hello World.cpgz"
```

N O T E

The code in Listing 20.3 is available for download from the book's Web site at www.wileydevreference.com.

Summary

In this chapter you learned about the System Events application and many of its suites of commands that are used to control system preferences and applications. The Process suite, which makes it possible to control non-scriptable applications, was also discussed.

Using Subroutines and Open-Ended Programming

Using Subroutines for Non-Linear Programming

on-Linear Programming refers to the execution of code in a sequence other than that in which it is arranged in a script file. Prior to this chapter, all code examples have been linear, with each line executing one after the other in the order in which they were written in a script document.

AppleScript uses subroutines to enable code to execute in a non-linear fashion. A *subroutine* is a collection of AppleScript statements that can be executed from one or more locations within a script. Although subroutines exist in the same document as a script, their code will not be executed as part of the script flow unless that script includes a *subroutine call,* which is an instance of the subroutine name, plus any required parameters.

When a script reaches the line of code that contains the subroutine call, it immediately skips to the subroutine and executes its code before returning to the line beneath the call, where it continues executing any remaining code in a linear fashion. This process is illustrated in Figure 21.1.

If the primary code does not include a call to the subroutine, the code within the subroutine will not be executed, even though it exists in the same script file, as illustrated in Figure 21.2.

NOTE
Subroutines are sometimes referred to as "handlers" because they handle a subset of script functions.

Figure 21.1

A flowchart showing a non-linear script flow with a subroutine

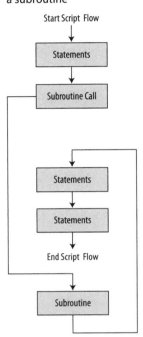

Subroutines play an increasingly important role as scripts grow; they reduce repetition and break code into more manageable chunks. Randomly chopping up lines of code, however, does not guarantee an efficient code structure. A developer must understand the importance and benefits of subroutines when creating a non-linear solution so that his solution takes full advantage of the benefits of subroutines without introducing excessive code.

Figure 21.2
A flow chart
showing a script
flow without a
call to a subroutine

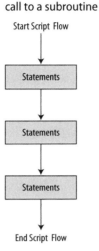

Working with Subroutines

You can identify a subroutine because it begins with the keyword on and ends with the key-word end. Each keyword is followed by the name of the subroutine. An open and close paren-thesis appears on the first line immediately after the subroutine name. Here is the formula of a subroutine:

```
On «subroutine name»()
    --  subroutine code
end «subroutine name»
```

NOTE
AppleScript automatically indents the lines of code between the on and end lines to create a visual cue of which lines are enclosed within the subroutine.

This example shows a subroutine named `helloWorldSubroutine` that will display a "Hello World" dialog box:

```
on helloWorldSubroutine()
   display dialog "Hello World"
end helloWorldSubroutine
```

As it stands, if the previous example is placed into a script document and that script was run, nothing will happen. In order for the code within a subroutine to be executed, code located elsewhere in the script must instruct the subroutine to run. A *subroutine call* is a line of code that includes the name of a subroutine, by itself or with other code, and instructs the script to execute the specified subroutine code before executing any remaining statements that appear after the call.

The following code shows a call to the subroutine from the previous example. If this code is placed within the same script document as that example, the subroutine will execute and the "Hello World" dialog message will appear:

```
helloWorldSubroutine()
```

To understand the space-saving power of a subroutine, place two calls to the subroutine like the one shown here:

```
helloWorldSubroutine()
helloWorldSubroutine()
on helloWorldSubroutine()
   display dialog "Hello World"
end helloWorldSubroutine
```

Although the `display dialog` statement is only included once in the subroutine, it will execute twice, once for each call.

Calling a subroutine from a tell application statement

All of the code within a `tell application` statement is directed to a specific application; therefore, a subroutine call placed there will not execute because the application has no knowledge of any other part of the script. This example shows a subroutine call contained within a `tell application` "Finder" statement that cannot execute the subroutine:

```
tell application "Finder"
  myFirstSubroutine()
  -- result = error "Finder got an error: Can't continue
   myFirstSubroutine." number -1708
end tell
on myFirstSubroutine()
   display dialog "Hello World"
end myFirstSubroutine
```

The subroutine call requires extra instruction to route the command out of the `tell` command and back to the script. You accomplished this by using the `of me` or `my` keywords. These keywords always refer to the script. The following example returns the entire script object as the result:

```
me -- result = «script»
```

Adding the `of me` or `my` keywords to the end of a subroutine call that exists within a `tell application` command will successfully route the command to the subroutine. Likewise, adding `tell me to` in front of the subroutine call will accomplish the same result. This example shows both keywords used to call the same subroutine:

```
tell application "Finder"
  myFirstSubroutine() of me
  my myFirstSubroutine()
  tell me to myFirstSubroutine()
end tell
```

CROSS-REF
The `tell application` command is discussed in Chapter 17.

Another method around this problem is to terminate the `tell application` statement, call the subroutine, and then start a new `tell application` statement. This involves more lines of code, but it avoids any possible confusion and helps keep statements untangled.

Exchanging data with subroutines

A subroutine does not have access to the variables used by the rest of a script, including other subroutines. Likewise, the script can't access variables that are contained within any of the subroutines. This is an advantage in that it avoids conflicts between two variables with the same name. However, in order for a subroutine to function as an integrated part of a script, it needs to be able to exchange data with the rest of the script. Fortunately, AppleScript has an answer.

Sending data to a subroutine with parameters

A *subroutine parameter* is a variable that is declared in the first line of a subroutine, which will accept a value passed from the code that is calling the subroutine. A subroutine can have as many parameters as are required and they can be any class of data. Three styles are available for including parameters in a subroutine: positional, labeled, and pattern positional.

TIP
Sending a `list` or `record` into a single parameter is a good way to save horizontal space on the first line of the subroutine and on all of its calls.

Using positional parameters

Positional parameters are parameters that receive input based on their position within the parameter string. This is the most common of the three available subroutine parameter types because it is relatively easy of use and frequently appears in sample scripts and books, including this one.

The *parameter string* is one or more parameters placed between the parentheses next to the subroutine name separated by a comma. This subroutine formula includes space for two parameters:

```
On «subroutine name»(«parameter1», «parameter2»)
   --  subroutine code
end «subroutine name»
```

When a subroutine includes parameters, the calls to the subroutine must include data in the same order. These values will be automatically placed into the parameter based on its position in the string. The following example shows a "Hello World"–style subroutine with a parameter called `textMessage` that is used as the dialog message. Rather than hardcoding a specific message into the code, the subroutine can display any message sent to it:

```
on helloWorldSubroutine(textMessage)
   display dialog textMessage
end helloWorldSubroutine
```

Adding these calls to the script with the previous subroutine and executing the script will create two dialogs, each with a different message:

```
helloWorldSubroutine("Hello World")
helloWorldSubroutine("Goodbye World")
```

You can add additional parameters to the parameter string by adding a comma and the name of the new parameter. This example shows a "Hello World" subroutine that allows a parameter to specify both the text of the message and the name of the button to be specified:

```
helloWorldSubroutine("Hello World", "Hello")
helloWorldSubroutine("Goodbye World", "Goodbye")
on helloWorldSubroutine(textMessage, nameButton)
   display dialog textMessage buttons {nameButton}
end helloWorldSubroutine
```

N O T E

When a subroutine does not have any parameters, nothing is placed between the open and close parenthesis.

Using labeled parameters

Labeled parameters are subroutine parameters with labels preceding them. The labels turn a subroutine call into a statement that is less technical and reads more like English, much the same way application commands are written. A subroutine can use AppleScript-defined labels or custom labels.

T I P

Labeled parameters only benefit a developer or users who might tinker with the code. However, it is usually not worth the complexity of setting them up to resemble English. Also, if there are no parameters, a subroutine must use empty parenthesis, which mixes parameter types.

AppleScript-defined labels

When a subroutine uses an AppleScript-defined label, the subroutine name appears with a space between the name, the label, and the parameter variable. The formula for a subroutine with labeled parameters is as follows:

```
On «subroutine name» «label» «parameter1»
  --  subroutine code
end «subroutine name»
```

For each additional parameter that the subroutine accepts, an additional «label» «parameter» is added to the formula. This formula includes two labeled parameters:

```
On «subroutine name» «label» «parameter1» «label» «parameter1»
  --  subroutine code
end «subroutine name»
```

Each label can only be used once per subroutine, but you can use as many labels as required.

The AppleScript language provides a lengthy list of keywords that can be used as labels. These include: about, above, against, apart from, around, aside from, at, below, beneath, beside, between, by, for, from, instead of, into, on, onto, out of, over, since, thru (or through), and under. This assortment is intended for the most common situations.

The following simple example uses the from keyword as a label for the parameter text-ToSearch. The subroutine call sends the value Hello World!, which is placed into the parameter variable:

```
getFirstWord from "Hello World!"
-- result = "Hello"
on getFirstWord from textToSearch
  return word 1 of textToSearch
end getFirstWord
```

When a subroutine requires more than one parameter, simply add another labeled parameter. The previous example is modified as follows to use both the at and from keyword to allow a choice of which word to return:

```
getWord at 2 from "Hello World!"
-- result = "World"
on getWord at numWord from textToSearch
  return word numWord of textToSearch
end getWord
```

A subroutine can use any of the available labels, even if they don't make sense. The previous example reads like English because the subroutine name lists three words in the order you would speak them followed by a keyword and text, making the entire call read like a short sentence. The label's only purpose is to facilitate this effect. The subroutine could easily be modified to make no sense, but it would still function correctly, as in this example:

```
getWord beneath "Hello World!"
-- result = "Hello"
on getWord beneath textToSearch
  return word 1 of textToSearch
end getWord
```

This illustrates the difficulty of using labeled parameters. Making the subroutine and its labeled parameters sound right is sometimes very difficult. If that end can't be achieved consistently in every case, then the benefit of this parameter style is lost.

Custom labels

When the default labels are not appropriate, you can define your own. In this case, you must include the `given` keyword followed by a custom label-parameter combination for each parameter, as shown in this formula:

```
On «subroutine name» given «label»:«parameter»
  --  subroutine code
end «subroutine name»
```

This subroutine creates a dialog box displaying any text that is sent to it in the custom labeled parameter `thisMessage`:

```
makeDialog given thisMessage:"Hello World"
on makeDialog given thisMessage:textMessage
  display dialog textMessage
end makeDialog
```

Adding additional parameters requires a comma followed by any number of additional label-parameter combinations, as shown here:

```
makeDialog given thisMessage:"Hello World", withButton:"Yes"
on makeDialog given thisMessage:textMessage,
   withButton:nameButton
  display dialog textMessage buttons {nameButton}
end makeDialog
```

Combined labels

The benefit of using labeled parameters becomes more apparent when you are building more complex subroutines. These two subroutine calls to a hypothetical subroutine illustrate the difference. The first shows positional parameters, while the second shows the English-like use of multiple positional parameters:

```
getNumberRange(listToProcess, numAbove, numBelow, blnRounding)
getNumberRange from listToProcess above 2 below 7 with rounding
```

When using multiple labeled parameters, you can modify their order without affecting the performance of the script. This subroutine call would work just as well as the previous example:

```
getNumberRange above 2 below 7 from listToProcess with rounding
```

Using patterned positional parameters

Patterned positional parameters are positional parameters that define a pattern to match when calling the subroutine. This has the effect of showing more details about the value(s) a specific parameter expects to receive. In this example, the second parameter is a single list made up of two variables, one for each button in the dialog box:

```
makeDialog("Hello World", {"Yes", "No"})
on makeDialog(textMessage, {nameButton1, nameButton2})
  display dialog textMessage buttons {nameButton1, nameButton2}
end makeDialog
```

TIP

While this approach to parameters is intriguing for defining complex parameters, it increases the horizontal size of the subroutine's first line and can cause wrapping. It's preferable to use positional parameters with a comment defining any complex variables over this approach.

Receiving data from a subroutine

A *subroutine result* is any data returned from a subroutine, which can then be used by the remaining portions of the script that called the subroutine. While parameters enable a script to send data to a subroutine, sending a result back from the subroutine completes the circle of data exchange.

If no result is specified in your code, a default result of the last line of the subroutine will be returned as the result of the subroutine. You may have noticed this when running the "Hello World" subroutine earlier in this chapter. The result is a record with a single field: the name of the button the user clicked, as shown here:

```
helloWorldSubroutine()
-- result = {button returned:"OK"}
on helloWorldSubroutine()
  display dialog "Hello World"
end helloWorldSubroutine
```

To customize a result, simply place it at the end of the subroutine. With a couple of minor changes to the previous subroutine, this version returns only the name of the button as a text string:

```
helloWorldSubroutine()
-- result = "OK"
on helloWorldSubroutine()
  set recData to (display dialog "Hello World")
  button returned of recData
end helloWorldSubroutine
```

You can also use the `return` command before the line of code that will be returned as the result. This enables you to stop a subroutine and return a result at a point before the end of the subroutine. This permits a subroutine to react to specific situations and return control to the calling script before reaching the end of its code.

The following script demonstrates this capability. It adds, subtracts, multiplies, and divides two numbers provided as parameters along with the name of an action that should be performed. If the action parameter is `add`, the script adds the numbers and immediately returns that as the result. If the action is `multiply`, it skips the first two `if-then` statements, multiplies the numbers, and returns that as the result. The subroutine only reaches the end of its code if the value in `nameAction` is not one of the four available.

```
performMath(5, 10, "add")
-- result = 15
performMath(5, 10, "multiply")
-- result = 50
performMath(5, 10, "perform magic")
-- result = "The action 'perform magic' is not an acceptable
    value!"
on performMath(num1, num2, nameAction)
  if nameAction = "add" then return num1 + num2
  if nameAction = "subtract" then return num1 - num2
  if nameAction = "multiply" then return num1 * num2
  if nameAction = "divide" then return num1 / num2
  return "The action '" & nameAction & "' is not an acceptable
    value!"
end performMath
```

The result of a subroutine can be any class of data. This includes a single variable of any type as well as a list of any number of mixed values, and one or more records with any number of fields of data.

To use the result of a subroutine in future lines of a script, simply place the result into a variable. There are two methods to achieve this. You can add a `set «variable»` in front of the call or set a variable to `the result` on the line of code immediately following the call. Both are shown in this example:

```
set numResult to performMath(5, 10, "add")

performMath(5, 10, "add")
set numResult to the result
```

Subroutine calls can also be used in a single line `if-then` statement in two similar ways. The result of the subroutine can be placed into a variable, which is used in a formula for the `if-then` statement. However, it can also be placed directly within the formula portion of the statement, as shown here:

```
if performMath(5, 10, "add") > 10 then
  display dialog "Hello World"
end if
```

In this case, the result of the subroutine is immediately compared to see if it is greater than 10 and, thereby displays the conditional dialog. This in-line usage of subroutine calls applies to other statements such as a `repeat` statement.

Identifying command handler subroutines

A *command handler subroutine* is a subroutine that reacts to a command such as `run`, `open`, `idle`, or any other AppleScript command. Instead of being triggered by a call to the subroutine, it responds to a command being issued.

Run

The `run` command is sent to a script when the run button is clicked on a script file that is opened with the AppleScript Editor, a script application is double-clicked by a user, or a loaded script is instructed to run. An empty script document has an implicit `run` subroutine. If there is no `run` subroutine when the run button is clicked, any code not inside of another subroutine will be executed as if it were inside of one.

CROSS-REF
The `load script` command is discussed in Chapter 16.

If a `run` subroutine exists, all code not contained within other subroutines must be contained within the `on run` and `end run` statements. The following script presents a "Hello World" dialog message when the script is run, just like examples in previous chapters:

```
on run
   display dialog "Hello World!"
end run
```

NOTE
It doesn't matter whether you use an explicit or implicit `run` subroutine. However, for the sake of consistency, it is a good idea to choose one and stick with it.

Open

The `open` command is sent to a script when a user drops files or folders onto its application icon or an `open` command is issued by a piece of code.

To access the paths to the files or folders dropped on the script application, a single command parameter can be included, following the `on open` portion of the subroutine. The following script illustrates the formula of an `open` command with a `listDroppedItems` parameter:

```
on open listDroppedItems
   -- subroutine code
end open
```

When this subroutine is included in a script that is saved as an application, the icon changes from a regular application icon to a "drop" application icon, shown in Figure 21.3; this notifies the user that it will react to items that are dropped on it.

Figure 21.3

A script application icon indicating that files or folders can be dropped onto the script for processing

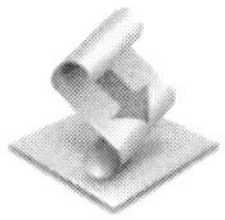

Anything dropped on the script icon will be placed into the parameter where it can be used by the script to perform tasks. The following script uses a `repeat` loop to display the path of every item that is dropped on it:

```
on open listDroppedItems
  repeat with a in listDroppedItems
    display dialog a as string
  end repeat
end open
```

A script can contain both a `run` and an `open` subroutine if desired. This can be done to facilitate testing the `open` command with the script open in the AppleScript Editor or as a convenience to the user. When the script is run, it can ask the user to select a file or folder for processing, as shown in this example:

```
on run
  set pathToFile to choose file
  open {pathToFile}
end
on open listDroppedItems
  repeat with a in listDroppedItems
    display dialog a as string
  end repeat
end open
```

Optionally, the `run` subroutine can perform a completely diverse set of functions if needed.

Idle

The `idle` command is sent to a script after a specified amount of time has passed without any script activity. When the idle time has expired, the command is sent and the subroutine code is executed. Then the script waits for the specified time before repeating this process.

TIP

Remember to select the Stay open check box in the Save dialog box so that your script doesn't quit after the first execution of the idle subroutine.

Using an `idle` command subroutine enables a script to continuously perform background tasks on a user machine or on an automation server. It can monitor folders, perform tasks on a schedule, or notify users of various events.

Using the `idle` command is as easy as using the `run` and `open` commands except that the final line of the subroutine must return the number of seconds that will pass before the command is repeated. The following script shows the formula for an idle subroutine:

```
on idle
  -- subroutine code
  return «idle time»
end idle
```

This script, when saved as a stay-open application, displays a "Hello World" dialog message every five seconds:

```
on idle
  display dialog "Hello World!"
  return 5
end idle
```

Because the `return` command can be used at different positions within the subroutine, it is possible to create a variable idle script. The amount of time required to lapse between executions of the subroutine can vary based on any criteria. This example waits twice as long on Mondays:

```
on idle
  set nameDay to day of (current date)
  if nameDay = "Monday" then return 10
  return 5
end idle
```

You also can include an equation to calculate larger time intervals:

```
return 5 * 60
```

Custom event handler subroutines

In addition to the `run`, `open`, and `idle` subroutines discussed thus far, AppleScript enables a script to intercept and override any built-in command by using an *event handler subroutine*. You accomplish this by putting `on «command»` and `end «command»` statements around the code that will substitute the built-in command.

The following example demonstrates a subroutine that will override the `current date` command. Instead of performing the built-in functionality, it will display a "Hello World" dialog message. With this code in a script, any `current date` command results in a dialog instead of returning the current date:

```
current date
on current date
   display dialog "Hello World!"
end current date
```

NOTE

While this feature will work with any command, it doesn't add anything that you can't do with a standard subroutine and, therefore, doesn't provide much in the way of practical benefit.

If you want the intercepted command to execute after your custom code, be sure to include a `continue` statement:

```
current date
on current date
   display dialog "Hello World!"
   continue current date
end current date
```

Commenting subroutines

All of the code contained within a subroutine, like any code, should be well commented. However, two additional types of comments should be added to subroutines. First, each subroutine should begin with a comment containing a single sentence that describes its general function in a clear but brief manner. Second, any complex `list` or `record` parameter should have a comment defining its structure to act as a reminder of the format of the data it contains.

This subroutine provides an example of both of these commenting recommendations:

```
on catalogProductBuild(nameDocument, recProductData)
   --   This subroutine will build a product box in a catalog
   --     recProductData = {
   --       nameCategory:"",
   --       nameItem:"",
   --       textDescription:"",
```

```
--      numPrice:"" }
--   commands here
end catalogProductBuild
```

CROSS-REF
Script comments are discussed at length in Chapter 5.

Exploring the Benefits of Subroutines

There are many positive benefits to using subroutines to organize code, and the ultimate benefit is that they make code more organized, manageable, and easier to interact with.

Easing developer tasks

A developer's primary focus should be the end-user's experience. It is critical to ensure that a script functions correctly and interacts with users in an easy-to-use and logical manner. Code-writing practices that help you, as the developer, can indirectly improve the user's experience.

Organizing code into subroutines can make a significant difference in how you interact with a script while planning, developing, testing, troubleshooting, and applying future upgrades. An improvement to any of these steps can positively affect the quality of a user's experience.

Delimiting the code structure

Like the use of comments and spaces between sections of code, subroutines help break a lengthy script into smaller, more manageable sections. This makes it easier to navigate through a script and can be compared to breaking a book into chapters, sections, paragraphs, and even sentences.

Eliminating repetition

Because a subroutine can be called many times from different parts of a script, it helps eliminate repetition that would otherwise plague a script. By removing unnecessary redundancy, the script becomes shorter in length and more manageable.

Reorganizing code

Sometimes during development, you will find that your original outline of the steps involved needs to be rearranged. A subroutine is a small, delimited group of code and you can easily move it around as needed. More important, a group of subroutine calls are significantly more portable than all the code that would be in their place within a linear script.

Dealing with complex logic

Breaking a complex problem into parts is a great way to work toward a solution. A giant, linear script rife with unruly complexity can appear to be an impossible foe. In contrast, a well-designed script that makes use of subroutines can be much easier to sort out. You can review, test, and rework each subroutine independently from the other subroutines or the primary script. Once each part works, testing them together with the entire script can be a breeze.

Handling future expansion

No matter how forward-thinking a script design might be, eventually every script will require a modification or an expansion. In fact, often a script will be developed over time, first automating a handful of simple tasks and expanding its reach slowly over time. Each step forward requires a review of what the existing script does and how best to expand it.

A well-designed modular script is much easier to expand. New subroutines can be dropped in, adding to or replacing other subroutines. You can temporarily disable one subroutine and try a new one with the option to revert the script to its original functions if problems dictate. Instead of hacking up a giant, monolithic script in a poor attempt at expansion, subroutines enable you to perform careful surgery to one portion of a script, monitoring its vital signs as you go.

Avoiding nested statements

Using subroutines to separate portions of a script that control different applications helps avoid nested `tell application` statements.

CROSS-REF

Avoiding nested `tell application` statements is discussed in Chapter 4. Controlling applications with scripts is discussed in Chapter 17.

Subroutines can also help you avoid lengthy nested `if-then` or `repeat` statements. If each level of a nested statement of either type calls one or more subroutine, it keeps the distance between the subsequent nested statements to a minimum, making the code easier to read. A script flow with large, linear conditional statements, like those illustrated in Figure 21.4, can be much easier to work with if the statements are compressed into subroutine calls, as shown in Figure 21.5.

Figure 21.4

The pattern of an `if-then` statement containing lengthy conditional statements, which should be converted into subroutines

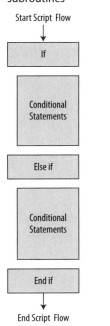

CROSS-REF

`If-then` statements are discussed in Chapter 13. The `repeat` command is discussed in Chapter 14.

Figure 21.5

A pattern of an
`if-then` statement
with conditional
subroutine calls,
reducing the vertical
height of the statement

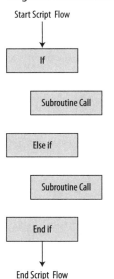

Reusing code

At some point, every AppleScript developer will encounter a situation that can benefit from previously written code. Reusing code saves time and subroutines make the coding process even more efficient.

Reusing code within a single script

This is the primary justification for using subroutines. Subroutines allow a portion of a script to be reused as many times as necessary within a single script. A subroutine containing a dozen statements can be called repeatedly using a single line of code, which greatly reduces the size of the script.

Reusing code from other scripts

Subroutines enable you to reuse code more efficiently. You can copy and paste a well-designed subroutine into a new script with ease. Because subroutines can accept input from the script calling them, they can be self-contained and very portable widgets of code.

Reducing testing requirements

While it is prudent to test every piece of a new script, subroutines that have been copied from a previously tested script are typically less prone to failure. The more code you reuse, the less time you will waste troubleshooting typos and other errors.

Allowing advanced script design

Subroutines make possible advanced script design concepts that would be otherwise impossible. Once a script is separated into several portions, it can become more open-ended and pave the way for viewing subroutines as part of a hierarchy.

Facilitating open-ended code

Because a subroutine can accept parameter-based input from, and can return data to, the line of code that calls it, it can perform functions in a more open-ended way. With the addition of a parameter and `if-then` statement, a subroutine that will save an image file as a TIFF (tagged image file format) file can be easily transformed to save an image file as any available image file type. With a little extra code, the subroutine becomes more flexible as parameters can vary from one call to the next.

CROSS-REF
Open-ended programming is discussed in Chapter 22.

Enabling a hierarchical code structure

A script without subroutines is simply a linear set of commands. Simply by breaking the code into parts, subroutines enable you to conceive and divide code into grouped hierarchical arrangements. Some subroutines can be considered "low-level" because they perform simple functions, while others can be thought of as workflow managers with several steps in between. This enables you to vary your focus from the most detailed, lowest level of development to the overall big picture with ease.

CROSS-REF
Hierarchical subroutine design is discussed in Chapter 23.

Resolving variable names conflicts

Variable names in one subroutine can't conflict with variables in other subroutines. A lengthy script without subroutines requires that each unique variable be given a unique name. If the script manages several data objects that are conceptually similar and you want them named in a uniform manner, the temptation is to name them something too long.

A linear batch of code with five variables that each contain the name of a report requires you to create five unique names. They can't all be named `nameReport`, so you might name them `nameReportSales`, `nameReportInventory`, and `nameReportContacts`. The more report variables your script contains, the greater the temptation to increase the name in length. If there are five different sales reports, `nameReportSales` might become `nameReport-SalesForAccounting` or `nameReportSalesForMarketing`, for example.

If you were to assemble, format, save, and print each report within a separate subroutine, you could name them all `nameReport` because they would not conflict with one another.

Designing a Non-Linear Script

Once you understand the benefits of using subroutines, you should take a moment to determine the best approach to designing and implementing a non-linear script. Simply chopping a script into arbitrary parts would be counter-productive and result in a disastrous mess.

The design of a non-linear script needs to follow the functional goals of developing non-linerally. It should reduce the number of lines of code in the script and make it easier to scan visually. It should make the code more manageable, with areas for expansion, while making parts reusable, flexible, and open-ended. If a subroutine structure does not accomplish at least some of these goals, it might be better off remaining a linear script.

Understanding when to delimit a script into subroutines

Deciding if a script might benefit from subroutines can be challenging. While it is impossible to posit a set of rules for every style and situation, there are a few situations that might indicate that you should use subroutines.

Obviously if any code is repeated within the script, subroutines can remove that repetition. Also, when a script grows beyond several dozen lines or has more than a dozen groups of commented code, it might be time to consider subroutines. Code with lengthy `if-then`, `repeat`, or `tell application` statements can also benefit from subroutines.

Alternatively, code that will require more than six to eight parameters or will become overly dependent on global variables should probably not be separated into subroutines.

CAUTION

Arbitrarily separating code into random subroutines can create a situation far worse than a script devoid of them. Be sure to keep the benefits of subroutines in mind. If using subroutines does not help you achieve these benefits, you might need to reorganize the subroutines or return to a linear script.

Looking at the methods of delimiting a script

When you decide that it is time to split a script into subroutines, you need to address where to make the divisions. You should consider several general methods before deciding how to structure your code.

By reuse

Separating code based on its capability to be reused is one of the easiest ways to get started using subroutines. Whenever a batch of code seems like a good candidate for reuse in other scripts, move it into a subroutine. Doing so makes it portable immediately because a subroutine is a self-contained unit you can easily graft into any script.

By application

You can split code that controls multiple applications into subroutines along application lines. Each batch of subroutines then performs functions in a specific application. For example, a group of subroutines could perform Finder tasks while another controls FileMaker Pro. Keeping each application's function clearly separated from one another helps you avoid nesting multiple `tell application` statements.

TIP

Adding comments to groups of statements is a great way to begin thinking about organizing and delimiting code into subroutines.

By function

Dividing code by function is another good option. One subroutine can extract data from a database while others process the data and place it into a page layout program.

By hierarchical position

If you view code as part of a hierarchy of commands, natural division lines will become more apparent. For example, some code might perform specific commands while other code might sit above it, acting as a manager. The more complex and lengthy the code, the more steps there will be in the hierarchy.

CROSS-REF

Learn about arranging subroutines into a hierarchical structure in Chapter 23.

Summary

In this chapter you learned about subroutines and the advantages of non-linear programming. You also learned how to identify situations that could benefit from subroutines and methods of delimiting a script into subroutines.

Introduction to Open-Ended Programming

S omething is considered *open-ended* if it allows for or is adaptable to change. A computer is the ultimate open-ended piece of hardware. If you are not sure why, just compare its feature set to a pocket calculator. A computer can be "taught" new functionality with every software install or upgrade, turning it into an ever expanding, multifunctional machine. It can edit video, record audio, manage pictures, process words, crunch numbers, create pages, send correspondence, transmit files, organize information, manage data, and any number of other functions you can imagine.

Operating systems are integral to the flexibility of computers. They support the fundamental functionality other software runs. AppleScript is a form of open-ended software that enables a user to customize third-party applications so they provide even more specialized functionality.

While you are learning to use the AppleScript language or when you are exploring an application's dictionary for the first time, most of your code will focus on very specific tasks. At the beginning, a "just make it work" philosophy is justified. However, at some point, you will want to begin making your scripts more open-ended to maximize their adaptive nature and expandability.

Open-ended programming is a method of writing code that anticipates and adapts to changes within its environment or can be expanded without significant retooling.

Not every script can or should be made more flexible. Small or narrowly focused scripts don't benefit enough to justify spending additional development time to make them more flexible. However, as a script grows in size, becomes more complex, and plays a critical role in a given workflow, a little extra attention to future changes can be extremely advantageous.

In This Chapter

Exploring open-ended script development

Looking at the benefits of flexible programming

Designing an open-ended script and subroutine

Building an open-ended image batch processor

Understanding the Benefits of Open-Ended Code

In technology and business, nothing is eternal. Hardware upgrades often require software upgrades while software upgrades can require better hardware. With each version of an operating system, new features appear and old ones are phased out or improved. Third-party software requires upgrades to stay relevant and offer new features, which in turn ensures customer loyalty. On top of all this technological turmoil, businesses change logos, styles, templates, business rules, page layout designs, Web site designs, and more. In short, change is everywhere and constantly trying to force your script into obsolescence. A script designed to anticipate change will be more flexible and, therefore, more viable over a longer period of time.

It is not possible to anticipate and include every possible scenario and that is not the meaning or intent of making something open-ended. Instead, using a handful of simple techniques can make even the most unexpected change much easier to absorb.

Makes recycling code easy

Narrowly focused code is difficult to reuse without major modifications. If a subroutine is fundamentally modified with each reuse, the trend of a narrow focus continues. Instead, writing open-ended code makes it easy to recycle old code for reuse in new scripts, often with little or no change. In addition, recycled code that remains unchanged in each reuse requires less testing than new code.

Improves script quality

An open-ended approach to writing scripts encourages the improvement of the quality of scripts in two ways.

First, building code with the expectation of future reuse encourages a higher quality of work from the start. It makes you regard a piece of code as an investment in future development rather than a simple one-use chunk of code churned out as quickly as possible.

Second, reusing code from past script projects gives you more time to improve the quality or feature set of new code. Features that may have seemed like a luxury that couldn't be justified may suddenly be within reach. There is more time to add advanced features to help diagnose issues, report problems, log activity, auto-update key components, interact more skillfully with the user, and more. If these new, more advanced features are also designed to be open-ended, they too can be reused in future scripts. Continually recycling code provides exponential rewards when every new script inherits something from the old.

Finding a Balance of Openness

A common misconception about open-ended programming is that it somehow leads to an infinite level of adaptability and preparedness. Achieving this is clearly impossible, as it is with all goals without an end.

For example, consider a situation where a script must simply place a short piece of text into a text box in a page layout program and apply a style sheet. This can be accomplished with a small collection of statements. Consider the folly of writing a script several pages long that will handle every possible situation and variation of how that text might at some time in the future be placed, styled, rotated, and wrapped, all in the name of "openness." Going further, you might decide to expand the code to handle any number of combinations of characters, words, sentences, and paragraphs. After all shouldn't it also be able to place the text into a single text box or parse it into any number of boxes? In addition to assigning text a style sheet, shouldn't it also

be able to create a new style sheet or apply font, size, and style properties directly? Going further, shouldn't it also be able to create, resize, rotate, or reposition the box according in an infinite number of possible combinations? You would have to consider countless other possibilities in order to address "everything."

Writing flexible code requires a careful balance of anticipating future needs and being practical. If your mind is racing with a never-ending stream of ideas of what a script might be called on to perform, you are probably looking too far.

One method of learning how to make scripts more flexible is to wait until a script you wrote actually requires some improvements or additional features. Paying attention to the modifications you have to make to implement the changes can often point to areas that should have been open-ended from the start.

Encourages consistency

When a new script contains parts that have been extracted from different scripts, inconsistencies will become more pronounced. Knowing that a new subroutine might be reused in future scripts may encourage you to be consistent in your technique, design, and naming scheme to allow a smooth transition from old script to new.

Justifies smaller scripts

The time and cost of development must always be weighed against the time required to perform a task manually. For example, it is hard to justify spending a full day developing a script that will only save you a few minutes each month. However, if that script can be built in a half an hour from mostly recycled code, it becomes more feasible.

Creating Open-Ended Code

Many easy techniques can make any piece of code more flexible. To demonstrate them, I will show you how to evolve a poorly designed group of statements so they are more flexible and open-ended.

NOTE

All of the code used throughout the examples in this chapter is available for download from the book's Web site at www.wileydevreference.com.

The script will manipulate five images in a folder, shown in Figure 22.1. The example script, shown in Listing 22.1, instructs the Finder to get the name of a file, calculates a new name in which Product # is replaced with Item Number, and changes the name of the file. Then it performs the same process on the four additional files. When finished, all of the image files will be renamed, as shown in Figure 22.2.

Figure 22.1

A folder of selected images ready for processing

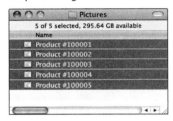

Figure 22.2

The folder of selected images after processing

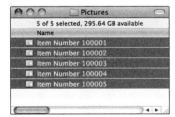

Listing 22.1

A poorly designed, hard-coded script that will replace text within a group of file names

```
tell application "Finder"

  set pathToItem to "Macintosh HD:Users:mmunro:Desktop:Pictures:Product
  #100001.png"
  set nameItem to name of file pathToItem
```

```
    set nameItemNew to "Item Number " & text 10 thru 19 of nameItem as
    string
    set name of file pathToItem to nameItemNew

    set pathToItem to "Macintosh HD:Users:mmunro:Desktop:Pictures:Product
    #100002.png"
    set nameItem to name of file pathToItem
    set nameItemNew to "Item Number " & text 10 thru 19 of nameItem as
    string
    set name of file pathToItem to nameItemNew

    set pathToItem to "Macintosh HD:Users:mmunro:Desktop:Pictures:Product
    #100003.png"
    set nameItem to name of file pathToItem
    set nameItemNew to "Item Number " & text 10 thru 19 of nameItem as
    string
    set name of file pathToItem to nameItemNew

    set pathToItem to "Macintosh HD:Users:mmunro:Desktop:Pictures:Product
    #100004.png"
    set nameItem to name of file pathToItem
    set nameItemNew to "Item Number " & text 10 thru 19 of nameItem as
    string
    set name of file pathToItem to nameItemNew

    set pathToItem to "Macintosh HD:Users:mmunro:Desktop:Pictures:Product
    #100005.png"
    set nameItem to name of file pathToItem
    set nameItemNew to "Item Number " & text 10 thru 19 of nameItem as
    string
    set name of file pathToItem to nameItemNew

end tell
```

The example script shown in Listing 22.1 is completely hardcoded and would take longer to write or to modify for each new batch of files that require this process than it would to rename the files manually. Next, I'll show you the ways you can change this script so it's more open-ended.

Use repeat loops to remove duplicate code

The first improvement to the script is to remove duplicate statements by using a `repeat` loop. The new script, shown in Listing 22.2, puts the five image file paths into the `listSelectedItems` variable and then performs the same four-step process to rename them.

CROSS-REF
The `repeat` statement is discussed in Chapter 14.

This step is mostly about eliminating redundancy rather than adding flexibility. However, in addition to compressing the script, including a variable containing the files to be processed is a first small step towards a more flexible script. To add additional images, simply add them to the list and the script will process them.

Listing 22.2

An improved script with a repeat loop

```
tell application "Finder"
  set listSelectedItems to {"Macintosh HD:Users:mmunro:Desktop:Pictures:
  Product #100001.png", "Macintosh HD:Users:mmunro:Desktop:Pictures:Pro
  duct #100002.png", "Macintosh HD:Users:mmunro:Desktop:Pictures:Prod
  uct #100003.png", "Macintosh HD:Users:mmunro:Desktop:Pictures:Product
  #100004.png", "Macintosh HD:Users:mmunro:Desktop:Pictures:Product
  #100005.png"}

  repeat with a from 1 to count items of listSelectedItems
    set pathToItem to item a of listSelectedItems as string
    set nameItem to the name of file pathToItem
    set nameItemNew to "Item Number " & text 10 thru 19 of nameItem as
  string
    set name of file pathToItem to nameItemNew
  end repeat
end tell
```

Use the Finder selection

The scripts shown in Listings 22.1 and 22.2 contain hardcoded paths. In order for the script to process any file, its path needs to be typed into the code, which is highly inefficient and completely defeats the purpose of writing a script.

Rather than typing all of the image file paths, the script shown in Listing 22.3 gets the user's current selections as the source material for the rest of the script. This simple technique makes the script far more flexible. You can now use it to process any selected file(s) without requiring any code modifications.

Listing 22.3

An improved script that dynamically processes the currently selected item(s)

```
tell application "Finder"
  set listSelectedItems to the selection
```

```
    repeat with a from 1 to count items of listSelectedItems
      set pathToItem to item a of listSelectedItems as string
      set nameItem to the name of file pathToItem
      set nameItemNew to "Item Number " & text 10 thru 19 of nameItem as
    string
      set name of file pathToItem to nameItemNew
    end repeat
end tell
```

Provide for an empty selection

Making one part of a script more open-ended can raise new potential problems. By using the
Finder selection, the script now needs to be able handle situations when the user has not made
a selection. To do so, you add an if-then statement that displays a dialog box informing the
user that he must select something to rename before running the script, as shown in the example in Listing 22.4.

CROSS-REF

Logical branching with the **if-then** statement is discussed in Chapter 13.

Listing 22.4

An improved script that conditionally notifies the user that nothing is selected

```
tell application "Finder"
  set listSelectedItems to the selection
    if listSelectedItems = {} then
    set textMessage to "You must select something to rename."
    display dialog textMessage buttons {"OK"} default button "OK" with
  icon 2
    return -- stops the script
  end if

  repeat with a from 1 to count items of listSelectedItems
    set pathToItem to item a of listSelectedItems as string
    set nameItem to the name of file pathToItem
    set nameItemNew to "Item Number " & text 10 thru 19 of nameItem as
  string
    set name of file pathToItem to nameItemNew
  end repeat
end tell
```

Allow folders to be processed

The script is currently limited to processing only files. If a user wants to modify folder names as well, he is out of luck. This small oversight can be easily remedied because a `file` and a `folder` can both be referred to as an `item`. With this small change, the script shown in Listing 22.5 can rename both files and folders.

Listing 22.5

An improved script that allows folders to be processed

```
tell application "Finder"
  set listSelectedItems to the selection
    if listSelectedItems = {} then
    set textMessage to "You must select something to rename."
    return display dialog textMessage buttons {"OK"} default button "OK"
   with icon 2
  end if

  repeat with a from 1 to count items of listSelectedItems
    set pathToItem to item a of listSelectedItems as string
    set nameItem to the name of file pathToItem
    set nameItemNew to "Item Number " & text 10 thru 19 of nameItem as
   string
    set name of item pathToItem to nameItemNew
  end repeat
end tell
```

Dynamically count the name's length

The script still assumes that the selected items have 19 characters in their names. If it encounters a file or folder with more characters, it will clip the name while items with fewer characters cause a script error. Neither is desirable. By adding a line to count the number of characters in the name, as shown in Listing 22.6, the problem is removed and the script takes one more step toward flexibility.

Listing 22.6

An improved script that calculates the item name dynamically

```
tell application "Finder"
  set listSelectedItems to the selection
    if listSelectedItems = {} then
    set textMessage to "You must select something to rename."
    return display dialog textMessage buttons {"OK"} default button "OK"
   with icon 2
```

```
    end if

    repeat with a from 1 to count items of listSelectedItems
      set pathToItem to item a of listSelectedItems as string
      set nameItem to the name of item pathToItem
      set numCharacters to count characters of nameItem
      set nameItemNew to "Item Number " & text 10 thru numCharacters of
    nameItem as string
      set name of item pathToItem to nameItemNew
    end repeat
  end tell
```

Use text item delimiters

Another area of concern is the fact that this script assumes that the first nine characters of the name of each item is the text that is to be replaced. Because the entire batch of sample files all start with Product #, everything works fine with this assumption. However, if the names of one or more selected items stray from this assumption, the script will produce some rather undesirable results.

CROSS-REF
Finding and replacing text with text item delimiters is discussed in Chapter 7.

Scripts should never assume things will be "perfect." If the goal is to find Product # and replace it with Item Number, the script should use a dynamic method to locate the text like using text item delimiters. If the desired phrase is not in the name or if it is in a different position, the code in Listing 22.7 will still function properly.

NOTE
As of Mac OS 10.6, the use of the delimiter feature, like all scripting addition commands, can't be used inside of a tell application statement. For this reason, the example in Listing 22.7 has been modified to contain multiple, separate tell application "Finder" statements.

Listing 22.7

An improved script that uses text item delimiters to perform the text replacement

```
tell application "Finder"
  set listSelectedItems to the selection
  if listSelectedItems = {} then
    set textMessage to "You must select something to rename."
    return display dialog textMessage buttons {"OK"} default button "OK"
  with icon 2
  end if
end tell
```

continued

Listing 22.7 *(continued)*

```
repeat with a from 1 to count items of listSelectedItems
   tell application "Finder"
      set pathToItem to item a of listSelectedItems as string
      set nameItem to the name of item pathToItem
   end tell

   set text item delimiters to {"Product #"}
   set listName to every text item of nameItem
   set text item delimiters to {""}
   set text item delimiters to {"Item Number "}
   set nameItemNew to text of listName as string
   tell application "Finder"
      set name of item pathToItem to nameItemNew
   end tell

end repeat
```

Use variables or script properties

Generally, it is a good practice to keep specific names in variables or in properties to avoid weaving them directly into code as literals. Placing these values into the `textToFind` and `textToReplace` variables, as shown in Listing 22.8, makes it easier to locate and modify the find and replace text values and it is a small step toward the next flexibility-inducing modification.

Listing 22.8

An improved script that uses variables to contain the find and replace values

```
set textToFind to "Product #"
set textToReplace to "Item Number "
tell application "Finder"
   set listSelectedItems to the selection
   if listSelectedItems = {} then
      set textMessage to "You must select something to rename."
      return display dialog textMessage buttons {"OK"} default button "OK"
    with icon 2
   end if

end tell

repeat with a from 1 to count items of listSelectedItems
   tell application "Finder"
```

```
      set pathToItem to item a of listSelectedItems as string
      set nameItem to the name of item pathToItem
   end tell

   set text item delimiters to {textToFind}
   set listName to every text item of nameItem
   set text item delimiters to {""}
   set text item delimiters to {textToReplace}
   set nameItemNew to text of listName as string
   tell application "Finder"
      set name of item pathToItem to nameItemNew
   end tell

end repeat
```

Query user input

One of the simplest ways to impact a script's flexibility is to make choices available to the user instead of hard-coding them into the code. In all of the previous examples, the script assumes that you want to find the value `Product #` and replace it with `Item Number`. Making these variables something the user can customize without any code changes is a huge step toward an open-ended script.

To do this, you display two variables asking the user to enter some text to find in the selected item names and some text to replace it with, as shown in Listing 22.9. Now anyone can use the script to find and replace any value in a file or folder on any computer.

Listing 22.9

An improved portion of the script that asks the user to enter find and replace values

```
set textToFind to (text returned of (display dialog "Enter text to find
   in selected item names" default answer ""))
set textToReplace to (text returned of (display dialog "Enter text to
   replace in selected item names" default answer ""))
```

Use subroutines

The simple act of using subroutines can go a long way toward making code both flexible and reusable. By placing the three major parts of the script into subroutines, as shown in Listing 22.10, you are left with seven lines that are custom to this script and three subroutines that are completely generic and reusable.

First, the `display dialog` lines that enable a user to enter the find and replacement text is converted into two calls to a single subroutine called `dialogInputGet()`. The dialog message is sent in as a subroutine parameter so the subroutine can be used twice in this script and any number of times in other scripts, each with a unique message.

The second subroutine, named `finderSelectionGet`, gets the user's selection, checks it, and passes back a value. If the selection is empty, this subroutine notifies the user and then sends back a value of `false`, which the primary subroutine detects and halts the script with a `return` command. If the selection is not empty, then the list of selected items is sent back so the primary script can send it to the final subroutine for processing.

The `finderNameReplace` subroutine accepts three parameters: the list of selected items, the text to search for, and the text to replace it with. Finally, the actual replacement is performed and the script is finished.

Listing 22.10

An improved script organized into subroutines

```
set listSelectedItems to finderSelectionGet()
if listSelectedItems = false then return

set textMessage to "Enter text to find in selected item names"
set textToFind to dialogInputGet(textMessage)

set textMessage to "Enter text to replace in selected item names"
set textToReplace to dialogInputGet(textMessage)

finderNameReplace(listSelectedItems, textToFind, textToReplace)

on dialogInputGet(textMessage)
  --  This subroutine will as the user to enter some text
  set textResponse to (text returned of (display dialog textMessage
  default answer ""))
  return textResponse
end dialogInputGet
on finderSelectionGet()
  --  This subroutine will get the finder selection and warn if nothing
  is selected
  tell application "Finder"
    set listSelectedItems to the selection
    if listSelectedItems = {} then
      set textMessage to "You must select something to rename."
      display dialog textMessage buttons {"OK"} default button "OK" with
  icon 2
      return false
    end if
    return listSelectedItems
  end tell
end finderSelectionGet
```

```
on finderNameReplace(listSelectedItems, textToFind, textToReplace)
  --  This subroutine will find and replace some text in a list of
    finder items
  repeat with a from 1 to (count items of listSelectedItems)
    tell application "Finder"
      set pathToItem to item a of listSelectedItems as string
      set nameItem to the name of item pathToItem
    end tell

    set text item delimiters to {textToFind}
    set listName to every text item of nameItem
    set text item delimiters to {""}
    set text item delimiters to {textToReplace}
    set nameItemNew to text of listName as string

    tell application "Finder"
      set name of item pathToItem to nameItemNew
    end tell
  end repeat
end finderNameReplace
```

Creating Open-Ended Subroutines

Subroutines have a natural tendency toward being open and reusable. You can implement several techniques when designing subroutines that will help them take advantage of this capability and improve the flexibility and reusability of the script in which they exist.

Divide code with logical groupings

The first step to designing open-ended subroutines is to actually create subroutines. However, there are numerous ways to divide code for such a purpose. Choosing the right method can make a big difference in how flexible and reusable your end result will be.

Model-View-Controller Programming Technique

Apple's recommended programming technique for interface-driven applications is the Model-View-Controller (MVC) design pattern. The idea is to keep code separate depending on its role in containing entities (model), displaying information in the user interface (view), and communicating between those two (controller). Apple's developer guide on the subject states:

"The benefits of adopting this pattern are numerous. Many objects in these applications tend to be more reusable, and their interfaces tend to be better defined. Applications having an MVC design are also more easily extensible than other applications."

Although scripts don't have an application interface, Apple's MVC design pattern can be an insightful concept when parsing code into subroutines. Subroutines can be parsed out of a script in much the same way as MVC recommends keeping object-related code separate from view-related code with a separate controller acting as the conduit between them.

When presented with a script that needs subroutines, try to keep code separated by type. There are a few basic types of code that should be separate from the others. This includes code for:

- **The primary script and management.** The code that manages the overall flow of the scripted process.
- **Feature management routines.** Code that is responsible for a specific feature.
- **Communication with the user through dialog boxes.** Code that interacts with a user.
- **Acquiring source material.** Code that loads, reads, and digests source material.
- **Manipulating material.** Code that manipulates the source material and creates the output.
- **Specific application code.** Code that interacts with a given application.
- **Reporting process results to a log or activity summary.** Code that manages reporting results to the user.

Separating code into all or some of these types can be a big help when deciding what should be spun off into a subroutine. Such separation also provides a precursor to building open-ended scripts.

CROSS-REF

Some of these parsing recommendations will make more sense once you read about subroutine hierarchy (Chapter 23) and multi-module solutions (Chapter 24), as they discuss some of their advantages.

Make smaller subroutines

The size of subroutines will always vary and there is no "right" size. However, creating smaller and more focused subroutines can increase the chance of a more flexible result, especially for code that performs a specific function.

Imagine a hypothetical script that assembles a list of files, copies them somewhere, renames the copies, zips them, uploads the zipped archive to a networked file server, and generates and sends an e-mail to report the completion. Merging all of these steps into a single subroutine would make it too specialized and, therefore, not useful beyond the immediate script. However, if each step was a separate subroutine and called from a primary run subroutine, they would each be useful, by themselves or in groups, in countless other scripts.

Name subroutines, parameters, and variables generically

The names used in subroutines can later be modified to broaden the scope of the code. However, keeping those names generic from the start is a good way to help encourage open-ended design. One trick is to always think one step more generically. For example, a generic reference to "this item" replaces "this disk," "this file," or "this folder," which are too specific. So, variables named `nameDisk`, `nameFile`, or `nameFolder` can all become `nameItem`, but only in a situation where the functionality might later be adapted to other objects. A subroutine that gets the name of a disk could use `nameItem` but code that gets the `ejectable` property of a disk can't be applied to folders or files so it can remain `nameDisk`.

In the following example, a subroutine gets the available space remaining on the start-up disk and uses very specific naming. Its name includes `startup` and it is hardcoded to get the name of the start-up disk:

```
on finderStartupDiskFreeSpaceGet()
  tell application "Finder"
    return the free space of the startup disk
  end tell
end finderStartupDiskFreeSpaceGet
```

By simply removing `startup` from the subroutine name, you open the possibility of future flexibility:

```
on finderDiskFreeSpaceGet()
  tell application "Finder"
    return the free space of the startup disk
  end tell
end finderDiskFreeSpaceGet
```

The Challenge of Name Planning

Trying to foresee the future and anticipate the naming requirements of tomorrow is a challenging task. It even afflicts a popular software title of the operating system we all know and love. Apple has done a fantastic job building development tools that are highly open-ended and flexible for almost any situation. And yet their application that sells and manages a user's music, television shows, movies, iPhone applications, podcasts, and audio books is named iTunes. I have no doubt that, had Apple been able to predict the amazing success of the iPod and the variety of material the program would come to manage, they would have named it something inclusive to that diversity. At this point, a name change might require a lot of work and a steep adjustment curve for all of the millions of users, which might explain why they have not yet done so.

So, if your naming isn't sufficiently forward-thinking, don't feel too bad. Just learn from the experience and apply this knowledge in the future.

Avoid branch-style openness

A common misconception about making a subroutine open-ended is that it is a good idea to use an `if-then` statement to execute one of many hardcoded results or courses of action. While there may be situations where such a statement is justified, in general, it is a misguided attempt at open-ended design.

Branch-style open-ended code is any code that uses an if-then statement to selectively perform one of a series of hard-coded statements. One or more of the subroutine parameters are used to instruct the script which branch of code to execute and, therefore, this type of subroutine typically requires new code added for each new condition. By contrast, *dynamic-style open-ended code* is any code that can dynamically adapt to new situations. In most cases, the subroutine parameters are used to construct portions of a path, object name, or command. The ability of the subroutine to continue functioning in new circumstances without modification is the best indicator of which style of openness it employs. Because a fully open-ended subroutine might still include an `if-then` statement for certain functions, the presence of or lack of a branch alone is not a singular indicator of the openness of the subroutine.

The following subroutine logs onto a specific networked volume using a hardcoded URL-style parameter for the `mount volume` command:

```
on serverMount()
   mount volume "afp://10.0.1.12/WTM Server/"
end serverMount
```

Adding a subroutine parameter that enables it to mount different volumes is a step toward making a more flexible piece of code. However, if the subroutine uses an `if-then` statement to run one of several hard-coded commands, it can only barely qualify as open-ended.

This example uses *branch-style openness* to provide the subroutine with the capability to open three servers, each with their own hardcoded command:

```
on serverMount(nameDisk)
   if nameDisk = "WTM Server" then
      mount volume "afp://10.0.1.12/WTM Server/"
   else if nameDisk = "WTM Transfer" then
      mount volume "afp://10.0.1.12/WTM Transfer/"
   else if nameDisk = "WTM AppleScript Resources" then
      mount volume "afp://10.0.1.12/WTM AppleScript Resources/"
   end if
end serverMount
```

While this approach does add a sense of flexibility, it fails to fully grasp the true benefits of open-ended design. For each new permutation the subroutine must handle, a code change is required. This defeats the purpose of making the code open-ended.

By rethinking the structure of the subroutine, you can transform it so it is fully parameter driven and uses *dynamic-style openness*, which will handle new circumstances without any code changes. First, you add a second subroutine parameter for the server address. Then both parameters are used to dynamically create the URL-style parameter for the single `mount volume` command. This example of the subroutine can truly be called open-ended:

```
on serverMount(textServerIP, nameDisk)
  mount volume "afp://" & textServerIP & "/" & nameDisk & "/"
end serverMount
```

Use subroutine parameters for variable input

Even if a subroutine's immediate needs are narrow in scope, try making any key value a parameter to allow for more flexibility. Rather than making a subroutine to delete a specific file, make it delete the file specified by a parameter. A subroutine that adds a picture box to page three of a specific page layout document should create a box of any kind on any page of any document.

In this example, the subroutine is hard-coded to add data into a specific field of the current record of a specific database. It is open-ended only due to the fact that it allows the contact name to vary from one use to the next:

```
on enterContactNameToCurrentRecord(nameContact)
  tell application "FileMaker Pro Advanced"
    tell window "Contacts"
      set cell "Contact Name" of record ID (ID of current record)
  of current table to nameContact
    end tell
  end tell
end enterContactNameToCurrentRecord
```

When you change the name and add two parameters, the subroutine can finally be properly called open-ended. It can enter any value into any field of any database's current record:

```
on dbFieldDataSet(nameWindow, nameField, textToEnter)
  tell application "FileMaker Pro Advanced"
    tell window nameWindow
      set cell nameField of record ID (ID of current record) of
  current table to textToEnter
    end tell
  end tell
end enterContactNameToCurrentRecord
```

TIP

When employing this method, try to not get carried away. There is certainly a benefit to making a robust subroutine that can flex to handle many variations of a specific function. However, you don't want to get caught up in the folly of trying to make a subroutine do everything, especially not all at once.

Use records for future parameter expansion

Each time a new parameter is added, all calls to the subroutine must be updated. If the subroutine is used in many scripts, as it should be, it can be a tedious chore finding and updating every call. To avoid this, add a `record` parameter at the end of the parameter list to allow for future expansion.

CROSS-REF

The **record** class is discussed in Chapter 12.

A record can contain an infinite number of field values while only taking up a single place among a subroutine's parameters. This provides a mechanism for expansion without affecting older calls to the subroutine. This formula shows a `recData` parameter that can gradually include additional instructions as the subroutine evolves:

```
on subroutineName(refLocation, nameItem, recData)
  -- subroutine code
end subroutineName
```

Any new data that will be added to the parameter will need to include an error-capture mechanism that uses a default value for situations when the new field is not included. Because older subroutine calls will not contain the new information, the subroutine must be allowed to function properly in such circumstances.

The following example shows an error-protected statement that attempts to extract a field named `nameFont` from the `recData` parameter. When an error occurs because the field is not present in `recData`, a default value is placed into the `nameFont` variable so the subroutine can continue without disruption:

```
on subroutineName(refLocation, nameItem, recData)
  try
    set nameFont to nameFont of recData
  on error
    set nameFont to "Verdana"
  end try
  --  subroutine code
end subroutineName
```

TIP

Try to avoid the desire to crowd every parameter into a single record. Although this technique would save space, some values should have their own parameter placeholders, indicating that they are not optional like **refLocation** and **nameItem** in the previous example.

Keep subroutines as portable as possible

Next to making them more flexible, the second goal of building open-ended subroutines is to make them easily reusable in other scripts. To do this, you need to keep as many subroutines as portable as possible. Not every subroutine can be portable, but many can and there are a few simple ways to achieve this goal.

Use fewer properties and global variables

Properties and global variables are useful for sharing a preset value or other information throughout a script. However, if those containers are not uniform across all of your scripts, a subroutine dependent on them makes it less portable and, therefore, more difficult to reuse. At the minimum, moving a subroutine to another script requires you to remember to bring along that extra baggage. If you want a piece of code to be easily reusable, you should avoid properties and global variables as much as possible.

Organize subroutines into a hierarchy

Create a hierarchical subroutine structure with project-specific code at the top managing the flow of the script and endowed with specific business rules. Subroutines that perform specific functions should be at the bottom and be as open-ended as possible.

CROSS-REF

Learn more about creating a hierarchical subroutine structure to keep subroutines portable in Chapter 23.

Creating an Open-Ended Image Batch Processor

Chapter 18 includes a script that uses the Image Events application to perform a couple of manipulations on a batch of image files. In this section, I show you some modifications you can make to the script to make it more flexible and open-ended.

Allow a user to select folders

From the beginning, the original batch processor code endorses a very narrow scope. The folder of source images and the output folder for modified images are both hard-coded into the script, as shown here:

```
set pathToImageFolder to "Macintosh HD:Users:mmunro:Desktop:Pache
    Images:"
set pathToSave to "Macintosh HD:Users:mmunro:Desktop:Pache
    Output:"
```

If a user wants to process images, he either needs to put them into this folder or modify the code so it points to another folder. You can easily eliminate this problem by allowing the user to select an input and output folder using a `choose folder` dialog message, as shown in Listing 22.11.

Listing 22.11

An improved portion of the script that allows users to select input and output folders

```
--  Choose input location
set textPrompt to "Choose a folder of images to modify:"
set pathToImageFolder to (choose folder with prompt textPrompt) as
    string

--  Choose an output folder
set textPrompt to "Choose a folder to save modified images:"
set pathToSave to (choose folder with prompt textPrompt) as string
```

Enable two additional selection methods

Building on the last modification, you can also adapt the script to allow the user to choose a folder or an individual file to provide even greater flexibility.

To provide this increased flexibility, you will modify the script in the following ways:

- The script will create a list of the two available options the user can choose from: process a single image file or a folder of images.
- The script will ask the user to select an image file or a folder of images.
- The line just above the start of the `repeat` statement, which used to get a list of items in the image folder, will be removed.
- The first line inside the `repeat` statement will be changed. The `listFiles` variable now has full paths for the items to be processed so you no longer need to add the image folder path in front of the current item.

These changes, shown in Listing 22.12, give the user greater flexibility in how he informs the script which images he wants to be processed. When this portion of the script is executed, the user will see a dialog box offering two choices like the one shown in Figure 22.3. Based on the user's selection, the `listFiles` variable will contain the choice of a file or a list of items in a selected folder.

Figure 22.3

A choose from list dialog box allows the user to choose what should be processed.

Listing 22.12

An improved portion of the script that allows the user to choose to process an image or a folder full of images

```
--  Choose input type and location
set listChoices to {"One Image", "Images in a Folder"}
set nameDefault to "Images in a Folder"
set dataChoice to choose from list listChoices with prompt "Process:"
   default items nameDefault
if dataChoice = false then return
set nameSelection to item 1 of dataChoice

--  Gather a list of files for processing
if nameSelection = "One image" then
  set textPrompt to "Choose an image file to modify:"
  set pathToImageFile to (choose file with prompt textPrompt) as string
  set listFiles to {pathToImageFile}
else if nameSelection = "Images in a Folder" then
  set textPrompt to "Choose a folder of images to modify:"
  set pathToImageFolder to (choose folder with prompt textPrompt) as
   string
  set listFilesTemp to list folder pathToImageFolder without invisibles
  set listFiles to {}
  repeat with a from 1 to count items of listFilesTemp
    copy pathToImageFolder & item a of listFilesTemp as string to end of
   listFiles
  end repeat
end if

--  Choose an output folder
```

continued

Listing 22.12   *(continued)*

```
set textPrompt to "Choose a folder to save modified images:"
set pathToSave to (choose folder with prompt textPrompt) as string

--   Setup variables for tracking success
set textSuccess to ""
set textFailure to ""

--   Process each file that was dropped
repeat with a from 1 to count items of listFiles
   set pathToItem to item a of listFiles as string
```

Choose manipulations

One blatant flaw in the original script is that it limits the image manipulations to two hard-coded functions: a horizontal flip and scaling by a factor of 25 percent, as shown here:

```
tell application "Image Events"
   flip refImage with horizontal
   scale refImage by factor 0.25
end tell
```

This restriction severely limits the usefulness of the script and requires code changes to perform a new command, perform a variation of these commands, or remove a command. You can remedy this shortcoming with another `choose from list` command, which enables the user to choose one or more options from a list of possible manipulations.

The new code, shown in Listing 22.13, offers the user one or more command options. The user can choose to flip the image horizontally or vertically and choose form one of four scaling options. The user can also choose any combination of these.

Listing 22.13

An improved portion of the script that allows the user to choose from a list of image manipulations

```
set textPrompt to "Perform which action(s):"
set listActionChoices to {"Flip horizontal", "Flip vertical", "Scale
   25%", "Scale 50%", "Scale 75%"}
set listActionChoices to (choose from list listActionChoices with
   multiple selections allowed without empty selection allowed)
if listActionChoices = false then return ""
```

Next, a `repeat` loop, shown in Listing 22.14, replaces the two lines that flipped and scaled the image. The new code steps through each selected action and performs the modification to the currently open image.

Listing 22.14

An improved portion of the script that performs only the user-selected image manipulations

```
repeat with a from 1 to count items of listActionChoices
   set nameChoice to item a of listActionChoices

   tell application "Image Events"
     --  Flip the image horizontally
     if nameChoice contains "Flip horizontal" then
        flip refImage with horizontal
     end if

     --  Flip the image vertically
     if nameChoice contains "Flip vertical" then
        flip refImage with vertical
     end if

     --  Scale the image
     if nameChoice contains "Scale" then
        set numScale to "." & last word of nameChoice as real
        scale refImage by factor numScale
     end if
   end tell
end repeat
```

Offering the user a choice of manipulations not only adds flexibility but also helps facilitate additional functionality over time. By simply adding another option with a corresponding `if-then` condition to the list of choices, the script can gradually evolve.

Select a custom scale percentage

Adding a choice of scaling options in the last example is helpful but somewhat limited because it only offers scaling in 25 percent increments. Expanding the list of choices to include every size, from 1 percent to 99 percent, would be too overwhelming, so you will add an option for a custom scaling.

To begin, add `Scale Custom %` to the list of choices. A new `if-then` statement will conditionally ask the user to enter a custom percentage when she chooses that option. Because
`listChoices` will contain the value `Scale Custom %`, you need to remove that and add an
entry that includes the customer number the user entered. A `repeat` loop handles removing
the entry and then you add `Scale Custom` back into the list with the number the user
entered. Finally, the scale portion within the `tell application` statement is appended to
include the new custom scale choice. All of these changes are reflected in Listing 22.15.

Listing 22.15

An improved portion of the script that allows the user to enter a custom scale percentage

```
--  Ask the user what manipulations they want to perform
set textPrompt to "Perform which action(s):"
set listActionChoices to {"Flip horizontal", "Flip vertical", "Scale
   25%", "Scale 50%", "Scale 75%", "Scale Custom %"}
set listActionChoices to (choose from list listActionChoices with
   multiple selections allowed without empty selection allowed)
if listActionChoices = false then return ""
--  Handle custom scale request
if listActionChoices contains "Scale Custom %" then
    set textPrompt to "Scale images by what percentage:"
    set textPercent to (text returned of (display dialog textPrompt
   default answer ".10"))

    set listActionChoicesTemp to {}
    repeat with a from 1 to count items of listActionChoices
        set nameChoice to item a of listActionChoices
        if nameChoice is not "Scale Custom %" then
            copy nameChoice to end of listActionChoicesTemp
        end if
    end repeat

    copy "Scale Custom " & textPercent as string to end of
   listActionChoicesTemp
    set listActionChoices to listActionChoicesTemp
end if

--  Process each file
set textSuccess to ""
set textFailure to ""
repeat with a from 1 to count items of listFiles
    set pathToItem to item a of listFiles as string
    try
        tell application "Image Events"
            -- Open the file and get its name
            set refImage to open alias pathToItem
            set nameImage to name of refImage
        end tell
```

```
    -- Remove the file extension from the image name for saving
    tell application "Finder"
        set textExtension to name extension of item pathToItem
    end tell
    set nameImageForSave to nameImage
    if nameImage ends with textExtension and textExtension ≠ "" then
        set text item delimiters to {"." & textExtension}
        set listTemp to every text item of nameImage
        set text item delimiters to {""}
        set nameImageForSave to listTemp as text
    end if

    tell application "Image Events"
        -- Confirm the file is an acceptible image type
        set recProperties to (properties of refImage)
        set dataFileType to file type of recProperties
        set listFileTypes to {BMP, GIF, JPEG, JPEG2, MacPaint, PDF,
Photoshop, PICT, PNG, PSD, QuickTime Image, SGI, TGA, TIFF}
        set blnImageFile to listFileTypes contains dataFileType
        if blnImageFile = false then error "Not an image file"
    end tell

    -- Process each image
    repeat with a from 1 to count items of listActionChoices
        set nameChoice to item a of listActionChoices

        -- Modify the image
        tell application "Image Events"
            if nameChoice contains "Flip horizontal" then
                flip refImage with horizontal
            end if

            if nameChoice contains "Flip vertical" then
                flip refImage with vertical
            end if

            if nameChoice contains "Scale" then
                if nameChoice contains "Custom " then
                    set numScale to "." & last word of nameChoice as
real
                else
                    set numScale to "." & last word of nameChoice as
real
                end if
                scale refImage by factor numScale
            end if

        end tell
    end repeat
```

continued

Listing 22.15 *(continued)*

```
        -- Save the modified image
        tell application "Image Events"
            set pathToSaveImage to pathToSave & nameImageForSave & ".
    jpg" as string
            save refImage as JPEG in file pathToSaveImage
        end tell

        --  Build the log entry
        set textForLog to nameImage & return
        set textSuccess to textSuccess & textForLog as string
    on error errText
        set textForLog to nameImage & " (" & errText & ")" & return
        set textFailure to textFailure & textForLog as string
    end try
end repeat
```

Allow the user to choose an output format

Now that the code provides the user with a choice of image manipulations, it's time to focus your attention on the output functionality. Currently, the script is hard-coded to save the modified image as a JPEG file even though the Image Events application can save images as eight different file types.

CAUTION

As of Mac OS X 10.6, Image Events is not able to save an image as a QuickTime image.

Allowing the user to choose an image format to save the modified image in is easy to do by adding another `choose from list` command as shown in Listing 22.16, and an `if-then` statement that saves the image based on their selection as shown in Listing 22.17.

Listing 22.16

An improved portion of the script that allows the user to choose from one of a list of output image formats

```
--  Ask the user to choose output format(s)
set textPrompt to "Save images as:"
set listSaveOptions to {"BMP", "JPEG", "JPEG2", "PICT", "PNG", "PSD",
    "QuickTime Image", "TIFF"}
```

```
set listSaveOptions to (choose from list listSaveOptions with empty
   selection allowed)
if listSaveOptions contains false then return ""
set nameSaveFormat to listSaveOptions as string
```

Listing 22.17

An improved portion of the script that saves the current image in the user-selected format

```
--  Save the modified image
  tell application "Image Events"
    if nameSaveFormat = "BMP" then
      save refImage as BMP in file (pathToSave & nameImageForSave & ".
  bmp" as string)
    else if nameSaveFormat = "JPEG" then
      save refImage as JPEG in file (pathToSave & nameImageForSave & ".
  jpg" as string)
    else if nameSaveFormat = "JPEG2" then
      save refImage as JPEG2 in file (pathToSave & nameImageForSave &
  ".jp2" as string)
    else if nameSaveFormat = "PICT" then
      save refImage as PICT in file (pathToSave & nameImageForSave &
  ".pict" as string)
    else if nameSaveFormat = "PNG" then
      save refImage as PNG in file (pathToSave & nameImageForSave & ".
  png" as string)
    else if nameSaveFormat = "PSD" then
      save refImage as PSD in file (pathToSave & nameImageForSave & ".
  psd" as string)
    else if nameSaveFormat = "QuickTime Image" then
      save refImage as QuickTime Image in file (pathToSave &
  nameImageForSave & ".qif" as string)
    else if nameSaveFormat = "TIFF" then
      save refImage as TIFF in file (pathToSave & nameImageForSave &
  ".tiff" as string)
  end if
  close refImage
end tell
```

Allow the selection of multiple output formats

Often, image files must be saved as multiple file types, which presents another opportunity to improve the script's flexibility. Instead of limiting the user's choice to a single output format, you can expand the code to allow multiple selections. A quick change to the `choose from list` command allows multiple selections, as shown in Listing 22.18.

Listing 22.18

An improved portion of the script that allows the user to select one or more output formats

```
set textPrompt to "Save images as:"
  set listSaveOptions to {"BMP", "JPEG", "JPEG2", "PICT", "PNG", "PSD",
  "QuickTime Image", "TIFF"}
  set listSaveOptions to (choose from list listSaveOptions with empty
  selection allowed and multiple selections allowed)
  if listSaveOptions contains false then return ""
```

Then, an un-nested `if-then` statement allows the script to save a file as any or all of the available choices. To work around some quirky behavior, the script needs to save the modified image into a temp file, close the image, and then open, save, and close for each file type. Therefore, you will add a `repeat` loop, which will run for each output format the user selected. This leaves you with the script shown in Listing 22.19.

Listing 22.19

An improved portion of the script that saves the current image as each selected output format

```
--   Save the image in the selected format(s)
set pathToTemp to pathToSave & "TEMP" as string
set pathToSave to pathToSave & nameImageForSave as string
tell application "Image Events"
  save refImage in file pathToTemp
  close refImage

  repeat with a from 1 to count items of listSaveOptions
    set refImage to open file pathToTemp
    set nameType to item a of listSaveOptions

    if nameType = "BMP" then save refImage as BMP in file (pathToSave
& ".bmp" as string)
    if nameType = "JPEG" then save refImage as JPEG in file
(pathToSave & ".jpg" as string)
    if nameType = "JPEG2" then save refImage as JPEG2 in file
(pathToSave & ".jp2" as string)
    if nameType = "PICT" then save refImage as PICT in file
(pathToSave & ".pict" as string)
```

```
    if nameType = "PNG" then save refImage as PNG in file (pathToSave
& ".png" as string)
    if nameType = "PSD" then save refImage as PSD in file (pathToSave
& ".psd" as string)
    if nameType = "QuickTime Image" then save refImage as QuickTime
Image in file (pathToSave & ".qif" as string)
    if nameType = "TIFF" then save refImage as TIFF in file
(pathToSave & ".tiff" as string)
    close refImage
  end repeat
end tell
--  Clean up
tell application "Finder"
  delete file pathToTemp
end tell
```

Make a drop application

Like the original version of this script in Chapter 18, this version still assumes that the script is running within the Script Editor. While this might be good when learning the language, it is not how the final script will be used. To make the script more realistic and more flexible, it should be saved as a drop application.

The option added earlier that allows the user to process a folder of files, a specific file, or the selected items can remain for maximum flexibility if the user chooses to launch the application without dropping files on it.

 CROSS-REF
Drop applications and command handler subroutines are discussed in Chapters 3 and 21.

The first step to making the script a drop application with a run option is to add a run and open command handler subroutine. The code that asks the user to choose an option will be placed into a run subroutine, as shown in Listing 22.20. Once it compiles a list of items to process, it sends them to the open subroutine.

Listing 22.20

An improved portion of the script that moves the user selection code into a run subroutine

```
on run
  --  Ask the user what they want to select
  set listChoices to {"One Image", "Images in a Folder"}
  tell application "Finder" to set listSelectedItems to the selection
```

continued

Listing 22.20 *(continued)*

```
set nameDefault to "Images in a Folder"
set dataChoice to choose from list listChoices with prompt "Process:"
 default items nameDefault
if dataChoice = false then return
set nameSelection to item 1 of dataChoice

--  Gather a list of files for processing
if nameSelection = "One image" then
  set textPrompt to "Choose an image file to modify:"
  set pathToImageFile to (choose folder with prompt textPrompt) as
 string
  set listFiles to {pathToImageFile}
else if nameSelection = "Images in a Folder" then
  set textPrompt to "Choose a folder of images to modify:"
  set pathToImageFolder to (choose folder with prompt textPrompt) as
 string
  set listFilesTemp to list folder pathToImageFolder without
 invisibles
  set listFiles to {}
  repeat with a from 1 to count items of listFilesTemp
    copy pathToImageFolder & item a of listFilesTemp as string to end
 of listFiles
  end repeat
else
  set listFiles to listSelectedItems
end if
open listFiles
end run
```

Next, the remaining portion of the code goes into an open subroutine with a listFiles parameter. If the user drops files on the application, the files go directly to the open subroutine. If the user launches the script application by double-clicking its icon, the run subroutine asks the user to choose an option of what to process:

```
on open listFiles
  -- remainer of the script goes here
end open
```

The script's report of what was or was not processed also assumes the script is running in the AppleScript Editor. When converting a script to an application, values that get returned as a result will no longer be visible to the user. So, the script needs modified reporting code that will create a text file on the desktop and open it so the user can see the results. Adding the code in Listing 22.21 to the end of the open subroutine generates a text file and opens it for the user, as shown in Figure 22.4.

Listing 22.21

New session logging code added to the end of the open subroutine that saves the log to the desktop and opens it after processing images

```
--  Create the new report and open it
set pathToReport to (path to desktop folder as string) & "Image Batch
 Processor Results.txt" as string
tell application "Finder"
  if (file pathToReport exists) then delete file pathToReport
end tell

set textResult to ""
 set textLine to "------------------------------------------------"
 if textSuccess ≠ "" then
   set textResult to textResult & "Successfully processed image(s):" &
  return & textLine & return & textSuccess & return as string
 end if
 if textFailure ≠ "" then
   set textResult to textResult & "The following image(s) failed to
  process:" & return & textLine & return & textFailure as string
 end if

open for access file pathToReport with write permission
 write textResult to file pathToReport
 close access file pathToReport
 tell application "Finder"
   open file pathToReport
 end tell
end open
```

Figure 22.4

The batch processing results stored in a text file

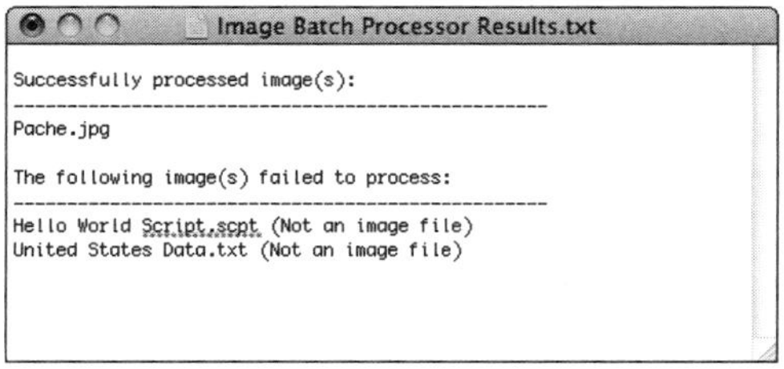

Use subroutines

The final improvement is to break the script down into specialized subroutines. This makes it easier to reuse, navigate, and later convert into a multi-module solution. However, I have saved this final step for the next chapter because it contains an ideal example of how to create a subroutine hierarchy to make a larger portion of a script even more open-ended.

Bring it all together

Integrating all of the changes to the image batch processor together into a final script leaves you with a script that is open-ended and more flexible, like the one shown in Listing 22.22.

Listing 22.22

The final version of the Image Batch Processor script that includes all the changes discussed in this chapter

```
on run
    --  Choose input type and location
    set listChoices to {"One Image", "Images in a Folder"}
    tell application "Finder" to set listSelectedItems to the selection
    set nameDefault to "Images in a Folder"
    if listSelectedItems is not {} then
        copy "Selected Images" to end of listChoices
        set nameDefault to "Selected Images"
    end if
    set dataChoice to choose from list listChoices with prompt "Process:" default
items nameDefault
    if dataChoice = false then return
    set nameSelection to item 1 of dataChoice

    --  Gather a list of files for processing
    if nameSelection = "One image" then
        set textPrompt to "Choose an image file to modify:"
        set pathToImageFile to (choose file with prompt textPrompt) as string
        set listFiles to {pathToImageFile}
    else if nameSelection = "Images in a Folder" then
        set textPrompt to "Choose a folder of images to modify:"
        set pathToImageFolder to (choose folder with prompt textPrompt) as string
        set listFilesTemp to list folder pathToImageFolder without invisibles
        set listFiles to {}
        repeat with a from 1 to count items of listFilesTemp
            copy pathToImageFolder & item a of listFilesTemp as string to end of
listFiles
        end repeat
    else
        set listFiles to listSelectedItems
    end if
```

```
        open listFiles
end run

on open listFiles
    -- Choose an output folder
    set textPrompt to "Choose a folder to save modified images:"
    set pathToSave to (choose folder with prompt textPrompt) as string

    --    Setup variables for tracking success
    set textSuccess to ""
    set textFailure to ""


    --  Ask the user what manipulations they want to perform
    set textPrompt to "Perform which action(s):"
    set listActionChoices to {"Flip horizontal", "Flip vertical", "Scale 25%",
"Scale 50%", "Scale 75%", "Scale Custom %"}
    set listActionChoices to (choose from list listActionChoices with multiple
selections allowed without empty selection allowed)
    if listActionChoices = false then return ""

    set textPrompt to "Save images as:"
    set listSaveOptions to {"BMP", "JPEG", "JPEG2", "PICT", "PNG", "PSD",
"QuickTime Image", "TIFF"}
    set listSaveOptions to (choose from list listSaveOptions with empty selection
allowed and multiple selections allowed)
    if listSaveOptions contains false then return ""

    --  Handle custom scale request
    if listActionChoices contains "Scale Custom %" then
        set textPrompt to "Scale images by what percentage:"
        set textPercent to (text returned of (display dialog textPrompt default
answer ".10"))

        set listActionChoicesTemp to {}
        repeat with a from 1 to count items of listActionChoices
            set nameChoice to item a of listActionChoices
            if nameChoice is not "Scale Custom %" then
                copy nameChoice to end of listActionChoicesTemp
            end if
        end repeat

        copy "Scale Custom " & textPercent as string to end of
listActionChoicesTemp
        set listActionChoices to listActionChoicesTemp
    end if

    --  Process each file
    set textSuccess to ""
    set textFailure to ""
```

continued

Listing 22.22 *(continued)*

```
repeat with a from 1 to count items of listFiles
    set pathToItem to item a of listFiles as string
    try
        tell application "Image Events"
            -- Open the file and get its name
            set refImage to open alias pathToItem
            set nameImage to name of refImage
        end tell

        -- Remove the file extension from the image name for saving
        tell application "Finder"
            set textExtension to name extension of item pathToItem
        end tell
        set nameImageForSave to nameImage
        if nameImage ends with textExtension and textExtension ≠ "" then
            set text item delimiters to {"." & textExtension}
            set listTemp to every text item of nameImage
            set text item delimiters to {""}
            set nameImageForSave to listTemp as text
        end if

        tell application "Image Events"
            -- Confirm the file is an acceptable image type
            set recProperties to (properties of refImage)
            set dataFileType to file type of recProperties
            set listFileTypes to {BMP, GIF, JPEG, JPEG2, MacPaint, PDF,
Photoshop, PICT, PNG, PSD, QuickTime Image, SGI, TGA, TIFF}
            set blnImageFile to listFileTypes contains dataFileType
            if blnImageFile = false then error "Not an image file"
        end tell

        -- Process each image
        repeat with a from 1 to count items of listActionChoices
            set nameChoice to item a of listActionChoices

            -- Modify the image
            tell application "Image Events"
                if nameChoice contains "Flip horizontal" then
                    flip refImage with horizontal
                end if

                if nameChoice contains "Flip vertical" then
                    flip refImage with vertical
                end if

                if nameChoice contains "Scale" then
                    if nameChoice contains "Custom " then
                        set numScale to "." & last word of nameChoice as real
                    else
                        set numScale to "." & last word of nameChoice as real
                    end if
```

```
                    scale refImage by factor numScale
                end if

            end tell
        end repeat

        --  Save the image in the selected format(s)
        set pathToTemp to pathToSave & "TEMP" as string
        set pathToSave to pathToSave & nameImageForSave as string
        tell application "Image Events"
            save refImage in file pathToTemp
            close refImage

            repeat with a from 1 to count items of listSaveOptions
                set refImage to open file pathToTemp
                set nameType to item a of listSaveOptions

                if nameType = "BMP" then save refImage as BMP in file
(pathToSave & ".bmp" as string)
                if nameType = "JPEG" then save refImage as JPEG in file
(pathToSave & ".jpg" as string)
                if nameType = "JPEG2" then save refImage as JPEG2 in file
(pathToSave & ".jp2" as string)
                if nameType = "PICT" then save refImage as PICT in file
(pathToSave & ".pict" as string)
                if nameType = "PNG" then save refImage as PNG in file
(pathToSave & ".png" as string)
                if nameType = "PSD" then save refImage as PSD in file
(pathToSave & ".psd" as string)
                if nameType = "QuickTime Image" then save refImage as
QuickTime Image in file (pathToSave & ".qif" as string)
                if nameType = "TIFF" then save refImage as TIFF in file
(pathToSave & ".tiff" as string)
                close refImage
            end repeat
        end tell

        --  Clean up
        tell application "Finder"
            delete file pathToTemp
        end tell

        --  Build the log entry
        set textForLog to nameImage & return
        set textSuccess to textSuccess & textForLog as string
    on error errText
        set textForLog to nameImage & " (" & errText & ")" & return
        set textFailure to textFailure & textForLog as string
    end try
end repeat
```

continued

Listing 22.22 *(continued)*

```
    -- BEGIN  MODIFIED
    -- ------------------

    --  Create the new report and open it
    set pathToReport to (path to desktop folder as string) & "Image Batch
Processor Results.txt" as string
    tell application "Finder"
        if (file pathToReport exists) then delete file pathToReport
    end tell

    set textResult to ""
    set textLine to "--------------------------------------------------"
    if textSuccess ≠ "" then
        set textResult to textResult & "Successfully processed image(s):" &
return & textLine & return & textSuccess & return as string
    end if
    if textFailure ≠ "" then
        set textResult to textResult & "The following image(s) failed to
process:" & return & textLine & return & textFailure as string
    end if

    open for access file pathToReport with write permission
    write textResult to file pathToReport
    close access file pathToReport
    tell application "Finder"
        open file pathToReport
    end tell
end open
```

Summary

In this chapter you learned about the benefits and techniques for creating open-ended code. You also learned specific techniques for making code, subroutines, and scripts more dynamic. Additionally, you learned how to rewrite the image batch processing script to be more flexible.

Designing a Hierarchical Subroutine Structure

A *hierarchical subroutine structure* is a method of dividing a script into subroutines based on functional type instead of execution order or other random criteria.

A linear script keeps code "equal" and restricts its position within a file to its order of execution. This makes it impossible to think of any statement or group of statements as being in a different category from the others. The only step you can take toward categorization is to group code into sections with comments and spaces, as shown in the script flow in Figure 23.1, which is adequate for smaller scripts.

Figure 23.1

A linear script flow with code separated into commented groups

In This Chapter

Exploring an advanced organizational view of subroutine design

Redesigning an image batch processing script with a hierarchical subroutine structure

Transferring a linear script to a subroutine-driven non-linear script presents a challenge: what criteria should be used to separate code into smaller pieces? Using commented groups as the basis for the organization of larger scripts will not result in an optimal, hierarchical structure, and it barely qualifies as being non-linear. Moving each group of code into a subroutine, as shown in Figure 23.2, makes it technically a non-linear script. However, because it was divided based on a grouping of linear code, it is still quite linear. Although this type of division results in minor benefits such as easier navigation of a code, it does not maximize the true value of using subroutines.

Figure 23.2

A script flow parsed into subroutines based on group execution order

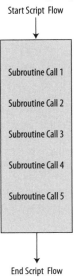

Simply mixing up the order of the group-based subroutines, as shown in Figure 23.3, doesn't make it more non-linear. The issue is not the order in which the subroutines exist, but rather the method used for their extraction.

Figure 23.3

A script flow with subroutines arranged in a "non-linear" fashion but still divided in a linear fashion

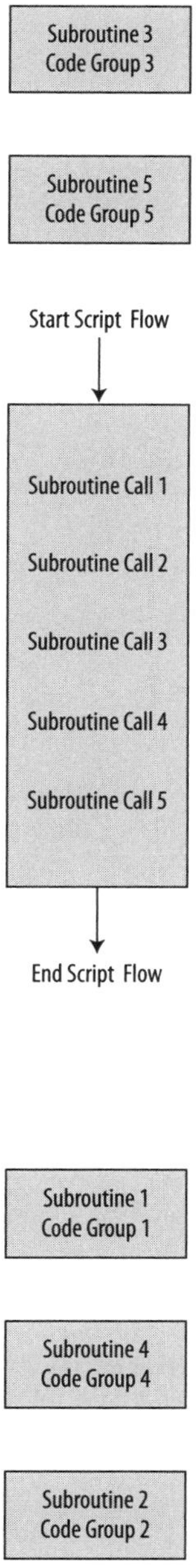

Subroutine 3
Code Group 3

Subroutine 5
Code Group 5

Start Script Flow

Subroutine Call 1

Subroutine Call 2

Subroutine Call 3

Subroutine Call 4

Subroutine Call 5

End Script Flow

Subroutine 1
Code Group 1

Subroutine 4
Code Group 4

Subroutine 2
Code Group 2

A slightly different organization that also adheres to execution order is a group of cascading subroutines, shown in Figure 23.4. The first subroutine runs the first group of code and then calls the second subroutine. That subroutine runs and calls the next one. One after the other, they execute in a chain and are still very much linear.

Figure 23.4

A script flow with subroutines arranged in a cascading order but still divided in a linear fashion

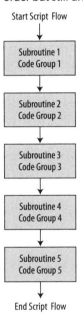

Start Script Flow

Subroutine 1
Code Group 1

Subroutine 2
Code Group 2

Subroutine 3
Code Group 3

Subroutine 4
Code Group 4

Subroutine 5
Code Group 5

End Script Flow

To show you how to achieve an ideal arrangement of subroutines, I will first explore the goals of idea subroutine hierarchy and how these goals determine which method you use to extract code into subroutines.

Defining the Goals of Subroutine Hierarchy

Achieving a hierarchical structure requires a new way of looking at script design. To understand the "how," you begin with the "why" by defining the goals of optimal code division.

Produce a flexible and expandable script

Simply using subroutines makes code more manageable, easier to navigate, and simpler to modify. Arranging code into a hierarchical subroutine format helps to accentuate these benefits. Subroutines at each level call a sequence of subroutines at the next level, providing a "table of contents" effect. This enables you to quickly trace a script's execution path and perform surgical modifications to key sections of such code.

Maximize reusable code

A primary goal of organizing subroutines in a hierarchy is to maximize the amount of code that is easily reusable, enabling you to copy and paste subroutines into new scripts. The lowest level code, which includes all code that controls applications, should be as open-ended as possible, and the same approach should be used upward through as much code as possible. In some cases, an entire script might be reusable with just a few modifications to properties.

Create portable code

Any code can be reused with enough effort. The hierarchy aims to make that reusable code as easily portable as possible. To be portable, code must be open-ended and parameter driven.

Achieve a separation of data from function

One of the ways code becomes more open-ended and portable is by separating data from function. Code that specifies the location of source material, the business rules guiding the script, and other project details should be separated from code that performs specific functions.

Facilitate a multi-module solution ideology

One of the most important benefits of using subroutine hierarchy is that it gives rise to more advanced script design concepts like multi-module solutions. Just as subroutines resolve difficulties with reusing code, subroutine hierarchies simplify multi-module solutions. Lower-level, single-function, application-specific subroutines can be moved into a completely generic subroutine library file while mid-level feature subroutines are prime candidates for script modules.

CROSS-REF
Designing multi-module script solutions is discussed in Chapter 24.

Identifying the Primary Levels of Hierarchy

Subroutine hierarchy can be broken down into three levels of code, as shown in Figure 23.5. The pyramid arrangement shows both the hierarchy and target size for each level. Ideally, subroutines with embedded project specific details will be as scarce as possible while open-ended code will exist in greater numbers.

Figure 23.5

The subroutine hierarchy pyramid

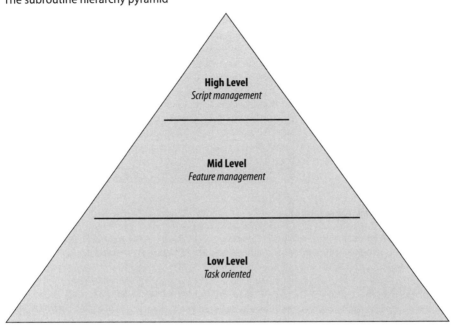

The three levels of code in a subroutine include:

- **High-level management code.** The *high-level subroutines* are smart, well informed, and very much in charge of a script's performance. They manage project specific material, invoke business rules, interact with users, and generally control the overall flow of events within a script. Code at this level should not perform actual functions and should never communicate with applications. Instead, it should send these tasks to a lower level, using parameters to convey information and instructions.

NOTE
The run and open subroutines are always considered high-level management subroutines, as are the main subroutine that these might call to manage the overall script functionality.

- **Low-level functional code.** The *low-level subroutines* contain very narrowly focused tasks and are unaware of the broad functions of the script, its other processes, or the information it manages and manipulates. They receive data and instructions, which they use to perform a function. Generally speaking, every subroutine at this level should be completely open-ended and easily portable. However, occasionally some low-level subroutines might exist that perform specific project-related functions.

NOTE
Subroutines at this level are the only subroutines that should communicate with applications, although the reasons for this will not become fully clear until Chapter 24.

- **Mid-level code.** The *mid-level subroutines* occupy a gray area that may have a mix of project-specific and open-ended qualities. This is the area of code that manages specific features of the script. In a perfect world, these subroutines are either completely open-ended or completely managerial and project specific. However, there will be some features that are more or less inclined to fall into one of those two categories.

Maintaining flexibility within levels

Not every script will conform to these three levels, nor should you attempt to make it do so. The more complex a script becomes, the less chance it will easily fitting into the pyramid structure. For example, a script that has several dozen "feature" subroutines in the mid level might require one or more "feature group management" subroutines that would squeeze between the top-level and the mid-level. Sometimes a "multifunction" subroutine will be added to perform a coordinated batch of single function subroutines. If the code is open-ended, it could be considered in a category squeezed in just above the low level.

Also, when a script is part of a multi-module solution, you may find the ideal hierarchy becomes rather complex. In such cases, a *script file hierarchy* might be required with each script having its own internal subroutine hierarchy. Some files might be very project specific, some might be completely open-ended, and others might be a mix of the two.

CROSS-REF
Learn about multi-module solutions in Chapter 24.

Following proper inter-level communication

A subroutine at any level should only call other subroutines at that same level or lower. This is important because you are trying to design a hierarchy and not a democratic network of subroutines. Because open-endedness is concentrated downward at the lower levels, communication between subroutines must migrate in this same direction.

Identifying Hierarchy-Related Issues

To achieve the goal of hierarchy, you must those identify elements that bind a subroutine to a project and those that keep it flexible and portable.

Project-specific elements

Project-specific elements are script components or other functionality that possesses detailed information or logic that only applies to the project at hand. This type of project management code is ideally locked into the highest level possible.

Accessing script properties

Script properties are a great place to store project-specific information. To keep lower-level code portable, they should not directly access properties. Only high-level code that manages the script processes should read or write to properties. Any property information that is required by lower-level code should be passed down as script parameters.

Interacting with global variables

Like properties, data contained in global variables are universally accessible to any subroutine within a script; however, global variables should be used with caution.

Global variables are especially bad when used as a method of data exchange between subroutines. When this is done throughout a script, global variables will "lock" all of the subroutines into a web, like that shown in Figure 23.6, making them much more difficult to extract and reuse. To copy one subroutine into a new script requires the painstaking identification of any global variables that the subroutine interacts with, any subroutines that place data into the global in the first place, and any subroutines that prepare that data. Then, everything needs to be reworked for the new script. Eliminating the use of global variables alleviates this entire mess and allows subroutine design to be more open-ended and less dependent on other parts of the script.

Figure 23.6

A web of subroutines connected to global variables as a method of data transmission

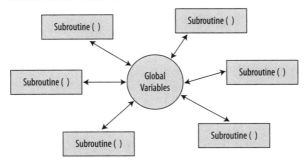

Ideally, data transfer between subroutines should be routed through subroutine parameters. Only the highest-level subroutines should access project-specific information stored in global variables and then pass them down, as shown in Figure 23.7. Because a call to a subroutine can include parameters that can deliver detailed information and instructions within the call to the subroutine, they are the most logical place to convey the information. Using a global variable as a method of data exchange between subroutines is a little like paying for a meal by placing your money on a table halfway between your table and the register and then walking up to the register and asking the cashier to get the money from that table. Because you are walking over there anyway, you could just hand over the money at the same time. When you multiply the number of global variables that could be required to handle all inter-subroutine communication in a complex script, keeping track of which money on the table belongs to who can become very confusing.

NOTE

There is a role for global variables, especially in multi-module solutions. Global variables are perfect for storing standard information that every script file in a multi-module solution will need access to such as a path to the project root folder or providing access to a library of open-ended subroutines.

Figure 23.7

A high-level subroutine accessing global variables and sending data down to lower subroutines through parameters

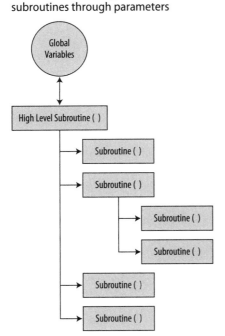

CROSS-REF

Learn more about how some global variables can be helpful sharing information in multi-module solutions in Chapter 24.

Accessing source material

The source material accessed by a script, such as data files, templates, folders of images, and more, are usually project specific. Code that knows where this material is located, how it is formatted, and the rules for preparing it for use should be reserved in the top level of the hierarchy. Subroutines that process this information should be as open-ended as possible, accepting data and instructions for processing it through subroutine parameters.

Collecting user input

When a script requires user input, the code that deals with project-specific details of this interaction should be restricted to the highest possible level. If the interaction is a commonly occurring procedure, a lower-level subroutine might be created to handle the input gathering with project-specific messages or button names being passed down to it from above.

Knowing business rules and other information

Any code with knowledge of business rules or other project-related details should be encoded into subroutines as high up the hierarchical chain as possible.

Loading other scripts

Subroutines that know which other module and library scripts need to be loaded should be as close to the top as possible. While the actual loading commands might be a lower-level subroutine, a script instructing it to open this library or that module would possess project-specific knowledge and should, therefore, be at the top of the hierarchy.

CROSS-REF

Learn how to load script modules in Chapter 24.

Open-ended elements

Open-ended elements are script components or other functionality that only possess the information required for them to perform narrowly defined tasks. Open-ended elements only have access to information that is passed down through parameters. Staunchly task-oriented code is ideally reserved for the lower levels while a general tendency toward open-endedness should expand to the highest possible level.

Performing specific tasks

Open-ended subroutines at the lowest level of hierarchy are intensely task oriented. They are unaware of the bigger picture and do not manage large features of a script. Their focus and concern is limited to their specialty.

A subroutine at this level is responsible for one simple task, such as confirming the existence of a folder in a specified location. While at first glance, it may not seem worthy of a whole subroutine, there are a few key benefits to having a subroutine dedicated to a single function.

A parameter could allow the calling script to specify that the subroutine should automatically create the folder if it does not exist. A record parameter can be included to allow additional folder properties to be set when the folder is located or created. For example, it might set the label color of the folder or automatically open the folder. By making the parameter a record, it can expand over time to include other, more advanced functionality. Of course, this expansion capability should be used cautiously so as not to venture too far from folder creation.

The script shown in Listing 23.1 performs the basic functionality described in this section. It allows a single line of code at multiple locations within a script to check for and/or create a folder and optionally assign it a label index and/or open it. Also, because the subroutine is open-ended, it can be pasted into any number of scripts and reused without modification.

Listing 23.1

A finderFolderExists() subroutine

```
on finderFolderExists(pathToParentFolder, nameFolder, blnAutoCreate,
    recData)
    --  This subroutine will check the existence of a folder and
    optionally create if it is missing.

    --  Setting: automatically open the folder
    set blnOpen to false
    try
        set blnOpen to blnOpen of recData
    end try

    --  Setting: automatically open the folder
    set numLabelIndex to 0
    try
        set numLabelIndex to numLabelIndex of recData
    end try

    set pathToParentFolder to (alias (pathToParentFolder as string)) as
    string
    set pathToFolder to ((pathToParentFolder & nameFolder & ":") as
    string)
```

continued

Listing 23.1   *(continued)*

```
tell application "Finder"
    --  Confirm or create the folder
    set blnFolderExists to (folder pathToFolder exists)
    if blnFolderExists = false and blnAutoCreate = false then return
false
    if blnFolderExists = false then
        set pathToFolder to (make new folder at (folder
pathToParentFolder) with properties {name:nameFolder}) as string
    end if

    --   Optionally open the folder
    if blnOpen = true then open folder pathToFolder
    --   Optionally assign a label index
    if numLabelIndex > 0 then
        set label index of folder pathToFolder to numLabelIndex
    end if
end tell
return pathToFolder

end finderFolderExists
```

An additional benefit to creating a subroutine specialized in a single function, such as confirming or creating a folder, is that it allows for the quick creation of a batch version of that subroutine like the one shown in Listing 23.2. Optionally, the batch functionality could be integrated into the original subroutine rather than standing alone.

Listing 23.2

A finderFolderExistsBatch() subroutine

```
on finderFolderExistsBatch(pathToParentFolder, listFolderNames, recData)
    --  This subroutine will create a batch of folders in a single location

    set pathToParentFolder to (alias (pathToParentFolder as string)) as
string
    set pathToFolder to ((pathToParentFolder & nameFolder & ":") as string)

    repeat with a from 1 to count items of listFolderNames
        finderFolderExists(pathToParentFolder, nameFolder, true,
{blnOpen:true, numLabelIndex:3})
    end repeat

end finderFolderExistsBatch
```

NOTE
The code in Listings 23.1 and 23.2 are available for download from the book's Web site at `www.wiley` `devreference.com`.

Limiting knowledge to parameters

Subroutines at the lower levels should be as open-ended as possible. They should be easily portable and highly reusable. This is accomplished by limiting their knowledge to the parameters they accept and any logic that is hardcoded within their code. As such, they do not have any knowledge of a few specific types of information.

First, they should not have direct contact with data stored in script properties as properties typically contain project-specific information. If a low-level subroutine needs to process data contained within properties, it should be passed down to them by higher-level subroutines. This "frees" them from the specifics of a script and enables them to become more universal.

The same is true of global variables. Using global variables within a single script file thwarts any opportunity to make portable and easily reusable subroutines. When designing a script to use a hierarchy, you should limit global variables to data used in every script you write or used to share information between script files in a multi-module solution.

NOTE
Open-ended subroutines should not have any knowledge of any project-specific logic or business rules beyond its immediate specialty or that information that is passed to it through subroutine parameters.

As you work your way up the hierarchical ladder, at some point it will become impractical or impossible to have parameters communicate everything. In other words, eventually, there will be a need for hard-coded business logic or other project specific code. The idea is not to ban details, but to try to confine them to the highest possible level.

Considering subroutine communication

Any communication with other subroutines should be carefully considered to ensure that they are directed down toward a lower level. The folder subroutine discussed earlier does not rely on any other subroutines because it is a lower-level, single-function subroutine. The fact that the batch folder subroutine calls this subroutine makes it one level higher.

A hypothetical script might have a hierarchy like the one shown in Figure 23.8. At the highest level, there is a primary subroutine called `projectStart()`. At some point during its execution, it reaches a point where it is time to build a project folder with a bunch of subfolders so it calls the `projectFoldersBuild()` feature subroutine. This subroutine first sends a command directly to the `finderFolderExists()` subroutine, instructing it where to build the project folder and what to name it. Then it calls the `finderFolderExistsBatch()` sub-routine, sending it a list of subfolders that should be created within the newly created project folder. Using a `repeat` loop, the batch subroutine sends each subfolder's name down to `finderFolderExists()`. When that subroutine is finished, control is returned back up the chain to `projectStart()`, which then runs other feature subroutines like `projectfol-derAddItems()`.

Notice that during this entire process all commands to subroutines went down. They can skip any number of levels as long as the commands trickle down. This approach aids the process of making subroutines easily portable. A subroutine at the lowest level can be reused elsewhere without concern for any dependencies it, or other subroutines, may have for it, because it has neither. A subroutine one level up can be reused as long as the lower level subroutine(s) it is dependent upon are reused with it.

Figure 23.8

The subroutine hierarchy of a hypothetical script

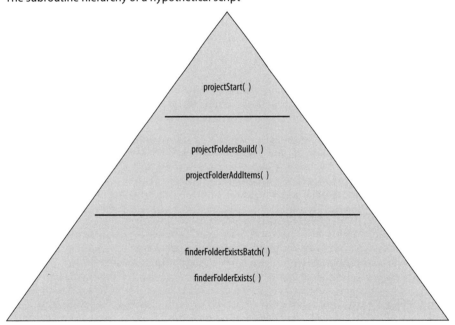

Limiting application interaction

Any interaction with applications should be limited to lower-level, single-function subroutines, that are highly reusable and upgradable, among other reasons discussed in Chapter 25.

> ## Raising the Hierarchical Bar
>
> It is possible to extract and reuse any code, as long as enough effort is exerted. The goal of designing a script into in a hierarchy is to make this recycling process as easy as possible for the largest portion of a script.
>
> Although I defined some issues or elements of a script as being "top-level" and others as being "bottom-level," assigning a level distinction to these elements may be slightly misleading. These associations are meant as a general guideline, but their actual implementation might vary from one script to the next. Most important, the lower-level objectives should apply to as much of a script as possible and not just the lower level. Likewise, the top-level goals should apply to as little of a script as possible. Therefore, a location-based goal is not equivalent to a hierarchy level.
>
> Think of "open-endedness" as a horizontal line within a script. Everything above the line can be project specific and everything below the line is open-ended. The goal is to keep that line as close to the top of the subroutine hierarchy as possible. The line would be at the bottom of a script that is completely project specific or at the top for a script that is completely open-ended. Most scripts will fall somewhere in the middle, as shown in the following figure.
>
>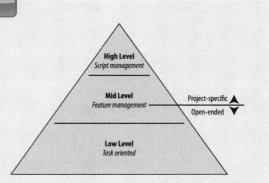
>
> A hypothetical script that is half open-ended and half project specific
>
> At first, you shouldn't worry too much about designing the perfect script. Instead, just write scripts. When they grow in size and you begin separating them into subroutines, try to make a few open-ended. When you start building other scripts, you will get a feel for which portions might have a wider use. When that happens, spend a little extra time making them self-sustaining, portable, and reusable. Eventually, you will be creating hierarchical structured subroutines like a pro.

Creating a Image Batch Processor with a Hierarchical Subroutine Structure

 In Chapter 18, you learned how to design a simple image batch processor script. You then learned how to upgrade this script in Chapter 22, which demonstrated how it could become more open-ended and, therefore, offer the user more control over which files were processed, how they were modified, which file types they were saved as, and where they were saved. Continuing this process in this section, you will again redesign the same script, this time dividing the code into subroutines using the hierarchical design structure discussed in this chapter.

Many improvements were made to the script in Chapter 22, including the separation of the implied `run` subroutine to an explicit `run` subroutine and the addition of an `open` subroutine. This change allowed the user to drop files directly onto a script application or to double-click and then select from a couple of options to guide the script to the items to process. The change, as illustrated in Figure 23.9, split the script into two subroutines based on how the user launched the script application.

NOTE
The Image Batch Processor script files are available for download from the book's Web site at
`www.wileydevreference.com`.

Figure 23.9

A flow chart showing the structure of the version of the batch
processor from the end of Chapter 22

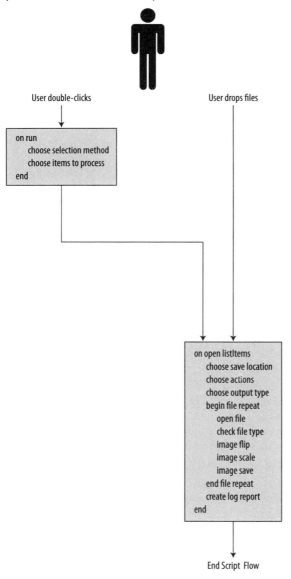

Earlier in this chapter, I discussed the unwise approach of dividing a script into subroutines based on execution order. The resulting script cascades control from one subroutine to the next in a clear lack of hierarchy, as shown in Figure 23.10. While the `open` subroutine has been separated into five subroutines, because they are arranged in the same order they were in before the separation, the script continues to be quite linear. Due to the script flow travelling in a straight line through each subroutine, the script is also lacking hierarchical structure.

Figure 23.10

A flow chart of a poorly designed image batch processor script with a cascading subroutine structure

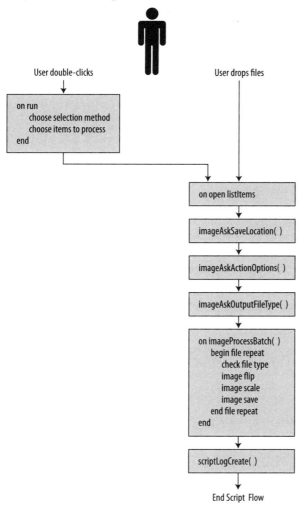

To design a version of the image processing script that uses the ideas discussed in this chapter, you need to rethink the flow chart to look something like the one shown in Figure 23.11.

Figure 23.11

A flow chart that shows the structure of a well-designed version of the script with a hierarchical subroutine structure

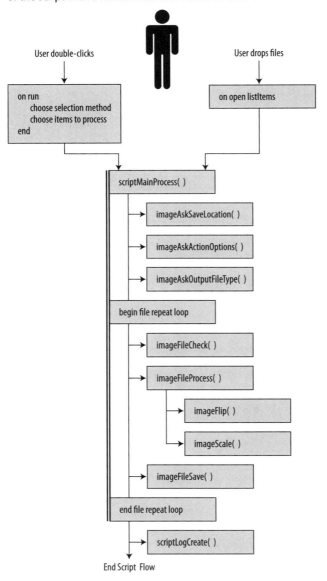

Notice that both the `run` and `open` subroutines immediately hand control over to the `scriptMainProcess()` subroutine, which then manages the script from start to finish. It contains the repeat loop, sending commands to subroutines for each specific function one step at a time. Some of the mid-level subroutines call lower-level subroutines, but this is different from a cascade. Instead of a steady string of subroutines, control goes back up the chain to the subroutine that is managing the tasks at a given level. So, `scriptMainProcess()` passes control to `imageAskSaveLocation()`. Once that subroutine is finished executing, control is reverted up to the main script, which then passes control to the `imageAskActionOptions()` subroutine and again to `imageAskOutputFileType()`. When `imageFileProcess()` gains control, it performs the image manipulations by calling `imageFlip()` and then `imageScale()` but then returns control back to the main script, which continues the process. Throughout the entire process, the organization of subroutines is hierarchical.

Outlining the new subroutine structure

The first step is to create an outline for the new version of the script. The new structure will have twelve subroutines in three different categories.

Level 1: Management subroutines

There will be two command handler subroutines: `run` and `open`. They will be greatly simplified to immediately route control to the primary subroutine that will manage the whole process. Technically this places these subroutines outside the realm of the hierarchical structure; however, they can be considered part of the top level.

The Level 1 subroutine responsible for primary script control will be called `batchMainProcess()`. It will accept a single parameter: a list of files that were dropped on the script application. If the user runs the script by double-clicking its application icon, this parameter will be empty, prompting the subroutine to perform the functions that were previously included in the `run` subroutine: letting the user select what he wants to process.

NOTE
This subroutine is project specific and not open-ended or portable.

Level 2: Feature subroutines

The new script will have two Level 2 feature subroutines. They include:

- **batchRunOption().** This subroutine, which was previously contained in the `run` command subroutine, will be executed if the user double-clicks the script application. It will ask the user to choose an option for selecting the images to be processed. The user can choose a single image, a folder of images, or their currently selected Finder item(s).

- **batchActionOptionsChoose().** This subroutine will ask the user which image manipulation actions he wants to perform on a batch of images.

Level 3: Single function subroutines

The new script will have eight single-function, low-level subroutines. All of these will be open-ended, reusable, and completely portable. These subroutines include:

- **finderFileExtensionRemove().** This subroutine will extract the "clean" name of an item without a file extension. This will be used later to save an image into various file types rather than adding a new extension after the current one.

- **imageSaveFormatChoose().** This subroutine will allow the user to select one or more file types in which to save each image in the batch.

- **imageFileOpen().** This subroutine will instruct the Image Events application to open an image file. It returns a list containing a reference to the open image and the name of the image.

- **imageFileCheck().** This subroutine will check a specified image's file type. It will help identify and halt processing for any file that is not a format Image Events can use.

- **imageFlip().** This subroutine will flip a specified image horizontally or vertically.

- **imageScale().** This subroutine will scale a specified image.

- **imageFileSave().** This subroutine will save a modified image to one or more of the eight file types that Image Events can save.

- **scriptLogCreate().** This subroutine will write an open a session log file that lists the files that were successfully processed and those that were not.

Rebuilding the script

Now that you have a good script outline, you can begin rebuilding the script with the new subroutine structure. Most of the code in this section is identical to the version of the script at the end of Chapter 22. However, it does include some additional and modified statements that are required to facilitate the new arrangement of code.

Building the command handler subroutines

Previously the run subroutine contained code that allowed a user to choose the material to be processed. This code moves into a feature subroutine to keep it contained as a semi-portable routine and to keep the command handler subroutines as short as possible.

Both the run and open subroutines include only a call to the primary batchMainProcess subroutine. While the open command simply relays the list of files dropped on the script application, the run command sends an empty list, which prompts the primary routine to ask the user what he wants to process.

The new script starts with the code shown in Listing 23.3.

Listing 23.3

The open and run command handlers

```
on run
    batchMainProcess({})
end run
on open listFiles
    batchMainProcess(listFiles)
end open
```

Building batchMainProcess()

The next subroutine manages the entire script process after the run and open routines call it. It is the longest subroutine in the new structure with two exceptions: a prompt for the user to choose an output folder and formatting of the session log data. This subroutine calls other subroutines rather than performing actions itself.

The subroutine, shown in its entirety in Listing 23.4, contains several steps, including:

1. **If the** `listFiles` **parameter is an empty list, indicating that no files were dropped, it calls the** `batchRunOption()` **subroutine.** If the result is `false`, indicating that the user canceled a dialog message, the entire script is aborted. If not, the script continues.

2. **Using the** `choose folder` **command, the script asks the user to select an output folder in which modified files should be saved.** This eliminates the chance of overwriting of the original files. If the user clicks cancel, the script automatically halts.

3. **The** `batchActionOptionsChoose()` **subroutine is called, asking the user to select one or more image modification action(s) he wants to perform on the batch of image files waiting to be processed.** If the result is `false`, indicating that the user canceled a dialog message, the entire script will be aborted. If not, the script continues.

4. **The script calls the** `imageSaveFormat()` **subroutine, which asks the user to select the file format(s) that the images should be saved as.** If the result is `false`, indicating that the user canceled a dialog message, the entire script will be aborted. If not, the script continues.

5. **Two variables are initialized for the session log, which will be created at the end of the process.** The first, `textSuccess`, will contain a list of files that are successfully processed. The second, `textFailure`, will contain a list of files that are not successfully processed and list the reasons why.

6. **The script is ready to begin processing the files.** To do so, it sets up a `repeat` loop that will run once for each item. A variable `pathToItem` is initialized with the path to the current item and a `try` statement that will protect the image processing code is begun.

7. **The path is sent to the** `imageFileOpen()` **subroutine and places the results into the** refImage **and** nameImage **variables.**

8. **The path is sent to the** `finderFileExtensionRemove()` **subroutine and the result is placed into the** `nameImageForSave` **variable.** This step removes the extension from the file name so an output image will only have one extension in their name.

9. **The reference to the open file is sent to the** `imageFileCheck()` **subroutine.** If the file is not an image file, an error will occur, making the code skip immediately to the `on error` clause of the `try` statement to record the error before continuing to the next file.

10. **Several values are sent to the** `imageFileSave()` **subroutine, which saves the current image in the selected folder as the selected file type(s).**

11. **If the subroutine performed Steps 7 through11 without an error, the name of the image is added to the list of successfully run subroutines in** `textSuccess`. If any of those steps caused an error, the image is added to the list in `textFailure`.

12. **The script skips back to Step 7 and repeats the sequence until there are no more images remaining to process.**

13. **The script formats the text headings for the session log and sends it to the** `scriptLogCreate()` **subroutine, which writes the information to a text file and opens it.**

Listing 23.4

The primary subroutine, which manages the entire script process

```
on batchMainProcess(listFiles)
    --    This subroutine will manage the processing of a batch of files

    --  If nothing was dropped on the script, ask the user to select
    items to process
    if listFiles = {} then
        set listFiles to batchRunOption()
        if listFiles = false then return
    end if

    --  Ask the user to select an output folder for processed images
    set textPrompt to "Choose a folder to save modified images:"
    set pathToSave to (choose folder with prompt textPrompt) as string

    --  Ask the user to choose the action(s) to perform
    set listActionChoices to batchActionOptionsChoose()
    if listActionChoices = false then return

    --  Ask the user to choose the file type(s) to save output
    set listSaveOptions to imageSaveFormatChoose()
    if listSaveOptions = false then return

    --  Process each file
    set textSuccess to ""
    set textFailure to ""
    repeat with a from 1 to count items of listFiles
```

```
        set pathToItem to item a of listFiles as string
        try
            --  Open the current file
            set {refImage, nameImage} to imageFileOpen(pathToItem)
            set nameImageForSave to finderFileExtensionRemove(pathToItem)
            imageFileCheck(refImage)

                --   Process the current image
            repeat with a from 1 to count items of listActionChoices
                set nameChoice to item a of listActionChoices

                --  Flip the image
                if nameChoice contains "Flip" then
                    imageFlip(refImage, nameChoice)
                end if

                --  Scale the image
                if nameChoice contains "Scale" then
                    imageFileScale(refImage, nameChoice)
                end if

            end repeat

            --  Save the modified image
            imageFileSave(refImage, nameImageForSave, pathToSave,
    listSaveOptions)

            --  Build the log entry
            set textForLog to nameImage & return
            set textSuccess to textSuccess & textForLog as string
        on error errText
            set textForLog to nameImage & " (" & errText & ")" & return
            set textFailure to textFailure & textForLog as string
        end try
    end repeat

    --  Format results and send to a session log file
    set textResult to ""
    set textLine to "-------------------------------------------------"
    if textSuccess ≠ "" then
        set textResult to textResult & "Successfully processed image(s):"
    & return & textLine & return & textSuccess & return as string
    end if
    if textFailure ≠ "" then
        set textResult to textResult & "The following image(s) failed to
    process:" & return & textLine & return & textFailure as string
    end if
    set pathToLog to (path to desktop folder as string) & "Image Batch
    Processor Results.txt" as string
    scriptLogCreate(pathToLog, textResult, true, true)

end batchMainProcess
```

Building batchRunOptions()

The `batchRunOptions()` subroutine, shown in Listing 23.5, is exactly the same as the `run` subroutine in the version of the script at the end of Chapter 22 with one small exception. Instead of calling the `open` subroutine and sending over the list of selected items, it simply returns the list of items that go back to the `batchMainProcess()` subroutine.

Listing 23.5

The batchRunOption() subroutine

```
on batchRunOption()
    --  This subroutine will as the user what they want to select (used
    if the script was double-clicked)
    set listChoices to {"One Image", "Images in a Folder"}
    tell application "Finder" to set listSelectedItems to the selection
    set nameDefault to "Images in a Folder"
    if listSelectedItems is not {} then
        copy "Selected Images" to end of listChoices
        set nameDefault to "Selected Images"
    end if
    set dataChoice to choose from list listChoices with prompt "Process:"
    default items nameDefault
    if dataChoice = false then return false
    set nameSelection to item 1 of dataChoice

    --  Gather a list of files for processing
    if nameSelection = "One image" then
        set textPrompt to "Choose an image file to modify:"
        set pathToImageFile to (choose folder with prompt textPrompt) as
    string
        set listFiles to {pathToImageFile}
    else if nameSelection = "Images in a Folder" then
        set textPrompt to "Choose a folder of images to modify:"
        set pathToImageFolder to (choose folder with prompt textPrompt) as
    string
        set listFilesTemp to list folder pathToImageFolder without
    invisibles
        set listFiles to {}
        repeat with a from 1 to count items of listFilesTemp
            copy pathToImageFolder & item a of listFilesTemp as string to
    end of listFiles
        end repeat
    else
        set listFiles to listSelectedItems
    end if
    return listFiles
end batchRunOption
```

Building batchActionOptionsChoose()

The `batchActionOptionsChoose()` subroutine, shown in Listing 23.6, asks the user to choose the action(s) he wants to perform on the batch of image files. Optionally, the user is asked to input a custom scale percentage. Then the list of selected actions is sent back to the main subroutine.

Listing 23.6

The batchActionOptionsChoose() subroutine

```
on batchActionOptionsChoose()
   --  This subroutine will ask the user to choose the action(s) to
   perform on the image batch
   set textPrompt to "Perform which action(s):"
   set listOptions to {"Flip horizontal", "Flip vertical", "Scale 25%",
   "Scale 50%", "Scale 75%", "Scale Custom %"}
   set listChoices to (choose from list listOptions with multiple
   selections allowed without empty selection allowed)
   if listChoices = false then return false

   --  Handle custom scale request
   if listChoices contains "Scale Custom %" then
      set textPrompt to "Scale images by what percentage:"
      set textPercent to (text returned of (display dialog textPrompt
   default answer ".10"))

      set listChoicesTemp to {}
      repeat with a from 1 to count items of listChoices
         set nameChoice to item a of listChoices
         if nameChoice is not "Scale Custom %" then
            copy nameChoice to end of listChoicesTemp
         end if
      end repeat

      copy "Scale Custom " & textPercent as string to end of
   listChoicesTemp
      set listChoices to listChoicesTemp
   end if
   return listChoices
end batchActionOptionsChoose
```

Building batchFileProcess()

The `batchFileProcess()` subroutine, shown in Listing 23.7, manages the execution of the selected actions on the current file. This subroutine accepts two parameters: a reference to the current image and the list of action choices the user selected. It performs a repeat loop through each action and instructs the appropriate single function subroutine to modify the image appropriately.

Listing 23.7

The batchFileProcess() subroutine

```
on batchFileProcess(refImage, listChoices)
    --  This subroutine will perform a sequence of manipulations to every
    file in a list
    repeat with a from 1 to count items of listChoices
        set nameChoice to item a of listChoices

        --  Flip the image
        if nameChoice contains "Flip" then
            imageFlip(refImage, nameChoice)
        end if

        --  Scale the image
        if nameChoice contains "Scale" then
            imageFileScale(refImage, nameChoice)
        end if

    end repeat
end batchFileProcess
```

Building finderFileExtensionRemove()

The `finderFileExtensionRemove()` subroutine, shown in Listing 23.8, performs a simple function. Using text item delimiters and the Finder's `name extension` command, it removes the extension from the name of a file specified in its `pathToItem` parameter. The new "clean" name is then sent back to the main subroutine to be used when saving the image file as a different file type.

Listing 23.8

The finderFileExtensionRemove() subroutine

```
on finderFileExtensionRemove(pathToItem)
    --  This subroutine will remove the file extension from the image
    name for saving
    tell application "Finder"
        set textExtension to name extension of item pathToItem
        set nameImage to name of item pathToItem
    end tell
    set nameImageForSave to nameImage
    if nameImage ends with textExtension and textExtension ≠ "" then
```

```
      set text item delimiters to {"." & textExtension}
      set listTemp to every text item of nameImage
      set text item delimiters to {""}
      set nameImageForSave to listTemp as text
   end if
   return nameImageForSave
end finderFileExtensionRemove
```

CROSS-REF

Text item delimiters are discussed in Chapter 7.

Building imageSaveFormatChoose()

The `imageSaveFormatChoose()` subroutine, shown in Listing 23.9, uses the `choose from list` command to ask the user to select the file type(s) to use when saving the image files.

Listing 23.9

The imageSaveFormatChoose() subroutine

```
on imageSaveFormatChoose()
   --   This subroutine will ask the user to choose the file type(s) to
   save images
   set textPrompt to "Save images as:"
   set listOptions to {"BMP", "JPEG", "JPEG2", "PICT", "PNG", "PSD",
   "QuickTime Image", "TIFF"}
   set listChoices to (choose from list listOptions with empty selection
   allowed and multiple selections allowed)
   return listChoices
end imageSaveFormatChoose
```

CROSS-REF

The `choose from list` command is discussed in Chapter 16.

Building imageFileOpen()

The `imageFileOpen()` subroutine, shown in Listing 23.10, simply opens the image specified in its `pathToItem` parameter and returns a reference to the open image and the name of the image.

Listing 23.10

The imageFileOpen() subroutine

```
on imageFileOpen(pathToItem)
    --  This subroutine will open an image and return the reference to
    and name of the image
    tell application "Image Events"
        set refImage to open alias pathToItem
        set nameImage to name of refImage
    end tell
    return {refImage, nameImage}
end imageFileOpen
```

NOTE

While it might seem odd to have a subroutine perform such a simple function, this technique becomes useful when building scripts that might someday be ported to another application or must be able to perform similar tasks is different applications of the same time. This topic is discussed further in Chapter 25.

Building imageFileCheck()

The imageFileCheck() subroutine, shown in Listing 23.11, confirms that the image referenced in its refImage parameter is one of the file types Image Events can manipulate. If not, an error is generated, which causes the main subroutine to skip the current image and add it to the list of items not processed.

Listing 23.11

The imageFileCheck() subroutine

```
on imageFileCheck(refImage)
    --  This subroutine will confirm that the specified file is an
    acceptable file type
    tell application "Image Events"
        set recProperties to (properties of refImage)
        set dataFileType to file type of recProperties
        set listFileTypes to {BMP, GIF, JPEG, JPEG2, MacPaint, PDF,
Photoshop, PICT, PNG, PSD, QuickTime Image, SGI, TGA, TIFF}
        set blnImageFile to listFileTypes contains dataFileType
        if blnImageFile = false then error "Not an image file"
    end tell
end imageFileCheck
```

Building imageFlip()

The `imageFileFlip()` subroutine, shown in Listing 23.12, will flip the image specified in its `refImage` parameter horizontally and/or vertically based on the value of its `textDirection` parameter.

Listing 23.12

The imageFileFlip() subroutine

```
on imageFlip(refImage, textDirection)
    --  This subroutine will flip an image in a specified direction
    tell application "Image Events"
        --  Horizontal flip
        if textDirection contains "Flip horizontal" then
            flip refImage with horizontal
        end if

        --  Vertical flip
        if textDirection contains "Flip vertical" then
            flip refImage with vertical
        end if
    end tell
end imageFlip
```

Building imageFileScale()

The `imageFileScale()` subroutine, shown in Listing 23.13, scales the image specified in its `refImage` parameter by the amount in its `textAmount` parameter. To preemptively handle situations where the latter might include a fractional amount or a whole number, it gets the last word of whatever the value is and then puts a period in front of it.

Listing 23.13

The imageFileScale() subroutine

```
on imageFileScale(refImage, textAmount)
    --  This subroutine will scale an image a specified amount
    tell application "Image Events"
        set numScale to "." & last word of textAmount as real
        scale refImage by factor numScale
    end tell
end imageFileScale
```

Building imageFileSave()

The `imageFileSave()` subroutine, shown in Listing 23.14, will save a specified image in one or more formats. Four parameters contain a reference to the current image, the non-extension bearing name to use when saving the image, the folder path to save the image, and a list of file types selected by the user. Using these values, the subroutine creates a temp file of the currently modified image and then opens, saves, and closes it once for each output file type. At the end, it instructs the Finder to delete the temp file.

Listing 23.14

The imageFileSave() subroutine

```
on imageFileSave(refImage, nameImageForSave, pathToSave, listOptions)
    --  This subroutine will save an in the specified format(s)
    set pathToTemp to pathToSave & "TEMP" as string
    set pathToSave to pathToSave & nameImageForSave as string
    tell application "Image Events"
        save refImage in file pathToTemp
        close refImage

        repeat with a from 1 to count items of listOptions
            set refImage to open file pathToTemp
            set nameChoice to item a of listOptions

            if nameChoice = "BMP" then save refImage as BMP in file
    (pathToSave & ".bmp" as string)
            if nameChoice = "JPEG" then save refImage as JPEG in file
    (pathToSave & ".jpg" as string)
            if nameChoice = "JPEG2" then save refImage as JPEG2 in file
    (pathToSave & ".jp2" as string)
            if nameChoice = "PICT" then save refImage as PICT in file
    (pathToSave & ".pict" as string)
            if nameChoice = "PNG" then save refImage as PNG in file
    (pathToSave & ".png" as string)
            if nameChoice = "PSD" then save refImage as PSD in file
    (pathToSave & ".psd" as string)
            if nameChoice = "QuickTime Image" then save refImage as
    QuickTime Image in file (pathToSave & ".qif" as string)
            if nameChoice = "TIFF" then save refImage as TIFF in file
    (pathToSave & ".tiff" as string)
            close refImage
        end repeat
    end tell
    --  Clean up
    tell application "Finder"
        delete file pathToTemp
    end tell
end imageFileSave
```

Building scriptLogCreate()

The `scriptLogCreate()` subroutine, shown in Listing 23.15, writes data into a session log file and opens it. It accepts four parameters: the folder path in which to save the log, the text data that should be written into the log, a boolean-driven indication of whether it should delete a file it if already exists, and a boolean-driven indication of whether it should automatically open the log.

Listing 23.15

The scriptLogCreate() subroutine

```
on scriptLogCreate(pathToLog, textToWrite, blnReplaceOld, blnAutoOpen)
    --  This subroutine will write data to a log file and open the log

    --  Optionally clean up old reports
    if blnReplaceOld = true then
       tell application "Finder"
          if (file pathToLog exists) then delete file pathToLog
       end tell
    end if

    --  Create the new report and open it
    open for access file pathToLog with write permission
    write textToWrite to file pathToLog
    close access file pathToLog

    --  Optionally open the log
    if blnAutoOpen = true then
       tell application "Finder"
          open file pathToLog
       end tell
    end if
end scriptLogCreate
```

Summary

In this chapter you learned about the different ways to divide a script into subroutines and heard a case for designing a hierarchical structure. You learned about the goals and levels of hierarchy. And you learned about dividing the image batch processing script created and modified in Chapters 18 and 22 into subroutines based on this idea.

Organizing Code into Modules and Libraries for Multi-Module Solutions

Introduction to Multi-Module Solutions

A *multi-module solution* is an AppleScript solution made up of more than one script file. The technique became a necessity years ago to overcome file size limitations; and dividing a script into separate parts has many positive benefits that make it desirable, even after file size restrictions were removed.

During the early years of AppleScript, script files were limited to a frustrating maximum file size of 32K. While this was plenty of space for creating small scripts, it was significantly restrictive for real-world solutions. Once a script reached the limit, developers were left with two options: shrink the size of the script or split the script into multiple files.

The first choice, shrinking the size of the script to conserve space, encouraged the use of cryptically named variables, the removal of comments and all extra spaces, and many other bad habits. The level of compression increased each time a script bumped into the size limit, taking the script down another level into the cryptic depths of obfuscation. Because the vintage Script Editor was devoid of a find and replace feature, many developers adopted these space-saving habits from the start, even with scripts that where well under the size limit. Some still use this popular approach to this very day, even though the size restrictions have long since vanished.

The second choice to conserve space, splitting the script into multiple files, is the subject of this chapter. A large script can be split into two or more separate files. The primary script can then load the other script(s) and instruct them to run or to execute specific subroutines, which can be executed just as commands are within an application. This approach is by far the better option, allowing scripts to continue to use a clear naming convention and retain comments and spacing between subroutines and grouped sections of code. It also encourages skilled developers to adopt a new focus on the structural design of script files, allowing some files to become libraries of specialized subroutines while other files manage processes or stored information.

Even though today there is no limit on the size of a script file, there are still many good reasons to continue creating script solutions across multiple files.

In This Chapter

Looking at the history, benefits, and types of multi-module scripts

Designing multi-module script solutions and inter-module workflows

Managing, testing, and troubleshooting complex script solutions

Understanding the Benefits of Multi-Module Solutions

There are many positive benefits to splitting a complex script into multiple files. As with subroutines, multi-module solutions help make code more organized, manageable, and easier for the developer to interact with.

Eases developer tasks

In some ways, breaking a script into several files can hinder a developer's efficiency by complicating the developer's interaction with and navigation of various code portions. Losing track of a subroutine's location becomes more pronounced as there are multiple files to search. Spotlight searches don't currently penetrate into compiled scripts so a find must be performed within the AppleScript Editor for each file that makes up the solution.

While this issue alone might cause some developers to avoid multi-module solutions altogether, if they keep an eye on design when deciding how to separate files, it can alleviate the problem. In fact, organizing code into separate script files, if done skillfully, can actually improve a developer's interaction with a solution. For example, separating code into multiple script files can:

- **Delimit the file structure.** Like the use of comments, spacing, and subroutines, separating a complex script into multiple files helps break the code into smaller, more manageable sections. When developers do it in a thoughtful manner, keeping similar routines together by type, scope, or hierarchy can make it easier to navigate through the complex structure of large solutions.

- **Facilitate collaborative development.** If a solution is encapsulated within a single script file, before other developers collaborate on it, the file must first be dissected and then later reintegrated. With a multi-module solution, members of a development team can simultaneously modify different modules.

- **Aid in visualizing the hierarchical structure.** If subroutines are grouped in separate files according to their hierarchical position, a multi-module solution helps emphasize the hierarchical structures within. This helps the developer visualize the hierarchy of the whole solution rather than trying to see groupings within a single, sprawling script file.

Allows advanced script design

In the same way that using subroutines enables you to rethink the arrangement of code into an optimal way, splitting a script into separate files makes advanced script design options possible. For example, organizing code into separate script files can:

- **Encourage standardization and better design.** A delimited script structure encourages the adoption of standards and a better overall solution design, and helps to alleviate some of the navigational and troubleshooting headaches of having a script span more than one file.

- **Focus specialized script file types.** When scripts are broken into separate modules, it becomes possible to consider specialized script types. Code in a single script can be organized by some criteria, but it is still a single file. When the material is separated, it becomes possible to consider a group of code as a specialized entity such as a library of subroutines or a module focused on a particular function.

- **Encourage open-ended file design.** In the same manner that subroutines encourage an open-ended, parameter-driven design, a multi-module solution encourages the same in the form of open-ended script files. New modules can be dropped in with little additional work when the basic structure is in place and allows it.

- **Allow the reuse of entire files.** Subroutines help create small portable packages of generic code that can be recycled in future scripts, just like multi-module solutions help to create small portable files of generic code that can also be reused. Rather than copying a batch of subroutines into a new project script, entire files can be brought in and reused with little or no modification.

Designing a Multi-Module Solution

A multi-module solution requires unique considerations about the types of files, how and where they are stored, and how they communicate to one another.

Defining types of script files

When a script is separated into individual files, the developer can group different types of script files. While developers can choose whatever division they prefer, most scripts fall into three general categories: modules, libraries, and data storage files.

Modules

A *module* is a script that contains mid- to high-level functions that manage one or more auto-mated processes. The primary script application that the user launches or drops items on is a module as is any other script file that bears the responsibly for managing one or more features. A solution might have one module, or dozens or hundreds of them arranged in a complex folder structure mirroring their hierarchical connection to one another.

Modules typically manage processes by running subroutines that exist within the same file or by loading other script files. They often have business rules and logic embedded within them.

NOTE

Subroutines that control communication with applications are usually stored within a library file and not a module, although they can be.

An AppleScript solution that builds a catalog in Adobe InDesign may include several modules that perform key portions of the build process (see Figure 24.1). To start the process, the user launches a primary Build Catalog script application module. Because it manages the overall process, this module asks the user which catalog she wants to build, which template to use, and any other relevant information. It also loads up the subroutine library files into global variables for solution-wide use and loads data files that contain information that helps guide the catalog process. Then it starts the catalog-building process by loading and running the appropriate module that handles each major step in the process.

Figure 24.1

A hypothetical AppleScript solution
that builds complex catalog files

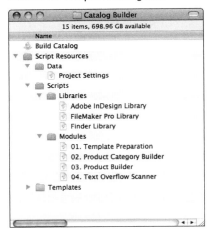

First, the Template Preparation module is instructed to copy, open, and prepare the selected template file. It modifies specific details of the master pages and performs any other preparatory tasks. When the module is finished, control is passed back to the primary module, which instructs the next module to begin its tasks. The second module performs a database search and extracts data for the products that will be included in the catalog. Then, the primary script loops through each category of product, passing data to the appropriate module to populate the catalog with product information and images.

In the same way that the primary script manages the modules for each step, those modules send commands to the application libraries, instructing them to perform specific tasks. For example, the second module instructs the FileMaker Pro Library script to open a database, perform a find and sort action, and then export data. The third and fourth modules send commands to the Adobe InDesign Library file.

Libraries

A *library* file is a script that contains a group of low-level subroutines that perform narrowly focused, specific tasks. Any data or instructional values are sent to a library subroutine through its parameters because, unlike modules, libraries are not aware of project-specific processes or logic. Library subroutines should be more open-ended, but that can vary depending on the way they are organized.

N O T E

Subroutine libraries can be organized by various criteria, such as application, function, client, project, or another project-related area of focus.

Data storage files

A *data storage file* contains specific project data in properties, which are loaded and used by modules. These can include preference-like pieces of information containing specific values that govern some aspect of how a solution should perform. They can also provide a place to temporarily store data generated during the course of a solution.

Generally, data storage files are only used when information is needed throughout many scripts in a complex solution. For simpler solutions, these values can be properties stored in the script module that used them.

Data storage files can also be used if there are several sets of similar data. For example, a solution that has several templates available might have one data storage file per template, which indicates key differences between them such as the name of master pages or style sheets.

N O T E

Data storage files can be considered somewhat analogous to localization files, which contain interface phrases for different languages.

C R O S S - R E F

Temporary data or other settings can also be stored in script-generated databases using the Database Events application, which is discussed in Chapter 19.

Exploring file structure options for complex solutions

By definition a multi-module solution has more than one file and must, therefore, have those files grouped together in some kind of folder structure. Two of the containment options keep all of the solution resources together while several others pare resources into a separate location from its primary script application.

CROSS-REF

Deployment locations for single script solutions are discussed in Chapter 4.

Integrating solution files in a single location

One option for the structure of a complex solution is to keep the primary script and all of the additional resources in a single location. This creates a highly portable solution and makes it easy to keep track of required material.

Storing files in a classic application folder structure

A *classic application folder structure* consists of a folder that contains all of the resources for a multi-module script solution in subfolders along with the primary script. This was the best choice for complex script and most third-party applications prior to Mac OS X, long before application or file packages and dedicated user folders appeared on the scene.

While this is probably the least favored option today, there may be situations still where it has an advantage. For example, if a non-developer user will be given access to solution files such as templates, data files, and perhaps even some script files, keeping the files easily accessible can prove to be advantageous. Sometimes it is useful to be able to see the entire solution structure within a single directory.

A hypothetical Catalog Builder solution might have a classic folder structure like the one shown in Figure 24.2. At the root level of the folder is the Build Catalog script and a `Script Resources` folder. The script provides easy access to the solution, while the folder contains a substructure that organizes data, templates, and various types of script files.

Figure 24.2

An example of a classic application folder with everything accessible and stored in a single location

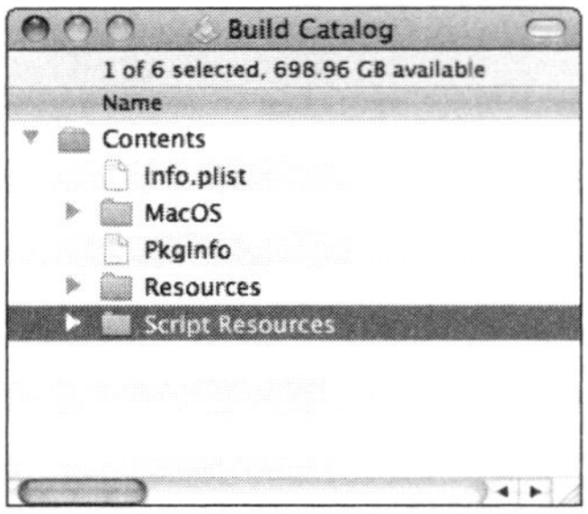

A script application can access material contained by the same folder in which it exists by using the `path to me` command. This command returns the entire path to the script application, which can then be pared down to get the path of the folder containing the script. From there, the script can access any material in the folder by appending the subpath. The script in Listing 24.1 demonstrates how to establish the path to the root folder and then acquire a list of folder contents for that folder and the `Script Resources` folder within it.

Listing 24.1

Calculating the path to the enclosing folder and locating files and folders contained within it

```
set pathToRoot to path to me as string
tell application "Finder"
  set pathToRoot to folder of file pathToRoot as string
  -- result = "Macintosh HD:Users:mmunro:Desktop:Catalog Builder:"
end tell

list folder pathToRoot without invisibles
-- {"Build Catalog.app", "Script Resources"}

set pathToScriptResources to (pathToRoot & "Script Resources:" as
    string)
list folder pathToScriptResources without invisibles
-- result = {"Data", "Scripts", "Templates"}
```

Storing files in an application bundle

 Another option that allows all solution resources to stay within a single location is to store files as an application or script bundle. When a script is saved as an application or a script bundle, it includes an embedded folder structure. You can open the embedded folder by Ctrl+clicking the script application and choosing Show Package Contents in the contextual menu that appears. Then, you can move files or folders into the `Contents` folder within. Keeping this material in a new folder instead of copying it into an existing default folder within the structure is a good idea.

Like a script in a classic application folder, a script application can access resources stored within its package with the `path to me` command. Once the path to the script is established, adding `Contents:` to it will establish the path to the internal package contents folder within the file. From there the script can access any material in the package by appending the appropriate subpath. The script in Listing 24.2 demonstrates how to establish the path to the contents folder and then acquire a list of folder contents for that folder and the `Script Resources` folder within it.

Listing 24.2

Calculating the path to the embedded folder structure and locating files and folders contained within it

```
set pathToRoot to path to me as string
set pathToRoot to pathToRoot & "Contents:"

list folder pathToRoot without invisibles
-- result = {"Info.plist", "MacOS", "PkgInfo", "Resources", "Script
   Resources"}

set pathToRoot to pathToRoot & "Script Resources:" as string
list folder pathToRoot without invisibles
-- result = {"Data", "Scripts", "Templates"}-- result = {"Data",
   "Scripts", "Templates"}
```

Separating resources from the primary script application

Sometimes certain script files are best separated from the primary script application that uses them, especially when they might be shared by multiple scripts installed in different locations. They can be tucked away inside one of the available library folders, the user's `Documents` folder, a server volume, and a script document bundle.

Resource Folder Structure

When script resources are stored in a folder separate from the primary script application, be sure to build a folder structure that allows for growth over time. Ideally, you would have a single folder that can contain all of the resources for any script that might be run on the computer. Even if you have only one solution, create a folder structure that will allow for the addition of other solution resources within the same folder. You can include subfolders for client name, script type, script name, and any other levels to allow for maximum expandability. Each new client or solution can be added to the structure without disturbing the solution resources already installed. The folder structure shown in the following figure illustrates a flexible resource folder structure. Any number of solutions for one or more companies can be stored in a single folder within the library folder.

A flexible resource folder structure

Storing resources in a library folder

Storing scripts in a `Library` folder is a good choice, especially for resources shared by multiple solutions. Ideally, the material would be stored in the user's `Library` folder so it will stay with the user as he moves his folder to a new computer or into a clean install. However, if multiple users on the same computer will use the resources, the material can be stored in the computer's `Library` folder.

You can choose any location within the `Library` folder to store your files, although creating your own folder immediately within the `Library` folder is probably the best option. That makes it easy to locate and keeps all of your material separate from the other material stored there. You can name it `AppleScript Resources`, `Script Resources`, or something unique to you, your company, or your client. You may also choose to create a folder inside the `Application Support` folder as it is intended for resources that support any application or process.

Storing resources in the user directory

Another location to store script resources is in a folder within the user's directory alongside `Documents`, `Library`, `Pictures`, `Music`, and the other folders found in this location. This may not be the best choice for every user, especially non-technical ones, because it enables them to access the material more easily, and they can erroneously delete or modify important material or add new, irrelevant material. However, for yourself or for qualified users who need regular access to these resources, the user's directory can be an ideal location.

Storing resources on a server volume

Storing script resources on a server volume is a great way to keep everyone's scripts up to date. When anyone launches a script application, it accesses other modules, libraries, templates, and any other required resource from a file server's directory. Modifications performed on any of the resources are instantly available to all the users without the need to download and install them. Only the primary application would need to be distributed.

The only downside to this storage location is that the application requires the file server in order to perform the automated tasks it is assigned. Logging onto the server automatically averts errors from missing resources as long as the user is connected to the network and the server is up and running. If not, the script is rendered defunct.

One way around this issue is to use the server as a delivery method while the script keeps a copy of all of its resources locally on the user's computer. When the script is launched for the first time during the day or week and the server is detected, it can copy the resources from the server to a folder in the user's directory. Then, it uses the local material to perform its tasks.

CAUTION

Be sure to keep the resources tucked safely in a folder that is not frequented by users on a regular basis. This keeps the material safe from destructive manipulation. Also, the folder containing the resources should include a text file warning or be named in a way that indicates that the material within is used for an automated process and should not be disturbed.

Integrated Resource Healing Functionality

Keeping a backup of resource folders is always a good idea. When a script will be used by a large number of users, it is essential. If someone deletes or irreparably damages his copy of script resources, you can simply install a fresh copy from your backup.

For complex solutions, you might choose to integrate a resource "healing" function that can automatically update a user's copy of resources from a backup copy installed within the script application, or in any of the locations discussed in this chapter. If a key file is not where it should be, the script can quickly duplicate a fresh copy to the appropriate location and continue processing.

This is an advanced feature and may not be feasible for smaller solutions. However, as your solutions grow, you may want to consider developing a generic healing subroutine that can be used globally within them. This type of function can also be coupled with an auto-update function to update a user's resources from an updated master copy.

Storing resources in a document bundle

 Storing script resources inside of a document bundle is more of a method of packaging them rather than a storage destination. Using a bundle keeps vital material safe from infiltration by irrelevantly saved material and from an accidental rearrangement of files and folders. The actual location of the bundle can be any of the locations mentioned within this section. This is a great way to embed resources inside of a script that will be attached to the script menu or other deployment locations that work with script files.

Understanding inter-script communication

Loading and using an external script is relatively simple. Once loaded, a script can get and set properties of the external script and instruct it to run a subroutine. The external script's subroutines can exchange data with local script calls exactly as they would if they were part of the local script.

NOTE

Listing 24.3 contains a script that is used in this section. The following examples assume that this script is saved on the desktop and is named `Hello World Script.scpt`.

Listing 24.3

A script used to demonstrate inter-script communication

```
global gTextGlobal

property textMessage : "Hello World"

on run
   display dialog "Loaded Script: Run"
end run
```

```
on open listItems
   display dialog "Loaded Script: Open " & (count items of listItems &
   "!" as string)
end open

on sayHelloWorld()
   display dialog textMessage
end sayHelloWorld

on globalValueDisplay()
   display dialog gTextGlobal
end globalValueDisplay
```

Loading an external script file

A script can load any number of external scripts by using the `load script` command and specifying a script file path. The entire contents of a script file can be placed into a variable, which can be the target of commands or subroutine calls.

The following code loads the `Hello World Script` file from the desktop and places it into a variable called `scriptHelloWorld`:

```
set pathToScript to "Macintosh HD:Users:mmunro:Desktop:Hello
   World Script.scpt"
set scriptHelloWorld to load script file pathToScript
-- result = «script»
```

The result shown is the script object «script», which represents the entire script file.

NOTE

A single external script can be loaded multiple times into different variables if needed. Each variable will contain a separate copy of the script.

Accessing properties of a loaded script

Once an external script is loaded into a variable, local code can read and write its custom properties. This example gets the value of the `textMessage` property of the external script by adding an `of «script»` clause after the property name:

```
textMessage of scriptHelloWorld
-- result = "Hello World"
```

The local script can also set the value of the `textMessage` property of the external script with the `set` command, as shown here:

```
set textMessage of scriptHelloWorld to "Howdy World"
-- result = "Howdy World"
```

NOTE

Properties of a loaded script are not the same as the properties of an object class such as a piece of text. A custom script property has a name and value declared in the external script, formatted like this: `property` `«name»:«value»`. The value can be any AppleScript object class.

Storing a loaded script into a file

Any changes to a loaded script's properties are made in the copy of the script and not to the actual script file. However, a script in a variable can be saved back to the same file or into a new file using the `store script` command.

The following example loads the script file, changes its `textMessage` property, and then saves it into a new file. Loading the newly saved script file and checking the property shows that it successfully saved the new message:

```
set pathToScript to "Macintosh HD:Users:mmunro:Desktop:Hello
    World Script.scpt"
set scriptHelloWorld to load script file pathToScript
set textMessage of scriptHelloWorld to "Howdy World"
set pathToSave to "Macintosh HD:Users:mmunro:Desktop:Howdy World
    Script.scpt"
store script scriptHelloWorld in file pathToSave
set scriptHelloWorld to load script file pathToSave
textMessage of scriptHelloWorld
-- result = "Howdy World"
```

When saving a script back into the original file, you must include a `replacing «ask/yes/ no»` clause, specifying the desired behavior for asking the user to replace the file, automatically replacing the file, or not replacing the original file. This example loads the external script, modifies its property, and then saves it, replacing the original file:

```
set pathToScript to "Macintosh HD:Users:mmunro:Desktop:Hello
    World Script.scpt"
set scriptHelloWorld to load script file pathToScript
set textMessage of scriptHelloWorld to "Howdy World"
store script scriptHelloWorld in file pathToScript replacing yes
```

CAUTION

When a script saves a copy of a loaded script with modified preferences, the changes will not be visible to a user who opens the saved script file. Rather, whatever value was there when the script file was manually saved will persist and can cause confusion. However, if the script reloads the saved, external script and accesses its properties, the changes are saved. Although it might seem like a bug, and can be rather confusing, this has been the case with AppleScript from the very first version.

Storing an embedded script into a file

An entire script can be embedded within a script file, alongside other code statements. These script objects can also be placed into a variable, executed, or saved using the `save script` command. This example shows a script named `embeddedScript`, which is inline with a script. A copy of the script is placed inside of a variable called `scriptTemp` and then stored into a script file on the desktop called `My Script.scpt`:

```
script embeddedScript
   -- script steps here
end script

set scriptTemp to script embeddedScript
set pathToScript to "Macintosh HD:Users:mmunro:Desktop:My Script.
   scpt"
store script scriptTemp in file pathToScript replacing yes
```

T I P

Using this technique, you can create multiple copies of an inline script template, each with different property values.

Running code in a loaded script

A parent script can run code within a loaded script as easily as it gets and sets external properties. To run a subroutine, the parent script needs to add an `of «script variable»` clause after the subroutine call, as shown in this example, which displays the text in the `textMessage` property in a dialog box (see Figure 24.3):

```
set pathToScript to "Macintosh HD:Users:mmunro:Desktop:Hello
   World Script.scpt"
set scriptHelloWorld to load script file pathToScript
sayHelloWorld() of scriptHelloWorld
```

If a script contains an implicit or explicit `run` command handler subroutine, the parent script can instruct it to execute with the `run` command. The dialog box shown in Figure 24.3 shows that the loaded script has executed its `run` subroutine:

```
run scriptHelloWorld
```

Figure 24.3

The run dialog box displayed by the loaded script

This can also be expressed in a `tell` statement like this:

```
tell scriptHelloWorld to run
```

Likewise, the parent script can instruct the loaded script to process Finder items by calling the open command handler subroutine and including a list of file or folder paths. The following example gets a list of items on the desktop and sends them to the open subroutine in the loaded script:

```
set pathToDesktop to path to desktop folder as string
set listItems to list folder pathToDesktop without invisibles
set pathToScript to "Macintosh HD:Users:mmunro:Desktop:Hello
    World Script.scpt"
set scriptHelloWorld to load script file pathToScript
tell scriptHelloWorld to open listItems
```

The resulting dialog box displays a count of items, as shown in Figure 24.4.

Figure 24.4

The open subroutine in the loaded script displaying the count of desktop items passed to it by the parent script

Loaded Script: Open 29 items!

Cancel   OK

Accessing global variables across multiple scripts

If a global variable exists in both a parent script and a script it has loaded, the values will be the same. Setting the value from either the parent or the child updates the value globally.

In this example, the gTextGlobal global variable is initialized to contain a sentence. Then the external script is loaded and instructed to run the globalValueDisplay() subroutine, which displays the global value proving the sentence exists globally across all scripts, shown in Figure 24.5:

```
global gTextGlobal
set gTextGlobal to "Hello World from a loaded script"
set pathToScript to "Macintosh HD:Users:mmunro:Desktop:Hello
    World Script.scpt"
set scriptHelloWorld to load script file pathToScript
globalValueDisplay() of scriptHelloWorld
```

It doesn't matter if the global value is set before or after the external script is loaded. If both scripts have a global variable with the same name, their values will always be synchronized.

Figure 24.5

A dialog box generated from a loaded script, showing the value of a global variable

Hello World from a loaded script

Cancel   OK

TIP

Script files containing a library of subroutines can be loaded and placed into a global variable. Then all scripts within a multi-module solution that have the global variable will be able to directly execute any of the subroutines in the library. This is one of the few justified uses for global variables in an open-ended script design.

Overcoming the Complexities of Multi-Module Solutions

Multi-module solutions create a complex and somewhat difficult environment, which at first can be overwhelming. This is especially true when you are tracking down errors. Imagine testing a complex catalog building script with several dozen separate script files and being presented with a dialog box that says "File not found" or "Can't get item 2 of { }"; and combing through dozens of files to figure out which file wasn't found or why a list is empty when the script expects there to be at least two items within it.

Rather than be discouraged by this dilemma, be inspired by it. There are relatively simple ways to overcome the complexities inherent within complex, multi-module solutions.

Employing good development habits

You can conquer much of the complexity inherent in multi-module solutions by adopting of couple of simple good habits.

Understanding the importance of naming and usage standards

Coding errors are most frequent when you write code for the first time. Whether you are automating an application for the first time or crunching some unfamiliar data, a new situation can foster confusion and, therefore, introduce bugs. Using consistent naming and usage standards can remove confusion from even the most unfamiliar situations and remove problematic issues from the start.

CROSS-REF
Naming and usage standards are discussed in Chapter 4.

Testing parts of the whole

One of the more obvious ways to avoid troubleshooting bugs in a huge solution is to test each small batch of new code in an isolated environment before inserting it into the solution. Any subroutine can be tested apart from the solution, especially low-level ones that carry out basic functions or don't rely on other subroutines. Higher-level subroutines that rely on other subroutines are easier to test within a solution as a whole, but their individual statements can be pre-tested prior to integration.

While this doesn't guarantee the fully assembled solution won't have any problems, it can definitely help to greatly reduce them.

Integrating an offsite test mode

All solutions should be thoroughly tested before they are deployed into a live workflow, especially complex ones. However, if the solution will be installed on a computer network other than the one used to develop it, testing it can be a challenge. Any resources that are not present on the development network present a formidable obstacle to adequate testing. For example, network server volumes, database resources, image files, and more may exist on a client's network but not on yours.

In this case, building an offsite-testing mode that temporarily locates resources and routes commands to your network can provide a means to perform "near-live" tests to shake out the majority of the bugs that may exist. A single global variable named `gBlnOffsiteMode`, or something like that, if set to `true`, can instruct a script to use secondary settings for folder paths, logon settings, database locations, and more.

CAUTION
Using an offsite mechanism is not a substitute for actual live testing. If the live paths are incorrect or resource names in the test environment don't match the live ones, the offsite test mode might succeed where the live one will fail. Testing offsite is meant to prove the validity of the logic and script functionality to help ease live testing, not replace it.

The actual implementation of the offsite mode can vary. Alternate paths can be set up in the same way the live ones are. For example, if a key resource path is a property called `pPath ToResources`, a second property called `pPathToResourcesOffsite` can contain the alternative path. A simple `if-then` statement can use the live folder path from a client's server or a test folder path on your development network accordingly, as shown here:

```
set pathToResources to pPathToResources
if gBlnOffsiteMode = true then
  set pathToResources to pPathToResourcesOffsite
end if
```

When using a choice of two static options, it is important to use a third variable in which to place the desired value. In this case, `pathToResources` is used to store either of the two static paths. This preserves the two options for the next use.

If the solution uses a data file to keep track of paths, you can create a mirror of that file to contain offsite paths so you don't have to create multiple offsite properties. You can use the offsite mode variable to load either the live file or the offsite file. If the properties within these files are named the same, the rest of the script will be automatically routed to the offsite file instead of the live one. This example sets a variable to a portion of a path to the settings file that exists within the root path of the script or its folder structure:

```
set pathSuffix to "Resources:Data:Project Settings.scpt"
if gBlnOffsiteMode = true then
  set pathSuffix to "Resources:Data:Project Settings Offsite.
    scpt"
end if
set pathToSettings to gPathToRoot & pathSuffix as string
```

If your solution uses aliases within the script resource folder to dynamically locate key resources on a server, this same technique applies. Simply create a duplicate folder with name-synchronized aliases pointing to your test resources and the solution can toggle between those and the "live" ones.

NOTE

An offsite-testing mode is not strictly reserved for paths. You can make addresses, accounts, and passwords for logging into databases, FTP (File Transfer Protocol) sites, and file servers available for both live and test modes using these same techniques.

Using logs for tracking

No matter how careful you are writing and testing, any solution, especially a complex one, can still contain bugs and non-developer related errors. An error in a multi-module solution can become a nightmarish search for the piece of code responsible. Script results and errors might show up in the AppleScript Editor when you are developing a script but scripts are not used that way. When the user launches a script application, a cryptic error might generate a dialog box with some error information, but it will not pinpoint what exactly caused the error and which file or subroutine is responsible. A custom logging process can solve this problem and include other reporting capabilities.

Using comprehensive error dialogs boxes can be adequate for many situations as long as you can count on users to communicate back every detail of the message, or to take a picture of the dialog box. However, dialog boxes can't display errors within the context of another activity or diagnostic information. Instituting a universal logging feature can be a big help in tracking down even the most obscure error message.

Depending on your preferences, a logging feature does not need to be limited to only reporting errors. It can record other events, such as starting a process, specific activity, or diagnostic data, with errors appearing in-line with them. Some of these events, such as a diagnostic log, can be designed to be turned off or on as needed to troubleshoot errors. Also, they can be one log file or written to their own files.

Error log entries

An *error log entry* is a script-generated message containing information about errors that occurred during the execution of the script. Ideally, the entries will include the name of both the subroutine that generated the error and the script file in which it exists. It should also have the actual text of the error and other information about the object that cause the errors. Figure 24.6 shows some sample error entries in an error log.

Figure 24.6

A sample error log with error entries

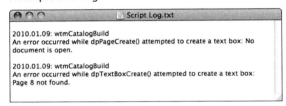

CROSS-REF
Script error details are discussed in Chapter 15.

Activity log entries

An *activity log entry* is a script-generated message indicating the start or end of some type of script activity. This might include an entry chronicling the start of a new phase of a script or that the script is beginning to manipulate a specific file. When included in the same log file as error entries, these can help provide a context for what the script was doing when the error occurred. For example, knowing that an error occurred after the script started to process a file named `Pache.jpg` helps to focus your search for an answer to the problem much better than knowing that "an error occurred during one of the files being processed." Figure 24.7 shows an example of an activity log with activity entries.

Figure 24.7

A sample activity log with activity entries

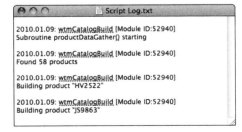

Diagnostic log entries

While an activity log records events relating to the material being processed, a *diagnostic log entry* records script events such as when a specific subroutine begins executing. Figure 24.8 shows some example diagnostic entries in a diagnostic log. Diagnostics should be controlled by a developer-accessible property because they would otherwise clutter up a log file.

Figure 24.8

A sample diagnostic log with diagnostic entries

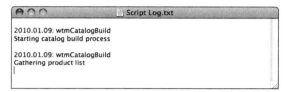

Session logs

A *session log file* is a script-generated text file that contains information about a specific auto-mated session. It might be a unique log used in conjunction with an error log or include an error log from a specific session. This type of log is especially useful for batch-processing scripts or other scripts that perform a burst of tasks in individual sessions and need a way to inform the user if each file was successfully processed. A sample session log is shown in Figure 24.9.

In addition to errors, a session log might include the date and time the script ran, the start and end times, the total time elapsed, a list of objects that were processed, and a list of tasks that were performed. It can include any or all of these in combination with any other information you think is pertinent to a particular process.

A script can save the data in a variable and create the text file when the tasks are completed or it can write the data in real time, making it available in the event of a crash or some other disaster.

Figure 24.9

An example of a simple session log

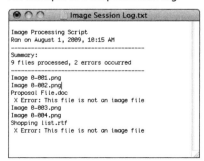

Building a Multi-Module Image Batch Processor

In Chapter 18 an Image Batch Processor script was created to perform a couple of manipulations to a batch of images. That script was made more open-ended in Chapter 22 and was parsed into a hierarchical subroutine structure in Chapter 23. In this section, the last version of the script is converted into a multi-module solution.

NOTE
In its current size and complexity, converting the Image Batch Processor script into a multi-module solution may seem like a burdensome and unjustified task. While somewhat true, it is presented here as a simple and convenient example of the concepts discussed in this chapter.

NOTE
The Image Batch Processor script described in this section is available for download from the book's Web site at `www.wileydevreference.com`.

Designing the new solution

The first step in designing the new batch processor is to identify any code that can or should be moved into an external module (see Figure 24.10). Clearly, the single function Image Events subroutines are open-ended and in adequate numbers to justify the creation of an Image Events Library file. While there is only a single Finder subroutine, that subroutine is placed into a Finder Library file to make it more portable and in anticipation of more subroutines joining it in the future.

Figure 24.10

The sections of code that will be extracted into separate modules

The two image manipulation functions, flip and scale, will each be placed into a module. While these modules will be rather small and unworthy of an entire file, it enables you to modify some key functionality and will aid a future transition to an open-ended multi-module solution in Chapter 25.

You will also move the logging function to a separate module. This will make it easier to share between every module in the solution and keep things segregated.

Building the Logging Module file

To help track errors and activity, a new log module will be built, which will be loaded into a global variable by the primary solution script and thereby be accessible to all files. This module will be designed to be completely open-ended, so it can be reused in any future solutions.

To begin, create a new script called Log Module and place it into the `/Script Resources/ Scripts/Other Scripts/` folder within the `Image Batch Processor` folder. This file will have two subroutines: one that creates a session log (much like the previous version) and one that logs events.

The script will have one property and two global variables, as shown in Listing 24.4. The `pTextModuleTitle` property contains the name of the module. The global variables include a path to the log folder and a path to the solution's root folder, which are both initialized by the primary script. All three of these will be included in each module for the new Image Batch Processing solution:

```
property pTextModuleTitle : "Log Module"
global gPathToLog, gPathToRoot
```

The `logEvent()` subroutine is responsible for writing a single event to the log. This might be an error that occurs in a subroutine anywhere in the solution or an activity notification.

To begin, set up the basic subroutine as shown in Listing 24.4. In addition to the start and end of the subroutine statement and parameters, include a `try` statement to protect the log statements that will be added next.

 NOTE
Because this subroutine is responsible for logging, if an error occurs, it is considered a development error and a dialog box will be generated. Unlike calls to this subroutine when an error occurs elsewhere in the solution, because this subroutine is responsible for logging errors, any error occurring here can't logged.

Listing 24.4

The logEvent() subroutine

```
on logEvent(nameLog, nameModule, listData)
    --   This subroutine writes an entry to the log.
```

continued

Listing 24.4 *(continued)*

```
try

    -- Log statements will go here
on error errText
  set textMessage to "Major Development Log Error: " & errText
  display dialog textMessage buttons "OK"
end try

return textModuleResponse
end logEvent
```

The `nameLog` parameter indicates the type of log entry. For this example, two entry types will be allowed: an error and an activity. This could be expanded to include additional diagnostic or other types of log entries as needed.

The `nameModule` parameter contains the name of the module containing the subroutine that encountered the error being reported.

The `listData` parameter contains a list of three values: the number of the error, the text of the error, and a message that indicates what the script was attempting to do when the error occurred.

As log statements are added into the subroutine shell shown earlier in Listing 24.4, the script starts with a simple confirmation that `listData` does in fact have three values. If it does, the script parses them out into separate variables as shown in Listing 24.5.

Listing 24.5

logEvent() confirms and parses the error data

```
--  Confirm that the listData parameter has X values in it
if length of listData ≠ 3 then
  set textMessage to "Major Development Log Error: " & errText
  display dialog textMessage buttons "OK"
end if

--  Parse the list of values
set numError to item 1 of listData
set textError to item 2 of listData
set textMessage to item 3 of listData
```

Now that the components of the error are in separate variables, the date and time are calculated, which will be written in front of the log entry, shown in Listing 24.6. First, get the current date and parse out the year, month, and day. Next, give both the month and day a leading zero if needed and then place them into a variable with the time added to the end. This gives you a `textTimeStamp` variable containing the date and time, formatted like this:

```
2010.01.09 @ 5:30:14 PM
```

Listing 24.6

The logEvent() suborutine's first step

```
--  Create the date & time stamp
  set dateCurrent to current date
  set textYear to (year of dateCurrent) as string
  set textMonth to (month of dateCurrent as number)
  if textMonth < 10 then set textMonth to "0" & textMonth as string
  set textDay to (day of dateCurrent)
  if textDay < 10 then set textDay to "0" & textDay
  set textDate to textYear & "." & textMonth & "." & textDay as string
  set textTimeStamp to textDate & " @ " & time string of dateCurrent
```

Now the actual log entry can be built using the date and time stamp and the three values parsed from `listData`. First initialize a variable named `textLog` to contain the date, time, a colon, and the name of the module followed by a paragraph return, as shown in Listing 24.7.

Listing 24.7

The logEvent() subroutine's second step

```
    --  Construct the log entry
  set textLog to textTimeStamp & ": " & nameModule & return
  set textModuleResponse to ""
  if nameLog = "Error" then
    set textLog to textLog & "An error occurred while " & textMessage
& ": "
    set textLog to textLog & "[#" & numError & "] " & textError &
return
    set textModuleResponse to "Error"

  else if nameLog = "Activity" then
    set textLog to textLog & "Activity: " & textMessage & return
  end if
  set textLog to textLog & return
```

An `if-then` statement controls the formatting of the log entry. If the name of the log is `Error`, it will format an entry like this:

```
2010.01.09 @ 5:39:02 PM: Log Events
An error occurred while Log Events module attempted to test a
    development error: [#0] A test error occurred
```

If the entry is reporting activity, it will format the entry like this:

```
2010.01.09 @ 5:39:02 PM: Log Events
Activity: Some test activity occurred.
```

Now that you have a formatted log entry, the script can write it to the log file, as shown in Listing 24.8.

Listing 24.8

The logEvent() subroutine writing the log data to the log text file

```
--  Write the entry to the log file
open for access file gPathToLog with write permission
write textLog to file gPathToLog starting at eof
close access file gPathToLog
```

To avoid frustration when testing logging code in other files, it's a good idea to test a new module, especially one with the critical task of logging. Because it does not have a `run` subroutine, you'll create one and use it to test an error and activity log entry. The code in Listing 24.9 instructs the log module to write logs to a file on the desktop named `Test Log.txt` and then writes test error and activity log entries.

Listing 24.9

Code to test logging functionality

```
on run
  set gPathToRoot to (path to desktop folder as string)
  set gPathToLog to gPathToRoot & "Test Log.txt" as string

  --  Test a fake error entry
  set numError to 0
  set textError to "A test error occurred"
  set textMessage to "Log Events module attempted to test a development
   error"
  set nameModule to "Log Events"

  set listErrorData to {numError, textError, textMessage}
```

```
logEvent("Error", nameModule, listErrorData)

-- Test a fake activity entry
set numError to 0
set textError to "N/A"
set textMessage to "Some test activity occurred."
set nameModule to "Log Events"

set listErrorData to {numError, textError, textMessage}
logEvent("Activity", nameModule, listErrorData)

end run
```

The session logging subroutine is placed into the new Log Module file exactly as it was in the previous version from Chapter 23. However, its name will be changed from `scriptLogCreate()` to `logSession()` to be consistent with `logEvent()`.

Error Feedback Mechanism

The `logEvent()` subroutine returns a value stored in a variable called `textModuleResponse`. This value is an empty string unless the log entry is reporting an error. In that case, the variable contains the word "Error."

This mechanism enables an error-causing subroutine to inform the subroutine calling it that an error occurred, thus giving higher-level code the option to pursue a different course. This technique works best if every subroutine returns a value. For subroutines that don't produce a result, an empty string can be returned if all goes well.

This example demonstrates the process. The main code calls a subroutine, which generates an error. The `try` statement sends the error information to the `eventLog()` subroutine in the log module. After logging the error, the log module returns the word "Error" which, in turn, is returned to the main code and placed into the `dataResults` variable. Before continuing with other statements, the main script checks the result of the subroutine to see if it contains the word "Error" and, if so, displays a dialog box and stops.

```
set dataResults to
   performSubroutine ()
if dataResults = "Error" then
```

```
   return display dialog "An
   error occurred"
else
   -- continue with other
   commands if no error
   occurred.
end
on performSubroutine ()
   try
      set a to b
   on error textError number
   numError
      set listData to {numError,
      textError,
      "performSubrouitne()
      attempted to do something."}
      return logEvent("Error",
      pTextModuleTitle, listData)
      of gLog
   end try
end performSubroutine
```

This provides a nice method for a script to monitor lower-level subroutines and take an alternative action in the event of an error.

Building the Finder Library file

Next the Finder Library file is created. This file will only contain a single Finder subroutine for now, but other subroutines can be added over time, such as the `finderFolderExists()` subroutine from the last chapter. It will also contain a small subroutine for routing events to the log module. Everything placed into this library file will be 100 percent open-ended and capable of reuse in any other solutions in which it might be needed.

To begin, create a new script called Finder Library and place it into the `/Script Resources/Scripts/Libraries/` folder within the `Image Batch Processor` folder.

The script will have one property and one global variable, as shown here:

```
property pTextModuleTitle : "Finder Library"
global gLog
```

The `pTextModuleTitle` property will contain the name of the module. The `gLog` global variable will contain the entire Log Module script, which will be loaded by the primary solution module.

NOTE

The Library files do not have the **gPathToRoot** global variable because they are low-level single function subroutines.

The `finderFileExtensionRemove()` subroutine can be pasted into the new Finder Library from the version in Chapter 23. A `try` statement is wrapped around the commands that will pass the appropriate data to the `logEvent` subroutine in the Log Module. The resulting subroutine is shown in Listing 24.10.

Listing 24.10

The finderFileExtensionRemove() subroutine

```
on finderFileExtensionRemove(pathToItem)
  --  This subroutine will remove the file extension from the image name
   for saving
  try

    tell application "Finder"
      set textExtension to name extension of item pathToItem
      set nameImage to name of item pathToItem
    end tell
    set nameImageForSave to nameImage
    if nameImage ends with textExtension and textExtension ≠ "" then
      set text item delimiters to {"." & textExtension}
      set listTemp to every text item of nameImage
      set text item delimiters to {""}
      set nameImageForSave to listTemp as text
    end if
    return nameImageForSave
```

```
on error textError number numError
  set listData to {numError, textError, "finderFileExtensionRemove()
attempted to remove an extension from a file."}
  return logEvent("Error", pTextModuleTitle, listData) of gLog
end try
end finderFileExtensionRemove
```

Building the Image Events Library file

The Image Events Library file contains all of the subroutines that perform a function with the Image Events application. Like the Finder Library file, every subroutine placed into this library file will be 100 percent open-ended and capable of reuse in any other solutions in which it might be needed.

To begin, create a new script called Image Events Library and place it into the `/Script Resources/Scripts/Libraries/` folder within the `Image Batch Processor` folder.

Like the Finder Library, this script will have one property and one global variable, as shown here:

```
property pTextModuleTitle : "Image Events Library"
global gLog
```

Each subroutine from the Chapter 23 version of the script can be pasted into this new file. Each will receive error protection like the Finder subroutine. Listing 24.11 shows the new version of the `imageSaveFormatChoose()` subroutine with error protection.

Listing 24.11

The imageSaveFormatChoose() subroutine

```
on imageSaveFormatChoose()
  --  This subroutine will ask the user to choose the file type(s) to
  save images
  try
    set textPrompt to "Save images as:"
    set listOptions to {"BMP", "JPEG", "JPEG2", "PICT", "PNG", "PSD",
  "QuickTime Image", "TIFF"}
    set listChoices to (choose from list listOptions with empty
  selection allowed and multiple selections allowed)
    return listChoices

  on error textError number numError
    set listData to {numError, textError, "imageSaveFormatChoose()
  attempted to ask the user to choose a file type to save images."}
    return logEvent("Error", pTextModuleTitle, listData) of gLog
  end try
end imageSaveFormatChoose
```

The only subroutine in this library that has changed is `imageFileCheck()`. In the previous version of the script, when a file was not an acceptable image format, this subroutine would generate an error, which would get captured by the error protection in the primary subroutine. That was fine when there wasn't any other error protection in the script. However, now that the script is logging errors to an error log, the `imageFileCheck()` subroutine will be modified to return a `true` or `false` value, indicating if a specific file is acceptable or not, as shown in Listing 24.12. The primary subroutine, now in a separate file than these subroutines, will be modified to look to this value as an indication of whether it should generate an error that will appear on the session log.

Listing 24.12

The new imageFileCheck() subroutine

```
on imageFileCheck(refImage)
  --  This subroutine will confirm that the specified file is an
  acceptable file type
  try

    tell application "Image Events"
      set recProperties to (properties of refImage)
      set dataFileType to file type of recProperties
      set listFileTypes to {BMP, GIF, JPEG, JPEG2, MacPaint, PDF,
  Photoshop, PICT, PNG, PSD, QuickTime Image, SGI, TGA, TIFF}
      set blnImageFile to listFileTypes contains dataFileType
      if blnImageFile = false then return false
    end tell
    return true

  on error textError number numError
    set listData to {numError, textError, "imageFileCheck() attempted to
  confirm an image file was an appropriate format."}
    return logEvent("Error", pTextModuleTitle, listData) of gLog
  end try
end imageFileCheck
```

Building the main Image Batch Processor file

With the two library files and the log module built, you can turn your attention to the primary image batch processor module. It will continue to be a drop application that will be the user's point of contact with the solution.

This new version will have several significant changes. Several global variables that make modules and libraries available must be initialized at the start. A new subroutine handles this. Also, because most of the single function subroutines were moved to library files and logging is removed, there will only be three of the original subroutines from this file remaining.

The new image batch processor file will be saved at the root level of the `Image Batch Processor` folder, which is at the same level as the `Script Resources` folder.

This script will have one property and five global variables, all shown here:

```
property pTextModuleTitle : "Image Batch Processor"
global gPathToLog, gPathToRoot
global gLibImage, gLibFinder, gLog
```

Like the other modules, the `pTextModuleTitle` property contains the name of the module for logging. The `gPathToLog` and `gPathToRoot` global variables will contain the path to the log file and the path to the solution root folder respectively.

With the introduction of global variables containing libraries of subroutines and other information, the script will need to run an initialization subroutine to set up everything for the rest of the solution. The `scriptInitialize()` subroutine, shown in Listing 24.13, locates the solution folder and places it into the `gPathToRoot` global variable. Next, it loads the script libraries and the log module, each into a global variable. Finally, it sets the `gPathToLog` global variable to the `~/Library/Logs/Image Batch Processor Log.txt` file.

Listing 24.13

The new initialization script

```
on scriptInitialize()
   -- Establish the path to the root folder of the solution
   set gPathToRoot to path to me as string
   tell application "Finder"
     set gPathToRoot to folder of item gPathToRoot as string
   end tell

   -- load the Finder Library
   set gPathTemp to gPathToRoot & "Script Resources:Scripts:Libraries:Fin
    der Library.scpt"
   set the clipboard to gPathTemp
   set gLibFinder to load script file gPathTemp

   -- load the Image Events Library
```

continued

Listing 24.13   *(continued)*

```
set gPathTemp to gPathToRoot & "Script Resources:Scripts:Libraries:Im
 age Events Library.scpt"
set gLibImage to load script file gPathTemp

--  load the Log module
set gPathTemp to gPathToRoot & "Script Resources:Scripts:Other
 Scripts:Log Module.scpt"
set gLog to load script file gPathTemp

--  Establish the log path
set gPathTemp to path to library folder from user domain as string
 set gPathToLog to gPathTemp & "Logs:Image Batch Processor Log.txt"
end scriptInitialize
```

The run and open commands will be pasted in exactly as they were in the last version of this script in Chapter 23. They both simply call the batchMainProcess() script, which manages the entire script process.

The new version of the batchMainProcess() subroutine, shown in its entirety in Listing 24.14, has a few modifications from the previous one:

- It now calls the new scriptInitalize() subroutine.
- It has a try statement around all of its code that will route errors to the Log Module. The try statement within the repeat loop that is used to report files that are not acceptable image formats remains.
- The call to imageFileCheck() now sits inside of an if-then statement that generates a session report error if the subroutine reports that the current image is not an acceptable type.
- The call to the session log reflects the new subroutine name, logSession() and includes a specifier that routes the command to the Log Module in the gLog global variable.

Listing 24.14

The new batchMainProcess() subroutine

```
on batchMainProcess(listFiles)
  --  This subroutine will manage the processing of a batch of files

  try
```

```
scriptInitialize()


--  If nothing was dropped on the script, ask the user to select
items to process
 if listFiles = {} then
   set listFiles to batchRunOption()
   if listFiles = false then return
 end if

 --  Ask the user to select an output folder for processed images
 set textPrompt to "Choose a folder to save modified images:"
 set pathToSave to (choose folder with prompt textPrompt) as string

 --  Ask the user to choose the action(s) to perform
 set listActionChoices to batchActionOptionsChoose()
 if listActionChoices = false then return

 --  Ask the user to choose the file type(s) to save output
 set listSaveOptions to imageSaveFormatChoose() of gLibImage
 if listSaveOptions = false then return

 --  Process each file
 set textSuccess to ""
 set textFailure to ""
 repeat with a from 1 to count items of listFiles
   set pathToItem to item a of listFiles as string
   try
     --  Open the current file
     set {refImage, nameImage} to imageFileOpen(pathToItem) of
gLibImage
     set nameImageForSave to finderFileExtensionRemove(pathToItem) of
gLibFinder
     if imageFileCheck(refImage) of gLibImage = false then error "Not
an image file"

     --  Process the current image
     repeat with b from 1 to count items of listActionChoices
       set nameChoice to item b of listActionChoices

       --  Flip the image
       if nameChoice contains "Flip" then
         imageFlip(refImage, nameChoice) of gLibImage
       end if

       --  Scale the image
       if nameChoice contains "Scale" then
```

continued

Listing 24.14 *(continued)*

```
            imageFileScale(refImage, nameChoice) of gLibImage
        end if

    end repeat

    --  Save the modified image
    imageFileSave(refImage, nameImageForSave, pathToSave,
listSaveOptions) of gLibImage

    --  Build the log entry
    set textForLog to nameImage & return
    set textSuccess to textSuccess & textForLog as string
  on error errText
    set textForLog to nameImage & " (" & errText & ")" & return
    set textFailure to textFailure & textForLog as string
  end try
 end repeat

 --  Format results and send to a session log file
 set textResult to ""
 set textLine to "-------------------------------------------------"
 if textSuccess ≠ "" then
   set textResult to textResult & "Successfully processed image(s):"
& return & textLine & return & textSuccess & return as string
 end if
 if textFailure ≠      "" then
   set textResult to textResult & "The following image(s) failed to
process:" & return & textLine & return & textFailure as string
 end if
 set pathToLog to (path to desktop folder as string) & "Image Batch
Processor Results.txt" as string
 logSession(pathToLog, textResult, true, true) of gLog

on error textError number numError
  set listData to {numError, textError, "batchMainProcess() attempted
 to process a batch of images."}
  return logEvent("Error", pTextModuleTitle, listData) of gLog
 end try
end batchMainProcess
```

Summary

In this chapter you learned about building AppleScript solutions that span across multiple script files. The history and benefits of this approach were discussed, and as an example of the technique, the Image Batch Processor script was upgraded to a multi-module solution.

25 Designing Open-Ended, Multi-Module Solutions

An *open-ended, multi-module solution* is a group of flexibly designed scripts packaged together as a single solution. This package is designed so it can be expanded easily and includes open-ended files that can be reused.

In the same way that an open-ended single file script is easily expandable and parts can be reused, a multi-module solution can be designed so entire files are open-ended, providing a simple way to add new modules into the solution with very little extra effort.

Planning for Change

Some people love to repeat the old adage that "The only constant is change." In the world of technological automation, this seems undeniably true.

The primary design goal of an open-ended solution is to design it from the start to allow for future expansion and changes. While it is impossible to anticipate every change that might occur, many common changes can be accommodated with a few simple techniques that greatly increase a solution's capability to adapt.

A solution that is designed to be static will require developer modifications for any change that might arise. Even the most flexible design may occasionally require code modifications due to a change; however, these code modifications can be reduced or eliminated with some careful planning and skillful design.

The two primary types of change a solution might encounter are explored in this section: business changes and development changes. This is not a complete list of every possible change, but it will help you know what to look for as you begin developing workflow automation solutions.

Anticipating business changes

If a script is intended to continue functioning beyond a year or two, it may eventually experience some business changes and should be designed to anticipate them.

25 In This Chapter

Building code to anticipate business and development changes

Upgrading the image batch processor application

Network resource changes

Periodically, equipment connected to computer networks will be upgraded or reorganized to better suite the future needs of a company. Eventually, the names, network addresses, or file structures of file, image, and database servers will change. There are several things you can do to make these changes easier for multi-module solutions to absorb.

Using a settings file

Don't hardcode network resource information in more than one place. Performing a find/replace for each change in dozens or hundreds of files can be a tedious exercise that begs for human failure. If more than one script will interact with network resources, place the details in the properties of a single settings file, such as the `Project Settings` file shown in Figure 25.1.

Figure 25.1

An example of a settings file used to store information prone to change

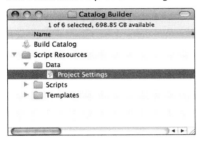

If the solution connects to a single server, the property names can be basic like these:

```
property pTextServerAddress : "10.0.1.0"
property pNameVolumne : "WTM Server"
```

If a solution connects to multiple severs, or if you want to plan for such a future scenario, you must modify your naming to allow for additional instances, as shown here:

```
property pServerImagesIP : "10.0.1.0"
property pServerImagesVolumne : "WTM Server"
property pServerTemplatesIP : "10.0.1.1"
property pServerTemplatesVolumne : "Automation Templates"
```

When the solution's primary script initializes the solution, it can load this data into a global variable, which can be accessed by every script in the solution. Once a change is updated in that single file, every module will continue functioning as expected and you can breathe a sigh of relief and thank yourself for your foresight.

CROSS-REF
Loading a script file is discussed in Chapter 16.

Using aliases to point to folders

When preparing for future server folder structure rearrangement, using a settings file containing paths to key resources is an option. Another choice is to use a folder full of aliases that point to key folder locations that will be accessed by the solution, as shown in Figure 25.2.

Figure 25.2

Keeping aliases to key solution locations in a folder can save a lot of time.

When a resource is moved, the only modification required is to update the alias so that it points to the new location. Because all of the scripts interact with a resource folder by finding the alias by name, they will continue to function. They simply need to resolve the original item of the alias, as shown here:

```
tell application "Finder"
    set pathToOutput to (original item of pathToAlias) as string
end tell
```

TIP
When using this method, be sure to name the aliases with generic descriptions of their functions. For example, if the solution output goes to a folder on a specific server, don't include the name of the server or even the name of the folder or resource. Any of these might change and you will be left with an alias whose name no longer makes sense and would require you to change its name and be faced with the task of updating all of the scripts that refer to that alias. Names such as Product Images, Catalog Templates, and Catalog Output are clear and don't contain any specific resource naming.

Selectable resources

Any solution that offers a user a list of items to choose from can be affected by change. For example, a list of product categories might change over time. If such a list is hardcoded into a script, the script will need to be updated and redistributed to every user each time a change occurs. In some cases this may not be such a huge chore; however, in a large company with dozens or hundreds of scripts using that category list, an alternative is required.

Sometimes, depending on the resource, you can grant any user access to modify the list. For non-technical clients, having such editing capabilities can be a welcome feature and results in them asking for development changes less frequently.

Using a server-based text file

Assuming every user has constant access to a file server, consider keeping a simple text file that contains a list of the selectable resources on that server. Any script that uses the list can read the file and instantly have the most up-to-date information.

CROSS-REF
Reading a text file is discussed in Chapter 16.

Using a server-based script file

For situations where a simple list isn't enough, a server-based script file can beneficial. For example, if a user-selected category must be translated into a file naming abbreviation, a script file can contain two synchronized property lists of values. The first list is used to present the user with a choice while the second one is used to locate the corresponding naming element. This script contains a simple example of two synchronized properties:

```
property listCategories : {"Fiction", "Non-fiction", "Sci-fi",
    "Children", "Parenting"}
property listFilePrefix : {"FN", "NF", "SF", "CH", "PT"}
```

Once the user has selected one of the items from the category list, this code uses a `repeat` loop to locate the corresponding file name prefix and create the file name:

```
set textSelection to "Sci-fi"
repeat with a from 1 to count items of listCategories
   set nameCurrentItem to item a of listCategories
   if textSelection = nameCurrentItem then
      set textPrefix to item a of listFilePrefix
      exit repeat
   end if
end repeat
set nameFile to textPrefix & "_2010_Cover.jpg" as string
-- result = "SF_2010_Cover.jpg"
```

When data is stored in a script file, it can also contain any necessary subroutines that help to process the user selection in more complex ways. Because every user's copy of the script loads a copy of the server-based script file, there is no need to worry about interference from others.

Page layout template changes

Desktop publishing files change quite often. Styles vary, themes come and go, and new product lines require new considerations. Catalog layouts might get a new design every year, requiring massive restructuring of a complex script. To avoid this, build flexibility into your script and work with designers to create a balance between the needs of automation and the need for design change. With a little forethought and cooperation, you will be surprised at how much less a change will affect your script.

Naming objects generically

Artists and programmers sometimes have trouble communicating. When it comes to template design and object names, this can be a problem. Artists tend to use informal and inconsistent style sheet names, literally named colors swatches, and leave master pages with a default name. If this type of naming is hardcoded into your script, even when using a settings file, it can be a recipe for disaster.

As a developer, you need to understand the needs of the users and those who work within the environment you are automating. However, you also may need to communicate information about the requirements of workflow automation and your need for consistency.

Clearly, you can't restrict or control design changes. You can help designers understand that you need a predictable environment in order to effectively streamline the process. Object naming is an area in which you should lay out an explicit set of rules.

Consider a catalog that uses an overall color scheme based on the season or a specific holiday. Static elements on the master pages will already have the desired color applied. However, if a script must assign the current color to dynamically placed elements, it will need to know which color to use. If a designer names the color Spring Theme in one template and Winter Chill in another, your script will need to be modified in order to accommodate each template.

One solution is to have the script check the color of a named default layout object and then use that color for the special items being placed on the page by the script. Another solution is to have everyone agree to use a generic name for the color, such as Catalog Color Theme. If this name is used consistently for each unique color in each template, the script will have no trouble assigning it to page elements.

Another example of this issue can be found with style sheets and other named resources. A style sheet for the category heading should be named something like Category Heading rather than Verdana 18 pt caps or Arial 24 pt blue vertical rotation, which are more difficult to remember and open up more room for error.

Should you fail to win over those responsible for template design, the alternative is to put all the settings that will change into a settings file — at least until you can make further appeals for consistent naming of design elements in future templates.

Using box names instead of numbers or ids

When a script will access text or image boxes on master pages, don't assume that the number or order of boxes will never change. They will! Always assign a name to the boxes so when new boxes are added, your script will continue to function as expected.

NOTE

This is another issue that you need to communicate with the template designer. Often, she will start from scratch to design a new template and all of the box names the script expects to find will be anonymous. The designer needs to understand that certain elements will need names and hopefully be convinced to assign the name or retain names from past templates by rearranging elements rather than starting from a blank document. In any event, you should review any new templates to make sure that they adhere to your script's naming expectations.

Assigning a box a name is pretty simple. Adobe InDesign has a script label feature, shown in Figure 25.3, that enables you to assign a name to a text frame or image box. With QuarkXPress, you can add a name to a box with a script like this one:

```
tell application "QuarkXPress"
    set refBox to the selection of master document 1
    set the name of refBox to "«NAME HERE»"
end tell
```

Figure 25.3

The script label palette for assigning an object name in Adobe InDesign

Company name changes

Because companies can be bought, sold, or merged, try to avoid using a company name within your scripts or solution resources. It is okay to brand the solution name or other prominent aspects a user might see; however, within scripts or resource files, try to avoid names that include the related company.

For example, rather than calling a logo `Write Track Media Logo.jpg`, try using `Logo.jpg` or `Company Logo.jpg`. If the company changes its name, the logo file might change, but the name the solution uses to locate it will continue to work without modification.

Personnel changes

One of the more sensitive considerations when planning for change is the fact that, over time, there will be changes in the personnel who use a script or are the recipient of messages from it. A simple script designed to be used by one person might later be shared with others. Also, employees may leave the company or get promoted to new position. There are several ways to anticipate this type of change.

Accessing user account information dynamically

One of the simplest ways to anticipate personnel changes is to not hardcode user names, local folder paths, or other personalized information within a script. Instead, a script can dynamically get the current user's full name, short name, home directory path, computer name, computer IP (Internet Protocol) address, and more with the `system info` command. You can also get paths to various folders within the user's Home directory by using the `path to (folder)` command and specifying the `user domain`.

CROSS-REF
Both the `system info` and `path to` commands are discussed in Chapter 16.

Keeping recipient lists flexible

When a script sends e-mail or other messages, try to use an easily modifiable design. For example, e-mail addresses can be stored in a settings file accessible to the script and to whoever is responsible for updating personnel changes. Using a generic name like `pRecTeamLeader` keeps all of the scripts using the property from requiring an update if the team leader is replaced, as shown here:

```
property pRecTeamLeader : {name:"John Doe", email:"john@cp.com"}
```

Another option is to use a group e-mail list that is always updated on a mail server when the individuals on a team change. Instead of adding each recipient to an e-mail, the script can simply send it to catalogteam@company.com.

Anticipating development changes

Just as a company experiences business changes, a long-lived script will inevitably require development changes.

Planning for resource name changes

Similar to the resource-naming–related topics discussed in the last section, some name changes will require development changes. You may be able to convince a designer to name style sheets in a logical manner, but you may not have this flexibility with other resources. For example, database table and relationship structural naming might be out of your control. A major change to the name of tables, fields, relationships, or other database components can require a lot of script modifications. Once again, use settings or a naming file with properties to store the actual name of the resource, like this property that contains the name of a database:

```
property nameContactsDB : "Contacts"
```

However, use this technique with some degree of caution. While it can relieve the stress of updating a few names that are used hundreds of times in dozens of scripts, it can cause development headaches when used to store hundreds of names used in a small number of scripts. Sometimes a simple find and replace is the best choice.

TIP

When an object will be script-accessed by name, something should be added to the name to remind everyone that a script expects the name to remain the same. A simple suffix of (AS) at the end of the name can be a reminder that an AppleScript uses the object. For example, a FileMaker Pro script might be named Build Inventory Report (AS) or an Adobe InDesign style sheet might be named Category Heading (AS). A simple reminder embedded in the name of key resources can help eliminate unplanned accidental name changes and the script errors they produce.

Anticipating additional modules

You will know a script is well received by users is when they ask you to expand its feature set. With a well-designed multi-module script, adding new modules can be a simple process.

Using folder contents to feed a list

When a solution includes a folder full of modules, you have the option to dynamically generate the list of the folder contents instead of hardcoding the list in a script. This has been referred to as "using the Finder as a database," although that is not the most accurate description.

Listing 25.1 illustrates an excerpt from a hypothetical script that presents the user with a list of options, each corresponding to module files in a folder. In this example, the list of available modules is hardcoded in the `listModules` variable of the script. Adding a module requires the script to be modified to keep the list of modules current.

Listing 25.1

Hardcoded example

```
set gPathToRoot to "Macintosh HD:Applications:Catalog Builder Script:"

--   Ask the user to select the modules to run
set listModules to {"Option 1.scpt", "Option 2.scpt", "Option 3.scpt"}
set listChoicesSelected to (choose from list listModules with multiple
   selections allowed without empty selection allowed)
if listChoicesSelected = false then return

repeat with a from 1 to count items of listChoicesSelected
   -- Locate and log the script module
  set nameModule to item a of listChoicesSelected
   set pathToModule to gPathToRoot & "Modules:" & nameModule as string
   set scriptTemp to load script file pathToModule

   --   Run the current script module
   tell script scriptTemp to run

end repeat
```

In contrast, the example shown in Listing 25.2 shows a portion of the script that dynamically compiles a list of options based on the folder containing the script modules. Using this approach, the list presented to the user will always be up to date because it is always based on the folder contents.

Listing 25.2

Dynamically generated example

```
--   Ask the user to select the modules to run
set pathToModules to gPathToRoot & "Script Resources:Scripts:Modules:"
set listModules to list folder pathToModules
```

You can use this technique throughout virtually every multi-module script solution. In addition to a list of script modules, a solution might dynamically generate a list of available templates, client categories, output locations, build application options (discussed in the next section), and any other kind of list that might be reflected in a folder's contents.

In the off chance that any of the items being listed are designed in a way that any user can modify them, this technique enables anyone to expand the functionality of a script solution without any knowledge of programming. For example, if a folder contains aliases for available output folders that are used to present a user with a choice for saving files, anyone can simply drop new aliases into the folder and instantly expand the solution.

Standardizing module structure

Another method for anticipating module changes is to design and use a standardized module structure. One of the easiest ways to do this is to make the name and parameters of the primary subroutine in the script identical across all modules in the solution.

You might be tempted to make this subroutine unique and specifically describe the script's functionality. However, doing so will require an `if-then` entry in the main script file so that it can run the correct subroutine, like the one shown in Listing 25.3.

Listing 25.3

An if-then driven module trigger

```
repeat with a from 1 to count items of listChoicesSelected
   -- Locate and log the script module
   set nameModule to item a of listChoicesSelected
   set pathToModule to gPathToRoot & "Modules:" & nameModule as string
   set scriptTemp to load script file pathToModule

   --  Run the current script module
   if nameModule = "Option 1" then
      tell script scriptTemp to run
   else if nameModule = "Option 2" then
      performFunction() of scriptTemp
   else if nameModule = "Option 3" then
      buildCatalog() of scriptTemp
   end if

end repeat
```

If all modules have a uniform primary subroutine, the main script can transform into the example shown in Listing 25.4 with a single command to run a subroutine in each module called `moduleStart()`. A new, properly formatted module can be dropped into the folder and the script will continue to function correctly.

Listing 25.4

A uniform module trigger

```
repeat with a from 1 to count items of listChoicesSelected
   -- Locate and log the script module
  set nameModule to item a of listChoicesSelected
   set pathToModule to gPathToRoot & "Modules:" & nameModule as string
   set scriptTemp to load script file pathToModule

   --  Run the current script module
```

```
    moduleStart() of scriptTemp

end repeat
```

You can resolve any input material requirements that are different from one module to the next by using a record parameter. This technique was discussed in Chapter 22 as a method for anticipating future parameter changes.

Anticipating application changes

One of the most disruptive development changes a multi-module solution can face is an application change, especially when that solution has application calls entangled throughout every script file. The semiannual version upgrade isn't the only manifestation of this issue. While less frequent, switching a solution to an entirely new application does occur, like the droves switching from QuarkXPress to Adobe InDesign, for example.

The issue becomes more apparent if numerous user groups request simultaneous support for multiple versions of an application or multiple applications. You may need to support QuarkXPress version 7 and 8 while also supporting Adobe InDesign CS3 and CS4. A smaller script can be easily duplicated for each application, but when a solution is comprised of dozens of separate modules all interconnected in a complex arrangement, duplicating it four times seems a nightmare of epic proportions. Then, imagine if the same environment supported three different e-mail clients and two word processing applications. However, unlikely that all of these would converge in a single context, it certainly can happen. Fortunately, there is a technique so easy to implement that it can be used in every multi-module solution, even those that may never encounter the issue.

A *user-selectable, multi-application solution* is a technique of putting all application-specific code into single-function, name-synchronized subroutines; arranging them into one subroutine library file per application; loading them into a single global variable per application type; and putting all of this under the user's control.

Setting up subroutine libraries

In a user-selectable, multi-application solution, each application category is represented by a subfolder in the `Libraries` folder, such as the `Desktop Publishing` folder shown in Figure 25.4. Within a subfolder, any supported version of an application is represented by a subroutine library file. These files might be simply be called QuarkXPress Library and Adobe InDesign CS4 Library as shown, but the folder could expand to include different versions of each if needed. All communication with the corresponding application must be performed by subroutines within a subroutine library file.

Every subroutine in a library would perform a single function in a completely open-ended manner. For example, a single subroutine would be dedicated to creating a new page including the task of assigning it a specified master page and showing the page. A separate subroutine would be responsible for deleting a page. Each subroutine in one library is synchronized to one in the other library, all with the same name and the same parameters. The only difference is the application they control to perform a given function. So, the Quark and InDesign libraries will each have a subroutine called `dpPageCreate()`.

Figure 25.4

A solution's Libraries ➪ Desktop Publishing
folder

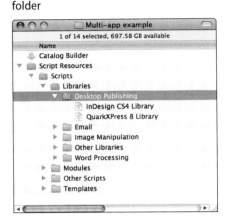

Configuring the main script

Every script module that will call subroutines within a library must have a global variable for that
application type. For example, a global variable called gLibDP, which stands for global library desktop publishing, would need to be declared in every script file. In addition to this declaration, the
main script file will need to ask the user to choose one of the available libraries in a given category.

The following example demonstrates the process of dynamically generating a list of desktop
publishing application libraries using the list folder command to offer the user a choice
with the choose form list command. Then, the selected library script file is loaded into the
appropriate library global variable, in this case, gLibDP:

```
--  Ask the user to chose a Desktop Publishing application
set pathToLibrary to gPathToRoot & "Script Resources:Scripts:Libr
   aries:Desktop Publishing:"
set listAppChoses to list folder pathToLibrary without invisibles
set nameApp to (choose from list listAppChoses with prompt "Build
   catalog with:") as string
--  Load the selected subroutine library
set pathToLibrary to pathToLibrary & nameApp
set gLibDP to load script file pathToLibrary
```

Calling subroutines in the library file

Because the open-ended, application-specific, single-function subroutines are synced between
similar applications, the calls to the subroutines they contain will work fine no matter which application library is loaded. This script shows a module asking a desktop publishing library to create a
new page by passing a reference to the document and the name of the desired master page:

```
dpPageCreate(refDocument, nameMasterPage) of gLibDP
```

Understanding the benefits of multi-application design

Applying a multi-application design to every application used by a solution can have many additional benefits. Even an application that would never have an alternative, like the Finder, can have new versions, which might require modifications. This process can be repeated for every application category including Email, Database, Image Manipulation, PDF, FTP, Media Library, Web, Calendar, Word Processing, and more.

This technique provides maximum versatility for upgrading or multi-application support, but it does a lot more. Because it requires application subroutines to be open-ended and it adheres to the hierarchical subroutine ideology, it is based on, and encourages, good solution design. It also allows any subroutine library to be reused in total or in parts in every solution you build.

Because all of your application-interacting subroutines are simple, single-function subroutines stored together in a library file, retesting them on a new version increment is easy. There will be no need to retest every solution you have, just the core subroutines that might be affected by the upgrade.

Finally, a more obscure side effect is that every script file in a solution that is *not* an application subroutine library can be created, edited, and compiled without requiring the presence of any of the applications. Developers without Adobe InDesign CS4 installed, for example, can still work on every other module of a script without a problem. Only the computers used to edit the actual InDesign library or to test the entire solution require it to be installed. If you work with a team of developers, this can reduce the expense of buying expensive software.

Upgrading the Image Batch Processor to an Open-Ended, Multi-Module Solution

 The image batch processor solution from Chapter 18 has evolved three times, most recently in the previous chapter, where it transforms into a multi-module solution. With a few additional changes, this solution can become a fully open-ended multi-module solution.

 NOTE
The Image Batch Processor script described in this section is available for download from the book's Web site at `www.wileydevreference.com`.

This final version of the image batch processor solution will have many changes. The folder structure, shown in Figure 25.5, will see a new `Templates` folder, a new `Modules` folder, and application category subfolders to allow for future multi-application support.

Creating the new module template

To begin, a template needs to be designed to accommodate the new external script module architecture. This template will be used to construct the Flip and Scale modules and allow you to quickly add additional action modules into the solution.

Figure 25.5

The folder structure for the new image
batch processor solution

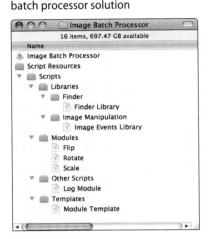

Entering the properties and global variables

The module template has several properties and global variables.

The `pTextModuleTitle` property contains the name of the module. Because you are building a template, it has a «Name» placeholder that will be replaced when building an actual module.

The next two properties are unique to action modules. The `pBlnCustomOption` property is used to allow a module to notify the main script if it has a custom option, such as Custom Scale. The property is `false` by default but can be switched to `true` for modules that support custom options. The `pListChoices` property lists the action choices a module can perform. These actions are extracted by the main script and displayed for the user to select.

```
property pTextModuleTitle : "«Name»"
property pBlnCustomOption : false
property pListChoices : {}
global gPathToRoot, gLog
global gLibImage, gLibFinder
```

The `gPathToRoot` global variable provides the module with the solution's root folder. This variable is standard on all script files except libraries and may not be needed in a specific module. The `gLog` global variable contains the log module. The `glibImage` and `gLibFinder` global variables contain the entire image and finder subroutine libraries, respectively. These are also included by default in case they are needed. For the image batch processor solution, the image library will contain the code that actually performs the image manipulation so it will be needed.

Building the subroutines

The module template has two standard subroutines whose names and parameters are uniform across all modules, allowing them to be interchangeable.

The `moduleStart()` subroutine, shown in Listing 25.5, is responsible for performing the image modification process. The `refImage` parameter contains a reference to the open image while `recData` contains the details about the action to be performed. Like every subroutine in this solution, the custom subroutine code is wrapped in a `try` statement that will send error information to the log module.

Listing 25.5

The moduleStart() subroutine

```
on moduleStart(refImage, recData)
   --  This subroutine will perform this module's primary function
   try

      --  Add actions here

   on error textError number numError
      set listData to {numError, textError, "moduleStart~«MODULE NAME»()
   attempted to «DESCRIPTION»."}
      return logEntry("Error", pTextModuleTitle, listData) of gLog
   end try
end moduleStart
```

The second standard subroutine, the `moduleStartCustom()` subroutine shown in Listing 25.6, performs any custom options that a module might offer. For example, because the original script offered a Custom Scale % choice, the forthcoming Scale module will need to support that option. (This is shown in the next section.)

Listing 25.6

The moduleStartCustom() subroutine

```
on moduleStartCustom(textChoice)
   --  This subroutine will perform any custom options
   try
      if textChoice = "«Custom Options»" then

      end if

      return textChoice
   on error textError number numError
      set listData to {numError, textError, "moduleStartCustom ~«MODULE
   NAME»() attempted to «DESCRIPTION»."}
      return logEntry("Error", pTextModuleTitle, listData) of gLog
   end try
end moduleStartCustom
```

Setting up the Scale module

The first new external module file is the Scale module. To begin, copy the Module Template script into the `Modules` folder. Rename it "Scale" and open it.

Entering the properties

The `pTextModuleTitle` property should be set to Image Scale or whatever you want this module to be referred to in log entries. Because this module includes a custom option, the `pBlnCustomOption` property should be set to `true`. Finally, the choices that will be supported by this module should be entered into the `pListChoices` property, as shown here:

```
property pTextModuleTitle : "Image Scale"
property pBlnCustomOption : true
property pListChoices : {"Scale 25%", "Scale 50%", "Scale 75%",
    "Scale Custom %"}
global gPathToLog, gPathToRoot
global gLibImage, gLibFinder
```

Building the subroutines

The `moduleStart()` subroutine is relatively easy to customize. The last version of the script contained the following code that sent a command to the image library to scale the image if the current action contained the word "Scale":

```
if nameChoice contains "Scale" then
    imageFileScale(refImage, nameChoice) of gLibImage
end if
```

In this version, the action code is inside a module dedicated to scaling an image, so you don't need the `if-then` statement. The information in the `recData` parameter will be the user's choice in the form of `Scale «%»` with `«%»` being the amount of scale the user wants to perform. This is placed into a variable and passed to the `imageFileScale` subroutine in the Image Events library, as shown in Listing 25.7.

Listing 25.7

The moduleStart() subroutine

```
on moduleStart(refImage, recData)
    -- This subroutine will perform this module's primary function
    try

        set textAmount to recData
        imageFileScale(refImage, textAmount) of gLibImage

    on error textError number numError
```

```
      set listData to {numError, textError, "moduleStart~Scale()
   attempted to scale an image."}
      return logEntry("Error", pTextModuleTitle, listData) of gLog
   end try
end moduleStart
```

The code that asks the user to select a custom scale percentage is moved into the `module-StartCustom()` subroutine, shown in Listing 25.8. If the user selects Scale Custom %, this subroutine asks the user to enter the amount by which the image should be scaled. The user's entry is then sent back to the main script.

Listing 25.8

The moduleStartCustom() subroutine

```
on moduleStartCustom(textChoice)
   --  This subroutine will perform any custom options

   if textChoice = "Scale Custom %" then
      set textPrompt to "Scale images by what percentage:"
      set textPercent to (text returned of (display dialog textPrompt
   default answer ".10"))
      set textChoice to "Scale Custom " & textPercent as string
   end if

   return textChoice
end moduleStartCustom
```

Setting up the Flip module

The flip module is even easier to set up because it has no custom option. To begin, duplicate the `Module Template` file into the `Modules` folder and rename it Flip. Then open it for customization.

Entering the properties

The module title is set to Image Flip and the two options, horizontal and vertical, are entered into the choices property, as shown here:

```
      property pTextModuleTitle : "Image Flip"
      property pBlnCustomOption : false
      property pListChoices : {"Flip Horizontal", "Flip Vertical"}
      global gPathToLog, gPathToRoot
      global gLibImage, gLibFinder
```

Building the subroutines

The `moduleStart()` subroutine, shown in Listing 25.9, gets the data from `recData` and passes it to the `imageFlip()` subroutine in the Image Events library.

Listing 25.9

The moduleStart() subroutine

```
on moduleStart(refImage, recData)
   --  This subroutine will perform this module's primary function
   try

      set textDirection to recData
      imageFlip(refImage, textDirection) of gLibImage

   on error textError number numError
      set listData to {numError, textError, "moduleStart~Flip()
   attempted to flip an image."}
      return logEntry("Error", pTextModuleTitle, listData) of gLog
   end try
end moduleStart
```

Modifying the image batch processor module

The final modifications will be to the Image Batch Processor script module. It needs to be modified to get the option choices from the actual module files, route custom choices to the appropriate module, and pass the chosen actions to their corresponding module.

Modifying the scriptInitialize() subroutine

The `scriptInitialize()` subroutine, shown in Listing 25.10, is modified slightly to accommodate future use of the multi-application library feature discussed earlier in this chapter. Both the Finder and Image Events libraries are placed into a corresponding library subfolder by application type. The Finder would only need an alternative if a newer version of the Mac OS makes radical changes to key functionality. However, placing the image library into a folder enables you to duplicate the library and create a version that works with any version of Adobe Photoshop or some other image manipulation software title.

Listing 25.10

The modified scriptInitialize() subroutine

```
on scriptInitialize()
   --  Establish the path to the root folder of the solution
   set gPathToRoot to path to me as string
   tell application "Finder"
      set gPathToRoot to folder of item gPathToRoot as string
   end tell
```

```
--   load the Finder Library
set gPathTemp to gPathToRoot & "Script Resources:Scripts:Libraries:Fi
nder:Finder Library.scpt"
set the clipboard to gPathTemp
set gLibFinder to load script file gPathTemp

--   load the Image Events Library (with future multi-app support)
set gPathTemp to gPathToRoot & "Script Resources:Scripts:Libraries:Im
age Manipulation: "
set listChoices to list folder gPathTemp without invisibles
if (count listChoices) > 1 then
    set nameApplication to (choose from list listChoices with prompt
"Process images with:") as string
else
    set nameApplication to listChoices as string
end if
set gPathTemp to gPathTemp & nameApplication
set gLibImage to load script file gPathTemp

--   load the Log module
set gPathTemp to gPathToRoot & "Script Resources:Scripts:Other
Scripts:Log Module.scpt"
set gLog to load script file gPathTemp

--   Establish the log path
set gPathTemp to path to library folder from user domain as string
set gPathToLog to gPathTemp & "Logs:Image Batch Processor Log.txt"
end scriptInitialize
```

Removing the old batchActionOptionsChoose () subroutine

The batchActionOpitonsChoose() subroutine added in a previous version will now be removed. This subroutine had a list of action options hardcoded within it and a routine that would ask the user to enter custom information. Because both of these functions are now moving to the individual external modules, this subroutine is no longer needed.

Adding a new scriptModuleList() subroutine

The new scriptModuleList() subroutine, shown in Listing 25.11, gathers a list of installed modules and a list of every action supported by every module.

Listing 25.11

The new scriptModuleList() subroutine

```
on scriptModuleList(pathToModules)
    --   This subroutine will generate a list of options from all
    available modules
    try
```

continued

Listing 25.11   *(continued)*

```
    --  Get a list of the available module files
    set listModules to list folder pathToModules without invisibles

    --  Setup lists to track modules
    set listActionChoices to {}
    set listActionModuleTracker to {}

    --  Compile a list of action choices for each module
    repeat with a from 1 to count items of listModules

        --  Load the current module and get its options
        set nameModule to item a of listModules as string
        set pathToModule to pathToModules & nameModule
        set scriptModule to load script file pathToModule
        set listChoices to pListChoices of scriptModule

        --  Add those options to the lists
        set listActionChoices to listActionChoices & listChoices
        repeat with b from 1 to count items of listChoices
            copy {nameModule, item b of listChoices} to end of
listActionModuleTracker
        end repeat
    end repeat

    return {listActionChoices, listActionModuleTracker}
on error textError number numError
    set listData to {numError, textError, "scriptModuleList()
attempted to generate a list of action choices."}
    return logEvent("Error", pTextModuleTitle, listData) of gLog
end try
end scriptModuleList
```

This subroutine returns a list of two values. The first value, `listActionChoices`, contains a "clean" list of the actions available to the user. The second value, `listActionModule-Tracker`, contains a list of two item lists that specify each action and which module is associated with, as shown here:

```
{{"Flip.scpt", "Flip Horizontal"}, {"Flip.scpt", "Flip
    Vertical"}, {"Scale.scpt", "Scale 25%"}, etc
```

This list will be used to match a selected action to the module that contains it, which is vital because the list the user selects from does not mention the module name.

NOTE
The new subroutines starting with "script" instead of "batch" indicate that they are open-ended and can perform a similar function for any script, even one that might not be a batch processor.

Adding a new scriptModuleChoicesCustomize() subroutine

Once the user makes a choice of one or more actions he wants to perform, the `scriptModuleChoicesCustomize()` subroutine loads and checks each associated module and, if it supports custom options, sends the selection to the module's `moduleStartCustom()` subroutine, as shown in Listing 25.12.

This subroutine requires three parameters to perform this function: the path to the `Modules` folder within the solution folder structure, the list of choices the user selected, and the list of every action with its corresponding module.

The module is given the current user choice through a single subroutine parameter. When finished, the module sends back that choice or the new custom version of that choice, which is inserted back into the list of actions the user selected.

The results of this subroutine are the selected actions, with any custom entered values in a list with their associated module name.

Listing 25.12

The new scriptModuleChoicesCustomize() subroutine

```
on scriptModuleChoicesCustomize(pathToModules, listChoicesSelected,
   listActionModuleTracker)
  --   This subroutine will check each module and run the customization
  subroutines were appropriate
  try
    --   Process each selected choice
    set listResults to {}
    repeat with a from 1 to count items of listChoicesSelected
      set textTemp to item a of listChoicesSelected

      --   Find the current action's module
      repeat with b from 1 to count items of listActionModuleTracker
        set listTemp to item b of listActionModuleTracker
        if item 2 of listTemp = textTemp then

          --   Check if the module has a custom option & run it
          set pathTemp to pathToModules & item 1 of listTemp as string
          set scriptTemp to load script file pathTemp
          if pBlnCustomOption of scriptTemp = true then
            set textTemp to moduleStartCustom(item 2 of listTemp) of
   scriptTemp
            set item 2 of listTemp to textTemp
          end if

          --   Add the {module, action} to the final list of selected
   actions
          copy listTemp to end of listResults
```

continued

Listing 25.12   *(continued)*

```
        exit repeat
      end if
    end repeat
  end repeat
  return listResults

  on error textError number numError
    set listData to {numError, textError,
  "scriptModuleChoicesCustomize() asked the user for a custom scale
  percentage."}
    return logEvent("Error", pTextModuleTitle, listData) of gLog
  end try
end scriptModuleChoicesCustomize
```

Modifying the batchMainProcess() subroutine

The `batchMainProcess()` subroutine has two changes to integrate into the new external module architecture: the process that presents the user with a list of choices and the process that performs the appropriate action will be replaced with new code.

Upgrading the user action selection process

First, the old code that called the `batchActionOptionsChoose()` subroutine will be removed:

```
        --  Ask the user to choose the action(s) to perform
        set listActionChoices to batchActionOptionsChoose()
        if listActionChoices = false then return
```

In its place the code shown in Listing 25.13 is added. The new code calls the new `scriptModuleList()` subroutine to get the list of action choices and the list of actions with their associated module names. It then presents the user with the actions and gets the user's selection, which is then routed to the new `scriptModuleChoicesCustomize()` subroutine. Finally, the results provide the official list of actions that need to be performed.

Listing 25.13

The new code for getting a user's selections

```
    set pathToModules to gPathToRoot & "Script
  Resources:Scripts:Modules:"

    --  Generate a list of action options
    set dataResults to scriptModuleList(pathToModules)
    if dataResults = "Error" then error "Unable to build an action list"
    set listActionChoices to item 1 of dataResults
    --  listActionChoices =
    --    {"Action Name", etc}
```

```
set listActionModuleTracker to item 2 of dataResults
--   listActionModuleTracker =
--      {{"Module Name", "Action Name"}, etc}

--   Ask the user to select from the list of actions
set listChoicesSelected to (choose from list listActionChoices with
multiple selections allowed without empty selection allowed)
if listChoicesSelected = false then return
--   listChoicesSelected =
--      {"Action Name", "Action Name"}

-- Perform custom options & build list with module names
set listActionChoices to scriptModuleChoicesCustomize(pathToModules,
listChoicesSelected, listActionModuleTracker)
if listChoicesSelected = false then return
--   listActionChoices =
--         {{"Module Name","Action Name"}, etc.}
```

Upgrading the image manipulation process

Next, this old code, which sent the appropriate command to the Image Events library, will be removed:

```
set nameChoice to item a of listActionChoices
--   Flip the image
if nameChoice contains "Flip" then
   imageFlip(refImage, nameChoice) of gLibImage
end if
--   Scale the image
if nameChoice contains "Scale" then
   imageFileScale(refImage, nameChoice) of gLibImage
end if
```

In its place the code shown in Listing 25.14 is added, which locates the module for the current action, loads it into a variable, and runs the `moduleStart()` subroutine with the action details the user selected.

Listing 25.14

The new code for performing the selected actions

```
set {nameModule, nameAction} to item b of listActionChoices

set pathToModule to pathToModules & nameModule as string
set scriptTemp to load script file pathToModule

set recData to nameAction
moduleStart(refImage, recData) of scriptTemp
```

The entire new version of `batchMainProcess()` is shown in Listing 25.15.

Listing 25.15

The new version of batchMainProcess()

```
on batchMainProcess(listFiles)
  --  This subroutine will manage the processing of a batch of files

  --  Initalize the script
  scriptInitialize()

  try
    --  If nothing was dropped on the script, ask the user to select
    items to process
    if listFiles = {} then
      set listFiles to batchRunOption()
      if listFiles = false then return
    end if

    --  Ask the user to select an output folder for processed images
    set textPrompt to "Choose a folder to save modified images:"
    set pathToSave to (choose folder with prompt textPrompt) as string

    set pathToModules to gPathToRoot & "Script
  Resources:Scripts:Modules:"

    --  Generate a list of action options
    set dataResults to scriptModuleList(pathToModules)
    if dataResults = "Error" then error "Unable to build an action list"
    set listActionChoices to item 1 of dataResults
    --  listActionChoices =
    --     {"Action Name", etc}

    set listActionModuleTracker to item 2 of dataResults
    --  listActionModuleTracker =
    --     {{"Module Name", "Action Name"}, etc}

    --  Ask the user to select from the list of actions
    set listChoicesSelected to (choose from list listActionChoices with
  multiple selections allowed without empty selection allowed)
    if listChoicesSelected = false then return
    --  listChoicesSelected =
    --     {"Action Name", "Action Name"}

    -- Perform custom options & build list with module names
    set listActionChoices to scriptModuleChoicesCustomize(pathToModules,
  listChoicesSelected, listActionModuleTracker)
```

```
    if listChoicesSelected = false then return
--   listActionChoices =
--       {{"Module Name","Action Name"}, etc.}

--   Ask the user to choose the file type(s) to save output
    set listSaveOptions to imageSaveFormatChoose() of gLibImage
    if listSaveOptions = false then return
--   Process each file

    set textSuccess to ""
    set textFailure to ""
    repeat with a from 1 to count items of listFiles
       set pathToItem to item a of listFiles as string
       try
          --   Open the current file
          set {refImage, nameImage} to imageFileOpen(pathToItem) of
gLibImage
          set nameImageForSave to finderFileExtensionRemove(pathToItem) of
gLibFinder
          if imageFileCheck(refImage) of gLibImage = false then error "Not
an image file"

          --   Process the current image
          repeat with b from 1 to count items of listActionChoices
             set {nameModule, nameAction} to item b of listActionChoices

             set pathToModule to pathToModules & nameModule as string
             set scriptTemp to load script file pathToModule

             set recData to nameAction
             moduleStart(refImage, recData) of scriptTemp

          end repeat

          --   Save the modified image
          imageFileSave(refImage, nameImageForSave, pathToSave,
listSaveOptions) of gLibImage

          --   Build the log entry
          set textForLog to nameImage & return
          set textSuccess to textSuccess & textForLog as string
       on error errText
          set textForLog to nameImage & " (" & errText & ")" & return
          set textFailure to textFailure & textForLog as string
       end try

    end repeat
--   Format results and send to a session log file
    set textResult to ""
```

continued

Listing 25.15 *(continued)*

```
  set textLine to "--------------------------------------------------"
  if textSuccess ≠ "" then
    set textResult to textResult & "Successfully processed image(s):"
& return & textLine & return & textSuccess & return as string
  end if
  if textFailure ≠ "" then
    set textResult to textResult & "The following image(s) failed to
process:" & return & textLine & return & textFailure as string
  end if
  set pathToLog to (path to desktop folder as string) & "Image Batch
Processor Results.txt" as string
  logSession(pathToLog, textResult, true, true) of gLog
on error textError number numError
  set listData to {numError, textError, "batchMainProcess() attempted
to process a batch of images."}
  return logEvent("Error", pTextModuleTitle, listData) of gLog
  end try
end batchMainProcess
```

Creating a new Rotate module

Now that the solution's external module infrastructure is designed and built, you can take advantage of the ease with which a new module can be added. To demonstrate this, you will build a Rotate module. To begin, make a copy of the Module Template in the `Modules` folder, rename it Rotate, and open it.

Entering the properties

The module title is set to Image Rotate. Because every possible rotation angle cannot be included, a custom option is added. Therefore, the `pBlnCustomOption` property should be set to `true`. Next, the list of available action choices is entered with a Custom rotation option, as shown here:

```
property pTextModuleTitle : "Image Rotate"
property pBlnCustomOption : true
property pListChoices : {"Rotate 45 degrees", "Rotate 90
    degrees", "Rotate 180 degrees", "Custom rotation"}
global gPathToLog, gPathToRoot
global gLibImage, gLibFinder
```

Building the subroutines

The `moduleStart()` subroutine passes the user's selection to a new `imageRotate()` subroutine, shown in Listing 25.16, that is put in the Image Events library. It converts the value in the `recData` parameter to a number and uses that number to set the image rotation.

Listing 25.16

The new imageFileRotate() subroutine

```
on imageFileRotate(refImage, recData)
   --  This subroutine will rotate an image a specified amount
   try

      set numDegrees to recData as number
      tell application "Image Events"
         rotate refImage to angle numDegrees
      end tell

   on error textError number numError
      set listData to {numError, textError, "imageFileRotate() attempted
   to rotate an image."}
      return logEvent("Error", pTextModuleTitle, listData) of gLog
   end try
end imageFileRotate
```

Next, the `moduleStart()` subroutine in the new Rotate module, shown in Listing 25.17, is configured to pass the second word of the user's choice (the number of degrees of rotation) to the `imageRotate()` subroutine that was added to the Image Events Library file.

Listing 25.17

The moduleStart() subroutine for the Rotate module

```
on moduleStart(refImage, recData)
   --  This subroutine will perform this module's primary function
   try

      set numDegrees to word 2 of recData
      imageFileRotate(refImage, numDegrees) of gLibImage

   on error textError number numError
      set listData to {numError, textError, "moduleStart~Rotate()
   attempted to rotate an image."}
      return logEntry("Error", pTextModuleTitle, listData) of gLog
   end try
end moduleStart
```

Finally, the `moduleStartCustomize()` subroutine, shown in Listing 25.18, is set up to ask the user to enter a custom rotation if the user selected that option.

Listing 25.18

The moduleStartCustomize() subroutine for the Rotate module

```
on moduleStartCustom(textChoice)
  --  This subroutine will perform any custom options
  try
    if textChoice = "Custom rotation" then
      set textPrompt to "Rotate images how many degrees:"
      set textDegrees to (text returned of (display dialog textPrompt
  default answer "15"))
      set textChoice to "Rotate " & textDegrees & " degrees"
    end if
    return textChoice
  on error textError number numError
    set listData to {numError, textError, "moduleStartCustom~Rotate()
  ask the user for a custom rotation."}
    return logEntry("Error", pTextModuleTitle, listData) of gLog
  end try
end moduleStartCustom
```

Further expansion and inspiration

This final version of the image batch processor still has a lot of room for improvement and further development possibilities. Many new modules can be added as can support for other applications, like Adobe Photoshop. Another improvement would be to set up a `Locations` folder within the solution folder structure that can contain a list of aliases to common output locations, letting the user choose from a list of these rather than simply picking a folder. Maybe an `Input` folder containing common locations of source material can be added to accompany the other choices the script currently allows.

It is also important to consider that you can use this new module-driven batch processor as a sort of template for building other similar complex scripts.

Whether you build new scripts from scratch using the techniques in this book, build new variations of this batch processor, or even create your own new and innovative techniques, the power of AppleScript will be with you … always.

Summary

In this chapter you learned about techniques to make multi-module solutions more open-ended and conducive to growth. The image batch processor was modified for a fifth time to demonstrate how easily you can apply these techniques to a well-designed multi-module solution.

Appendix: AppleScript Web Resources

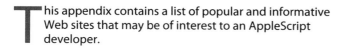

This appendix contains a list of popular and informative Web sites that may be of interest to an AppleScript developer.

Apple's Developer Resources

Apple's Developer Connection Web site is a resource-rich repository of information and tools related to Mac OS X development. It also contains a wealth of introduction, instruction, examples, and other AppleScript related documents.

Developer Connection main page

The main page of the Developer Connection site is:

```
http://developer.apple.com
```

Currently, the site has three "Dev Centers": iPhone, Mac, and Safari. Clicking into the Mac Dev Center or typing AppleScript in the Search ADC box enables you to navigate to many useful pages.

AppleScript documentation and resource main page

Apple's Developer Connection AppleScript main page provides access to many useful articles, links, reference libraries, mailing lists, and business resources. It is found at:

```
http://developer.apple.com/applescript/
```

In This Appendix

AppleScript resources on the Internet

NOTE

To shorten the URLs for pages on Apple's developer Web site, the prefix ~ replaces: `http://developer.apple.com/mac/library/`.

Introduction to AppleScript overview page

The Introduction to AppleScript Overview page provides a broad introduction to AppleScript and other automation technologies for Mac OS X. It is found at:

```
~/documentation AppleScript/Conceptual/AppleScriptX/
AppleScriptX.html
```

AppleScript language guide

Apple's language guide is a comprehensive, well-written document that contains a wealth of useful information. It is found at:

```
~/documentation/AppleScript/Conceptual/AppleScriptLangGuide/
introduction/ASLR_intro.html
```

AppleScript release notes

Keeping track of bug fixes and feature enhancements is a lot easier with Apple's release notes for AppleScript. This list includes every version of Mac OS X from 10.0 up through the current version. The release notes are found at:

```
~/releasenotes/AppleScript/RN-AppleScript/Introduction/
Introduction.html
```

Mailing Lists

Several mailing lists are available for AppleScript-related topics of discussion. These lists are a great place to post questions, foster conversations, or search for answers. You can browse all mailing lists and/or search past postings.

Apple's AppleScript Users

The AppleScript Users mailing list is for developers of every skill level who want to discuss anything related to writing scripts with AppleScript. This mailing list is found at:

```
http://lists.apple.com/mailman/listinfo/applescript-users
```

Mac Scripting Systems (MACSCRPT)

The Mac Scripting Systems (MACSCRPT) mailing list is for discussions of the various scripting systems available for the Mac OS, including AppleScript. It is found at:

```
http://listserv.dartmouth.edu/scripts/wa.exe?A0=MACSCRPT
```

Alternative Script Editor Software

Apple is not the only company who makes a Script Editor. There are a couple of popular alternatives.

Script Debugger

Late Night Software makes the highly popular Script Debugger application. This application provides a vast number of tools and shortcuts to aid in script writing and debugging that makes it well worth the purchase price. Script Debugger is found at:

```
www.latenightsw.com/sd4/index.html
```

Smile

Another popular script editor is Satimage's Smile. This application provides a programming and working environment for AppleScript with many unique features. Smile is found at:

```
www.satimage.fr/software/en/downloads/index.html
```

Additional Scripting-Related Sites

These AppleScript related Web sites are not lacking in usefulness.

MacScripter

MacScripter contains a wealth of information related to scripting on the Mac OS, including news, tutorials, scripting discussions, code exchange boards, resources, and a plethora of discussions pertaining to frequently asked questions. It is found at:

```
http://macscripter.net
```

UI Browser

Prefab Software's UI Browser provides a simple interface that enables you to visually explore and identify interface elements within any open application. It also provides code snippets that can help you learn how to script any application, even those without script support. It is found at:

```
http://prefabsoftware.com/uibrowser
```

MacTech's Visual Basic to AppleScript guide

This interesting guide provides Visual Basic developers a comparison and migration guide to convert to the AppleScript language. It is found at:

```
www.mactech.com/vba-transition-guide/index-toc.html
```

Write Track Media

Mark Conway Munro is the founder of Write Track Media, Inc., a company that creates professional quality workflow automation and data-management solutions to eliminate repetition and allow users to focus on their highest creative potential.

For more information about the company, to join the mailing list, or to send a message, visit:

`www.writetrackmedia.com`

The site has a special *AppleScript* book-related page at:

`www.writetrackmedia.com/books`

Index

Everything You Need to Craft
Killer Code for Apple Applications

Whether you are a seasoned developer or just getting into the Apple platform, Wiley's Developer Reference series is perfect for you. Focusing on topics that Apple developers love best, these well-designed books guide you through the most advanced and very latest Apple tools, technologies, and programming techniques. With in-depth coverage and expert guidance from skilled authors who are proven authorities in their fields, the Developer Reference series will quickly become your indispensable Apple development resource.

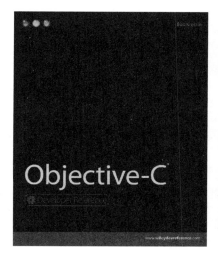

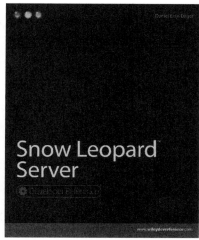

The Developer Reference series is available wherever books are sold.

Take the Book with You, Everywhere

How to purchase

Go to www.wileydevreference.com and follow the link to the iTunes store.

Wiley's Developer Reference app is free and includes Chapter 21, "Using the Game Kit API" from *Cocoa Touch for iPhone OS 3*. When you're ready for a full Developer Reference book, you can purchase any title from the series directly in the app for $19.99.

Want tips for developing and working on Apple platforms on your iPhone? Wiley's Developer Reference app puts you in touch with the new Developer Reference series. Through the free app you can purchase any title in the series and then read, highlight, search, and bookmark the text and code you need. To get you started, Wiley's Developer Reference app includes Chapter 21 from *Cocoa Touch for iPhone OS 3*, which offers fantastic tips for developing for the iPhone and iPod touch platforms. If you buy a Wiley Developer Reference book through the app, you'll get all the text of that book including a searchable index and live table of contents linked to each chapter and section of the book.

Here's what you can do

- Jump to the section or chapter you need by tapping a link in the Table of Contents
- Click on a keyword in the Index to go directly to a particular section in the book
- Highlight text as you read so that you can mark what's most important to you
- Copy and paste, or email code samples, out of the book so you can use them where and when needed
- Keep track of additional ideas or end results by selecting passages of text and then creating annotations for them
- Save your place effortlessly with automatic bookmarking, which holds your place if you exit or receive a phone call
- Zoom into paragraphs with a "pinch" gesture